THE LIFE AND DEATH OF
BENJAMIN ROBERT HAYDON
1786—1846

Oxford University Press, Ely House, London W. 1

GLASGOW NEW YORK TORONTO MELBOURNE WELLINGTON
CAPE TOWN SALISBURY IBADAN NAIROBI LUSAKA ADDIS ABABA
BOMBAY CALCUTTA MADRAS KARACHI LAHORE DACCA
KUALA LUMPUR HONG KONG TOKYO

B. R. Haydon 1816   J. E. R.

THE LIFE AND DEATH OF

BENJAMIN ROBERT HAYDON,

Historical Painter,

1786—1846,

BY

ERIC GEORGE

SECOND EDITION
With additions by Dorothy George

Too great intentions set thy thoughts on fire
OVID's *Metamorphoses*
(Geo. Sandys's translation)

OXFORD
AT THE CLARENDON PRESS
1967

FIRST EDITION 1948

SECOND EDITION 1967

© *Dorothy George 1967*

Printed in Great Britain

TO
MY WIFE

PREFACE TO THE SECOND EDITION

SINCE this book was published in 1948 there have been great additions to the Haydon saga. The most important of these is Professor W. B. Pope's edition of the full text of the Journals (p. 315), the source of the supplementary chapters.[1] George Olney's *Benjamin Robert Haydon, Historical Painter* (University of Georgia Press) appeared in 1952. Miss Alethea Hayter, using the full text of the Journals, produced *A Sultry Month, Scenes of London Literary Life in 1846* (Faber & Faber 1965), a conversation piece with Haydon's suicide as its focal point.

The revaluation of Haydon's work, of which beginnings are noted here, has gone further. An edition of the *Autobiography and Journals* (Macdonald 1950), the latter abridged, has an introduction by Malcolm Elwin challenging Aldous Huxley's introduction to the 1926 edition. More recently, Frederick Cummings has treated Haydon's work as a contribution to British art deserving the specialized attention of the art historian in three articles: 'Poussin, Haydon and the Judgement of Solomon' (p. 385); 'Nature and the Antique in the *Assassination of Dentatus*;[2] and 'B. R. Haydon and his School'[3] which describes a more inspiring and a 'better and more regular system of instruction' than that of the Academy Schools. Pen designs for pictures are the subject of 'Some unrecorded Haydon drawings and their context in the Autobiography'[4] by Yvonne Ffrench; these drawings were exhibited at the Alpine Club in November 1958. Other notable articles are biographical: that by Quentin Bell (p. 365) and P. J. Barlow's 'Benjamin Robert Haydon and the Radicals'[5] on the abortive Birmingham picture (p. 206).

[1] In 1931, while doing research for a thesis on Haydon, Professor Pope rediscovered the Journals in the possession of Frank Haydon's daughter. She eventually decided against allowing them to be used. When she died in 1935, Mr. Maurice Buxton Forman bought the Journals and in 1946 he took them to South Africa. In 1951 he sold them to Professor Pope who had told him of the 1931 discovery.

[2] *Journal of the Warburg and Courtauld Institutes*, xxv, 1962, pp. 147–577.

[3] Ibid. xxvi, 1963, pp. 367–80.

[4] *Apollo*, London and New York, November 1958.

[5] *Burlington Magazine*, September 1957. See *Diary*, iii, p. 618 n.

Since 1948 'lost' paintings and drawings have come to light. Professor Pope provides a chronological checklist of paintings begun by Haydon,[1] a total of 204 items, replicas, and variants being listed under the original work.

I am much indebted to Mrs. T. K. Jones, Assistant Archivist, Jesus College, Cambridge, for her researches on Frank Haydon in the college records, and to Mr. E. K. Timings, Principal Assistant Keeper, the Public Record Office, for his information on Frank's official career. Dr. Ursula Hoff, Keeper of Prints and Drawings, the National Gallery of Melbourne, has very kindly inquired into the present state of *Aristides* and *Nero* (p. 388). Information from Hans Fletcher, Assistant to the Librarian, Royal Academy, and from J. F. Hopkins, Librarian of the Society of Antiquaries, is recorded elsewhere. With great kindness Mr. Jack Gold overcame difficulties to enable me to see his picture, *Solomon*, and to have it photographed. I have also to acknowledge the permission of the Harvard University Press for my many quotations from *The Diary of Benjamin Robert Haydon*.

Apart from the additions this is a reprint of the first edition. The plates have been re-engraved, four have been added, four omitted (two caricatures and the letter to Leigh Hunt), four half-page illustrations are now whole page. The frontispiece is in half-tone instead of collotype.

M. D. G.

July 1966.

[1] *Diary*, v, pp. 587–601.

PREFACE

I HAD hoped to use for this book those long-lost *Journals* of Haydon's that have recently come to light.[1] Tom Taylor's extracts were copious, and there can be little doubt that he did his work well; he eliminated much intolerable repetition, but left out many things that would have been of interest as too personal for publication while many of the people Haydon wrote about were still living.[2] Unfortunately they are not accessible, and there seems no present prospect of their publication. Further information has also become available since this book was printed in a number of letters between Haydon and two men who are revealed as his benefactors in the last years of his life. I am greatly indebted to Mr. R. R. Rawson of Melbourne for telling me of this correspondence. He writes, 'There are about two hundred original letters of Haydon's, most of them written to R. Twentyman, but some perhaps to —— Bennock,[3] during the years 1842 to 1846. Twentyman and Bennock were two London business men who were probably Haydon's main financial supporters just prior to his death.' He adds, 'Twentyman came to Australia in either 1846 or 1847 and brought with him several of Haydon's paintings as well as his letters.' Two of these paintings are *Nero* and *Aristides*—the two shown at the Egyptian Hall at the moment when Barnum exhibited Tom Thumb in an adjoining room. They have thus a sinister and tragic importance in Haydon's life. Unfortunately their present position, 'locked in a small private room' in the Melbourne Aquarium, where they can be seen only by artificial light, makes suitable photographs unprocurable.

I wish to express my especial thanks to Mr. Edmund Blunden for his kindness in drawing my attention to many sources of information about Haydon. I am greatly indebted to Mr. A. C. Sewter for lending me photographs of Haydon's pictures and to Professor Bodkin of the Barber Institute of Fine Arts to whom he had handed these over; also to Mr. E. K. Waterhouse for lending me his photograph of *Dentatus*. Above all I am indebted to my wife.

[1] See below, p. 6.   [2] See below, pp. 6-7.   [3] See below, pp. 74, 308.

His Majesty the King has graciously permitted the reproduction of the *Mock Election*. I have also to acknowledge the kindness of the Marquess of Normanby and of Earl Grey for allowing me to reproduce pictures in their possession. Sir Robert Witt has most kindly lent his drawing of Haydon by Harlow for reproduction. Acknowledgements for permission to reproduce pictures and drawings are due also to the following institutions and corporate bodies: St. Mary's Seminary, Ohio; the Laing Art Gallery, Newcastle-on-Tyne; the City of Birmingham Museum and Art Gallery; the Corporation of the City of Norwich; the Tate Gallery; the National Portrait Gallery; and the Trustees of the British Museum. The editor of the *Spectator* has kindly given me permission to reprint passages from my centenary article on Haydon.

ERIC GEORGE

November 1947

CONTENTS

LIST OF PLATES

Frontispiece

BENJAMIN ROBERT HAYDON. From the drawing by
G. H. Harlow in the Witt Collection. *By courtesy of
Sir Robert Witt*

At end of book

I. INTRODUCTORY

Ali al cuor
TASSO
(Haydon's motto)

BENJAMIN ROBERT HAYDON left behind him an autobiography and twenty-six folio volumes of MS. containing his *Journals*. In these he described his daily actions, his hatreds and friendships, his successes and failures, his hopes, fears, ecstasies and miseries, with self-revealing minuteness. This work gives its author, with his handsome head and rather short legs, the right to a prominent position in that international gallery where hang the great literary portraits of the world.

Haydon chose to be a painter, but it is through the pen and not the brush that he is most likely to be remembered. He professed to make truth his leading principle in writing his autobiography, yet his enthusiasm for the subject, and his defective vision—blinded (when he was looking at himself) as it were by excess of light—led him into neglecting certain fundamental laws of perspective and proportion, necessary with so much appearance of realism elsewhere. His account of his life needs correcting at every turn in the light of outside information; he suffered from a passionate sense of grievance which affected his view, so that his explanation of both private and public events is constantly distorted. The Haydon of the *Autobiography* is not the man his enemies or even his friends saw. No one had guessed his torments, and few had realized the extent of his vanity. His story is highly dramatic, but to appreciate it fully it is necessary to elucidate, and to establish the main rhythms. Analysis of his actions and their motives, as described by himself and commented upon by others, forms an interesting study. In his boyhood he contracted the disease of ambition. With a rich endowment of gifts that might have won him success in half a dozen ways he made a choice of profession which proved disastrous and, letting his fancy run riot in dreams of glory, he indulged his malady, till, growing out of proportion to the talents upon which it rested, it finally broke his heart.

Like many ambitious but unsuccessful men he counted much on posterity, believing it would make amends for the lack of appreciation he had received in his lifetime. It was for this reason chiefly that he wrote his autobiography. It is interesting to know that he had thoughts of publishing it in his lifetime and that the form it took in one particular at least owes something to the wise advice of Elizabeth Barrett, to whom he showed the MS. She writes (1843), 'If you publish now, you must soften a little— and I would moreover, if I were you, abbreviate and subdue certain parts of your MS . . . particularly the opening of it where you speak boldly and openly of your own genius. I like the con- sciousness of genius, and I do not object to the truth under any aspect. But you must be aware that the world and the great mass of readers are irritated by assertion into denial; and are apt to call all such gloryings, if not mistaken sanity, mi[s]poken bad taste. I would therefore if I were you, *spare the provocative*. Now remember—this is not to advise insincerity, but simply one shade more of *reserve*!—and really it just strikes me that you have every reason for returning my counsel back to me, and that I am growing impertinent. . . . When the lion roars, he need not say "I am a lion": we know it while we stand beside the wood. And the conventional tactics and proprieties of this age are such, that if he SHOULD say "I am a lion", all the monkeys on the palm trees are sworn to cry out . . . "No lion! but a jackall".'

One cannot discuss a painter without talking about his pic- tures; but in Haydon's case their interest is more psychological than aesthetic. They were the key-note of his existence; round their lurid exaggerations revolves the restless spirit of the man who made them, hullaballooing for attention; now riding on the crest of the wave in exultant self-glory, now submerged in seas of debt and failure, yet struggling to the end with a courage so indomitable that few could read of it and withhold their admiration. Even to think of him apart from his pictures is an impossibility, they influenced every action of his life, and for their sake he sacrificed himself and all those who were dear to him. Standing before one of those enormous works, such as the *Lazarus*, one broods on the pathos of human aspiration, on the changes of fashion, on the men and women who once looked with awe at its dark spaces, and were shocked into silence by its principal figure.

Haydon proudly called himself an 'historical painter'. The phrase 'history painting' occurs in the later part of the seventeenth century, but is most properly applied to the dark melodramas of the eighteenth. It implies the representation of an event, historical or mythological—the death of Chatham or the birth of Venus. It was universally admitted to be the highest form of art; in effect it tended to the portentous and horrific. For its true expression it was necessary to 'raise nature', to 'heighten' emotion, which it was best to do on a very large scale. From the prestige in which it was held it followed that the vainest and most ambitious artists tended to become history painters. Though the other painters did not like the highest when they saw it, they recognized that history painting was the highest, and among its exponents are to be found some remarkable instances of vanity. Barry, though admitting Raphael's supremacy with human beings, considered he had the advantage of Raphael when it came to divine persons. Benjamin West did not wish to boast, but he could not fail to see that the chance which the time of his birth gave him of studying the works of Raphael and Pheidias enabled him by combining the principles of both to surpass either. While: 'What fire, what magic . . . !' cries Haydon, looking at his day's work, 'I bow and am grateful.' He wished to get the broad style of imitating nature he saw in the great masters—in Titian, in Correggio, Michael Angelo, Tintoretto, Rembrandt. 'Founded as I am,' he remarked, 'I know I could improve on it.' Haydon's interest lies not so much in the unusualness of such self-deception, as in his explicit confession of a state of mind not uncommon among painters, but not generally published to the world.

However, in England at the beginning of the nineteenth century historical painting was on the wane. A 'low, Dutch taste' was spreading, and smallness of scale and highness of finish had become fashionable. Haydon set himself to change all this. The stage-coach that left Plymouth for London on the evening of 14 May 1804, brought not only an embryo artist but a prophet and reformer, one called to his task from above: 'I took up the Art by His inspiration,' he wrote. 'My object has ever been to refine the taste, to enlighten the understanding of the English people and make art in its higher range a delightful mode of moral elevation.' He believed himself the heaven-appointed physician sent to restore the patient; in the event the cure he attempted, by proving so disastrous to himself, struck the death-blow at the style he practised.

The date of Haydon's arrival in London is important. Though history-painting was dying it was not dead, and there were those who were ready to welcome a young man who professed to revive it. When foreign artists came to England they first inquired who were our history-painters, and condemned us for our lack of them. Haydon had more reputation on the Continent than in this country. French and Italian painters have always been impressed by size, and there was a largeness about him, he thought in enormous terms. In his eyes a large scale was essential, so he worked on it, even when he had not a penny and knew the picture could not sell. If he failed in one gigantic effort, then: 'At it again!' was ever his motto, a huger picture still would be begun, with less money. Such a plan could not succeed, and the enthusiastic schoolboy, brought up against the hardness of facts, perforce took on some of the attributes of a grown-up person.

Haydon's life at many points illuminates the social history of the time, and his importance lies as much in what he preached as in what he practised. His judgement of ancient works of art was good and his enthusiasm intense; he earnestly desired that this country should have as high a place among the nations in painting as it had in poetry, and he hoped to bring this about both by his pictures and by encouraging the people and the patrons to take more interest in what he called 'the Art'. In some respects his propaganda was effective. His were the first popular lectures on art, and they brought the earliest rays of light into the northern manufacturing towns. Art schools were founded at his instigation, and the wealthy merchants were stimulated to think of pictures as things on which to spend their money. Cobden said the North would have waited twenty years more for their art schools but for Haydon. The old type of noble patron was being superseded by the new rich, and Haydon's popularity wherever he went, and his enthusiastic eloquence, were certainly not without effect. He obtained a few commissions for himself in the North, but the best of the fruit came later and was gathered largely by the Pre-Raphaelites. It is satisfactory that their admiration and sympathy for his work and his unhappy fate repaid something of their indirect debt to him. As his son said, what he sowed others reaped. Two other things he had much at heart: State encouragement of art, and art-education at the universities.

His life-long struggle for the former brought only misery to himself, and small benefit to anyone else, and the latter did not come to pass in his day. His idea was that people were too much in awe of the connoisseurs, and that wealthy young men of the governing classes should no longer be content to be barbarians (for so he thought them) in such things, but should take an intelligent interest in them. The apathy about everything connected with art among Ministers was complete. Haydon alone and unsupported for some twenty years agitated for improvements in these matters.

It was his unfortunate habit to 'tell the truth to power', as he expressed it. The Academy and the British Institution, or British Gallery, were the two important bodies in art. He began with them, and both to a great extent deserved his censure. The Academicians of that day were too often definitely hostile to great art, and Haydon asserts that he found Lawrence purple with rage in the newly opened National Gallery saying, 'I suppose they think we need teaching'; while Stothard remarked, 'This will do for us!' The Institution (founded in 1805) was a body of wealthy connoisseurs with whom Haydon was at one time influential, being the only artist admitted to their meetings. But he quarrelled with them too, since he considered their outlook narrow and their methods fatal, and did not hesitate to say so. Perhaps he was right. They lent their old masters for exhibition to educate the people and for the benefit of students, but since they were unwilling that the students should copy them they suggested that they should paint 'companion pieces' to the exhibits—one of which was Titian's *Bacchus and Ariadne*.

Even readers of the *Autobiography* will not altogether realize the important part played by Haydon in the spread of art-education, but in the matter of the purchase of the Elgin Marbles he has had rather more than his due. That he was quicker than almost anyone else, even than anyone else, to understand their value, must be admitted, but he claims to have tipped the scale in the question of their purchase by the nation, and the credit of this has often been conceded him. This claim will hardly stand examination.

Haydon's remarkable social gifts brought him into contact and often friendship with some of the most eminent men of his day; his London was the London of Keats, Lamb, Leigh Hunt and Hazlitt, and his intimate friends all seem to have agreed about his conversation. It was brilliant, witty, graphic, and wide in the range of its subjects. He is reputed to have been able to bring what he described before one's eyes; giving the impression of truth and sincerity in all he said. These gifts were in some ways a snare; London society had a dangerous glamour for the Plymouth bookseller's son. In his *Autobiography* two phrases stand out by reason of their frequency, they are 'My day of glory', and 'Rank, beauty, and fashion'. A lady 'of the highest rank' once told him, 'We look to you, Mr. Haydon, to revive the art'. He was to look back sadly on that remark when he realized how much so little had meant to him, and how little so much expectation had brought. It was the rank of that lady that made her remark so convincing. The phrase occurs again and again, to the point of absurdity, and yet he knew more of the great world than this naïve admiration would imply.

The life he led suited him strangely; 'I am sorry to say', he wrote, 'my ambition ever dwindles unless kept alive by risk of ruin.' He throve on disaster, he looked upon it as the darkness of the night which would make his day of glory, when it came, all the brighter. That day of glory—the idea of it—was the focus of all his aims; without its lure he would not have been Haydon. It may be said to have made its appearance twice in his life, and he never lost the belief that it would come again.

He began writing his *Autobiography* in 1841, at the age of fifty-five, and went on for about two years, carrying the story up to 1820, when it stops abruptly; for the rest there are the *Journals*. He knew he had mismanaged his life and wanted his biography to be a warning; 'I write this life', he said, 'for the student. I wish to show him how to bear affliction and disappointment by exhibiting the fatal consequences to myself who did not bear them.' From the original MSS., since believed to have been lost,[1] Tom Taylor, in 1853, published the *Autobiography and Memoirs of B. R. Haydon*. In it he suppressed much that would have added to our knowledge of the time; partly fearing to give offence, and partly with the object of reducing to a readable size the vast mass of material. Elizabeth Barrett said of it after his death, that it was 'as unfit as possible for the general reader—fervid and coarse at once, with personal references blood-dyed at every page. I only know', she added, 'that

---

[1] These have come to light, and a new and fuller version is, it is understood, in preparation. See Preface.

without great modification the Memoirs should not appear at all.' This great modification Taylor accomplished, but enough was left, and from it there emerges so remarkable a personality that an excuse is hardly needed for an analysis of his own strongly biased picture of himself. In his own eyes he was a man of the highest and most disinterested ideals, sacrificing everything for the good of others, yet cruelly ill-used. The impression he leaves is of a man weak in his reliance on the opinion of others, yet courageous to the point of heroism in his battle with difficulties. 'If I had not a body of iron, a heart of steel, a mind of fire, I should long since have been dead, and die I shall at last from the agonies of racked ambition.' That is what he told Miss Mitford, and of him she said that the last century had given birth to only two men: Napoleon Buonaparte and Benjamin Robert Haydon. And to this extent we may agree with Miss Mitford, that in the lives of both there are the elements of Greek tragedy.

II. THE BOOKSELLER'S SHOP

Not all the curses which the furies breathe
Shall make me leave so rich a prize as this.
                                    MARLOWE

HAYDON writes, 'My father was the lineal descendant of one of the oldest families in Devon, the Haydons of Cadhay. The family was ruined by a chancery suit, and the children were bound out to various trades. Among them was my grandfather, who was bound out to Mr. Savery, of Slade, near Plymouth. He conducted himself well, and gained the esteem of his master, who in time made him his steward. In a few years he saved money, and on the death of Mr. Savery set up a bookseller's shop in Plymouth, where he died from disease of the heart.'

This claim has been generally accepted, and Tom Taylor quotes it without comment; it was published in more than one newspaper after Haydon's death, and was a tradition in the family. But Haydon's eldest son Frank, examining the evidence many years later, came to the conclusion that the whole thing was a myth. He says the investigation is interesting as an 'illustration of his [B. R. Haydon's] conscientiousness under difficulties in the investigation of facts, and his extraordinary rashness in the interpretation of them'. Frank shows that the Robert Haydon of Cadhay, whom the painter assumed to have been his great-grandfather, died without issue. 'Yet to this day', writes Frank, 'my father's groundless assumption, thus proved to be erroneous, is actually accepted by many members of my family as perfectly correct.' There is no need to go into all the evidence Frank brings against the claim, but it is quite conclusive that no ancestor of his was the son, legitimate or illegitimate, of any of the Haydons of Cadhay. Gideon Haydon, the last possessor of Cadhay, so far from coming to complete ruin, as Haydon says, appears from his will to have died very comfortably off. Moreover Haydon's grandfather, Robert, was apprenticed to Mr. Savery when he was nine, six years before the chancery suit (and the subsequent 'ruin' of the family, which was supposed to

8

have been the reason of this apprenticeship) took place. The rest of the account may stand.

Robert married Mary Baskerville (a descendant of the printer) who is said to have been a woman of great energy and violent prejudices. On Robert's death Haydon's father succeeded to the business, and married a Miss Cobley, daughter of the vicar of Ide, near Exeter. The Cobleys seem to have been an enterprising family, and through them Haydon had a slight connexion with the Russian Court: one of the daughters married a Captain Mordwinoff of the Russian Navy, who rose to the rank of admiral, to become later the head of the Admiralty and President of the Council. Through him one of the sons got a commission in the Russian Army, and distinguished himself by an act of daring at the siege of Ismailoff, rising eventually to the rank of general.

Haydon was born on 25 January 1786, and, in his *Autobiography*, he thus introduces himself to the world: 'Many years ago, my sister sent me a journal of my father's, which he had kept for a number of years. . . . On the 23rd of January, 1786, my father thus writes: "Hay supped with me and left at twelve. *Dear Sally poorly*." My mother was called "Sarah", and every husband, from this gentle hint of my father's, will anticipate the approaching catastrophe.

'The next day: "Very dirty weather; wind W.S.W.," says my father. "Sally taken bad—hope it will end well with her."

'Called on Squire.

'And the next: "Sally taken in labour, and at nine at night was delivered of a fine *boy*. Is as well as can be expected."

'And so my father's journal launches me fairly on the world.

'The most important as well as the most trivial notes in my father's journal generally concluded with the state of the wind.

' "Poor Mrs. Burgess died in childbed," says he in one part— "poor Tom Burgess much afflicted: wind W.N.W." I do not know how it is, but that statement of the wind always alleviated any pain I felt at the afflictions he related. There was a consolation in finding that the course of the wind went on. One contrasted the cool perseverance of the wind doing its duty with the griefs of my father's friends.'

There was another child, Harriet, who seems to have been the younger. Haydon was an exceedingly self-willed and passionate little boy, who always got his own way, and fought for it if he did not get it. In one of his rages he was shown a book of engravings, when he at once became very silent and interested, and would not part with it for the rest of the day. His mother soon fell under the spell of his magic, and taught him the fatal lesson—that if he was sufficiently determined to get anything, he got it. This fact once grasped, Benjamin developed upon it a rule of conduct which worked admirably for some years.

His childhood coincided with the Great War, when French prisoners crowded the gaols of Plymouth, and sold guillotines made out of their meat bones with which he and his little friends amused themselves by beheading Louis XVI forty times a day. Once he found his mother crying on the sofa; when asked why, she replied, 'They have cut off the Queen of France's head, my dear.' His first effort in art was an ambitious piece drawn straight from contemporary history: *Louis Taking Leave of His People,* which he copied from a print of the day. Haydon's earliest notions of art were derived from his father's shop. The business had had its vicissitudes; his father soon after taking it over became bankrupt, owing partly to the treachery of a friend, partly to a phase of dissipation into which the shock of this threw him. But he pulled himself together, saved the business, and became a respected citizen—one important enough for an appreciative notice after his death in the *Gentleman's Magazine* (1813), which stresses his good nature and popularity. His shop was a meeting-place for the male gossips of the neighbourhood—naval and military officers, the local gentry, and the most important tradesmen. It was presumably owing to this that B. R. Haydon senior was able to supply the early and remarkably accurate information of engagements both by sea and land to the *Bristol Journal,* which he continued to do for many years without remuneration. He was a thorough-going Englishman, well known for his loyalty and public spirit, 'When Loyalty', as his son says, 'was no common virtue during the *French* Revolution.' He delighted to enrage a little hunchbacked Republican schoolmaster, who taught his son to write, by affecting to despise his arguments too much to answer them; merely throwing his leg over the little man's head as a sign of contempt. This turned the writing-master's face red with passion. 'In this school of John Bull feeling I was brought up', says Haydon, 'and I have never swerved in my feelings all my life. I am as thorough a John Bull as ever breathed. I have been brought up with the Army and the Navy, have ever gloried in their successes; for my creed had ever been—always beat the French *first* and then negotiate. This comprehends the whole of my politics—and ever will.'

Haydon senior took into partnership one of his wife's brothers, a pleasant idle man, whose casual attitude to money suggests that it was from the Cobleys that Haydon inherited his own peculiarities in this respect. Cobley had an estate in Devonshire, which he sold. Being devoid of foresight he did not invest the money, which would have been an independence for life, but kept it in a portmanteau and spent it guinea by guinea till it was gone. In this condition he came to visit the Haydons, where, finding every comfort, he remained for thirty years and died in possession of the business.

The Haydons were not only booksellers, stationers, and printers; they were also bookbinders, printsellers, sellers of artists' materials, of music and musical instruments, of mathematical instruments, of the trinkets known as toys, and of patent medicines. These miscellaneous activities did not add to the dignity of the business though they were doubtless well fitted to the Plymouth of the 'seventies and 'eighties.

During the French wars the town was to grow with startling rapidity, and the existing book-shops seemed inadequate. A Plymouth guide-book records in 1812: 'The number of booksellers is considerable: but most combine the trades of bookbinders, stationers, music-sellers, printers, medicine venders &c., which in the metropolis are considered derogatory to the business of a bookseller. In the year 1807, Messrs. Rees and Curtis, from London, opened a shop here, and have carried on the bookselling business upon a more extensive scale than had been done before by any person in Plymouth. The shop is well stocked with books of every description, and they have a constant supply of new and standard works from town.' This entry doubtless connotes a vast decline in the status and profits of the Haydon business (a decline which came at a critical moment of Haydon's career); for in the 'eighties and 'nineties it had been in a prosperous way, and was, according to Haydon, the principal shop of its sort in Plymouth. An advertisement couched in a magniloquent style characteristic of the family found its way into a London newspaper (1788): 'M. and B. Haydon, Stationers and Printers to his Royal Highness Prince William Henry [afterwards William IV], at No. 2 Pike-street,

Plymouth return thanks for the distinguished patronage they have received for near half a century. Solicitous and anxious to please, they acquaint them that they are lately arrived from London, and having had an opportunity of visiting all the capital print-shops in town, they have selected the most beautiful and elegant variety of ENGLISH and FOREIGN ENGRAVINGS ever seen in the West of England, from the following great masters, viz. Guido, Rembrandt, L. de Vinci, Raphael, S. Rosa, Claude, Sir J. Reynolds, Bunbury, Cipriani, Gainsborough, Cosway, Xc.'

Engravings were often wretched travesties of the original pictures and very bad guides for young artists, while their authority seemed to sanction ridiculous anatomical exaggerations. However, it was from these elegant prints that Haydon received his first lessons in taste. Fenzi also, the head man in the binding office, a powerful Neapolitan, had his hand in it. He used to talk of the wonders of Italy, and baring his muscular right arm, say, 'Don't draw de landscape; draw *de feegoore*, master Benjamin.' So master Benjamin, on the advice of a friend, began to read anatomical books, and set himself to draw 'de feegoore'.

His ambition seems to have flared up immediately: at the age of about twelve, he used to talk to himself in the fields; to fancy himself a genius and a historical painter; to look in the glass and conclude he had an intellectual head. Then he would forget about it and go to play cricket. But during convalescence after an attack of measles the longing for his 'divine art' came back to him. He looked in his drawing-book at the date of his last drawing with sorrowful regret, and set to work, resolving never to leave it again. This resolution he kept.

Like Sir Joshua Reynolds he went to Plympton Grammar School, where for the last six months of his time he was head boy of the school, and seems to have been popular, as he formed a drawing class, and used to march about correcting the other boys' drawings; while once he drew a picture of a hunt on the wall of the schoolroom so well that Dr. Haynes let it remain for some weeks.

On leaving school he was bound apprentice to his father for seven years, 'And now', he says, 'began that species of misery I have never been without since—ceaseless opposition.' His father's business brought in a handsome income, or so at least Haydon says, and he had only to pursue his course and independence was certain. But now that he was legally bound his detestation grew daily. Opposition roused in him fury and misery, and a kind of desperate fever of determination to get his own way. He rose early and wandered, chafing, by the sea; he sat up late and brooded on his ambition. He hated day-books, ledgers, bill-books, and cash-books; he hated standing behind the counter, and insulted the customers; he hated the whole town and every one in it. He saw his father had more talent than the asses he was obliged to bend to. He knew his honourable descent, and despised the 'vain fools' who patronized him. Finally, after a customer had offered him less than the legitimate price for a book, he dashed it back on its shelf and walked out of the shop, which he never entered again.

Now what? Back to the shop he would not go! His father saw it was hopeless: 'He was a good, dear, fond father,' he discussed future prospects with his son and asked if it was not a pity to let such a fine property go to ruin. 'I could not help it.' 'Why?' 'Because my whole frame convulsed when I thought of being a great painter.' 'Who has put this stuff in your head?' 'Nobody: I always have had it.' 'You will live to repent.' 'Never, my dear father; I would rather die in the trial.' At the thought of being a great painter, be it noted; not at the longing to paint. His malady had him fast in its grip already.

His plan was fully formed: historical art was dying in England, he would bring it back to life. He would raise his country to as glorious a position in the highest branch of painting as it held in every other way, his name should stand on the roll of honour for ever. His whole frame convulsed at the thought. Dead silence!—at dinner, at tea, at bedtime. Friends, aunts, uncles were called in and consulted. His language was always the same: his resolution 'no tortures of the rack would have altered'.

Then he had an illness, which in a few weeks ended in chronic inflammation of the eyes. For six weeks he was blind, and his family in misery. He recovered his sight, but never perfectly; had another attack, recovered slowly from that, but found that his natural sight was gone. Throughout life Fate took a delight in dealing him such cruel blows, and to this first one he reacted as he would always react: Now, said his family, that settles it, you can't see. 'I can see well enough,' said he. 'And see or not see, a painter I'll be, and if I'm a great one without seeing, I shall be the first.' His looks were not affected, his eyes being always remarkable for their brilliance.

'It would have been quite natural', he remarks, 'for an ordinary mind to think blindness a sufficient obstacle to the practice of an art, the essence of which seems to consist in perfect sight, but—"when the divinity doth stir within us", the most ordinary mind is ordinary no longer.' He found he could not shoot as he used to do, but it never struck him that he would not be able to paint. He intended to paint.

When he was well he bought two plaster casts, of the Discobolus and Apollo—the first he had seen. He looked at them so long that he made his eyes ill, he doted on them, he dreamt of them. He began wandering about the town in restless misery in search of books on art. Then he came upon a copy of Reynolds's *Discourses*. They placed so much emphasis on well-directed labour that he fired up at once, he read them through in the early morning, and came down to breakfast with his mind made up. He had listened to the Syren-voice that had discovered the one utterly compelling phrase for his case: 'Nothing is denied to well-directed labour, nothing is to be obtained without it.' 'The spark which had for years lain struggling to blaze', he says, 'now burst out for ever.'

A terrific scene followed; he stated his intention in a style and with an energy that demolished all arguments. 'My mother', says he, 'regarding my looks, which were probably more like those of a maniac than a rational being burst into tears. My father was in a passion and the whole house in an uproar. Everybody that called during the day was had up to bait me, but I attacked them so fiercely that they were glad to leave me to my own reflections.' In the evening he told his mother his resolution quietly, and left her.

His next step was entirely characteristic of his future behaviour; he hunted the shop for anatomical works, and seeing in a catalogue that there was a copy of Albinus for sale at Plymouth hospital, and knowing it was no use asking his father to buy it for him, he determined to bid for it and then to appeal for the money. The book was knocked down to him for two pounds, ten shillings. He came home and laid the case before his mother, who cried much at this further proof of his resolution, but promised to get his father to consent. His father paid with black looks.

The whole of this affair is a true picture of him in little; all the qualities which appear for good and ill in after life were displayed now. He would have his way at any cost, which till half-way through his life generally meant the cost of others; after that Nemesis took a hand and began to make him pay himself.

Having got his book another of his qualities showed itself; he set to work with fury to learn artistic anatomy. His energy was incessant. He used to get his sister to hear him, and they walked about the house, their arms round each other's necks, she asking 'How many heads to the deltoid?' 'Where does it rise?' 'Where is it inserted?' and he answering. By these means, in the course of a fortnight he had got all the muscles by heart.

One morning as he lay awake in bed, the door slowly opened and his mother came in with a look of sleepless anxiety. She sat down by the bedside and, taking his hand, said that his father blamed her much for having promised that he should go to London, that he had been talking all night, and had said that Benjamin should have everything he wished if he would give up the scheme. She added, 'You are our only support, and in the delicate state of your poor father's health God only knows how soon I may be left alone and unaided. It will break my heart, if, after all my care and anxiety for your infancy, you leave me just as you are becoming able to comfort and console me.'

He was deeply affected, but checking his tears, he told her in a voice struggling to be calm, that it was no use trying to dissuade him. 'Do not, my dear mother,' said he, 'think me cruel; I can never forget your love and affection; but yet I cannot help it—I must be a painter.' Kissing him with wet cheeks and trembling lips she said in a broken voice she did not blame him, she applauded his resolution, but she could not bear to part with him. He then begged her to tell his father that it was useless to oppose him. She rose sobbing and left the room. The instant she was gone he jumped out of bed, and falling on his knees, prayed God to forgive him if he was cruel, but to grant him firmness, purity and piety to go on in the right way for success.

His father worn down with sickness, the sad effect, says his son, of trying to drown remembrance in wine, tottered about him while he collected his books and colours; and on the 13th of May he booked his place in the mail-coach for next day. Affection for home, he says, was smothered, not extinguished: he thought only of London—Sir Joshua—Drawing—Dissection —and High Art.

The following day, as evening approached, he missed his

mother. At last the guard's horn announced the coming mail, and he rushed upstairs calling her, but was only answered by violent sobbings from his own bedroom; 'God bless you my dear child,' was all he could make out. The guard became impatient; he went slowly downstairs, shook his father by the hand and jumped into the coach. On 14 May 1804, at the age of eighteen, his heart bursting with such confidence as made victory seem almost in his grasp, Benjamin Robert Haydon set out on his career.

III. ART STUDENTS

I want, I want!
WILLIAM BLAKE

THE key to Haydon's character is vanity—enormous, but not ignoble. That being realized almost every act of his life becomes significant. For its gratification he was willing to work till he dropped; if it were thwarted he struck with passionate resentment at the person or institution that stood in his way, thereby standing directly and disastrously in his own way. His belief in his high destiny was so absolute that he thought of himself as a conqueror, one who need fear no one because success was assured in the end. 'I believe I have been so acted on from seventeen to fifty-five', he wrote, 'for the purpose of reforming and refining my great country in Art.' He thought that the eyes of the world were upon him, that there was something in him which marked him off from other men. His sense of a kind of swelling glory was so overwhelming that he could not doubt its message; greatness, or rather the image and superscription of greatness, haunted his soul. His heroes were the great conquerors: Napoleon, Caesar, Alexander. For the sake of his profession he added Michael Angelo and Raphael; he responded genuinely enough to their art, he understood and loved the beauties of Raphael—loved them passionately, that was the secret of his success in impressing others with his own greatness; but it was the princely splendour of Raphael that most fired his imagination.

His capacity for suffering was as great as his capacity for elation; it rose at times to a violent power that is impressive, and it, too, served the ends of his vanity. If the world crushed him, then his blood should cry to heaven, and he would live for ever in the glory of martyrdom. His opinion of himself was divided—half artist, half national hero. He was self-seeking and self-centred, but there was a generosity about him; he was a fine, spirited boy, who wanted the moon. He worshipped the great masters, but he meant to be of their number. On his arrival in London he instantly set to work to bring it about.

Having found his rooms, and breakfasted, he went off at once

17

to Somerset House, where the Royal Academy then held its exhibitions. Mounting to the great room he looked about for historical pictures. Opie's *Gil Blas* was one centre, and a ship-wrecked sailor-boy by Westall the picture of the year; he thought all else beneath contempt, and marched away, saying, 'I don't fear you!'

He had a letter of introduction from his uncle Cobley to Prince Hoare, who would be able to give him further introductions to a number of influential people. But he waited; till his longing for work had been satisfied he had no time for society.

Life and the affairs of life thrilled him, and he had a zest and curiosity about what was going on hardly inferior to that of Pepys; he had just arrived in the greatest city of the world, yet he shut himself up in his rooms working from dawn till late at night. Directly he left Somerset House he found a plaster shop, where he bought the Laocoön's head and some arms, hands, and feet, darkened his window, unpacked Albinus, and before nine next morning was hard at work. For three months he saw nothing but his books, casts and drawings. His enthusiasm was unbounded, and his devotion to study 'that of a martyr'. He got out of bed directly he awoke, at three, four, or five, and drew till ten or eleven at night, with intervals only for meals and an hour's walk in the afternoon. Once he was so long without speaking to a human creature that his gums became painfully sore from the clenched tightness of his teeth.

'I was resolved', he says, 'to be a great painter, to honour my country, to rescue the art from that stigma of incapacity which was impressed upon it. However visionary such aspirings may seem in a youth of eighteen, I never doubted my capacity to realize them. I had made up my mind what to do. I wanted no guide. To apply day and night, to seclude myself from society, to keep the Greeks and the great Italians in view, and to endeavour to unite form, colour, light and shadow, and expression was my constant determination.' 'I never doubted my capacity' and 'I wanted no guide'—with unerring hand he begins touching in the salient features of his portrait. Merely to be a great painter was not enough, he intended to be an apostle of art. To him already his own work and the art of his country were the same thing. It called for prayer: on the Sunday after his arrival he went to church and, says he, 'in humbleness I begged for the protection of the Great Spirits to guide, assist and bless my endeavours, to open my mind and enlighten my understanding. I prayed for health of body and mind and on rising from my knees felt a breathing assurance of spiritual aid which nothing can describe. I was calm, cool, as if crystal circulated through my veins. I returned home and spent the day in mute seclusion.'

At last he went to see Prince Hoare, who received him 'most affectionately'. Haydon says of him, 'He was a delicate, feeble-looking man with a timid expression of face, and when he laughed heartily he almost seemed to be crying.' He was a man of means, who had studied in Rome in order to be a painter, but finding he had no natural ability, he fell back on writing farces and adaptations of Spanish and French pieces, which he had set to music. He was kind to Haydon throughout his life, and now gave him letters of introduction to Northcote and Opie. Haydon began with Northcote of whom Frederic Haydon said that 'he had a power of insinuating suspicion and distrust, such that, had he lived in the early ages, he would have sown dissension between Castor and Pollux'. Haydon was taken through a dirty gallery into a dirtier painting-room, where he saw a tiny, wizened figure in an old blue-striped dressing-gown, his spectacles pushed up on his forehead. He eyed Haydon keenly through bright little eyes, opened his letter, read it, and then in the broadest Devon accent said: 'Zo, you mayne tu be a peinter doo-ee? What sort of peinter?' 'Historical painter, sir.' 'Heestaurical peinter! Why yee'll starve with a bundle of straw under yeer head!' He then pulled his spectacles down and read the note again, and looking maliciously at Haydon said: 'I remember yeer vather, and yeer grandvather tu; he used tu peint.' 'So I have heard, sir.' 'Ees; he peinted an elephant once for a tiger, and he asked my vather what colour the inzide of's ears was, and my vather told—un reddish, and your grandvather went home and peinted un a vine vermillion.' Chuckling delightedly at Haydon's confusion at this odd story, he went on to ask him what he was doing. On hearing that he was studying anatomy he told him Sir Joshua didn't know it, so why should he want to know what Sir Joshua didn't? This roused Haydon: 'But Michael Angelo did, sir.' 'Michael Angelo! What's he to do here? You must peint portraits here!' Haydon's mouth clinched: 'But I won't!' 'Won't?' screamed the little man, 'but you *must*! Your vather isn't a monied man is he?' 'No, sir; but he has a good income, and will maintain me for three years.' 'Will he? Hee'd

better make 'ee mentein yeezelf.' 'Shall I bring you my drawings, sir?' 'Ees, you may.' And Haydon took his leave. So ended
his first interview with this little creature. He liked Northcote
nevertheless, and went to see him frequently; he was very entertaining, and one day, in a fit of good humour, gave Haydon an
introduction to Smirke. Smirke and Opie were both kind to
him, and offered him much advice, but, 'it was curious', says he,
'the power I had of sifting all advice, and discarding everything
which interfered with my own decisions'.

His next introduction was to Fuseli, with whom he had much
in common and with whom for many years he was intimate.
Fuseli was at this time sixty-four; he had had a varied life: born
at Zurich of a gifted family, at one time in orders, he was both
scholar and author, was neat in his appearance and much liked
by women. His character was a mixture of scepticism, erudition,
blasphemy, obscenity and kindness. He had married a model
and they lived happily together, except at one period when the
too friendly attentions of Mary Wollstonecraft threatened his
wife's peace of mind. He was one of the very few men who kept
the affection and respect of William Blake throughout his life.
He had a great reputation for the terrible: his picture *The Nightmare* was famous throughout Europe, and he dealt almost exclusively in such subjects. Prince Hoare's fears lest Fuseli might
injure his morals had excited in Haydon's mind a picture of him
as of a sort of gifted wild beast. Just before he made his first call he
received a letter from his father which ended with the words:
'God speed you with the terrible Fuseli.' On setting out he was
nervous and blundered on in a state of intense preoccupation,
hardly knowing where he was going, till he found himself at
Fuseli's door. Here he paused to collect his courage, when sum-
moning all his resolution he jerked the knocker up so suddenly
that it stuck in the air. After looking at it for a moment he drove
it down again with such violence that the impact resounded
like the report of a musket. This brought the maid rushing up
in astonishment. He was taken into a gallery on the walls of
which were pictures which froze his blood, and he fancied
Fuseli himself must be a giant. Hearing footsteps, he turned and
saw a small, bony hand slide round the edge of the door, followed by a little man with white hair and a leonine head, dressed
in an old flannel dressing-gown with a piece of rope round his
waist. Somewhat reassured, all his apprehension vanished when

Fuseli said in the mildest and kindest way: 'Well, Mr. Haydon, I have heard a great deal of you from Mr. Hoare.'

Fuseli took his place as Keeper of the Academy Schools in 1805, after the Christmas vacation, and Haydon became a student there at the same time. On the first night he found to his dismay that he could not see at a distance. He had not noticed it in his small room, but at fifteen feet he could not distinguish a feature. He afterwards remedied this by spectacles, using three pairs and adding them one after another, or taking them off, as he was farther away or nearer. It was a serious disability and interfered with his work more than he would admit.

Haydon does not seem to have been a sociable student; he was too intent on his work for general popularity, but he made two friends, Wilkie and Jackson. Jackson (afterwards an able and successful portrait painter) introduced him later to Lord Mulgrave (his own patron) and to Sir George Beaumont. At the end of the first term Haydon set himself a scheme of study for the vacation, which entailed some twelve or fourteen hours' work a day. But he was no sooner launched on this than a letter came from home to say that his father was dying. He packed immediately, and, calling at Fuseli's on his way to the coach, talked so energetically that Fuseli said: 'By Gode, you talk well; wryite me.' On arrival he found his father better but much exhausted. His mother pressed him to her heart and cried hysterically, 'Don't leave us again—don't leave us again.' She held him away, laughing and sobbing; then pulled him close, whispering almost inaudibly, 'Don't leave me, don't leave me!' He was dreadfully affected, but determined to command himself, and succeeded. Haydon's ruthless ambition brought suffering to almost everyone connected with him, as it did to his mother now.

Determined not to waste a moment he got bones and muscles from the surgeon of the hospital, and was hard at work again that very night. Then began a period of torture: a massed attack was launched by all his family, relations, and friends to drive him from his purpose. They gave him no peace, scolding, advising, reproaching and appealing the whole day through. At last he told his father that if he wished he would stay, but only as a principle of duty, as he would certainly leave him in the end. Old Haydon was much moved, but said he had decided to gratify his invincible passion; promising, though he could not well afford to support him, that he would do so till he could support himself. Haydon was deeply touched and at once wrote to Fuseli and Jackson. Fuseli had been run over in the street, and says in his answer: 'The lucky escape I have had from an accident, which threatened death, or worse, is more endeared to me by the prospect of being suffered a little longer to be useful to such characters as yours.' Jackson replied from the Academy: 'There is a raw, tall, pale, queer Scotchman come, an odd fellow, but there is something in him; he is called Wilkie.' 'Hang the fellow!' thought Haydon, 'I hope with his "something" he is not going to be a historical painter.' On reaching town he eagerly discussed the new student with Jackson, who told him Wilkie had painted a picture at Edinburgh, from Macbeth. This worried him still more. 'What does Fuseli say?' he asked. 'O,' said Jackson, 'he thinks dere's someting in de fellow.'

At school next day Wilkie was an object of curiosity to Haydon: he was 'tall, pale, quiet, with a fine eye, short nose, vulgar humourous mouth, but great energy of expression'. After they had all been drawing a little, he got up, looked over Haydon and sat down again. Presently Haydon rose, looked over Wilkie, and sat down. A few days later they got into conversation, started discussing, then arguing, and finally went off and dined together. So began the only close friendship Haydon ever had with another artist. Other fellow students were Hilton, Mulready, and William Collins (the father of Wilkie Collins). Etty was there about the same time though Haydon does not mention him. Wilkie, Jackson and Haydon soon became intimate.

However immersed in his own concerns Haydon may have been he was always ready to enter emotionally into public affairs, and the news of the Battle of Trafalgar and the death of Nelson filled his mind and disturbed his feelings for days. He watched the solemn, black-velvet-covered barge moving slowly up the river, and saw the huge procession from Whitehall to St. Paul's, which took six hours to pass; though he was disgusted with the decorations—so costly, and in such execrable taste.

Wilkie's precocity, and the fact that he had had already several years' study in Scotland, soon carried him far beyond his friends. He was at this time painting (for Lord Mansfield) *The Village Politicians*, which began to make a stir. Jackson, who appears to have been entirely free from jealousy, spoke so highly of it to Lord Mulgrave and Sir George Beaumont that they went to see it while it was still in progress. It pleased them so much that they each gave Wilkie a fresh commission, one for *The Blind Fiddler*, and the other for *The Rent Day*. *The Village Politicians* was exhibited at the Academy where it had a great success; and, with characteristic generosity, Haydon was almost as pleased as Wilkie himself. But his friend's success stirred his own ambition, which kept him awake and allowed him no peace. The two met daily, and one morning when Haydon went to breakfast with Wilkie, he was astonished to find him sitting stark naked on the bed, drawing himself in the looking-glass.

At the end of the season Wilkie and Jackson went to stay with Lord Mulgrave, to meet Sir George Beaumont and a party; while Haydon went into the country and fell violently in love. He forgot his drawing and painting, while he rode with his charmer in the 'delicious neighbourhood', or read aloud from Milton and Shakespeare in 'grassy nooks by the rippling sea'. With delight he unbound her hair, watched with fascinated eyes as she bound it up again, her ivory arms bent back over her head, while she bewitched his ears by her thrilling laughter at his passionate oaths of fidelity. Into this Eden came a letter from Wilkie, dated from Mulgrave Castle, saying that it would perhaps give him pleasure to know that he was often the subject of conversation; that Jackson had spoken very highly of him to Lord Mulgrave, who wished to commission him to paint a subject which he admired for its grandeur: *The Death of Dentatus*. This was success indeed! A great historical work ordered before he had painted a picture. Not a moment was wasted in sending the good news home, where it was received as a triumph.

To be fit for *Dentatus* he must prepare himself by painting a trial picture. A six-foot canvas was ordered, and on this he immediately set to work. A fateful moment had come: on 1 October 1806, at the age of twenty years, nine months, taking his brush in his hand, he knelt down and prayed to God to bless his career, to grant him energy to 'create a new era in art, and to rouse the people and patrons to a just estimate of the moral value of historical painting'. He rose with that peculiar calm which always accompanied such deep emotions, and looking fearlessly at his unblemished canvas, dashed down the first touch 'in a species of spasmodic fury'. He stepped back: 'Now', said he, 'I have begun; never can that last moment be recalled.' He felt it was a turning-point in the history of art.

This picture was the *Flight into Egypt*; in it he meant to learn all that was necessary before beginning the much larger *Dentatus*. He considered the subject a pretty one if poetically treated, 'and', says he, 'I had so treated it: above were two angels regarding the group, and in the extreme distance the pyramids at the break of day. The whole was silently tender; the colour was toned and harmonious—the drawing correct.' It was an attempt to combine 'all parts of the art as a means of conveying thought, in due subordination. It had colour, light and shadow, impasto, handling, drawing, form and expression.' It took him six months to paint, and when he saw it again twenty-five years later he confessed himself astonished. It was sent to the Academy where it was well hung, and it was bought a year after by Mr. Thomas Hope. He had taken endless trouble, scraping out and repainting over and over again; and here Wilkie, with his born instinct for procedure, was of the greatest assistance. They formed a habit of almost daily criticism of each other's work; each taking it in good part if it started with a little judicious praise. After a sop of flattery a severe mauling could be endured.

Haydon's professional equipment is puzzlingly unequal. In some ways, in commissioned portraits for instance, he often suffered from a strange incompetence, yet in figure pictures he never went through the stage of failure and muddle of which most students know something. As he said himself, the difficulties of a first attempt are enormous, yet he got through this creditably, satisfying Lord Mulgrave, who confirmed his commission for *Dentatus*.

The youthful vanity displayed in Haydon's prayer is less exceptional than might be supposed. Young painters are rather given to such presumption, more so probably than young musicians, writers, or architects. It may seem odd that painting, the most difficult of all the arts from the point of view of craftsmanship, should induce this confidence in beginners, but so it is. The better painting is, the easier it looks; the difficulties are only fully apparent when incompetence setting gaily forth comes face to face with chaos. It is the countless concealed difficulties that the novice does not and cannot realize, difficulties so serenely overcome by a great master that they do not appear to exist. Haydon's peculiarity was not so much that he failed to see these excellencies in the work of the great masters as that he thought he saw them in his own, that he kept this belief throughout the whole of his life, and made it public.

IV. RIDING FOR A FALL

Il y a, dans les arts comme dans les lettres, une fausse respectabilité qui s'attache non pas au talent qu'on deploie, mais au genre dans lequel on l'exerce.
AUGUSTIN FILON

I know that if Art rises here, it must rise on the principles of Dentatus *and* Lazarus.—HAYDON TO MISS MITFORD, 1823.

THE student phase was nearly over and Haydon appeared as a budding genius. Society was interested; he was to be seen at the Beaumonts and the Mulgraves. Lady Beaumont was delighted with him, she discovered he had an antique head. Lord Mulgrave found him such good company—Haydon had a gift for listening as well as for talking—that he often asked him to dine alone. Sir George was impressed by his steady power of work, his exalted aims, and his determination to lay for himself a firm foundation of draughtsmanship. He dropped into a habit of writing long letters to him from Coleorton full of excellent advice.

Haydon was a little too inclined to differ from the opinions of the great: Lord Mulgrave said before a large company at dinner one evening that he did not admire Milton; Haydon defended him—Lord Mulgrave drew up and looked solemn, Sir George and Lady Beaumont quiet and surprised, Wilkie pale and agitated. But he was asked again almost at once, so no harm was done. Then, too, he understood Milton as Lord Mulgrave did not, and he had in him, still in embryo, conversational gifts far above those of any Mulgraves or Beaumonts; so it was hard for him to pretend ignorance (as Sir Joshua Reynolds always did) when the great were discussing some subject about which he knew more than they.

There was a change of government, the Whigs were turned out, and Lord Mulgrave went to the Admiralty. Haydon and Wilkie dined there constantly, started *chapeaux bras*, 'did the dandy and the buck', saw their names in the *Morning Post* as guests of the First Lord, met Ministers and their ladies, generals and ambassadors, men of talent and beautiful women, and rose daily in hope and promise. When dinner was announced, and

25

all of superior rank had gone in, Lord Mulgrave would say with an air, 'Historical painters first—Haydon, take so-and-so.'

The student-period is a raw one in most people's lives, yet such were Haydon's looks, his enthusiasm, his brilliant talk, and his belief in himself, that he was taken on trust and believed to be the coming man. Many years later Thackeray wrote: 'Mr. Haydon, by dint of telling the world he is a great painter, has made them believe it.' Or, as the *Quarterly* reviewer put it, 'he was treated with distinction on the sole ground that he professed to revive the art of historical painting in England'. He was employing that innate, outstanding gift of his, the gift of making people believe in him.

As has been said, the student phase was nearly over, but before leaving the schools he sowed, so he believed, the first seeds of his life-long feud with the Academy. The students wished to make a presentation to Fuseli, as a sign of their appreciation of his teaching. Haydon was chosen to make the speech, and so appeared as the leading spirit in an affair that roused the jealousy of the other Academicians. That it actually did so seems evident from the fact that they 'passed a law' forbidding the students ever again to exercise their judgement in such matters, as it belonged to the Academicians, and the Academicians alone, to decide on the merits of their officers. Haydon believed, with no tittle of evidence, that they never forgave him. The serious result (for him) was, that he never forgave them. He could not believe that what he did was unimportant to others, and not to admire him was an unforgivable offence.

Not all Haydon's spare time was spent in the exalted circles which, for him, revolved round the Admiralty; he had humbler friends. Wilkie introduced him to some half-dozen students from Scotland, who lived together in a house in Rathbone Place, among whom were Allan, afterwards Sir William Allan, President of the Scottish Academy, and a Frenchman, Du Fresne, a brilliant, charming fellow with whom Haydon became intimate. Perhaps the most interesting member of the set was Liz, a pretty girl who lived with her mother on an upper floor of the same house. She had the mind of a man, and joined in all their evening parties, read their books, and took part in their discussions. She also made tea for them and did their shopping. Naturally enough she did not improve her reputation by this behaviour, which at that time could have, for most people, but one interpretation. But she ignored what others might think, and cared more for an argument about pictures or music than for being made love to. She afterwards married the Frenchman.

The time had now come to begin *Dentatus*. This was to be a test piece, and no pains must be spared. There was something terrifying about the large white canvas that was to be covered, somehow or other, with an epoch-making masterpiece, and Haydon's heart quailed at the difficulties that lay ahead. Always wise in his advice, Wilkie suggested that a course of portrait painting would be a useful preparation for the many heads which the picture contained; and as Haydon was thinking this over a letter came begging him to return home at once as his father was again seriously ill. On arriving he found that his father had survived the crisis, and was in a fair way to recovery. Here he resolved to paint his friends at fifteen guineas a head, and soon made quite a lot of money. He then discovered another disconcerting thing: he could not paint the ordinary commission-portrait. His eyesight may well have had something to do with this, but not everything. Witnesses agree that there was something ridiculous about Haydon's portraits; for one thing he made them much too large; for another he tried to impose the grand style on them. Realizing his disability, the grapes at once became sour, and he gave up seriously trying. Yet he wrote to his father a few years later: 'I am never daunted, frightened, or depressed, at difficulties, however great. Difficulties and dangers are to me stimulants for exertion. It is undeserved neglect, or disappointment, that tempts me to complain of life. I mean by difficulties that, supposing I were a soldier, privation of food, long marches, desperate battles, losing my legs, being ordered for the forlorn hope, etc., or bringing my troops into a situation where they must be destroyed unless relieved by an immediate conception of my own; or of being a painter, as I am, undertaking work which I find myself unprepared for, being obliged to exert myself incessantly to render myself adequate, trying to express the most refined and difficult expressions, painting one head or any part ten times over before I do it rightly. All these are the delights of my soul; but if after having accomplished them I find the world insensible to their excellence, I droop, feel depressed, am weary of life, and then in a tumult of indignation console myself with the hope that one day their value will be understood.'

Much of this is true; he did meet difficulties with admirable courage, but portrait painting was the exception. Here he seemed to find a difficulty which he knew in his heart he could not overcome, and he never properly tried. Instead, he fell back on the weak and dishonest pretence that it was beneath his dignity as a historical painter to trouble about portraits, which, it is only fair to him to say, were at that time apt to be held in low repute. Finding he could not do it, hating the Academicians who made large fortunes by this means, his loathing of it rose later in life almost to the point of insanity, so that the thought of a sitter made him want to vomit, and he would scrawl with his brush, trying to paint as badly as possible. It was a disastrous disability; he might have started an important connexion on this visit, which he could have fallen back on in times of want. The local gentry were disposed to patronize him on account of his acknowledged industry and the success he had already had in London.

During this visit his mother became suddenly very ill. He tells the truth as usual with complete frankness when he says, 'Incessant anxiety and trouble, and her only son's bursting away from her at a time when she had hoped for his consolations in her old age, gradually generated that dreadful disease angina pectoris. . . . Her doom was sealed, and death held her as his own whenever it should please him to claim her. Her fine heroic face began to wither and grow pale,' and she wished to consult an eminent surgeon in town; though everyone knew that nothing could be done. He painted her portrait, and, as she sat, every now and then saw a tear rise and trickle down her cheek. It was arranged that he and his sister should take her to London, breaking the journey at Wells to stay with her brother. This brother, who was a prebend of Wells, took care of a man called Cross, a deaf and dumb artist, who in early life had made a fortune by miniature painting. Cross as a young man loved Haydon's mother and proposed to her, but she, being already engaged, refused him, and they had never met since. Poor Cross, who could neither read nor write, could not understand her reason for leaving him, and 'had brooded for thirty years over affections wounded as if for the mere pleasure of torture'. Their meeting was very touching. As Haydon left the room a tall handsome old man passed through the hall; opening the door he saw Haydon's mother, and then, rushing over to her, pressed her to his heart, uttering unintelligible expressions of rapture. 'He was in an agony of joy and pain, smoothing her hair and pointing first to her cheek and then to his own, as if to say, "How altered!" Then, flinging himself forward on the table he burst into a paroxysm of tears, as if his very heartstrings would crack.'

They pushed on as fast as possible, and stopped for the night at Salt Hill; the very mention of which place was to convulse Haydon's heart till the end of his life. That night he and his sister slept in chairs in their mother's room. At half-past two he woke from anxiety and found the fire nearly out. His mother was awake, and seeing Harriet move in her chair started up to cover her with a shawl. This exertion brought on a most terrible attack. Haydon took her in his arms and propped her up in a reclining position on the bed. He alarmed the inn and sent off an express for a surgeon, but finding him long in coming ran down and, taking a horse with only a halter, galloped off by the direction of the hostler to the surgeon's house. He found him, though someone was on the point of death, warming his boots with a lighted paper! When he got back his mother was dead. He put his sister in another room, sent everyone away, locked the door, and gave himself up to an agony of grief.

Resilience was one of Haydon's most marked characteristics. 'Nothing depressed him long,' his son Frederic said of him. There is no need to doubt his love for his mother, nor his grief at her loss, but he believed he was treading the first steps of a triumphal march and he could not mourn her long. On his return to London he changed his rooms, taking a first floor at 41 Great Marlborough Street, which lies in the angle between Regent and Oxford Streets. He was now twenty-two, and he remained in these rooms for nine years. Then began one of the happiest periods of his life. His health was perfect (it was always good, except when he had taken absurd liberties with it), he was being made much of by a number of important people, he was beginning the work he had set his heart on, and he was being paid for it. All that was necessary was to prove himself, and he had no misgivings.

So in these fortunate circumstances he set to work on *Dentatus*. As a work of art this picture calls for no discussion (although it is a striking achievement for a boy of his age), but its importance in Haydon's life was immense. In the long effort it cost him he discovered, so he believed, the eternal principles of art, at any rate they were those upon which he based the rest of his life's work; while the feud between himself and the Academy which arose out of it affected the whole of his career. He gives us a glimpse of his mind and of the lines upon which it was beginning to travel. He reflected, he says, deeply on the nature of the subject, which represented Dentatus defending himself from the assassins who had been engaged to murder him. Lord Mulgrave had chosen this subject for its grandeur and because it had never before been attempted. Lucius Siccius Dentatus, called the Roman Achilles, had fought for his country for forty years, had been present in one hundred and twenty engagements, receiving forty-five wounds, but no rewards; this injustice at length aroused the people's indignation. The Decemvirs, jealous of his popularity and afraid of his power, secretly resolved to make away with him, and he was trapped when alone in the defile of a mountain by a large band of assassins. Getting his back to a rock he killed fifteen and wounded thirty before one of his assailants, climbing above him from behind, crushed him with a huge boulder.

The moment Haydon chose was this last—when the soldier is in the act of raising the rock above his head. It was a subject exactly to appeal to him, for he revelled in scenes of violence; in such subjects 'sublime' art found its most natural expression. On his arrival in London he had made a list of subjects he intended to paint. As they throw a light on his mind it is worth taking a look at them. There are thirty-eight; they are not all lurid, and include such quiet themes as 'Milton playing on his Organ'; 'Adam reconciling Eve after her Dream'; 'Joseph and Mary resting on the road to Egypt'; and several others. Yet the general tendency is towards the horrific: 'Samson pulling down the Philistines'; 'The Spirit of Caesar appearing to Brutus'; 'A Woman contemplating the body of a man she has just murdered'; 'Scene in a madhouse'; 'A Mother dashing down a Precipice with her Child'; 'Hercules recovering his senses, and finding his Family murdered by his side'; 'Antigone and her Mother and murdered Brother'; 'Duncan's murder'. Such were the themes he selected for his pictures, and, after all, many of those chosen by Delacroix were equally bloody.[1]

---

[1] Some years later (1821) Haydon, wanting subjects from Scottish history, wrote to Sir Walter Scott, who suggested the death of old Jock-of-the-Side, a great and unconquered swordsman, who expired in the arms of his daughter when he saw his son slain and his own famous two-handed sword in the hands of the victor.

He intended by this work to introduce a new era in art, and for the rest of his life remained convinced that he had done so. For a century the failure to produce great historical paintings (for West, whose pictures were much admired, even by such men as Reynolds, was an American, and Barry's work was defective), had been looked upon as the serious flaw in the art of this country. Haydon meant to remedy that deficiency. With the production of this picture he would show that England had given birth to a painter who could rival the artists of any school ancient or modern. It was a glorious enterprise. So, most solemnly and with deep reliance on God, Haydon set out to revive 'the Art'. He 'felt that the figure of Dentatus must be heroic, and the finest specimen of the species' he could invent. But how could this be achieved? Fuseli gave him nothing but generalizations, he could not explain a single principle. He had nature; but if he copied her his work was mean; if he left her it was mannered. How was he to build a heroic form like life yet above life? He puzzled over it, painted, rubbed out, and painted again. The antique, as he knew it, was too unlike nature. He noticed that, as his model moved, muscles showed and disappeared which were not to be seen in the antique. He was wretched. His 'hero' was done, after a fashion, but not well done, when one day Wilkie called and suggested that they should go to see the Elgin Marbles, for which he had an order.[1] Haydon had no more idea of what he was going to see 'than of anything he had never heard of', and walked in with the utmost nonchalance. The Marbles were in a dirty pent-house in a yard at the back of Lord Elgin's house in Park Lane. As he entered, at the first glance, he was overwhelmed; here were the principles for which he had been looking. He saw the alterations of the form, according to the action, as in nature, yet heightened to something that transcended nature. He felt the future, he told himself that they would prove to be the finest things on earth. It seemed 'as if a divine truth had been inwardly blazed' upon his mind. Haydon must be given his due for this. He really appears at this time to have been almost alone in his appreciation. There was a strange apathy, even opposition, at first, and no one else, apparently, realized what had arrived in England. Lord Elgin

---

[1] The Marbles were arriving in England between 1803 and 1812. It is strange that Haydon appears to have known nothing about them before this time, 1808.

had thought the Marbles wonders out in Greece, but he doubted his own judgement when the connoisseurs spoke slightingly of them. Their effect upon Haydon was immense, he may be said to have fallen in love with worshipping adoration. Through Lord Mulgrave he got permission to make drawings. He was the first to be allowed to do so, and as he was to make a great point of this later it is well to fix the dates; he began in March 1808,[1] West came in September and, later still, Lawrence; no one else seems to have applied. Haydon drew and studied from them almost with violence. The first result was to make him disgusted with his figure of Dentatus, and he breathed again when he had rubbed out 'the abominable mass'. He passed the evening 'in a mixture of torture and hope; dozed all night and dreamed of the Marbles'. He rose at five in a fever of excitement and tried to sketch the Theseus from memory. He drew from the Marbles ten, fourteen and fifteen hours at a time, staying often till twelve at night, holding a candle and his board in one hand and drawing with the other, and then he would go home 'cold, benumbed and damp', his clothes steaming up as he dried them; and so, spreading his drawings on the floor he would put a candle on the ground and drink his tea in an ecstasy of excitement, looking first at his picture then at his drawings, while he 'pondered on the change of empires'. 'And then,' says he, 'lifted up with my own high urgings of soul, I have prayed God to enlighten my mind to discover the principles of those divine things—and then I have had inward assurance of future glory, and almost fancying divine influences in my room have lingered to my mattress bed and soon dozed into a rich balmy slumber. . . . I arose with the sun and opened my eyes to its light only to be conscious of my high pursuit; I sprang from my bed, dressed as if possessed and passed the day, the noon, and the night in the same dream of abstracted enthusiasm; secluded from the world, regardless of its feelings, unimpregnable to disease, insensible to contempt.'

Many of these drawings are to be seen at the British Museum; they vary considerably in merit, but on the whole they are good, careful, student's work. With such long hours it is not surprising if some are inaccurate. The best are those which were done with

[1] *The Journal of Hellenic Studies* prints a letter from Haydon to Lord Elgin, dated 23 June 1807. Haydon had been asked by Lord Elgin to meet Flaxman at the Museum to discuss the restoration of the Marbles. The date is probably a mistake for 1809.

a few rapid strokes, in which occasionally he has seized the essentials with ease and power.

His Diary at this time is filled with expressions of enthusiasm: 'How the Greeks attended to every variety in the body produced by the slightest movement! The more I study them the more I feel my own insignificance. May I improve in virtue, purity and industry; let me admit no degrees of excellence, nothing but indisputable greatness on solid scientific principles—the house built on the rock.'

He then tried to put some of this newly acquired knowledge into practice in his principal figure: 'For Dentatus I selected all the muscles requisite for human action, no more nor less, and then the members wanted for *his* action, and no more nor less. I put a figure in the corner of a lower character, that is, more complicated in its forms, having parts not essential, and this showed the difference between the form of a hero and a common man.' One critic when the picture was exhibited described Dentatus as an old hump-backed Scotchman.

It must be repeated that whatever the merits or demerits of *Dentatus*, and this applies to others of Haydon's pictures, his exaltations and agonies over them show the man. It is for this that its history is given here. It is small blame to Haydon that he did not understand how to obtain the ease and economy of Pheidias—he meant to employ the principle of the Marbles, by which only those muscles in momentary use are tensed and show. He failed in this.

The load of difficulty grew, but he plodded on. One day Fuseli called, and noticing the enormous solidity of the drapery, drew a prop for it with a piece of white chalk on the canvas. Haydon took the drapery out for about the twentieth time. Indeed weight is the leading impression of this figure; Haydon had exaggeration in his blood and always overdid everything. He says: 'Enlarged the shield which gives a more irresistible weight to the figure—a more thundering air.' And again: 'I wish to express a lofty contempt among his other characteristics.' He was indignant with the people who told him he could not expect to paint like Titian, or draw like Michael Angelo, at a second attempt. 'But I will try; and if I take liberties with nature and make her bend to my purposes what then? . . . I have heard Nelson used to say, "Never mind the justice or the impudence, only let me succeed." If I had the power I would spit fire at such insignificant wretches! I have no language to express my indignation at them. What Homer dared I'll dare. . . . Genius is sent into the world not to obey laws but to give them! . . . God grant that this be not presumption!'

Yet he was deeply perturbed, and resorted constantly to prayer: '. . . and prayed to God to give me strength of mind and vigour of body to go through the work with a firm spirit, not to be daunted by any difficulties, however great . . . but to consider how soon I may die, and if unexpectedly, that I may be taken doing all a human being can to advance the art and raise the reputation of my dear country.'

Any hint or dread of failure raised in him the cry of the martyr; he instantly saw himself as the sole hope on which his country's honour hung trembling. It made it all the more incumbent on God to help him. 'After a night of continual restlessness and reflections literally excruciating—for my mind is quite on the rack about my hero—I rose in a fever of anxiety and set to work. . . . God grant I may be in the right path.'

Still more weight for Dentatus: 'On the helmet of one of my figures I have put some light airy ostrich feathers which give a more ponderous look to my hero.'

'A man of real genius will not suffer Nature to put him out. He will make Nature bend to him; he will make his own use of Nature; he will force her into his service.'

One wonders what Haydon would have become if he had not been chastened by adversity, 'When you find people inclined to treat you with respect', he says, 'never check it from modesty, but rather increase it by a quiet unassuming air of conscious worth. A man does not perceive his own improvement or the difficulties he has conquered until some young beginner[1] brings him his first efforts, asking for advice. You find then that you must carry your conversation back ten years to the level of his comprehension.' He was in fact becoming, or in danger of becoming, a spoiled darling of society. He was dining two or three times a week with Lord Mulgrave, often alone, while his studio was crowded with 'rank, beauty, and fashion' to such an extent that there were days when he could hardly work, but spent his time talking and explaining. The manners of high life fascinated him, and it is little wonder if his

[1] In this case the 'young beginner' was Eastlake, afterwards President of the Royal Academy. Haydon himself was twenty-two.

head became slightly turned by the 'beauty and sweetness' of the women who came to marvel at 'the extraordinary picture by a young man who had never had the advantage of foreign travel'. At table he was 'talked to, looked at, selected for opinions, and alluded to constantly'. He would receive compliments and bow his humble acknowledgements; then a discussion would take place about the merits and fiery fury of Dentatus; then all agreed it was 'so fine a subject'; then Lord Mulgrave would claim the praise for the selection; then people would whisper: 'He himself has an antique head'; then they would look and some would differ; then the noise the picture would make when it came out; then Sir George would say, that he had always said: 'A great historical Painter would at last arise,' and that Haydon was he. Looking back thirty years later he says sadly: 'Believing all this to be gospel truth, and never doubting the sincerity with which it was said, I anticipated all sorts of glory, greatness and fame. I believed that the Academy would hail with open arms so extraordinary a student. . . . I believed that they could not, would not, envy the reputation and advance of the very sort of talent they all agreed was wanted in the English School.'

Never for one moment does he seem to have doubted the merit of his finished picture. He said later in life, 'The production of this picture must and will be considered as an epoch in English Art. The drawing in it was correct and elevated, and the perfect forms and system of the antique were carried into painting, united with the fleshy look of every-day life. The colour, light, and shadow, the composition and telling of the story were complete. . . . The Academicians said I had attempted too much. But had I not succeeded? Leigh Hunt said it was a bit of old embodied lightning.'

He must have been making enemies all this time without knowing it; he admitted that he became a little 'montée' [sic], that he talked rather more grandly to the artists, that he looked down upon poverty, did not 'relish the society of the middle classes, and thought their manners gross and their breeding hideous'. It would undoubtedly be annoying for older painters to hear perpetually the praises of an utterly untried boy, and to know that his studio was crowded with pretty women and titled people. It must have been maddening for Fuseli to be told by the *Examiner* to study 'the property of Haydon's hues forms and expressions of passion as exemplified in *Dentatus*'. While few could have endured it if he then practised what he preached later: that those who possess great talents should 'endeavour to make their fellow-men bear their inferiority by sweetness, gentleness, and benevolence'.

At last the picture was finished and the time came to send it to the Academy. With ill-advised zeal Sir George and Lord Mulgrave called on a member of the hanging-committee to ask that it should be given a good place. According to Fuseli it was first put into the same position as *The Flight into Egypt* of the previous year, but while he was absent it was taken down and given the centre of a wall in the Ante-room. Haydon and his friends had expected too much. Nothing but the place of honour would have satisfied *him*. He really believed his picture epochmaking, and to have it tucked away in the Ante-room as if it were unfit to hang with the better works was an intolerable insult. But there was in fact no reason at all why he should have felt himself insulted; he says his picture was hung 'in the dark'; a complete inaccuracy; the Ante-room at Somerset House was well lit by a top light, and several of Sir Joshua Reynolds's important pictures had been hung in Haydon's place. Writing more than forty years after, the *Quarterly* reviewer had not forgotten the displeasing impression it made, as of a sort of 'forced abortive grandeur'. The Academicians considered it 'a glaring picture'.

Haydon's claim that *Dentatus* was a masterpiece is absurd; nevertheless it is a sufficiently wonderful performance for a second attempt, and one can hardly doubt that it was better than other historical pictures in that exhibition. Those familiar with the immense difficulties to be overcome in carrying out so large and elaborate a composition will give Haydon at the age of twenty-three their respect.

No doubt his own fury and sense of insult communicated itself to his patron, for he says Lord Mulgrave seemed to consider that he had been duped.

Haydon had reached a watershed in his life. From it ran two streams, the one flowing through prosperous country, the other a foaming torrent, forcing its violent way over rocks and through terrible gorges to end in a marshy swamp. James Ward had a picture rejected in 1804. He told West that he blamed no one. Four years after, he was elected an A.R.A., and in 1811 a full Academician. Haydon had a picture hung in a centre in the

Ante-room—and he allowed it to poison his life. His attitude is scarcely sane. Resolutely, his lips twitching with bitterness and with fury in his heart, he turned his back on the cheerful stream and began picking his way down the precipitous torrent. His enormous vanity had had a wound it could not bear.

Society neglected him; no longer did pretty women hang on his words, or ask for explanations of this and that in his picture and listen to his opinions on High Art. But all that was needed was a little patience, and success and recognition would have been certain. He had as yet taken no fatal step, had only let his indignation show too clearly in his talk and behaviour; but there was a storm brewing within which was presently to burst out to his undoing. He became dull and solitary; he dined with Lord Mulgrave occasionally, but believed he was treated as if under a cloud. Sir George stood by him and said roundly that not one of the Academicians could have painted so good a picture. But he had risen into the seventh heaven, where crowds of beauties had 'put up their pretty glasses and lisped admiration' of his efforts, and the contrast was too bitter to be endured. 'I walked about my room,' he wrote later, 'looked into the glass, antici-pated what the foreign ambassadors would say, studied my French for a good accent, believed that all the sovereigns of Europe would hail an English youth with delight who could paint a heroic picture. Exactly as I knew the soundness of the principles developed in Dentatus, I believed the praises I heard were evidence of the sagacity of the praisers, forgetting that the same terms would have been applied to the portrait of a race-horse or of a favourite pug, and that my flatterers knew no more about the principles I had discovered than I did before I began.' Again and again in the *Journals* are unveiled the inmost thoughts, in all their unreasonable egotism and bitterness, of a man who, as Elizabeth Barrett said, saw 'maniacally in all men the assassins of his fame'.

Was not this an epoch-making picture, based on eternal laws understood by no one else, and rediscovered by him under the influence and guidance of the divine works of Pheidias? Was it not painted by the first artist ever permitted to draw from those remains? 'And this picture', he cries, 'was ruined in reputation through the pernicious power of professional men, embodied by royalty for the advancement of works of this very descrip-tion. I, the sincere devoted artist, was treated like a culprit, deserted like a leper, abused like a felon and ridiculed as if my pretensions were the delusions of a madman.' Such thoughts were, in his own telling phrase, but 'the dark starts of a nightmare'; no one had treated him like a culprit, or abused him like a felon. What painter that has ever lived has not been disappointed at the way some picture has been hung?

Were it not for Wilkie's remarks, there would seem to be nothing to show that the Academicians treated him badly till he himself attacked them. Many years later William Bewick asked Wilkie if he thought Haydon was justified in his complaints of the treatment he received from the Academy about *Dentatus*? Wilkie replied, "Oh, yes, yes, he was ill-used—badly treated in that matter, but he should never have heeded, passed it by, and got in. He might have then pursued a deep scheme of retaliation, if he had liked, upon the various parties who behaved so shamefully on that occasion; for he has vast powers, stores of varied acquirements, and a command of language that none in the Academy can combat with. . . . But you see, Mr. Bewick, I am myself of the Academy, and it is a rule that "birds are not to foul in their own nests", so, if you please we will change the subject.'

Then gazing through the window, and with a long-drawn desponding sigh he muttered, 'Pity—what a pity!'

One shudders in reading the *Journals* a second time at some reckless action, which, had he but known, was to lead to disaster. A picture forms itself in the mind of a man brilliantly gifted to make a success of life, with delightful qualities that won love and admiration, with a capacity for enjoyment such as few people have, throwing his chances away because he did not at once get quite the reward he thought he deserved, and because his vanity claimed an impossible glory. 'I was an only son,' he wrote later to Sir Walter Scott. 'I never knew the want of a wish ungratified.' That was the tragedy—any thwarting of his will crazed him. He could not tolerate it, and would fight with any weapon he could lay hands on. The Academy became for him from that time a 'coiled snake', an 'association of vanity, monopoly and intrigue'.

V. BITTER FRUIT

I am wrong'd here monstrously.

BEN JONSON

HAYDON'S fits of despair were as violent as his bursts of elation, and before he could react he had to sink into the depths. His friends feared for his sanity, he felt 'the hollow glitter' of society, and became 'sullen, retired, and musingly thoughtful'. He began to think he was 'under a curse, and doomed to be so'. His 'brain was affected' and the 'splendour and refinement of high life' disgusted him.

From this morbid condition he was roused by a visit to his family at Plymouth in which Wilkie joined. Cyrus Redding, the journalist, met him for the first time during this holiday, and the account he gives of their swimming and walking expeditions suggests anything but despondency on Haydon's part. Redding was much attracted and found him full of enthusiasm about his work, the Marbles, the beauties of the country, the sunrise over the Lara, and Wilkie's attempts at swimming (which Redding considered the least adroit he had ever seen). He wondered that the two men should be friends, and considered Haydon in every way the superior, mentally, socially, physically. They met in the shop, and Haydon had him up at once to 'the spacious drawing-room above it', where they found Wilkie, uncouthly at his ease, talking trivialities (the only things he could talk) to Harriet, and entirely unconscious that he was with a pretty girl. In reading Redding's account it is impossible to believe that the man he is describing could ever be 'sullen, retired, and musingly thoughtful'. Redding was not a brilliant writer, but he conveys an impression of brilliant vitality, nevertheless, in this young artist who felt the hollow glitter of society, and believed himself under a curse. The point is important because it is clear that the *Journals* show a side of him that the world seldom saw.

By the end of five weeks he had recovered his spirits, and set out with Wilkie for Coleorton to visit Sir George and Lady Beaumont. Here he had the mortification of finding himself out-

39

classed, not only by Wilkie, but by Sir George (and one dreads to suspect even by Lady Beaumont), in the sketches all made daily from the scenery in the park. It was their habit to compare their work in the evening, when they would cut each other up in fine fashion. 'So, without saying a word,' he writes, 'I painted, full of fire and life, the head of a favourite horse of Sir George's, and bringing it in when the party were waiting for dinner, I had the satisfaction of demolishing their little bits of study, for the size of life, effectually done, is sure to carry off the prize.'

Next day Wilkie came in with a beautiful study (quite small) of an old woman of the village, so honours were divided, 'but', says Haydon, 'they all allowed that nothing could exceed the eye of my horse'.

It was a pity that the members of this friendly party should so soon have fallen into dissension. This came about through Haydon's next picture. *Macbeth* was an unfortunate business from start to finish. Sir George had commissioned it while Haydon was working at *Dentatus*, and now, riding one day at Coleorton, he said, 'What size do you intend to paint *Macbeth*?' 'Any size you like, Sir George.' 'Would a whole length be large enough?' 'Certainly, it is larger than I had contemplated, and I should be highly gratified at being allowed to paint the picture such a size.' The picture was begun, and well advanced, before Sir George returned to town. When he saw it he showed constraint: 'This is the full size of life?' 'No, Sir George, a little less.' He came again with General Phipps and they both abused, and even ridiculed, saying, 'Figures less than life look dwarfish.' 'His first impression', says Haydon 'had been that the figures were life-size if not larger.' Then, very illogically, he insisted on having a smaller picture. Wilkie advised submission, but to Haydon a smaller picture was not only defeat, it was the selling of his principles. They all met at Lord Mulgrave's, and he in the kindest manner said, 'Haydon, if you will consent to oblige Sir George, you will please us all.' Sir George's face expressed rigid indifference; if he had given one look Haydon said he would have been vanquished. But he said nothing, Haydon said nothing; Lord Mulgrave, astonished, changed the conversation. At leaving, Lord Mulgrave shook him kindly by the hand and whispered, 'Yield', looking more than he whispered. All his friends walked home with him, begging him to consent. In his lonely painting room he 'mused on the grooms heavy in slumber; the king sleeping in innocence; Macbeth striding in terror; the vast shadow of the listening Lady Macbeth' (the figure itself had not been put in), till getting inspired as midnight approached, he marched about in agitation, and swore he would not yield. 'Full of the glory of resistance to injustice' he went to bed and fell asleep. The whole of the next day he spent staring at his picture; a model came and waited for him to begin work, but seeing his dazed condition, asked with an expression of surprise if he should go. Haydon said, 'Yes', and the model, eyeing him as if he thought he was mad, went.

Making a great effort over himself, he called on Sir George and offered to paint a small picture. Sir George, who was dressing to go out, looked blank, and replied, 'Ah—yes, indeed—yes, indeed—yes, yes—I am happy—yes. I am going out instantly.' He left town, and Haydon wrote to ask him to withhold his decision till the picture was finished. He then rose 'breathing like a young lion which has just burst the net which fettered him'. Sir George returned to London and for six weeks Haydon let him alone, till, tired of this, he began to talk 'with great indignation', hoping it would reach Sir George's ears. As this produced no effect, he resolved, by his own admission 'against all breeding and delicacy', to show the correspondence. Sir George was wonderfully tolerant; he called, but finding Haydon out, sent an invitation to dinner. There was a brilliant company and Haydon was treated with great attention. During dinner Sir George began talking of Pope's letters, then, turning a little towards Haydon, he said, 'It is very strange, but I have a great aversion to people showing letters; nothing, you know, is so indelicate.' 'Certainly,' said Haydon, 'but there are cases, you know, Sir George, which oblige a man to show letters in self-defence.' In the drawing-room 'Lady Beaumont', says Haydon, 'was enchanting. Patting my arm, with the engaging pressure which sets a man on the *qui vive*, she rallied me on the propriety of docility in early life. "Yes," I replied, "but is there not a docility amounting to servility?". . . I was fearless, young, and proud of a quarrel with a man of rank which would help to bring me into notice. This was foolish in the extreme but it was natural. Full of high and virtuous principles, knowing I had all along meant to do what was right, I felt disgusted at injustice, and seized the first opportunity of showing that the artist was the man to be listened to and not the connoisseur, forgetting that the connoisseur was generally the man of rank and wealth . . . and that though the world would enjoy the exposure of a man of rank in secret, it would take good care to shake its head in public at the presumption of the artist. In fact victory is defeat in such cases, and the artist will always find it so.'

In the meantime he had had an extra piece added to the canvas, making it larger still, so that when Sir George and Lady Beaumont called to see what could be done it was clear that they could not possibly hang it in their house. It was finally agreed that Sir George was to be allowed to refuse the picture when it was finished if he did not like it, but would consider himself engaged for a smaller one, the price to be settled by arbitration. When it was finished Sir George came, but declined it, though he offered Haydon £100 for the trouble he had taken, or else to paint another picture. 'Foreseeing', says Haydon, 'that any further connexion would bring me nearer ruin than I was already (for I had incurred £600 of debts, and when he first ordered the picture I did not owe one shilling . . .), and taking everything into consideration, I resolved to decline both offers, and did so briefly.'

It was a pretty disastrous piece of work. He had succeeded, at the very beginning of his career, in alienating the sympathy of his two powerful patrons, though Sir George did afterwards relent, and took the picture; a fact which Haydon neglects to tell us in his *Autobiography*. In mentioning this James Elmes adds that Sir George behaved throughout as a substantial friend.

In explanation of Haydon's behaviour it must be remembered that to him *Macbeth* was a work of genius. Leigh Hunt, while admitting faults, as that the page's hand was 'for a pickaxe rather than a train or a feathered bonnet', that Macbeth's muscles were 'too much obtruded', nevertheless admired the, 'in parts, Titianesque colouring, and masterly drawing', the 'nobly expressive upper part' of Macbeth, and Lady Macbeth with her lifted finger throwing a gigantic shadow on the wall. Some years later Elmes described in the *Annals of the Fine Arts* how he had recently seen the picture in Sir George's house, and the splendid impression it made. He greatly admired the swollen veins on the hands of the sleeping grooms, a result of their drunken debauch: and Macbeth's hands, grasping the daggers with 'supernatural clutch', and 'the monster's gasping and heaved-up chest'. Such things were that heightening of nature necessary to sublime Art, and to many did not seem the exaggerations of weakness. But everyone did not admire. The *Edinburgh* reviewer speaking of it after Haydon's death, says, 'We have a perfect recollection of the unfavourable impression it made on the public. The attitude of Macbeth, in the act of staggering back when about to enter the chamber of Duncan, struck the eye as awkward and ungraceful even to painfulness.' There is a drawing for the legs of this figure in the British Museum which is distressing in its clumsy violence. It repels at sight, and anything more remote from the spirit of the Elgin Marbles could not be imagined. But in reading his own account it is difficult not to believe that one is being privileged to watch the progress of some great masterpiece: 'I advanced and fell back and advanced again; Macbeth's head I painted and repainted, and it was at this period I confirmed by perpetual deductions the principles of a standard figure'—principles on which, he adds later, 'I reared the figure of Macbeth.' 'My want of money was now great,' he continues. 'My expenses were dreadful. I moulded torsos for the chest of Macbeth. I moulded knees for the sleeping grooms. I made studies without end; hands over and over again—from nature, from the antique. Models sat till night. My lamp often burnt till deep into it. In fact my love of art, my enthusiasm, were those of an inspired being self-sacrificed to a great principle. . . . Nothing could exceed my enthusiasm, my devotion, my fury of work—solitary, high-minded, trusting in God, glorying in my country's honour. . . . Day and night, night and day, I streamed on in a flow of thoughts and conclusion that would not disgrace my understanding or my heart now at fifty-seven.' After reading this it comes with something of a shock to find him saying a little later of these same first six months of 1811, 'If I review them with rigour what will they exhibit but one scene, with few exceptions, of vice and idleness.'

Just when he most needed it, harassed and ill as he was from this long dispute, a piece of good fortune came to him: the Directors of the British Institution offered a hundred-guinea prize for the best historical picture, and awarded it to *Dentatus.* 'The reader', he says, 'has read of the cruelty and tyranny with which it was treated by one institution and surely will feel pleasure in learning that I got my fair reward at last by the proper feeling of another.' Lord Mulgrave had paid him two hundred guineas for the picture, so after all *Dentatus* did not do so badly.

Haydon wrote to Wordsworth long after, 'I cannot help believing in that awful support I received thirty-seven years ago in my obscure lodgings when painting "Macbeth" in just the same condition. In agony of mind I opened the Bible, vowing to myself the first passage I saw should regulate my die for life. To my joy then, and ever since, I saw: "Fear thou not, I am with thee. Be not dismayed, I am thy God. I will strengthen thee, yea I will help thee, yea I will uphold thee with the right hand of Righteousness." This passage has blazed in my brain night and day ever since. Hesitation never enters my mind if for a moment I hear "go on" audibly, as if whispered.' To his undoing he heard it now, and, 'hesitation never entering his mind for a moment', he says he *began* to borrow. His father had written to tell him he could not continue his allowance; he had tried to cry off before, 'but', says Haydon, 'I was iron-minded and bent not'. There is something novel in the idea of an iron-minded borrower, but eventually old Haydon put his foot down and refused point blank to send any more money. The business was less prosperous, and Harriet's claims had to be considered; Haydon argued that if *Dentatus* had won the hundred-guinea prize, *Macbeth* ought to win the three-hundred-guinea prize which was now being offered. So he borrowed thirty pounds from Leigh Hunt's brother, John ('as noble a specimen of a human being', he says, 'as I ever met in my life'), and thirty pounds from a friend of Wilkie's. 'Yet what was I to do?' he cries; 'was I to relinquish all the advantages of so many years study and thought merely because now came one of those trials of which life is so full?' He lived to write bitterly, '*Here began debt and obligation, out of which I never have been, and never shall be, extricated, as long as I live.*'

A comment is called for here. He was desperately aggrieved by the *Macbeth* incident, and wished to prove that his misfortunes in life arose out of ill-usage over his first two important pictures. He wanted to show that it was Sir George's behaviour that drove him to begin borrowing. But he had always borrowed; he was seventy pounds in debt before he had finished his first picture. In noting the air of martyrdom with which he excuses his borrowing thirty pounds from Leigh Hunt's brother, and thirty pounds from a friend of Wilkie's, and the sense of wrench therein implied, as of the first downward step, it will not do to forget the money he had borrowed already (and never repaid) from his first pupil, little Charles Eastlake, aged fifteen.

His next step was to call his landlord, Perkins, to whom he explained his position, asking him to wait till *Macbeth* was done. Perkins said, 'You paid me when your father supported you, and I see no reason not to believe you will do so when you can support yourself.' Haydon adds, 'I had begun to feel more independent from the very position my father had placed me in.' He was now living upon his friends. At the end of the year (1811) he wrote, 'Macbeth being thus concluded after a long struggle, without assistance from my father and wholly by dint of borrowing from my friends, I scrutinized my debts before beginning a new work and found they were £616 10s., of which £200 was due to my landlord for rent.' His position was very serious, and, what was worse, his mind was blazing with rage and bitterness against Sir George, the Academy, and the connoisseurs. In this state of mind, driven mad by the lack of reputation without which he could not live, and for which, as Elizabeth Barrett said 'he wrestled, and struggled, and kicked, forgetting grace of attitude in the pang', he took another fatal step: he made an attack in the Press on Payne Knight and the Academy. He began by attacking an article by Payne Knight on Barry, which had come out in the previous year. Before sending in his letter he got into touch with Soane, who had been called to order for some remarks he had made about a building of Smirke's, and was so enraged that he wrote a pamphlet, which he showed to Haydon, saying 'Shall I precede or follow?' 'Whichever you please,' said Haydon, 'only I make my début on Sunday next.' As Soane's pamphlet was ready, it was agreed over a bottle of wine that Haydon should begin next Sunday, and that Soane, who was violent, should follow or precede as he thought best. To have the backing of an Academician was an important aid. On Sunday, 27 January Haydon's attack on Payne Knight, signed 'An English Student', came out in the *Examiner*, followed by that on the Academy, the Sunday after; and 'never since the Art was established', says he, 'were its professors in such a hubbub of fury and rage. From this moment the destiny of my life may be said to have changed.' Soane failed him, so Haydon bore alone the consequences of his enormous folly.

Haydon's attack on Payne Knight was merely a piece of gratuitous quarrelsomeness. Knight's article had appeared eighteen months before and had probably been forgotten by everyone. In it he had praised Rembrandt more highly than Haydon thought he deserved; and Haydon, as his manner was, took it as a personal offence that such pictures as Rembrandt's (which nevertheless he admired) should be put on a level with *true* historical pictures, such as his own and Raphael's. So pernicious a doctrine was 'prejudicial to the advance of High Art in this country', and must not be tolerated: 'You praise the Picture of Rembrandt, sir, as all men praise such pictures who know they are in a lower rank in spite of their wishes. Michael Angelo and Raphael excelled in the intellectual excellencies of the Art, therefore in the highest. Rubens, Vandyke, Tintoretto and Rembrandt in the mechanism of the Art, and therefore in the lowest. . . . Let connoisseurs say what they will, they cannot, they are not, they must not, be put on a level with Michael Angelo and Raphael.' This cogent reasoning (we are told) 'demolished' Payne Knight; but his victor had not finished with him even then. Knight had had the audacity to assert that greatness of size was no advantage in a picture, 'but', says Haydon, 'we affirm without fear of refutation, that *greatness* added to *goodness*, and correct and finished excellence with real sublimity, the full size of life will more powerfully affect human feelings, than the same correctness and the same arrangement on a scale less than life'. Throughout his polemical career Haydon was to mistake affirmation for argument, and rhetoric for reasoning.

The attack on the Academy is a fine example of rancour arising from wounded vanity: making an enemy with every stroke of his pen he sneers at 'the palpable absurdities of the Exhibition, at the little girls feeding chickens and the little boys feeding pigs and children fetching water from the well'. If Payne Knight had sneered at *these*, Haydon tells him, he would have shown greater feeling for the taste of the country than by doubtfully sneering at the grand style 'which alone can give rank to "this England in art"'. Then, forgetting still further the thin pretence that by 'the art of the country' or 'the grand style' he meant anything other than his own work, he launches out against the R.A.s: '. . . there is a set whose imbecile prejudices against the rising Students are apparent, and against the Institution [which had awarded him the premium for *Dentatus*], and against any person and every place that will foster or protect them; composed of all those who find that travelling to Italy, copying in the Vatican, lounging in the coffee-houses, will not give them that power which nature has denied them; composed of all those who have struggled a short time in the higher walks of art, then sunk into picture dealers, and then sunk into nothing —hence the hatred of the Academicians to the Gallery [The British Institution], because it will afford an opening to those who exhibit careful and legitimate excellence.'

This letter made it impossible for the committee to give its £300 prize to Haydon for his *Macbeth* without seeming to endorse his laudation of the Institution at the expense of the Academy, with which it was, and wished to remain, on friendly terms; while his attack on Payne Knight (an influential member of the committee) clinched the matter. Most characteristically he wrote these letters just before competing, thereby utterly ruining his chance of success. He lost all his influence, which had been considerable, with this powerful body of patrons, who had formed their society, not only for exhibitions of the old masters, but to encourage modern art. 'As the result of these letters,' he says indignantly, 'my picture was caricatured, my name detested, and my peace harassed, so great was the indignation that all merit was denied to *Macbeth*! I was looked at like a monster, abused like a plague, and avoided like a maniac. I had imagined the truth would have been felt by all, and that all would bless him who showed her to them. . . . But every stipulation with his destiny for safety must be dismissed by him who is ambitious of being a great reformer. I therefore glory in having done it when I did. I would rather have perished at that age in doing it than have waited till it was safer. I was twenty-six years of age when I attacked the Academy, I exposed their petty intrigues, I laid open their ungrateful, cruel, and heartless treatment of Wilkie, I annihilated Payne Knight's absurd theories against great works . . . and having swept the path, I laid down rules to guide the student, which time must confirm—rules, the result of my own failures, collected and digested within six years— rules, which posterity will refer to and confirm, early acquired without master or instructor, settled in spite of folly, and put forth in spite of ignorance or rank.'

He had exposed no intrigues, he had laid down no rules, and had none worth laying down. The cruel treatment of Wilkie consisted in hanging his pictures in excellent positions and making him an Associate at an early age, but Haydon had singled him out for exception, and made him seem a party to this attack against the very institution he was most anxious to please. 'But

Wilkie,' he cries, 'Wilkie to uphold whose genius in the sincerity of my glowing heart I would have stood before a battery of blazing cannon and have been blown to splinters rather than have degraded his power—Wilkie shrank back terrified, and in order to exculpate himself joined in the abuse of me. . . . Yet he must be excused. He begged me not to do what I did. He entreated I would not defend him. It might be cowardly to decline walking with me in the streets, as he did, but he ought not to be blamed for endeavouring to screen himself from the consequences of violence which he was not to blame for and foresaw.' Wilkie wrote to expostulate, pointing out that Haydon had laid himself open not only to the charge of spleen and disappointment, but to railing at the Academy in order to ingratiate himself with the British Institution; and that he had, with the worst possible taste, run down one of the men who was competing with him for the premium. His bitterest enemy could not have done him greater damage. The attack was entirely unprovoked and unnecessary, a mere explosion of temper, yet he professed to glory in it to the day of his death; 'for though', he says, 'in moments of depression I wished I had taken Wilkie's advice, I should not then have acquired that grand isolated reputation, solitary and unsupported, which while it encumbers the individual with a heavy burden, inspires him with vigour proportionate to the load'. About the Academy he was scarcely sane. 'Such a tendency exists in the Academy', he wrote, 'to see nothing but what is wrong in my actions, that it amounts to a morbid insanity.' As the Blackwood reviewer said, 'Haydon often gives the impression that he has suffered some heinous wrong at the hands of the Academicians—there seems no ground whatever for this assumption.' He would hear no argument for the defence, and became furious at the bare attempt to excuse its alleged transgressions. 'Thus then', he wrote, 'for the rest of my anxious life my destiny was altered. I had brought forty men and all their high connexions on my back at twenty-six years old, and there was nothing left but "Victory or Westminster Abbey". I made up my mind for the conflict and ordered at once a larger canvas for another work,'

VI. FORLORN HOPE

Though Mars himself, the angry god of arms,
And all the earthly potentates conspire
To dispossess me of this diadem,
Yet will I wear it in despite of them.

MARLOWE

AS Haydon was walking one day down the Haymarket, in the greatest anxiety about a debt, he met Prince Hoare, who spoke of the Academy and said, 'They will deny your talents and deprive you of employment.' 'But', said Haydon, 'if I produce a work of such merit as cannot be denied, the public will carry me through.' 'They know nothing of the art.' 'That I deny, the merest shoeblack would understand *Ananias*.' Hoare shook his head. 'What are you going to paint?' 'Solomon's Judgement.' 'Raphael and Rubens have both tried it.' 'So much the better. I'll tell the story better.' Hoare smiled, and, putting his hand on Haydon's shoulder, said, 'How are you going to live?' 'Leave that to me.' 'Who is to pay your rent?' 'Leave that to me.' 'Well,' said Hoare, 'I see you are ready with a reply. You will never sell it.' 'I trust in God.' Hoare shook hands, as if Haydon was light-headed, and saying, 'If you are arrested send for me,' walked away.

At first the desperate nature of his position prevented Haydon from working and he would sometimes sit for hours in a sort of daze, doing nothing. But these fits passed, and in a few weeks he began again. Early in April his canvas for *The Judgement of Solomon* arrived, and its great size; 12 ft. 10 in. by 10 ft. 10 in., so thrilled him that he soon forgot his worries in the excitement of a new work.

If *Dentatus* had been a partial success, and *Macbeth* a disaster, *Solomon* was a triumph. The painting of this picture (now lost, but by all observers considered his best), in conditions of great difficulty, with no money except what he could borrow from his friends and the dread of a debtor's prison in the background, was an achievement he always looked back on with pride. It took him two years, and by the end of that time he had reached his limit, in health and resources and courage. What he had said

49

to his father about leading a forlorn hope was true, all his fine qualities came out under the strain. The situation roused in him that strange mixture of courage with quailing of the spirit, a kind of sobbing valour, the presence of which makes itself felt in the later volumes of the *Journals*.

When Prince Hoare asked Haydon how he was going to live, and he answered, 'Leave that to me', he should have said, 'Leave that to my friends'.

He now went to Wilkie and told him he wanted the common necessities of life; Wilkie looked at him with horror. Haydon asked for £10, Wilkie shook, got nervous and stammered out he could not spare more (he had lent some £30 already). Haydon pressed, Wilkie persisted he could not; he kept saying, 'I told you so, I told you so.' Haydon walked out without another word. What was he to do? How could he go on? He owed his landlord £200; would he allow it? How was he to dine, to live in fact? Where was he to get his dinner that day? He had just rubbed in a large picture, should he throw up the whole thing, retire to small lodgings and do anything for a living? But if he did he could never make enough to pay his debts; besides he loathed the thought, it was defeat; and how could he bear the sneers of the students to whom he had preached that failure should stimulate and not depress? How could he bear his own reflections when he compared himself with Julius Caesar? Is that how Napoleon would have behaved? Never! and should it be said of him that he had given in at the first brush? Something instantly surged within him, and—'striding with wider steps' (he must have been reading his Homer), 'I determined', he said, 'to bear all—not to yield one particle of my designs—to go at once for my model—to begin to-morrow and to make the best of my situation. "Well done," said the God within, and instantly I was invincible.' He went to the house where he dined, intending to dine without paying that day. He thought the servants were less attentive than usual. He thought the other diners eyed him curiously, he thought the meat was worse. His heart sank as he said falteringly: 'I will pay you to-morrow.' The girl smiled and seemed interested. As he was escaping with 'a sort of lurking horror', she called after him, 'Mr. Haydon, Mr. Haydon, my master wishes to see you.' 'My God,' thought he, 'it is to tell me he can't trust.' In he walked like a culprit. 'Sir, I beg your pardon, but I see by the papers that you have been ill-used; I hope you won't be angry—I mean no offence; but—you won't be offended—I just wish to say, as you have dined here many years and always paid, if it would be a convenience during your present work, to dine here till it is done—you know—so that you may not be obliged to spend your money here, when you may want it—I was going to say you need be under no apprehension—hem! for a dinner.' Haydon's heart filled. He told him he would take his offer, and the good man, whose forehead was perspiring, seemed quite relieved. While 'from that hour', says Haydon, with one of his not infrequent perfect touches, 'the servants (who were pretty girls) eyed me with a lustrous regret and redoubled their attentions'.

'Now,' said he, as he walked away with an elastic step, 'now, for my landlord.' He called up Perkins and laid his desperate case before him; Perkins was quite affected. Haydon said: 'Perkins, I'll leave you if you wish it but it will be a pity, will it not, not to finish such a beginning?' Perkins looked at it and muttered, 'It's a grand thing; how long will it be before it's done, sir?' 'Two years.' 'What, two years more, and no rent?' 'Not a shilling.' Perkins rubbed his chin and muttered, 'I should not like ye to go—it's hard for both of us; but I will say this you always paid me when you could, and why should you not again when you are able?' 'That's what I say.' 'Well, sir, here is my hand, I'll give you two more years, and if this does not sell, why then, sir, we'll consider what is to be done; so don't fret but work.' These were two vast loads off his mind, and he knelt down and prayed, and rose up 'refreshed and buoyant'. He spent the evening greatly affected, weeping when he contrasted this behaviour with that of his friend for whose reputation he had 'sacrificed everything'. Directly he awoke the following morning he flung himself on his knees: 'O, God Almighty, who so mercifully assisted me during my last picture . . . enable me to conceive all the characters with the utmost possible acuteness and dignity, and execute them with the utmost possible greatness and power. . . . O God, in pecuniary emergences Thou hast never deserted me; still in such moments stretch forth thy protecting hand.'

No sooner was he launched on his new picture than his health gave way. The long strain and disappointment of *Macbeth*, the excitement of the letters to the *Examiner*, and, now, an entanglement with 'an infernal woman' which shattered his peace of

mind, left him with habits so broken, and a mind so agitated
that a rest became necessary. With the Hunts' assistance (they
paid for his journey) he visited an uncle in Cheddar, where he
soon recovered. His sister joined him—her prospects at home
were unhappy (she married a Dr. Haviland soon after), and his
were gloomy; he could not offer her a home with him, and they
said good-bye 'with suppressed feelings affectionate and melancholy'. Yet at the sight of the smoky pall that hung over London,
and the sense of its energy, ambition and vigour, his spirits rose
as he considered the great scheme to which he had dedicated
himself. Towards that *Solomon* was only a stepping-stone. He
had conceived a plan and formed a resolution which became the
first object of his ambition, and for which he fought with a
persistence that would not be easy to parallel year after year till
the day of his death. Lord Mulgrave had sent him a ticket for the
opening of Parliament by the Prince as Regent for the first
time. It was a grand affair. Haydon went again in the evening
to hear the debates, and it was while listening to Lord Wellesley,
and noticing the 'miserable tapestry which surrounded him'[1]
that he conceived a series of designs to adorn the sides of the
House. He became gloriously abstracted and visualized the whole
series at once, to represent the different forms of government,
good and bad, 'the horrors of anarchy; the injustice of democracy; the cruelty of despotism; the infamies of revolution; the
beauty of justice; to conclude with limited monarchy and its
blessings'. It was for such an opportunity that he lived, and he
laid his plan before every Minister down to Lord Melbourne and
Sir Robert Peel. To have received such a commission would
have solved all his difficulties and would have satisfied his vast
ambition. It was a fatal evening for him. The hopes he then conceived were to be the breaking of his heart. Henceforth public
patronage for art was to be the first object of his existence; he
soon taught himself to believe that he was completely disinterested, and that he was working single-mindedly for the glory
of the nation and the instruction of the people, not for his own
hand. The bed-rock of his contention was that the Government
was willing to spend thousands on sculpture for buildings, but
would not vote a penny for pictures. His conception matured

[1] These are the famous and beautiful tapestries representing the Defeat of
the Armada. See the engravings by Pine in his *Tapestry Hangings of the House
of Lords*, 1739. The portions saved from the fire of 1835 are at Hampton Court.

daily, and he made many sketches, till at last he brought it to something like completion.

He believed (and he was by no means alone in doing so) that only by large pictures could the country ever take its place as a great nation in art. Haydon asks where Raphael would be if only his smaller pictures remained, and answers: Nowhere. It is difficult to know exactly how large a share personal ambition played in the matter; one thing is certain: it was not that alone. Even at the end of his life when he knew he would not participate he still ardently longed to see his scheme go through. This plan once formed, the idea was never absent from his mind. In the meantime he struggled on at *Solomon* which was to prove his fitness for the greater work.

He was living entirely on credit. His landlord had had no rent for three years, and did not press, and he was treated as an honoured guest at the house where he dined and could not pay.

Solomon was painted in a small room, with insufficient space to raise it up. For the upper part he had to stand on a table, and for the lower to go down on his knees. Painters of those days often speak of working eight or ten hours on a winter's day. How was it done? They only had candles or argand lamps, and to paint by the dim, yellow light must have been amazingly difficult. Lawrence boasted that on one occasion he painted for thirty-six hours at a stretch, and by the end of the time he was so exhausted that he could scarcely see. In January (1813) Haydon says, 'Dark day—hard at work: the light could hardly make its way through the blanket of a sky.'

Haydon's method of painting was peculiar: he used large, round, concave spectacles, so powerful as greatly to diminish objects, of these he had three pairs on his head all the time he worked. He would mount his steps, study his model through one pair of glasses, then, pushing them all back on his forehead, paint, with his naked eye close to the canvas. After some minutes he would pull down one pair of glasses, and look at his model, then, stepping to the ground, walk slowly backwards to the wall to study the effect, pulling down first the second and then the third pair as he got further away. Next, with one pair only, he looked long and steadily at the reflection of his picture in a looking-glass (which exaggerates faults of balance and drawing), and then mounting his steps began to paint again. It is little wonder he made mistakes in proportion, or that he found portrait painting difficult. He took great pains in arranging the position of his model before he began to work, making many changes so as to get harmony of light and shadow. When he had settled the composition of his picture he made an oil sketch, and from this he roughly scumbled in the whole on the canvas in raw umber, apparently without any squaring-off. This generally took a day.[1] When this was dry he began with the head of one of the principal figures, completing it at a sitting. Thus day after day he went through the whole, finishing as he went, but reserving the right to heighten his colour, or deepen his shadow in the final glazings.[2] Throughout his life he studied every figure, for whatever subject (portraits excepted), in the nude, and then clothed it or draped it where necessary. His son, in comparing him with other painters he had seen working, said the thing that always most impressed him was 'his marvellous rapidity' and 'intense precision' of touch.

'It was', says Frederic, 'as if he had seen in his mind's eye the effect of every touch before he had set his palette.' He never began till he had thought out exactly what he meant to do, then, when he took up his brush, 'his mind overflowed, he flew at his work like a man inspired with fiery impulse, talking to himself in a rapid whisper and utterly lost to all the world around. . . . He never seemed for a moment to naggle or hesitate. If the result were not satisfactory he became greatly agitated. I have seen big drops of perspiration come out on his brow. Another touch or two, and then perhaps he would dash it all out and breathe again freely. In painting the human form or that of animals he always had the living model before him. His horses were brought into the house, and stabled for the day on the ground floor. After he had hit the exact expression he wanted he would never touch it again, but swish down his palette and brushes and say, "There, thirty years of experience are in that, and yet how infinitely below what I aim at! But I shall not do better." And then he would fling open the shutters and begin to write.'

The last remark is a little puzzling. It seems to have been the custom to use very little light when painting; Reynolds used only one small window, nine feet from the ground; while

[1] So his son says, but it is an obviously impossible estimate for a large picture with many figures, such as *Solomon*.

[2] Transparent films of paint taken over the picture to deepen the tone or strengthen the colour.

pictures of Dutch artists in their studios often show tiny windows.

Haydon let anyone see his pictures at all stages. 'The instinctive feeling of the untutored', he used to say, 'is often to be preferred to the delusions of mere artists.'

He worked steadily through the whole of 1813, secure for food and lodging, but with no ready money except what he borrowed, or got by pawning his possession, which he did till he had scarcely anything left. His books, his clothes, his prints, and his watch, all went. The Hunts kept him going with unfailing kindness though they were at this time in prison for the libel on the Prince. Haydon spent many evenings with one or other of them (they were in different prisons), and on leaving would go 'through the clanking of chains and the crashing of bolts to the splendid evenings at the British Gallery', to be distressed by the contrast. The Hunts were among the first of his many literary friends, followed by Hazlitt, whom he met at Northcote's. As they walked away together Hazlitt praised *Macbeth*; Haydon asked him to come in. 'Thence', says he, 'began a friendship for that interesting man, that singular mixture of friend and fiend, radical and critic, metaphysician, poet and painter, on whose word no one could rely, on whose heart no one could calculate, and some of whose deductions he himself would try to explain in vain.'

Others of his friends were Barnes (of *The Times*), Charles Lamb, Horace Smith (*Rejected Addresses*), Wordsworth, Southey, Coleridge, Serjeant Talfourd, Samuel Rogers, Sydney Smith, and Miss Mitford, all of whom he met about this time or soon after. A friend of another sort of whom he was to see a great deal was the celebrated Maria Foote, who, in 1814, made her debut at Covent Garden, as Amanthis, in *The Child of Nature*. A Plymouth girl, their two families had long been intimate; and Haydon describes himself later as being perpetually about with her, and through her seeing much of other actresses, whom he characteristically liked and disapproved of. 'Certain delightful qualities in women', he says, 'are usually attended with certain tendencies to vice. If you love the one you must risk the other.' Her chief importance to him however is that she introduced him to his future wife.

Hazlitt, who was mortified at his own failure as a painter, lost no chance of 'damping the ardour, chilling the hopes, and dimming the prospects' of others, and Haydon sometimes found him an infinitely depressing companion. 'Why did you begin it so large?' he would ask, of *Solomon*, in a miserable hesitating voice, 'a smaller canvas would have concealed your faults. You'll never sell it.' 'No,' Northcote would say, 'I'll bet my very life you never do.' 'Why—why—why not?' Lamb would stutter. 'In our meetings,' says Haydon, 'Hazlitt's croakings, Leigh Hunt's wit and Lamb's quaint incomprehensibilities made rare scenes. Lamb stuttered his quaintness in snatches, like the fool in Lear, and with equal beauty'; An onlooker would have added as part of the rarity of the scenes Haydon's own talk and high spirits and fits of laughter at Lamb's jokes, in which he rolled on the ground. If Wilkie were there he would contribute his share with his inevitable, 'Re-e-eally? dear, dear!'

Haydon's excellent description of the christening party for Hazlitt's son, throws so much light on himself that it may be given here:

'In the midst of Hazlitt's weaknesses his parental affections were beautiful. He had one boy. He loved him, doted on him. He told me one night this boy was to be christened. "Will ye come on Friday?" "Certainly," said I. His eye glistened. Friday came, but as I knew all parties I lunched heartily first and was there punctually at four. Hazlitt then lived in Milton's House, Westminster, next door to Bentham.

'At four I came but he was out. I walked up and found his wife ill by the fire in a bed-gown—nothing ready for guests and everything wearing the appearance of neglect and indifference. I said "Where is Hazlitt?" "Oh dear, William has gone to look for a parson." "A parson; why, has he not thought of that before?" "No, he didn't." "I'll go and look for him," said I, and out I went into the park through Queen's Square, and met Hazlitt in a rage coming home. "Have ye got a parson?" "No, Sir," said he, "these fellows are all out." "What will you do?" "Nothing." So in we walked, Hazlitt growling at all the parsons and the church. When we came in we sat down—nobody was come—no table laid—no appearance of dinner. On my life there is nothing so heartless as going out to dinner and finding no dinner ready. I sat down; the company began to drop in—Charles Lamb and his poor sister—all sorts of odd, clever people. Still no dinner. At last came in a maid who laid a cloth and put down knives and forks in a heap. Then followed a dish of potatoes, cold, waxy, and yellow. Then came a great bit of beef with a bone like a battering-ram, toppling on all its corners. Neither Hazlitt nor Lamb seemed at all disturbed, but set to work help-

ing each other; while the boy, half-clean and obstinate, kept squalling
to put his fingers into the gravy. Even Lamb's wit and Hazlitt's disquisitions, in a large room, wainscotted and ancient, where Milton had
meditated, could not reconcile me to such violation of all the decencies
of life. I returned weary, and placing a candle on the floor of my room
soon recovered under the imposing look of my picture and retired to
bed filled with thought.'

This is one of many glimpses Haydon gives of himself—many
such nights was he to look back on with that malady of regret
for youth and the past which it is the way of the years to bring.

Let scepticism close its eyes for a moment, and among the
shadows of that dark painting-room in Great Marlborough
Street, lit by the light of its single candle, placed on the floor,
let Haydon be imagined as he stood that evening nearly a century and a half ago, a cheap teacup in his hand, his shadow
thrown back sharply at his feet to lose itself in the poor mysteries
where are his sagging bed and tiny wash-stand. While he sips
and swallows his thoughts soar into realms of majesty where his
Solomon—the triumph of the English School—hangs in a figura-
tive picture gallery that exists, not in any special place, but in
the admiration of mankind with Raphael's *Transfiguration* and
Correggio's *Marriage of St. Catherine*. Round him as he stands
in his shabby clothes are the facts of penury, in his soul the facts
of imagination—glory, supremacy in art, and the buzzing applause of the world.

The actor and his setting might well be chosen without any
alteration to represent on the stage the aspiration of youth; and
let us be grateful that such exaltation as he felt is granted not only
to the very few who have been gifted to bring it to earth in
concrete form by the magic arrow of genius. He might almost
stand as the type of those (how many millions) who have longed
but could not achieve. He is pre-eminent in the passion with
which he wanted, and in the life-long struggle he kept up, as
also in the courage with which he faced his difficulties. But above
all he was articulate, and could express the hope and despair
which have been common in greater or less degree, to all the
others. Few laymen are aware of the miseries of the artist—
which equal the wretchedness of the saint who believes he has
fallen from grace—when he sees the vision he thought he had
within his grasp, drowned in baffling incompetence.

His friend Wilkie may stand for another type of artist, the

unaspiring, successful type, satisfied with painting well, having his work appreciated, and making a good income. He was satisfied with success. Haydon wanted the glamour of success. He almost preferred to endure poverty and danger and neglect because they would add to his glory when he finally achieved.

On Christmas Eve he began the head of Solomon at ten in the morning and worked straight on till three o'clock on the following morning when it was finished. His model left after six hours, exhausted. All the heads were now done; the young mother's head had been painted four or five times before he was satisfied. The picture had begun to have an imposing look, but his necessities were dreadful; he had been nearly four years without a commission and three without any aid from home, but the Hunts had assisted him at the cost of great personal deprivation. 'It was something to be grateful for,' he says, 'and grateful I was to my Great Protector.'

One day while he was working news was brought of his father's death; he read the letter, but his mind was so intensely occupied that it made no impression on him. He went on painting till he had finished, and then his loss burst upon him. He always regarded the head he painted this day as the best he ever did. Some of his most successful work was done under similar harassing conditions. More than a month of 1814 had passed and his picture had to be ready for one of the spring exhibitions. His application, in spite of his failing health, he says, was 'dreadful'; stimulated by an enthusiasm whipped by despair into a state almost of delirium, and living for a fortnight on potatoes, because they were the only thing he could digest, he broke down, nor did he ever quite get back his originally perfect health. His picture was finished except for the toning, but his eyes were so affected that he could see no longer.

His next anxiety was about a frame: he sent for Carpenter, his frame-maker, told him how his landlord had felt it his duty to assist a young man who was doing such fine work, and put it to him that he could do no less. The old man said, 'You have always paid me: I will.' Adams, his oculist, advised generous diet, and wine, which he could not buy. Haydon sent for a wine merchant, showed him *Solomon*, told him he was in bad health, and appealed to him whether he ought after such an effort to be without the glass of wine which his medical man had recommended. 'Certainly not,' said the wine merchant, 'I'll send you two dozen; pay me as soon as you can, and recollect to drink success to Solomon the first glass you taste.'

While he was in this state the picture began to make a noise; old West, the President, called and was affected to tears by the young mother. 'But get into better air; you will never recover with this eternal anxiety before you. Have you any resources?' 'They are exhausted.' 'D'ye want money?' 'Indeed I do.' 'So do I,' said West, 'they have stopped my income from the King, but Fauntleroy is now arranging an advance, and if I succeed, my young friend, you shall hear. Don't be cast down—such a work must not be allowed to be forgotten.' Later on the same day fifteen pounds came from West.

The question now was where to send the picture. Wilkie advised the Academy. Haydon said he would perish first. He eventually decided on the Water-Colour Society (in Spring Gardens), which then admitted oil-paintings. The day approached. The picture was unstretched, rolled, and taken safely to the gallery, where it was re-stretched and put up in a centre position with nothing near it. With a frame 'wasted and hectic', with 'quivering eyes, and a trembling hand' he prepared to glaze it on the days allowed.

The opening day came: as he tottered down the Haymarket he leaned on a post and said: 'What shall I do if it do not sell?' 'Order another canvas,' said his inward voice, 'and begin a greater work.' 'So I will,' he thought, and thenceforth lost all despondence. Before half an hour a gentleman came up and offered £500, 'Will you take it?' Haydon's heart beat; his agonies of want pressed, but it was too little, he trembled out, 'I cannot.'

On the third day as he walked into the room he looked across at his picture and saw the word SOLD upon it. He almost fainted.

The picture was bought for seven hundred guineas by Sir William Elford, Miss Mitford's correspondent, and an old friend of Sir Joshua's. It appears that Sir George Beaumont and Holwell Carr had been deputed to buy it for the British Gallery, but were just too late.

As Haydon was standing in a daze up came Sir George and holding out his hand said, 'Haydon, I am astonished. You must paint me a picture after all. Yes, indeed, you must; Lady Beaumont and I will call—yes, indeed.'

When he got home he found his table covered with 'cards of

fashion—noble lords, dukes, ladies, baronets, literary men'. The picture received high praise in the *Morning Chronicle* from Hazlitt, who accepted it as a proof of genius. There is David Wilkie's opinion of many years later, 'That is truly a great work—well gone into in all its parts, nothing is slighted, nothing little, and it combines tenderness and delicacy of feeling with real power over his materials and art. Ah, it is grand! with affecting sentiment, and would have done honour to Rome and Venice.' Leigh Hunt in the *Examiner* devoted a long article to it, saying, 'This painter is justly classed among the great masters of Art.' The *Spectator* said, 'About Haydon's capacity for achieving greatness there is no question'; and Fuseli, 'By Gode, it is the finest ting dat eaver any Englishman painted!' 'Tell Haydon I am astonished,' said Turner to a friend, and Miss Mitford, thirty years later, wrote that after the exhibition of *Solomon* 'he was considered the most promising artist in England'. Callcott assured him that no people had a higher respect for his talents than the Academicians, and that he was quite mistaken if he imagined they had not. Some of them seem to have made overtures, which he was bitterly to regret later not having met; but his victory, which he characteristically overestimated, swelled his vanity to such a degree that he assumed a lofty indifference and lost his last chance. So delighted was he with himself that he had the immense picture taken to Surrey gaol and set up there to show Leigh Hunt.

He was pretty nearly at the end of his tether. 'These elevations', he says, 'to the heights of glory from the lowest depths of misery are dreadful cuts into the constitution. I slept with horrid dreams and startling restlessness. My landlord's honest joy was exquisite to me. I paid him £200 [out of £400], and he drew on me for the balance. John O'Groat held out his big hand and almost cried. I paid him £42 10s. My baker spread my honesty and fame in Mark lane . . . I paid him every shilling. My tailor, my coal-merchant, my private friends were all paid. In short £500 went easily the first week, leaving me with £130. It did not half pay my debts [he admits to owing £1,100], but it established my credit. Many private friends forbore to press, the Hunts the foremost.'

People of every description now crowded to see him; some had known his father; some had nursed him as a baby; fathers brought their sons that he might look at their drawings; authors sent him their works; his sister came to town to share his fame, and he pressed her to his heart, 'overwhelmed by the dreadful and painful burst of reputation after such long, struggling obscurity'. 'The success of Solomon', he says, 'was so great and my triumph so complete, that had I died then my name must have stood on record as a youth who had made a stand against the prejudices of a country, the oppressions of rank, and the cruelty and injustice of two public bodies.'

'It was a victory in every sense of the word,' he wrote thirty years later; 'in my pursuit I had proved the power of inherent talent, and I had done good to the great cause, as far as I could do it. I did not command bayonets and cannons; would to God I had! But what I did command I wielded with firmness and constancy. . . . I had been tried and not found wanting. I held out when feeble and faint and blind, and now I reaped the reward.'

This achievement was surrounded with glamour for Haydon for the rest of his life; as the years passed *Solomon* grew greater and greater in his estimation: 'In looking again after long absence', he writes in 1840, 'at this wonderful picture, painted at twenty-six and twenty-seven, and brought out at twenty-eight, I candidly acknowledge I am astonished. Taking into account all my difficulties, necessities, want of instruction from any master, my youth and the fact that I had only painted three pictures before, when I look at the execution, the manner and firmness of the touch, I no longer wonder at the uproar it made at its appearance. Good God! Ought I to fear comparison of it with the Duke of Sutherland's Murillo or any other picture? Certainly not.'

And again, in 1842: 'Called in to see my dear old painting-room, at 41 Great Marlborough Street, where I painted my Dentatus, Macbeth, Solomon, and part of Jerusalem. Perkins, my dear old landlord (who behaved so nobly through Solomon) was dead. The house was bought and undergoing repair; the rooms stripped and desolate; the cupboard, the little room where I slept, and the plaster-room, with all their associations, crowded on me. . . . I thought once of putting up a brass plate, "Here Haydon painted his Solomon, 1813". For want of engraving the picture is now forgotten.'

Not only so, but lost. Like its author *Solomon* had a varied fate. Elford sold it to a Mr. Prideau for £800. In his will (1846) Haydon says: 'William Newton . . . holds pictures and books

and prints, and the Judgement of Solomon, which is the property
of the assignees of the late Mr. Prideau of Plymouth, bankrupt;
he took possession of the picture at the Western Exchange, and
paid the rent due, on my insolvency in 1830. His claim is for
warehouse-room, for which he paid.' This explains the constant
references to it in the *Journals*: (1826) 'Where is your Solomon,
Mr. Haydon?' 'Hung up in a grocer's shop.' (1836) 'My Solomon is rotting in a carpenter's shop.' Or, at other times, in a hay-
loft, or a barn. Later (1853) Taylor tells us that it is in an honoured position in Sir Edwin Landseer's house in St. John's
Wood. And Frederic Haydon who published his Memoir in
1876 says the picture was then the property of Louisa, Lady
Ashburton. The present Lord Ashburton has no knowledge of it.

Haydon and Wilkie made plans to start for Paris at once.
Harriet was to stay with Wilkie's mother and sister, who were
now in London. He felt an immense relief.

Napoleon was overthrown and was going to Elba. All the
nations were in Paris; the Louvre was in its glory, with the loot
of half the galleries of Europe. 'No human being', says Haydon,
'hereafter can ever enter into the feelings of Europe when we
heard Napoleon was in retreat; it cannot be comprehended.'

On 26 May the friends set out for Brighton. But before leaving another canvas was on the easel, and *Christ's Entry into Jerusalem* had been rubbed in.

VII. PARIS, 1814

But where is he, the modern, mightier far,
Who, born no king, made monarchs draw his car.

BYRON

AS the friends approached Paris, thoughts of the dreadful scenes that had happened there since 1792 crowded on Haydon's imagination. He was going to visit that 'bloody and ferocious capital, in which refinement and filth, murder and revolution, blasphemy and heroism, vice and virtue alternately reigned triumphant'.

But these stern thoughts were dissipated at the sight of two old Frenchwomen with short petticoats and wooden shoes, which set the young Englishman laughing outright.

Everything had 'a deserted, forlorn, insecure appearance': and after driving through the outskirts at their leisure, they entered the city 'by one of the most dreadful entrances this side of the infernal regions'.

'For my part,' says Haydon, 'I was passionately affected. I had read everything from the first sitting of the National Convention to the dethronement of Napoleon, and was now plunging into the inextricable confusion of the Rue Saint Honoré, in the middle of the day, shaken to my heart's core.'

The first impression was one of hopeless confusion; 'cabs, carts, horses, women, boys, girls, soldiers, carriages, all in endless struggle; streets narrow, houses high, no flat pavement. Russians, Poles, Germans, Italians, English, Jews, Turks, and Christians, all hot, hurried, and in a fidget. In the midst now and then you might see a beautiful French girl, with her little black apron and trim black-haired head, stopping in the middle of the crossing, affecting to be frightened, darting about her eyes for help, tucking her petticoats round her slender form, and before you can come to her aid, she steps lightly between the carriages, and trips along in gaiety and triumph.'

They drove to their hotel in the Rue Villedot, where Wilkie was greatly shocked—a pretty maid-servant showed them through a suite of rooms hung round with indelicate prints.

63

The next day they went to the Louvre. Intense was Haydon's excitement as he dashed up the steps, and deep his scorn as he looked back and saw Wilkie quietly walking on at his usual pace. Wilkie stopped at 'some Jan Steen', and Haydon rushed on breathless, looking at nothing till he came to Raphael's Transfiguration. His first feeling was of disappointment, it looked 'small, harsh and hard' (13 ft. x 8 ft.). Even Titian's Peter Martyr (19 ft. x 12 ft.) was smaller than he had expected. A serious fault! However, getting over this, he gradually felt their wonder.

They changed their expensive hotel for cheaper rooms, and here, as soon as they were settled, Wilkie fell ill, overcome by the excitement and strain of the journey. By their landlord's advice Haydon went for a 'distinguished physician', whom he eventually ran to earth at midday, in a café, playing dominoes. The physician came at once, saying to his antagonist, 'Attendez un moment, mon cher.' When they got back there was a difficulty: Haydon talked French better than he understood it, Wilkie did neither. At last the doctor, in a fury, thundered out, 'Parlez-vous Latin?'

'Oui, Monsieur.' 'Ah, ah!' And soon they came to the point. A prescription was given, a fee paid, and away went Haydon to a chemist, where to his wonder the medicine was put into a champagne bottle.

He went out till the evening, leaving Wilkie to his medicine, which he drank in large glass-fulls, with such good result that when Haydon came back he found him quite recovered, and in roars of laughter, trying to teach his landlady to speak English by the system of repeating 'Peter Piper picked a peck of pepper off a pewter plate'.

The interest and attraction of the streets were so great that they left small time for the Louvre, and Haydon with Wilkie wandered about absorbed in the scene before him, finding every step excited some mighty association.

'Every church,' he writes, 'every place, every street, and every corner was remarkable for some slaughter, or struggle, or wonder connected with revolution and blood; yet everywhere a sense of despotism pressed on your mind. There was in everything a look of gilded slavery and bloody splendour, a tripping grace in the women, a ragged blackguardism in the men and a polished fierceness in the soldiers, which distinguished Paris as the capital of a people who combine more inconsistent vices and virtues than any other people on the earth.

'At this moment, too, there was with all this an air of mortified vanity and suppressed exasperation which was natural. By the side of the Russian, Austrian, Prussian, and English officers, the remnant of Napoleon's army had a look of blasted glory, of withered pride and lurking revenge, which gave one a shudder of the sublime, and it was clear to anyone of the commonest sagacity that they must seize the first opportunity of trying to regain their lost position.

'In the middle of the day the Rue St. Honoré was the most wonderful sight. Don Cossacks chiefs loosely clothed and moving as their horses moved, with all the bendings of their bodies visible at every motion; the half-clothed, savage Cossack horseman, his belt stuck full of pistols and watches and hatches, crouched up on a little ragged-maned, dirty-looking, ill-bred, half-white, shaggy pony; the Russian Imperial guards-man pinched in at the waist like a wasp, striding along like a giant, with an air of victory that made every Frenchman curse within his teeth as he passed him; the English officer with his boyish face and broad shoulders; the heavy Austrian, the natty Prussian; and now and then a Bashkir Tartar, in the ancient Phrygian cap, with bow and arrows and chain armour, gazing about from his horse in the midst of black-eyed grisettes, Jews, Turks and Christians from all countries in Europe and Asia. It was a pageant that kept one staring, musing and bewildered from morning till night.

'On looking down the Louvre one day, full of people of all nations, I said: "Now, Wilkie, suppose you did not know any nation present, what would be your impression from the look of the English?" Wilkie looked a minute, and contemplating their sedate, respectable monied look by the side of the Russians and French, said: "Dear, dear, they just look as if they had a balance at their bankers."'

They visited Versailles and saw the Great and Little Trianon, and Haydon went by himself to Rambouillet, where he saw the Emperor's secret closet, which produced in him one of the best of those musings in which he so excelled.

The thought of Napoleon was always profoundly stimulating to Haydon, he saw in him the fulfilment of an ambition as great even as his own, and he constantly affirmed himself to be of the Napoleon species. He wrote to Leigh Hunt:

'From this drawing-room I entered a private room of small dimen-sions. This was Napoleon's private closet for repose and reflection, where he used to retire when exhausted, and to which no one was admitted but the Empress.

'The little room seemed a complete illustration of the mind and feelings of this extraordinary man. Opposite the window was an elegant arch, under which stood a most luxurious satin couch, with the softest pillows. Round the arch were painted in gold the names Austerlitz, Marengo, Friedland, &c. and down the side the arms of all the states tributary to France, with groups of warlike implements; and "N.N.N." with laurel crowned the head. When Napoleon lay in indolent seclusion on this luxurious couch, he was reminded of conquered monarchs and his greatest battles. I was exceedingly interested, and felt as though admitted to the centre of his soul, on a spot where his demon spirit had yet an influence. He could never have risen from such a couch but with his mind filled with vast designs, fevered blood, and his brain in a blaze. Why, I thought, might he not have resolved in this tremendous silence on the murder of D'Enghien, on the gigantic enterprise against Russia? I entered into the secret feelings of one who was first the admiration then the terror, and then the detestation of the world. . . .

'*There* he revelled in dreams of dominion and conquest, of murder and blood; and when his mind and imagination were fired with a sort of gory, gleaming splendour, perhaps sent for the Empress.'

In this passage Haydon has unconsciously given his readers an insight into his own mind; such imaginings were part of the texture of his thought; such a luxury of purple and gold was what his soul craved for, such dreams of gory, gleaming splendour.

The idea of Napoleon haunted him all the time he was in Paris; he saw Gérard's portrait, 'A horrid yellow for complexion; the tip of his nose tinged with red; his eyes fixed and stern, with a liquorish wateriness; his lips red dirt; his mouth cool, collected and resolute. All the other heads in the room looked like children beside him, Wilkie said, and so they did. . . . Napoleon, in this infernal portrait, had not the least look of mercy, breeding or high mindedness.' Again, 'Gérard's horrid head of Napoleon has haunted me. All who approached him were evidently his victims; that bloody, glassy eye looked you through without mercy.'

On 3 July Wilkie went home and Haydon missed him badly:

'My dear Wilkie sets off for England this day; in spite of his heaviness of perception and total want of spirit, his simplicity, his honesty of manner, his good sense and natural taste endear him to one. I feel low at his departure though I shall soon see him again. . . . I felt melancholy after Wilkie's departure. . . . There was hardly a day but we had a dispute, and yet we were better pleased with each other's society than with the society of others.

'Notwithstanding Paris was filled with all the nations of the earth, the greatest oddity in it was unquestionably David Wilkie. His horrible French, his strange, tottering, feeble pale look, his carrying about his prints to make bargains with printsellers, his resolute determination never to leave the restaurants till he got all his change right to a centime; his long disputes about sous and demi-sous with the dame du comptoir; whilst madame tried to cheat him, and as she pressed her pretty fingers on his arm without making the least impression, her "Mais, Monsieur", and his Scotch "Mais, Madame", were worthy of Molière.'

Liveliness of observation and a keen sense of the ludicrous are among Haydon's most attractive qualities. His shrewd intuition of the quality of people, his racy gift of narration, his zest in all that is going on, the telling brevity of phrase with which he will sometimes hit off a peculiarity, or the rolling redundance of adjective after adjective with which at others he will bedizen his sentences in a kind of crimson-velvet-gorgeousness all his own, are his proper means of expression as an artist. When he tried to write finely for the Press he fell unto fustian and rhetoric. when he tried to write finely to impress his literary friends he came perilously near being ridiculous: he tells Hunt (in prison) that he thinks of him often with 'the most melancholy and exquisite sensations', that after his day's work he generally lays his head on his hand, draws near the fire, and muses on him till midnight, seeing him, 'as it were, in a misty vision'. 'I imagine myself', he continues, 'quietly going to you in the solemnity of evening; I think I perceive your massy prison, erect, solitary, nearly lost in deep-toned obscurity, pressing the earth with supernatural weight, encircled with an atmosphere of enchanted silence, into which no being can enter without a shudder. As I advance with whispering steps I imagine, with an acuteness that amounts to reality, I hear oozing on the evening wind, as it sweeps along with moaning stillness, the strains of your captive flute; I then stop and listen with gasping agitation, afraid to move, afraid to stir, lest I lose one melancholy tone, or interrupt by the most imperceptible motion one sweet and soothing undulation.' How refreshing it is to turn from these 'sublime' imaginings and read that he heard a black-haired St. Giles's lady in the park halloo to her friend 'in a voice burly with vice and drink. "I say, Sal——, come up here, and I'll show yer the place where Bob and I *parted*." ' But sublimity did not always come amiss to Haydon, though it needed more than Hunt in the Surrey gaol to stir it. Let the sun be setting in purple gloom as he paces 'with wider strides' in some spot where Napoleon brooded, and he will muse in a spirit so exactly adapted to the occasion that the reader is carried away.

'It being a beautiful summer evening,' he writes, 'I retired to the Jardin Anglais [at Fontainebleau], and stretching myself out close to the soothing tinkle of a beautiful fountain, meditated on Napoleon and his fall till night had darkened without obscuring the scene. . . .

'Right opposite . . . was a little column, against the setting sun, with a golden eagle grappling the world: this was surely to remind him in his solitary walks of the great object of his life. Though detesting Napoleon's government, I was affected with something like sympathy for his private habits.

'The heads of Raffaele and Michael Angelo, Alexander and Caesar adorned my bedroom, and often in the night I have felt their influence in my mind.

'It was the same feeling in Napoleon which made him set up this eagle grappling the earth. I sympathized with this romance of his nature, and I paced his favourite walk, drinking in sensations of ambition and glory, as if I were to be the next curse of the world.

'The evening was delicious; the fountain worthy of Armida's garden; the poetry of my mind unearthly for the time, when the crash of the Imperial drums, beating with a harsh unity which stamped their voices as those of veterans of war, made my heart throb with their stormy rattle. Never did I hear such drums, and never shall I again: there were years of battle and blood in every sound.'

How well too, and with how amused a sympathy he describes the women. He went by diligence to Fontainebleau: 'Inside were six Frenchwomen, and finding by my *tournure* I was English, they all assailed me and the domineering pride of my country. We had a very pretty little affair. England was too rich for the happiness of France.

' "Oh oui, Paris etait trahie." One lady swore it. Another knew Marmont had received 3,000 francs; "Pardon, Madame, it was 3,500," said an older with a look of great importance. . . . Peace was then discussed, and peace had been the salvation of England and would ruin France. "Sans doute, sans doute", echoed all twirling their ruffles, and darting their little black eyes at me with such impudent triumph and coquettish prettiness that they had it all their own way. There is a charming affectation in everything a Frenchwoman does which, although you cannot esteem it, you would not they should lose for the world. Every little creature has her tiny reticule and black apron, and away they go, tripping and mincing as if they trod on needles: "Are your women pretty?" asked the prettiest among the six.'

He made friends everywhere:

'In the evening I strolled on the parade: more dreadful looking fellows than Napoleon's guard I have never seen. They had the look of thoroughbred, veteran, disciplined banditry. Depravity, indifference and bloodthirstyness were burnt on their faces; black moustaches, gigantic caps, a slouching carriage and a ferocious expression were their characteristics. If such fellows had governed the world what would have become of it? They were large, tall and bony, but narrow-chested. . . . On returning again to the palace after the parade, where I had been eyed with a good deal of curiosity by officers and men, some of the guard came into the yard. Recognizing me they collected round me, and their familiar and frank bearing soon took away all dislike.'

Haydon had just been through a terrific strain and had been so ill and exhausted that he hardly had strength to finish his picture, but could anything be less suggestive of fatigue than these entries? Or than the following? He had settled to return to Paris *en poste*, which he had thought meant in a post chaise, when, hearing the crack of a whip, he went into the yard and found a fine tall postillion on a rough little horse, holding another for him.

'It was not for milord to appear abashed; so mounting at once, off galloped my leader and off galloped I, he cracking his whip all through the streets. The guards were lounging about, and some recognized me as the Anglais who had played skittles with them.
'The postillion was a complete character, and when we got out of the town I determined to try his mettle; so I pushed on at full gallop: he passed me and I passed him again, but I got in, after a complete race, before him to the posthouse. Once on the road, with the air of a Talma, he drew up and told me how that Chateau on the hill was purchased by a parvenu during the revolution, and how when the Bourbons came back, the purchaser said to the princess who was the owner: "Madame la Princess! j'ai acheté ce bien-ci, seulement pour vous et vos enfants— je le céderai—c'est tout à vous."
' "N'est-ce pas bien généreux?" said he, "Oui," said I.
' "Monsieur, j'étais courier de Napoleon de Paris à Moscou," and before I could reply he was off, and I after him, and overtook him, no doubt because out of compliment to milord he had, as he assured me, given me the best horse.

'He was a fine fellow, handsome and active, with a broad-brimmed, leathern, black, shining hat. Raving from the excitement of horse exercise, I went into the posthouse, calling "Vite, vite!" They thought I must be from the army: so horses were always ready in a moment. I got to Paris in a heat.'

On the visit he and Wilkie had met Bervic, the celebrated line engraver, Denon, L'Anglés and Nicolopolo of the Institute, Gérard, Prudhon, Guerin, and Gros all of whom had shown them 'great civilities'. But the times were so overwhelming that they accepted very few of the invitations they received.

Haydon felt this visit had done him immense good, chiefly from the chance it gave him of seeing so many masterpieces in the Louvre. He came back to England with a strong conviction of the superiority of his own country, its ways and its women: 'The manners of the Frenchwomen are exquisite; but they had all more or less beard, which ruined their grace and diminished the charm of their eyes. They were at this time so wrapped in frill, and lace, and muslin, and bonnet, that they looked like skeletons in petticoats. Never did I see the superiority of an Englishwoman so evident before.'

Soon after his return he went to an evening party at the Institute and wrote, 'The beauty of the women, the exquisite, fresh, nosegay sweetness of their looks, their rich crimson velvet, and white satin, and lace, and muslin, and diamonds, with their black eyes and peachy complexions, and snowy necks, and delicious forms, and graceful motions, and sweet nothingness of conversation, bewildered and distracted me. *What* the nobility have to enjoy in this world!! What has not the Prince?'

He felt the superiority of the English towns too: 'The contrast between Brighton and Dieppe was wonderful, Brighton gay, gambling, dissipated, the elegant residence of an accomplished prince with its beautiful women and light huzzars, its tandems and terriers; Dieppe dark, old, snuffy and picturesque, with its brigand-like soldiers, its sibylline fish-fags, its pretty grisettes, and its screaming and chattering boatmen. The houses of Brighton present their windows to the ocean to let in its freshness and welcome its roar, whilst Dieppe turns her back on the sea, as if in sullen disgust at the sight of an element on which her country has always been beaten.'

VIII. POETS' PRAISE

Haydon! Thou'rt born to immortality!
JOHN HAMILTON REYNOLDS

ON his return to England Haydon found that the excitement of his holiday had been so great that his health was by no means improved. He went to Hastings for a rest, and while there had the delight of hearing from the Mayor of Plymouth that he had been awarded the freedom of his native city—'as a testimony of respect for his extraordinary merit as a historical painter, and particularly for the production of his recent picture, the Judgement of Solomon'. Moreover, the British Institution had, on the suggestion of Sir George Beaumont seconded by Lord Mulgrave, voted him 100 guineas as a mark of admiration for the same picture. So at twenty-eight he could look back on the ten years since he came to London and feel he had not done so badly. His successes were rather those of notoriety than of tangible fact, and he seemed almost to prefer it to be so. If only he had swallowed his resentment and sent *Solomon* to the Academy he would almost certainly have been elected, and his whole life would have been different. The attention he had already got, and would continue to get, by his attacks on the Academy ill-repaid him for its antagonism, and the gratification of his vanity in having a quarrel 'with a man of note' was a poor exchange for the friendship of Sir George Beaumont. He could not afford to arouse so much needless ill-will, as he was later to discover to his regret. He never looked dispassionately at facts and considered how he could make the best use of them, nor, like his hero, Napoleon, was he content 'to follow the march of events'. He lived in an imaginary world, and he brought the state of mind of the stage-hero to the affairs of daily life. Whatever he did—pawning his watch, or getting his meals on credit—was seen across the footlights in terms of the applause of some future audience. It was that future audience, entirely sympathetic to him, which made these things possible, almost welcome. He felt certain of its praise—his diary would ensure that. To have been merely a successful or even a good

painter would never have satisfied him; he wanted to be alone—
'that lonely position, isolated and grand', counted so enormously
for his vanity that the ways of ordinary achievement really were
barred to him. He needed a defeated rival, or success had no
salt. His was not a single-minded love of his work for its own
sake; his 'glorious art' was always a means to an irrelevant end;
he talked incessantly about his love for it, but it was inseparable
from a desire for self-advertisement. And it was the approval
of people of 'rank and fashion' that he cared about more than
that of other artists.

With the completion of *Solomon* he reached one of his peaks,
his road for the next six or eight years ran along on a comparatively high level, but it did so over ground that was becoming
hollow. Those pictures which took years to paint could not
possibly repay him financially, nor cover the cost of living while
he did them. He always hoped they would bring him commissions, but they did not do so till he reduced their scale, and by
then he was deeply and irrevocably in debt. His pictures impressed but only half-pleased; his position in society was rather
similar, he made himself felt but was only half-liked. But he
had created a belief in himself, and many were willing to help
him by lending him money. His infectious enthusiasm carried
his friends with him, his society was stimulating, his courage
and determination were admired, and he was felt to have been
badly used. There is no reason for disbelieving what he says
about the crowds who called on him after the success of *Solomon*,
people wanted to know him; and it was during the six years
before his marriage that he enjoyed his greatest social importance. His breakfasts became famous; his studio was open on
Sunday afternoons, and was crowded by artists, literary men,
actors, and distinguished people of all sorts, never forgetting
those of rank, beauty, and fashion. Haydon's life, and he gloried
in it, was full of these violent contrasts. A few months before
he had been plodding away at *Solomon*, almost at his last gasp,
using his blankets and tablecloth for draperies for his lay-figure
—and now these breakfasts.

Here is a fairly true picture of his life when he was embarking
on the six-years' effort which was to produce *Christ's Triumphal
Entry into Jerusalem*: a large number of friends, much coming
and going about his studio, a good deal of entertaining on his
own part, and a great deal of going out, with rather an excessive

amount of Maria Foote. He regarded it differently: looking
back, he wrote, 'My enthusiasm at this time was intense. I held
intercourse only with my art and my great Creator. I shunned
society. I looked on myself as called to produce a great reform,
and I devoted myself to it with the passionate self-seclusion of
an ascetic.'

But that sort of asceticism costs money, and he had barely
begun his new picture when he found himself once more on the
rocks. This did not upset him, and he wrote, 'The more I reflect
on my nature, the more I am convinced of my adaptation to
great difficulties. I am once again without a farthing. I have paid
off the greater part of my debts. The price of *Solomon* was so
inadequate, that my models and journey have swept off most of
the rest. So far from being depressed, my breast broadens at the
contemplation of conquering. I look upon all difficulties as a
stimulus to action. I have £200 to pay the 21st of next month.
As yet I have not a sixpence towards it; but in God I trust, who
has always relieved me. Let me but be successful in realizing my
conception of my day's labour, and what shall subdue me but
extinction? In this mood of defiance I finished the Samaritan
woman [in *Jerusalem*], in a way which excited a great sensation
in the art.'

Help came in the form of a commission of 500 guineas from
a Mr. George Philips (afterwards Sir George) for a picture to be
painted at Haydon's leisure, when he should have time from his
big work, the money being paid in instalments in advance. The
picture was to be placed in a drawing-room where quadrilles
were danced, and after due consideration between the two the
subject of *Christ's Agony in the Garden* was decided on as the most
suitable. This would have been more of a relief to his mind if
he had seen more occasion for anxiety; as it was it supplied him
with ready money for his models and other expenses. Having
got his money from Phillips he delayed till he had finished
Jerusalem, and when done the picture was not a success, indeed
he considered it the worst he ever painted. He had the grace to
be ashamed of such a return for Phillips's generosity, for when it
arrived the family so objected to a sacred subject in a drawing-
room that it was condemned and hidden. It is now in the South
Kensington Museum, in a room where pictures are hung for
which there is no space in the public galleries. There are present
in the background qualities both of imagination and design, but

nothing can be said for the principal figure, which is a shapeless mass of red drapery, and above it a head only worthy of a Christmas card.

If Haydon thought that he would achieve immortality, his literary friends did their best to encourage this belief, and it was now that there arrived the first of that spate of sonnets, which was soon to pour in on him. It came from Wordsworth, 'occasioned, may I say inspired', says the poet, 'by your last letter'. It is dated 21 December 1815:

> High is our calling, Friend! Creative Art
> (Whether the instruments of words she use
> Or pencil pregnant with ethereal hues)
> Demands the service of a mind and heart
> Though sensitive, yet in their weakest part
> Heroically fashioned to infuse
> Faith in the whispers of the lonely muse,
> While the whole world seems adverse to desert.
> And oh when nature sinks as well she may,
> From long-liv'd pressure of obscure distress,
> Still to be strenuous for the bright reward,
> And in the soul admit of no decay,
> Brook no continuance of weak-mindedness,
> Great is the glory for the strife is hard.

'Now, reader!' cries Haydon, 'was not this glorious? And you, young student, when you are pressed down by want in the midst of a great work remember what followed Haydon's perseverance.'[1] Of the poems addressed either to himself or to his pictures Haydon had in all—three sonnets from Wordsworth, four from Keats, one from Elizabeth Barrett, two from Miss Mitford, one from Leigh Hunt, one from John Hamilton Reynolds, one from George Stanley, a poem by the same in seven verses congratulating him on his defence of the Elgin Marbles, one sonnet in Italian from an anonymous admirer, some Latin verses from Charles Lamb, an Epicedium from R. H. Horne, a sonnet by Francis Bennock, a poem in three verses by Charles Boner and one in four verses by George Croly on the picture of *Christ Entering Jerusalem*. Could any other painter show such a mixed string of pearls and gewgaws threaded in his own lifetime? Of them all it seems to have been Leigh Hunt's sonnet that gave Haydon most satisfaction; it was written on the

[1] See Appendix.

fly-leaf of Haydon's copy of Vasari's *Lives of the Painters*, dated
20 October 1816.

> Haydon, whom now the conquered toil confesses
>   Painter indeed, gifted, laborious, true,
>   Fit to be numbered, in succession due,
> With Michael, whose idea austerely presses,
> And sweet-souled Raphael, with his amorous tresses;
>   Well hast thou urged thy radiant passage through
>   A host of clouds; and he who with thee grew
> The bard and friend, congratulates and blesses.
>
> 'Tis glorious thus to have one's own proud will,
>   And see the crown acknowledged that we earn;
> But nobler still, and nearer to the skies,
>   To feel one's self in hours serene and still
> One of the spirits chosen by heav'n to turn
>   The sunny side of things to human eyes.

Haydon was enraptured, 'This to my feeling', he wrote, 'is
full of inspired energy and pathos it affected my imagination
and my heart. "'Tis glorious thus to have one's own proud will".
It is, it is, "And *see* the crown *acknowledged* that we earn" It is.'
    In reading Haydon's manuscript letters one realizes that the
careful punctuation in Taylor's edition of the *Autobiography*, so
correct even in the most disturbed and harrowing entries, must
be credited to Taylor and not to Haydon, whose letters (generally written on big pieces of drawing paper, about four times the
size of ordinary letter paper) ramble on in a large sprawling
illegible hand, with a dash now and then, and a comma or a
full stop when he happens to feel like it.
    He continues:

> Thy sonnet Bard and Friend, in truth I read
> Till the last moment of my going to bed,
> And when at length the candle was put out
> Long to myself thy sonnet did I shout
> And still in sleeping on the sonnet dreamt
>
> And when before I well knew what I meant
> Thy sonnet I muttr'd—(trust in what I say)
> At the first dawning of the creeping day
> When lads and lasses 'gin to rake the hay,
> And lovers drop and doze after long amorous play.

'About this time', Haydon continues, 'his mind received a sudden direction to poetry, in consequence as he himself *candidly* acknowledged of a sublime and beautiful sonnet addressed to him from his friend, the poet, Hunt: but whether it was from want of the early habit of inspiration, or whether his mind long unaccustomed to the modes of expressing his ideas in one which could not so happily convey his feelings as another, it must be acknowledged (and we speak without dreaming of depreciating so gigantic a capacity) that he never arrived at that felicity of diction and terseness of language so requisite to a great poet, in fact he never wrote as he painted, or to speak more aptly he wrote as his friend would have painted and his friend would have painted as he wrote.' (BULPIUS', *Life of Haydon and Hunt*, Vol. 8, Fol. 1, p. 483.)

Haydon wrote again a few days later:

'. . . the more I reflect on your sonnet, the more I am convinced it is the very best thing you have done. It has all the principles of your style without the least excep; it is tender and familiarly affectionate, and elevated—truly sublime—you have expressed the distinction of character between Michael Angelo and Raphael, by the very measure of the lines, setting aside the sense and I must repeat to you that "congratulates and blesses" convey such regard and fulness of heart as if you had just written it when we had escaped to the shore after being rolled and dashed about in a boiling smoky ocean and occasionally lent a hand as we accidentally met in the turbulence of the sweeping wave—this is exactly my feeling on this part—it will stand by its excellence—independentally [*sic*] of our making it do so by ours—adieu my dear Hunt. B. R. HAYDON.'

The steady progress of Haydon's work was rudely broken by the enormous events of the time: Napoleon had returned from Elba and had got possession of the throne. On 19 June Jackson called and told Haydon that he had met the Duchess of Wellington at Lord Mulgrave's the evening before, and that they had talked anxiously of the Duke. 'What does she say?' asked Haydon. 'She said', answered Jackson, 'that she felt perfectly tranquil as she knew he was now in his element.'

A few days after, on 23 June, Haydon spent the evening with John Scott. He stayed rather late; on his way home to Great Marlborough Street, as he was crossing Portman Square a messenger from the Foreign Office came up and asked, 'Which is Lord Harrowby's? The Duke has beat Napoleon, taken one hundred and fifty pieces of cannon, and is marching on Paris.' 'Is it true?' asked Haydon, quite bewildered. 'True,' said he.

'Which is Lord Harrowby's?' Forgetting in his joy that they were not in Grosvenor Square, he said, 'There', pointing to the same point in Portman Square as Lord Harrowby's house occupied in Grosvenor Square, which chanced to be a Mrs. Boehm's, where there happened to be a rout. In rushed the messenger, and away dashed Haydon back to Scott's. He found the house in darkness but knocked till Scott put his head out of the window, he then cried out, 'The Duke has beat Napoleon, taken one hundred and fifty pieces of cannon and is marching on Paris.' Scott began to ask question, but Haydon said, 'None of your questions; it's a fact.' And then they both shouted 'Huzza!'

The next day his model, Sammons (ex-corporal of the Life Guards, and afterwards Haydon's servant), came to sit and they both tried to do their duty, but Sammons was in such a fidget about his regiment's charging, and Haydon in such a heat that he had to let him go. Haydon read the *Gazette* the last thing before going to bed, dreamt he was fighting all night, got up 'in a steam of feeling' the next morning and read the *Gazette* again, ordered a *Courier* for a month, called at a confectioner's and read all the papers till he was faint.

He could not think of the Duke and the British troops without tears. 'Their constancy and firmness, his genius and prudence, the manner in which they had worked their way to their splendid reputation against the prejudices of Europe and the insolence of the French was passionately interesting.'

'Have not the efforts of the nation', he asked himself, 'been gigantic? To such glories she only wants to add the glories of my noble art to make her the grandest nation in the world, and these she shall have if God spare my life.'

The victory possessed his imagination; he read the *Gazette* through again the next day four times without stopping. And again on the following day till he knew it by heart. He rushed about and could not work, his breast swelled and his eyes filled with tears when he thought of the British army, he gloried in the prowess of his country; his ambition to do in art what the soldiers had done in arms roared skywards in his mind; and as for the French! 'Vain, insolent, thoughtless, bloodthirsty, and impetuous by nature—so susceptible to glory as to have their little sense blinded by that bubble—a people who are brilliant without intensity, have courage without firmness, are polite without benevolence, tender without heart—pale, fierce, and elegant in their looks, depraved, lecherous and blasphemous in their natures! Good God!' He imagined a vast statue of Britannia on the cliffs of Dover looking severely towards their wretched country.

During all this time the question of the Elgin Marbles had gone on fermenting. In the autumn of 1815 Canova had come to London and had given his emphatic verdict in their favour. Canova's prestige was at that time immense, and his admiration had done much to convince the Academicians, some of whom had been unappreciative. Haydon was delighted. He got an introduction and asked Canova to his studio. He looked upon this visit as a victory for himself, 'What became now of all the sneers at my senseless insanity about the Marbles? My opponents among the Academicians shrunk up . . . it was a great thing and checkmated the Government. I, unknown, with no station or rank, might have talked myself dumb; but Canova, the great artist of Europe, to repeat word for word what I had been saying for seven years! His opinion could not be gainsaid.'

Haydon's championship of the Marbles was well known, he had identified himself with them and it was a great score for him to have such a proof of his rightness, it brought him again into the limelight he loved and was the best possible advertisement for him. 'The Academicians', he says, 'were silenced. In high life they dared not speak. All classes were so enthusiastic and so delighted that though I had lost seven months with weak eyes, and had only accomplished the penitent girl, the mother, the centurion, and the Samaritan woman, yet they were considered so decidedly in advance of all I had yet done, that my painting-room was crowded by rank, beauty and fashion and the picture was literally taken up as an honour to the nation. A committee was promised early in the next session, and we all prepared for the last charge—victory or death.'

IX. THE MARBLES

I am convinced that to reach the highest degree of perfection as a painter, it is necessary, not only to be acquainted with the ancient statues, but we must be inwardly imbued with a thorough comprehension of them.

RUBENS

If the greatest artist the world ever saw, did not execute this, I know not who did.

HAYDON (*Letter to Lord Elgin*)

IN the beginning of 1816 the Elgin Marbles controversy came to a head. The subject is not only of national importance, but of importance in Haydon's life; it will be well to go into it from the beginning.

When Lord Elgin received his appointment as ambassador to the Porte, he consulted Harrison, the architect,[1] how he could best employ his visit for the improvement of architecture and sculpture in this country. Harrison suggested that casts should be taken of the sculptures, and also of the Ionic columns of the Parthenon to show how the Greeks turned the volute at the angle of the pediment. This plan was laid before Dundas, Grenville, and Pitt; they refused to advance the money, and Lord Elgin decided to take the responsibility himself. Realizing that he could not afford to employ artists and moulders from England, he sent Lusieri, of Palermo, to engage Roman workmen, and three of these were established in Athens in August 1800, where they soon began to mould, to draw and to measure. But they found great obstructions, only being allowed into the Acropolis on payment of five guineas a day to the Governor. During the French occupation of Egypt Turkish hatred of the Christians was intense, but vanished so far as the English were concerned, when, after their victories, they handed the country over to the Porte, and all difficulties disappeared at Lord Elgin's wish.

Up to this moment he had had no other views but those with which he had left England, but his artists began to tell him stories of the daily destruction by the Turks, which was taking place

---

[1] He built the Court House at Chester on the model of the Propylaeum of the Acropolis.

under their eyes; how several of the works of sculpture had been injured during their stay; how the Turks often fired their muskets at the figures from the plain; polished the heads of the statues into round shot, and pounded fallen figures into lime to build their houses with. They said that every English traveller broke off a bit of an arm, a leg, or a nose as a relic. A whole temple near Ilyssus, which had been in existence a short time before, had so totally disappeared that not even the foundation was visible. He was in a difficult position: he saw that if something was not done soon there would be nothing left; yet he foresaw the inferences which would be drawn at home by the envious and ill-disposed; he knew his political opponents would accuse him of furthering his own private objects by taking advantage of his position; he realized the outcry there would be from travellers who liked to indulge their lamentations over Turkish barbarity and Greek oppression, and that he would rouse the jealousy of all those foreigners who would have liked to do what he had done; and also he knew the jealousy of collectors would be irritated at the superiority of his collection over theirs.

Deciding that the bold step was the only rational one he applied at once for leave to model and remove, also for a special licence to dig and excavate. This was at once granted. The substance of the firman is, 'That in order to show their particular respect to the Ambassador of Great Britain, the august ally of the Porte . . . they gave to his Excellency, and to his secretary, and to the artists employed by him the most extensive permission to view, to draw, and to model the ancient temples of the idols, and the sculptures upon them: and to make excavations, and to take away any stones that might appear interesting to them.'

Lord Elgin ordered the erection of scaffoldings and the removal of what was in hourly danger of destruction; the Turkish Government never showing displeasure at any removals, while the people were pleased because three hundred workmen were employed daily. This was not the first attempt to remove the figures; in 1687 Konigsmark had tried to take away the great horses of Minerva; but the ropes broke, and they were dashed to pieces. M. Choiseul Gouffier, the French Ambassador, had actually taken down a metope, which he left on the ground when the Revolution broke out, and which Lord Elgin brought away for him. Haydon saw this in his house in the Champs-

Élysées. So much', he says, 'for the common sense in the objections the French presumed to make, and every other nation.' This time the Marbles were safely taken down and brought to Porto Leone, a distance of five miles—a difficult proceeding, for, as Lord Aberdeen said in his evidence, there was only one cart in Athens, and that was unfit for heavy loads. They were embarked for England in fine weather, but the Greek pilot ran the ship on a rock off the island of Cerigo and the Marbles went down in several fathoms of water. However, divers from the neighbouring islands were hired, and after immense persistence every case was recovered, with not a single fragment missing.

The Marbles were first placed in Privy Gardens, and had no sooner arrived than ill-will made itself felt. The artists were not for the most part hostile, though they seem to have taken a long time to realize their value, but the connoisseurs, with Payne Knight at their head, immediately began to throw cold water on them, denying their authenticity as the work of Pheidias, and their value as works of art. Payne Knight was at that time very powerful as an arbiter of taste; he was a rich man, a collector of bronzes and intaglios and an authoritative writer on those subjects. He delivered his opinion on the Marbles while Lord Elgin was a prisoner amongst other English in France (1803-1806), an unlucky circumstance for their reception in this country. After Lord Elgin's return to England the two met at a dinner at the Duke of Sutherland's and Payne Knight called loudly across the table, 'You have lost your labour, my Lord Elgin; your Marbles are overrated—they are not Greek, they are Roman, of the time of Hadrian, when he restored the Parthenon, and even if Greek, they are by Ictinus and Callicrates, and not by Pheidias, who never worked in marble at all; they are, perhaps, executed by their workmen, hardly higher than journeymen, and throw no light on the details and construction of the body.' Lord Elgin did not feel himself qualified to argue on the matter, and merely bowed. Coming from such a quarter this pronouncement had great effect, the other connoisseurs and society generally were afraid to admire where Payne Knight condemned. The Government, too, hesitated to spend a large sum of public money on works the authenticity of which was disputed by a leading authority.

For the next eight years opinion was uncertain, and inclined

to follow Payne Knight's lead. During this time Haydon acted
on occasion as Lord Elgin's agent, and was offered the duty of
curator in 1809. In 1811 the Marbles were moved to a shed in
the back yard of Burlington House. The artists seem gradually
to have realized their beauty; in this year West, in his presiden-
tial discourse to the Academy students, spoke of them with the
very highest praise, but when Canova arrived, in 1815, his instant enthusiasm finally tipped the scale in their favour. The
Government began to see that they might make themselves
ridiculous if they did not buy, and a committee was appointed
in the following year.

The Phigaleian Marbles had arrived while the Elgin Marbles
were in Park Lane and Payne Knight and his friends at once
cried them up against the Elgin Marbles. In an unsigned article
in the *Morning Chronicle*, presumably written by Knight,
occurred the sentence, 'They are believed to be the only examples extant of an entire subject of the admirable school of
Pheidias, and exhibit the sublimity of poetic imagination, united
to the boldness and power of execution, resulting from extensive
practice in the greatest school of antiquity.' To which Haydon
answered, the following Sunday, in the *Champion*, 'This is
written, I suspect, by the same man who said "The Elgin
Marbles were the work of journeymen, not worthy the name
of artists in a less fastidious age." Now so far from these Phyga-
leian Marbles being the only work of Pheidias, they have not the
slightest pretentions to be considered by his hand at all,' and
ends by saying, 'United with the Elgin Marbles, their errors will
do no injury to the student, and both together will form the
finest museum in Europe.'

Lord Elgin told Haydon that the effect of this letter was
'decided'.

When the committee began its sittings in 1816 Haydon who
had been named by Lord Elgin as one of his witnesses, was not
called, 'his other two witnesses', he says 'were dismissed after
a word or two; whilst those who were unfriendly to Lord Elgin,
or doubtful of the Marbles had every facility given them for
unfavourable reply. Lord Elgin was literally bullied like a culprit.' There is nothing in the official report of the committee's
investigation to bear out these assertions, almost all the witnesses
called were favourable to the sculptures, and not merely favourable but enthusiastic. The principal witnesses were seven artists,

who all placed the Marbles in the very highest rank, saying they
were an acquisition of the utmost value and importance to the
nation. These artists (all Academicians) were called: Benjamin
West (he wrote his deposition, as he was not well enough to
attend), Joseph Nollekens, John Flaxman, Richard Westmacott, Francis Chantrey, Charles Rossi, Sir Thomas Lawrence.
The questions asked were the same to all—whether, in the opinion of the witness, the Marbles were the work of Pheidias, and
what value they had as works of art. The seven artists and Payne
Knight were the only witnesses who presumed to offer opinions
on these questions, others were asked about the removal of the
statues in Athens, and whether Lord Elgin had acted in his private or official capacity. He said the facilities to remove were
granted to him as a private person, but Dr. Philip Hunt, his
chaplain, and William Hamilton seem in their evidence to imply
that this was not so. But the Marbles were shipped as his private
property. With regard to Haydon's assertion that Lord Elgin
'was literally bullied as if he had been a culprit' there is no suggestion whatever of this in the report (it will be remembered
that he had used this expression about himself when *Dentatus*
was hung in the Ante-room). It is not possible to hear the tone of
voice or the manner in which the questions were asked, but the
questions themselves were perfectly polite and legitimate, dealing only with his authority for removal, his costs, his use of his
official position, and the actual danger of destruction to the
Marbles. It must be borne in mind that it is throughout Haydon's object to give the impression that things were going badly,
and that the Marbles would not have been bought but for his
subsequent intervention. Even Payne Knight had modified his
assurance. He admitted that the frieze was the finest example of
its kind in the world, and praised the metopes highly; but there
can be little doubt that he was actuated by motives of vanity
and jealousy because a layman had dared to trespass on his
domains. He had no ground whatever for his assertions that the
Marbles were of the time of Hadrian. His evidence is marked
by ignorance and flippancy: when asked if he was acquainted
with Lord Elgin's collection he answered, 'Yes. I have looked
them over.' He made a parade of scholarship only to show that
he had either not understood, or had intentionally misquoted,
the passages he produced to prove his case. In a letter published
in the *Annals* in which Payne Knight replies to Haydon's attack

he writes, 'As for believing this mass of architectural sculpture to be the work of Phidias, it is a sort of belief which defies argument.'

The attack took three forms:

'(1) Lord Elgin stole the marbles.

'(2) He neither stole them, nor bought them, but received them as a present to Great Britain, and that he is therefore guilty of a fraud in attempting to sell to the public what is the property of the public already.

'(3) That instead of being regarded as a benefactor to the arts he should be execrated as the most savage and mischievous of vandals for having profaned the Temple of Minerva, ruined what even the Turks had spared, and mutilated, for purposes of his own profit, the perfect and glorious masterpieces of Athenian glory.'

To which may be added Payne Knight's contention that they were worthless as works of art.

The firman, quoted above, proves the falseness of the first charge.

With regard to the second, not only did Lord Elgin defray out of his own pocket the heavy cost of the wages of three hundred Athenian workmen employed daily for nearly fifteen years; but he had also to *propitiate* the Sultan's mother, to whom Athens had been assigned as her dower, and the captain Pacha. Also he had to purchase consent of the civil governor of the Acropolis, for, as he expresses it, 'Permission issuing from the Porte for any of its distant provinces is little better than an authority to make the best bargain you can with the local authorities.'

The first two charges thus disposed of there remained the third: that of vandalism.

Byron's rantings express all there is (or is not) to be said on this score, in view of the fact that there would have been nothing left for Byron, or anyone else, to sentimentalize over if the figures had not been removed before they were irretrievably ruined:

> Lo! here despite of war and wasting fire,
> I saw successive tyrannies expire
> 'Scaped from the ravage of the Turk and Goth,
> Thy country sends a spoiler worse than both.

> Survey this vacant, violated fane;

Recount the relics torn that yet remain:
These Cecrops placed, this Pericles adorned,
That Adrian rear'd when drooping science mourn'd,
What more I owe let gratitude attest—
Know, Alaric and Elgin did the rest,
That all may learn from whence the plunderer came,
The insulted wall sustains his hated name:
For Elgin's fame thus grateful Pallas pleads,
Below, his name—above, behold his deeds!

'Oh! ladies,' cried Haydon many years later in his lecture on the Elgin Marbles, 'is there an eye dry, or a heart which flutters not with sensibility, at the conception of the intellectual tortures which must have afflicted those delicate-minded people, the Turks, when they saw the fragments of the mighty genius of Phidias, so long the objects of their daily delight for centuries, torn from their ardent embraces, and placed where they could no longer exhibit that intense enthusiasm for their beauty and perfection by knocking off their noses, or grinding their heads into cannon shot?' Even Payne Knight in his evidence volunteered that the nation owed a debt of gratitude to Lord Elgin for saving the Marbles, which would certainly have been destroyed.

So far as can be judged by the official report opinion (Knight's excepted) seems to have been unanimous concerning the great value of the sculptures, and this makes one sceptical with regard to Haydon's claim that it was his famous letter, for famous it was, to the *Examiner* and the *Champion* (it was published in both) which turned the scale in their favour. His account in his 13th lecture is characteristic, and is worth quoting:

'Lord Elgin', he says, 'was very impatient for me to be examined and kept riding down and inquiring when it was to be; and every day he was promised, and every day passed off as before. This is Knight's influence I said to —— "I am sure it is," said he. Banks says, "You will not be examined out of delicacy to Knight." "Very well," I replied, "I who have been the only artist admitted to draw years before any one else was, except West—who have painted a picture, Dentatus, on the principles I discovered there—am denied an opportunity of giving the result of my knowledge to the committee; it is unjust to Lord Elgin and to myself: I'll appeal to the public."—— smiled as if incredulous of my power. I told Lord Elgin, "I'll make Knight remember the Elgin Marbles to his grave." He looked solemn, and even half smiled.

I went home, musing on that strange incredulity of one's species when one announces a capacity to see deeper than one's older friends. I retired to my painting room, with my great picture of Jerusalem before me, and wrote immediately the most effective letter of my life. "It has saved the marbles," said Lawrence, "but it will ruin you!" True enough; for neither the royal family, nobility, nor patrons, ever forgave the truths which poured out with the ink as I dashed my thoughts on the paper before me. The effect in high and middle life was sweeping and effective.'

The letter which occupies over nine printed pages is headed: '*On the judgement of connoisseurs being preferred to that of professional men.—The Elgin Marbles, Etc.*'

It is an attack on Payne Knight, and a determined attempt, prompted by a sense of injured vanity at not having been examined by the committee, to force himself into prominence over the Marbles and their purchase by the nation. It would naturally be galling to a temperament like Haydon's, after having been among the first, if not the first, to appreciate the Marbles at their proper value, and being as he was, associated with them in the public mind, to have the whole thing settled without being consulted. He was miserable if he was long out of the limelight, he admits himself that he was 'always panting for distinction, even at a funeral (for I felt angry at Opie's that I wasn't in the first coach).' So, of this letter—there was really no need for it so far as the Marbles were concerned; to judge from the unanimity of opinion, with the one exception, among the witnesses, they would assuredly have been bought for the nation. Payne Knight needed no 'demolishing', his single word against all the rest, not to speak of such overwhelming testimony as Canova's, could not conceivably have prevented their purchase. But Haydon's opinion had not been asked, therefore something must be done at once, before it was too late, before the Marbles were bought in fact, to show that without his interference they would never have been bought at all.

To make a powerful enemy, to antagonize through him the other patrons and connoisseurs, was nothing in comparison with being ignored and playing no part in the purchase of his beloved Marbles. And the letter did undoubtedly make a stir, it was translated into Italian and French, and, says Haydon, 'it was dispersed over Europe. Rumor found it and another on the Illyssus in the Magliabecchian Library, and Lord Elgin told me,

Danneker, the German sculptor, showed it to him; . . . the great Goëthe spoke of it when he noticed my Essay on the Venetian and Elgin Horse's heads; and the criticism can be found in his works.'

The letter begins with a criticism of the education of the 'higher classes' in matters of taste, and continues:

'I have been roused to these reflections from fearing that the Committee of the House of Commons on the Elgin Marbles will be influenced by the opinion of Mr. Payne Knight, and other connoisseurs, in the estimation of their beauty. Surely they will not select this gentleman to estimate the beauty of these beautiful productions! Are they aware of the many mortified feelings with which he must contemplate them? Do they know the death-blow his taste and judgement have received in consequence of their excellence being established in public opinion? Have they been informed that at first he denied their originality? Surely they can never be so little acquainted with human nature as to expect an impartial estimate from any human being under such circumstances. Perhaps they never heard that Mr. Payne Knight at first denied their originality; then said that they were of the time of Hadrian then that they were the works of journeymen, not worthy of the name of artists; and now, being driven from all his surmises by the proper influence of all artists and men of natural taste, doubts at last they may be original, but are too much broken to be of any value!'

There follows a long dissertation on the beauty of the sculptures and their economy of means to ends. He goes on:

'These are the productions which Mr. Payne Knight says *may be* original!—May be!—There are some men who have that hateful propensity of sneering at all which the world holds high, sacred or beautiful; not with the view of dissipating doubt, or giving the delightful comfort of conviction, but to excite mysterious belief in their own sagacity, to cloak their own envy, to chuckle if they can confuse, and revel if they can chill the feelings. . . . No man leaves off from what they have written, but with the dark starts of a nightmare—a distaste for beauty, a doubt of truth, an indifference towards virtue and a confusion about religion: and most of all, a pang, and a deep one, to see the mistake nature made, in giving a portion of capacity to beings of such heartless propensities. . . .

'I should consider myself a traitor to my art and my country's taste, and the dignity of my pursuit, if I suffered them to pass unnoticed: to these divine things I owe every principle of art I may possess. . . .

'Such a blast will Fame blow of their grandeur, that its roaring will swell out as Time advances; and nations now sunk in barbarism and ages yet unborn, will in succession be roused by its thunder, and refined by its harmony—pilgrims from the remotest corners of the earth will visit their shrine, and be purified by their beauty.

B. R. HAYDON.

'P.S. . . . I most sincerely hope, that this fatal proof of Mr. Payne Knight's complete want of judgement in refined art, will have its due effect; that it will show they are the most likely to know an art to its foundation, who have given up their life to the investigation of its principles; and will impress the noblemen with this truth, that by listening to the authoritative dictates of such men, they risk the disgrace of their exposure.'

Lord Elgin said that Knight was done up; and shaken in public opinion was the whole clique.

'The public voice', says Haydon, 'so completely and enthusiastically responded to this letter, that the patrons were afraid to let me see their displeasure; but I saw concealed anger lurking beneath the elegance of their manner; . . . In a week my painting room was again crowded with rank, beauty, and fashion, after two years' desertion, to such excess, that I ordered the fore door to be left open! Lord Mulgrave, always regarding me, had just at the very moment the letter appeared, laid a plan before the Directors to send me to Italy. It would have been done, but the moment the letter appeared, he said to a friend, "What is he about?" "Upon my word I don't know, my lord." "Here have I been planning to get him a handsome income for three years, and send him to Italy, and out comes this indiscreet and abominable letter!"

'. . . I acted as I had always done, and always will do, for the sake of the art, and the honour of my country.'

The Marbles were bought for £35,000. Lord Elgin's expenses were estimated at £74,000. (Haydon gives £52,000.) The collection was valued at £30,000, the £5,000 being added as compensation to Lord Elgin. The Government of this time resembled the governments that succeeded it for many years to come in its boorish stupidity, meanness and lack of vision where works of art were concerned. Those Members of the House who opposed the motion all paid lip-service to art, and none disputed what was by then established beyond question—the inestimable value of the Marbles. Their opposition arose from their sense of 'the unbecoming manner' in which Lord Elgin had obtained the Marbles, and from an unwillingness to spend any money on works of art at a time of pecuniary stress. Brougham went so far as to say that he would oppose their purchase even if they were to be had for £10,000, because the country could not at

that time afford even so much, while other speakers said they
would oppose however affluent the country might be on account
of the unjustifiable way in which the Marbles had been acquired.
Croker made a forcible speech in favour of purchase, for which
he was warmly thanked by Lord Elgin. If any one man deserves
the credit it is he and not Haydon; for the value of the Marbles
as works of art, which was the whole subject of Haydon's letter,
was not disputed by any speaker. When the House divided
(7 June) eighty-two voted for the motion, and thirty against it.

This insensibility among the governing classes to the importance to the nation of acquiring priceless works of art was shown
in other instances: when Sir Thomas Lawrence died in 1830,
his wonderful collection of old-master drawings, which had
cost him £40,000 (Redgrave says £60,000) was offered to the
nation for £18,000. The Academy offered £1,000, and Sir John
Soane £1,000 towards the purchase, yet the Government refused
the balance and the collection was sold to a dealer who made a
fortune out of it. However little value many of Haydon's pictures
may have, however displeasing his vanity and egotism may be,
the country owes him a debt of gratitude for the courageous,
single-handed battle he fought against such disgraceful ignorance
as this. He was right in clamouring for some sort of art education
at the universities; the aristocracy and the Ministers were barbarians, as Talleyrand said they would be if they did not buy
the Lawrence collection. He had begun his campaign already,
and was to carry it on during the rest of his life with unflagging
zeal, and an insect-like persistence that almost wearies while it
arouses admiration.

One must sympathize with Haydon's feelings at being passed
over, his knowledge and enthusiasm had been greater than those
of any Academician, and it was most unfair that he should not
have been examined, especially as he had been nominated by
Lord Elgin. It is very strange, that a private person and a com-
moner should have received so much consideration at Lord
Elgin's expense, for it must have been from tenderness to Payne
Knight's feelings that Haydon was not called; if he had been he
would not have written his letter, and would have been sent to
Italy for three years. The possible effects of such a visit on his
work need not be considered. Except in his humorous subjects,
he was on the way to becoming a conventional imitator of the
late Italians, and a visit to Italy could only have confirmed what

was already inevitable; but from a worldly point of view the result might have been important. It was thought almost essential for a history painter to go to Italy, and he would probably have had considerable success on the continent. Canova wanted him to come to Rome, where the friendship and good opinion of such a man would have carried great weight, and we know from Eastlake that he was thought very highly of both there and in Paris. He would never have settled abroad, his love of England was far too great, but he would perhaps have come home with an enhanced reputation which might have procured him patrons. He had not much time, a profound change of taste was on the way, which would make all he stood for obsolete, yet here he was offending people right and left, and throwing away his last chances. The only things that can be said for his letter are that it was a good advertisement, and gave rise to a belief (unfounded in my opinion) that it was owing to Haydon that the Marbles were bought, which is precisely what he intended, and his name has been associated with their purchase ever since. 'My views', he says, 'were now completely before the world. . . . I was an object of curiosity whenever I appeared in a public place. My vanity was tickled; and the Academicians when I met them at a conversazione, or a rout, slunk by, pale and contemptible, holding out a finger as they passed.' Poor Academicians! But one wonders why, since they had been examined and he had not.

X. THE BORROWER

It is always so pleasant to be generous, though very vexatious to pay debts.

EMERSON

IT cannot be too often repeated that whatever may now be thought of Haydon as a painter, in the early part of his life at least he was regarded by many of his contemporaries, and those not the least qualified to judge, as an undoubted genius, who, more than any other artist, was engaged in a great undertaking. It is necessary to remember this in considering the whole questions of his debts and his attitude to borrowing. He was not an ordinary sponger, was not extravagant in personal matters, and was free from self-indulgence. 'His moderate desires', as Miss Mitford called them, were soon satisfied, but he believed his efforts to 'educate the taste of the people' and to 'raise the art' of his country entitled him to employment and a living wage, and many of his friends believed it too; hence their otherwise unaccountable willingness to go on lending him money which they must have known they would never see again. Here the question of blame or praise is irrelevant, but some analysis of this important side of his character is called for.

There was nothing in Haydon's borrowings of the sordid mystery of Godwin's financial affairs, or of Sheridan's wild extravagance. To himself he must have seemed more like Pitt, utterly neglectful of his own financial interests for the good of the nation. His extravagance was almost exclusively connected with his art and, later, with his children's education. About the former he was reckless. Bewick tells how, when he was painting *Jerusalem*, he would pay his Jewish models anything they liked to ask, often using several together, to study the light and shade on the groups. If he saw a beggar he fancied for one of the heads in his crowd, he would hire a hackney coach and take him home at once for fear of losing him. His mouldings for *Macbeth* are another instance. When, many years later, he was commissioned to paint *The Duke of Wellington Musing on the Field of Waterloo,* he had the saddle and bridle and all the accoutrements specially made by the Duke's saddler (since his Grace would not lend)

91

and placed them on a horse to paint from—and then threw a large cloak over them so that in the picture only a few inches of the saddle can be seen. He also went (taking his wife) to Belgium, to study the background on the spot; and got the Duke's tailor to make him a pair of trousers similar to those worn by his Grace. Deciding during a sea-trip to Margate that his next comic picture should be a Margate steamer after a gale he immediately engaged the entire band to sit; and this for a picture he never painted.

The question arises, how was he able to borrow so much, by what magic did he extract all those pounds from his friends' pockets? It astonished even him. 'Think of my influence with my species,' he wrote later, 'to induce them to trust me for papers, canvas, chalk, labour, rent, models, to get collectors to pay my taxes, and landlords to abstain from rent; but I always show them my work, and they acquiesce. . . . But it is not *my* influence. It is not *human*.' He employed a double form of appeal: his genius—at once an honour and an asset to his country, and his ill-usage. This myth of his ill-usage was one he cultivated assiduously throughout his life. It was generally believed, and it is astonishing to what an extent he was able to impress all classes with the idea. He told Miss Mitford that he had once been shown one of his own books by a bookstall-keeper, with a sketch of his own on the fly-leaf, 'Which', said the man, 'I suppose is by Haydon himself. Ah! Sir, he was badly used—a disgrace to our great men.' 'But he was imprudent,' said Haydon. 'Imprudent! Yes, of course; he depended on their taste and generosity too much.'

Serjeant Talfourd believed (wrongly as it happened) that Charles Lamb took his *Ralph Bigod* from Haydon, but since Talfourd knew Haydon well, had lent him much, and felt sure of it, what Lamb says of Ralph may serve as a likeness of Benjamin. Lamb speaks of 'a certain instinctive sovereignty' about the men who borrow, 'What a careless even deportment hath your borrower! What rosy gills. . . .' He owned that in walking with his friend he had often been struck by the numbers of faces they met 'who claimed a sort of respectful acquaintance' with him. It seemed these were 'his tributaries; feeders of his exchequer: gentlemen, his good friends . . . to whom he had occasionally been beholden for a loan. Their multitude did in no way disconcert him.' . . . 'Then Bigod had an *undeniable* way with him. He had a cheerful, open exterior, a quick jovial eye, a bald forehead, just touched with grey (cana fides). He anticipated no excuse and found none.' ... 'When I think of this man; his fiery glow of heart; his swell of feeling; how magnificent, how *ideal*, he was: how great at the midnight hour; and when I compare him with the companions with whom I have associated since, I grudge the saving of a few idle ducats, and think that I am fallen into the society of *lenders* and *little men*.' Haydon's borrowings during the painting of *Jerusalem* the *Spectator* asserts to have been £600 a year. 'I have been told again and again,' wrote Elizabeth Barrett, 'that to give money *there*, was to drop it into a hole in the ground.'

He was occasionally unsuccessful: Cyrus Redding numbered among his acquaintance '. . . a distinguished literary character, whose pecuniary resources were not overabundant', Haydon asked for an introduction to this personage. A day or two later he called to beg for a loan. Redding's friend was just leaving town and could not spare the money, 'which', says Redding, 'was fortunate, as he would never have seen it again'. But the incident lost Haydon Redding's friendship. Then, too, his manner of repaying his debts, on the somewhat rare occasions when he did so at all, was peculiar, 'In one hour and a half', he wrote, 'I had £10 to pay upon my honour and only £2 15s. in my pocket. I drove to Newton, paid him £2 15s., and borrowed £10. I then drove away to my friend, and paid him the £10, and borrowed £5 more, but felt relieved I had not broke my honour.' He spared no one; as has been said, when Eastlake, aged fifteen, came to him as a pupil, Haydon almost immediately began borrowing from him. Another pupil, Edward Chatfield, innocently put his name to a bill to oblige Haydon and was 'thereby mulcted of a considerable slice of his modest fortune'. In 1822 Edwin Landseer, yet another of his pupils, won a prize of £150 from the British Institution. As he was under age the cheque was sent to his father. A few days later Haydon called and told a moving story of temporary distress, pointing out that Edwin could not use the money for some time, and begged for a loan of half the sum. The Landseer parents had a high respect for him and lent £75, Haydon handing over a post-dated cheque for the amount. Many years later at a dinner party at Landseer's, when the talk happened to turn on Haydon, the incident was recalled, and Edwin, turning to his sister, said,

'Jessie, bring me Haydon's dishonoured cheque.' The story well illustrates the characters of both.

The £70 he owed before he had finished *The Flight into Egypt* shows that Haydon began borrowing at once. But, as Mr. Oppé says, the marvel is that the artists managed to survive their early years. George Richmond in 1831 earned £207 in eleven months by teaching, and painting seventy-three portraits. Etty had borrowed £4,000 from his brother before he was forty-five, when he first reached an income of £500 a year. Haydon, who had neither a brother like Etty's nor a gift for portraiture like Richmond's, was less fortunate, and went to the moneylenders.

His quarrel with Wilkie in 1821 is interesting for the light it throws on his attitude to borrowing from his friends, and (as both have left an account of it) on his peculiar idea of 'truth' in relation to a dispute between himself and anyone else.

Haydon writes in March 1829:

'Spent an hour with Wilkie very delightfully. We got mutually kind to-day, and mutually explained. The only quarrel we ever had was about that arrest. I was too severe and he too timid. We ought to have made allowances for our respective peculiarities. He had been my old friend. He had dined with me the night before. We had drunk success to my marriage. We parted mutually friendly. The next morning I was arrested by a printer, to whom I had paid £120 that year, for the balance of £60. It was the second time in my life. The bailiff said, "Have you no friend sir?" "Certainly," said I, and at once drove to Wilkie's. Where ought I to have driven? Whom ought I to have thought of? "I thought it would come to this," said Wilkie; and after a great deal of very bad behaviour he became my bail. When roused I am like a furious bard of ancient days. I poured forth such a torrent of sarcasm and truth that I shook him to death. Wilkie told me to-day it sank deep into his mind, and never left him for months.'

Here is Wilkie's account:

'*12th November, 1821.* Had a call this morning from Mr. Haydon, to say that he had just been *arrested*, at the suit of Rennell the printer, for a debt of £66, and the sheriff's officer had brought him out in his gig to see if I would bail him. I expressed much dislike to this; but rather than see him go to prison, said, that if he would get another as good I would be one to bail him, but would not bail him alone. He therefore *promised* that he would get Mr. Perkins, of Great Marlborough Street, to join me, or some other friend equally good. In consequence of this, and his assurance that he would use every exertion to raise the money to discharge the debt, and his repeated promise that he would not leave town till it was discharged and the bond destroyed, I acquiesced, and put my name with his to the bond. In the afternoon I called at Perkins's, to ask if Haydon had called on him. He said he had: but that he being out did not see him. Of course, he could not be bail for him. I was led to call on Perkins to ascertain this in consequence of having received a very unbecoming letter from Haydon, filled with upbraidings, promises, and threats; and at the same time submitting to ask for secrecy, but neglecting entirely what it was most his duty to have informed me of namely, whether he had found anyone else to join me in bailing him. Haydon's conduct on this occasion appears strikingly offensive, and brings me to the determination of giving up his acquaintance.'

Haydon clearly thinks all the right is on his side, and is sure that everyone who reads his account will agree. He never had the slightest objection to borrowing, almost preferred it in fact to making the money himself. After he came out of his first imprisonment he made a sketch in chalk of a friend and was 'paid for it'. He writes to tell Miss Mitford of his humiliation, 'It was', he says, 'the first time I ever took money for a drawing in my life. I felt a wrench of feeling, but my own reflection proved to me it was more manly and honourable to take money for a drawing than to borrow it.' So one would suppose. With even greater astonishment one learns that at this very time (1816), when sowing the seeds of future disaster by borrowing from moneylenders, he refused a commission of five hundred guineas for a picture of *Edward the Black Prince* because it might interfere with *Jerusalem*; he accepted his first half-dozen pupils without fees, though most could well have afforded to pay, and he passed on another small commission of sixty guineas to one of them because it was beneath his dignity to paint small pictures. Then again, he seldom had his pictures engraved, though this was a recognized source of income for artists—the engraving of West's *Death of Wolfe* brought the publishers £15,000 in fourteen years, out of which West took his royalties. Rather than do these obvious things he borrowed from poor generous John Hunt and others of his friends. Later in life, when his prestige was declining, he made most of his money by raffling his pictures, and became expert in writing the whining, self-pitying letters which were broadcast among his wealthier patrons to induce them to subscribe. This side of him seems inconsistent with his character; it might have been expected that his vanity would prevent his exposing himself to the snubs and humiliations inseparable from such a way of living. At his death the amount of his debts is stated to have been £3,000, but this cannot represent anything like the whole. No account is taken of the debts to friends rich and poor who 'forbore to press', as he puts it, the number of whom was legion. No one was safe from him, he borrowed from everyone who would lend, and those who escaped did not do so for want of being asked, but only through sheer fortitude. The number of his creditors at the time of his first imprisonment (1823) is given as 150, but many of the friends who had lent would not have appeared publicly against him. On the other hand it is fair to say that he did, after his bankruptcy, pay many debts from which he was legally freed, landing himself in fresh difficulties by so doing.

Taylor publishes, on the occasions of Haydon's arrests, extracts from balance sheets of receipts and expenditure during the year, or years previous. They do not seem worth quoting in full, not being convincing documents, though they contain some interesting information. Haydon's average income between 1831 and 1836 was nearly £770; and he attributes his insolvency in the latter year to heavy law costs, loss sustained by the exhibition of his Reform Banquet picture, and to having been attacked by *Frazer's Magazine*. His debts at the time of his first arrest in 1823 are stated to have been £636, and at that of his second arrest in 1827, £1,767; between which times he had earned £2,547. Between 1824 and 1827 he had spent £3,679; details being: cash for furniture £190; wearing apparel for the whole family (there were five children) £60 per annum; servants wages £30 per annum; travelling and incidentals £20 per annum; schooling for two children £60 per annum; professional expenses £400 per annum; rent and taxes £151 per annum; and law expenses in the four years £280. At his marriage his wife brought a small income of £52 (interest on £1,000 left her by her first husband), which was lost in 1830 by the bankruptcy of the lawyer in whose hands her executors had placed it.

Taylor gives an 'Extract from Balance-sheet filed in Insolvency in the year 1830' which purports to be a true statement by Haydon of the money earned by him between 1810 and 1830.

The first column of figures (representing earnings from 1810 to 1825), including £1,571 net profit for the three exhibitions of Jerusalem, is not added up but comes to £6,200 12s. 10d. Taylor says this document 'throws light on the amount of Haydon's professional income'—it contains these items, 'From friends £350'; 'Received from friends £200'; 'From friends £50'. Why Haydon thought proper to stop short at these three entries, giving this arbitrary selection of money so 'earned', is not clear. The next column is a statement of his income between January 1826 and May 1830, and in it the same nice discrimination is shown, 'Mr. Wilkie (loan) £12.' 'Subscription, Parties unknown £20.' Then he adds up his column of figures and arrives at the conclusion that he has earned in these four and half years £10,746 4s. 6d., but the actual total is £8,100 11s. 0d. Frederic tells us that his father detested mathematics.

Among the entries occurs the incredible statement, '1826 and to July 1827—By cash received for Alexander £5,250'. The highest sum Haydon ever got for a picture was by raffle for *Xenophon*, which sum is given as £840 in the text of his *Journals* and as £947 in this balance sheet. *Solomon* sold for 700 guineas, and 1,000 was offered for *Jerusalem* in Haydon's absence, but was refused by Sammons, Apart from these, 500 guineas was his top figure for an important work. *Alexander* was a small picture, referring to it he writes to Miss Mitford, 'Alexander in a nutshell; Bucephalus no bigger than a Shetland pony, and my little girl's doll a giantess to my Olympias!' £5,250 is clearly a mistake for £525; yet he not only accepts the total resulting from its inclusion for his four and a half years' earnings, but throws in another £2,646, gratuitously, from pure miscalculation. If the figures given in the statement are correct (except for this mistake) he earned in these years not £10,746 4s. 6d. but £3,375 11s., yet he submitted the former sum in his statement and did not notice his error. That the total was intended to bear some relation to the sums above seems likely because in the final balance sheet for the years 1831 to 1836, where there are only six rows of figures instead of twenty-seven (the details being merged into a total for each year), he has added it up rightly, showing a result of £4,617 2s. 3d. for the six years, and this makes the sum I have arrived at—£3,375 for the four and a half previous years seem reasonable.

Haydon lost large sums by the private exhibitions of his pic-

tures. By the exhibition of *Christ's Entry into Jerusalem* he made
£1,571, and by that of Lazarus £440, before it was seized, but
on all his other private shows he either just covered expenses or
lost heavily. In 1823, after his first imprisonment, he made £614
by portraits (by far his best portrait year apparently), but these
portraits having been exhibited he never made so much in a
year again. His price seems to have been twenty-five guineas
for a head and shoulders, £50 for a half (or three-quarter)
length, and £100 for a whole length.

There can be no doubt that during all the early part of his life
at least Haydon counted on painting a picture of such trans-
cendent merit that Ministers, patrons, and the people would fall
down and worship, and then vote him State support. Let us
listen to him soliloquizing (1815):

'I took again the state of my exchequer into review, and asked myself
shall I paint for money, or by borrowing as I did when engaged on
Solomon (having honourably discharged what I then borrowed), keep
my mind in its high key, and go on watching, exciting, and regulating
the public mind? The battle about to be fought (I said to myself)
is a great battle. I cannot suffer my attention to be turned off. The
question, however, is, if my attention was not more turned off by the
harass of want than by the temporary devoting of time and thought
to a portrait or small picture now and then.

'The first moral duty is honestly to provide oneself with bread and
cheese; but is there any dishonesty in borrowing of friends you have
paid before, that you may persevere in a great plan which is for the
public benefit? No, certainly not. But the repayment is a contingency.
But if your friend be willing, why not? But is it more manly to make
a livelihood for yourself by a judicious exertion of your talents, than to
depend on the earnings of your friend who may be more prudent? Still
the excitement of a noble object is so overwhelming that to paint
smaller works in the intervals of great ones is not rest enough. I always
felt when I wanted rest, that the only thing to restore me was absence
of thought. This is my excuse for requiring that aid I asked; still it is
a fallacious principle and one I deprecate in all other cases but my own.'

This last remark is not a joke; his gifts were, he believed, so
wonderful that a moment wasted on lesser work was something
to be avoided at all costs. 'There can be no doubt', he continues,
'I ought to have been helped by the State. . . . No doubt there
were means of earning what I wanted by occasionally devoting
myself to portraits and small subjects. But that always divided
my mind. . . . Be that as it may I was resolved to go through my

work—to raise loan after loan to complete it—to set my life upon a chance, and to bear the hazard of the die.'

This idea that he ought to have been supported by the State, was one that he held all his life; and it was the hope, utterly unfounded, that it might happen that led him into anticipating this support by borrowing. He was not alone in this opinion; Wordsworth thought that a large sum of money ought to be granted to Haydon to enable him to go on with his work, while Rippingille writes (1846), 'The death of poor Haydon will be regarded in other nations even with greater horror than in this, whilst it may be fearlessly asserted that no painter of his powers could have fallen under a similar fate in any other country in the civilized world.'

Sir George Beaumont wrote often to urge him to paint a portrait now and again, and a few small pictures; one such letter ends, 'Indeed my dear sir, you must attend to this necessary concern, or circumstances more mortifying than what I recommend cannot fail to attend you.' Haydon says, 'This letter was prophetic; but all my friends were always advising me what to do instead of advising the Government what to do for me. Now a different course, I have no hesitation in saying, would have prevented my necessities, and developed what powers I had. Dear Sir George's advice was kind and good, but it was yielding the question of public support; and as I had made up my mind to bring that about by storm, I disdained Sir George's timid caution and flew at my picture come what might.'

It was early in 1816 that he took the fatal step, and went to a moneylender. He borrowed £120 at 5 per cent for three months. He owed £200 to his landlord, borrowed £100 to make it up, and paid £22 10s. for the favour, thus increasing his rent by that sum. When this bill of £122 10s. fell due he had received £100 on commission, but was obliged to borrow £22 10s. to make up the total; for this he paid £6, so here again was added £6 to the £22 10s. making £28 10s. on £200 rent. He soon borrowed another £100 from a different moneylender at 40 per cent and was now regularly involved. So much for himself. What about his friends?

There were two classes from which Haydon borrowed, the rich and the poor; those who could afford to lose and those who could not. The first included such men as Coutts and Harman, wealthy people, who looked upon their loans as gifts to deserving genius, which they hardly expected to see back, and for which apparently they did not press. The second included among others two of his pupils. This is the blackest mark which his contemporaries scored against Haydon. What exactly did he do? It is necessary to go back a little. Early in 1816 William Bewick (no relation of the wood engraver), aged twenty, came to London to get into touch with Haydon for advice and instruction. He was poor, and Haydon at once took him without a fee. He was infinitely kind. Of all the distinguished people Bewick met 'none', he says, 'excited higher admiration, or exercised a more profound influence on my mind than Haydon'. He wrote to Bewick's father letters showing the deepest interest in his son's career, received the young man always in the kindest way at his house, and promised him every assistance in his power. 'I cannot give you an idea of my feelings,' Bewick wrote to his brother, '. . . Mr. Haydon has given me some precious advice, in fact more by half than I could have expected from a father.' And in another letter:

'I wish I could describe my feelings at receiving such friendship from this great man. He has even gone so far as to lend me money; and when I offered it him again he would not take it. I told him I really did not know how I should be ever able to recompense him for all he had done for me. His answer was, "Only be industrious, and succeed in your art, that is all I require." Think, dear John, what must be my feelings to be thus honoured by such a man, while his acquaintance is courted by all the noble in the land.'

And again:

'What I am to do I do not really know. I was at Mr. Haydon's to tea on Monday last. We talked matters over, he thought like a father, and with as much concern as if I had really been his son, he confessed to me that he had only £5 left. "However," says he, "I'll let you have five shillings, that will help a little," think of a man like this letting me have five shillings out of the only five pounds he had. He likewise offered to pass his word for the payment of a quarter's living at an eating-house; but as I was so unsettled, and did not know whether I should change my lodgings, I thought it not advisable to accept this offer. . . .

'What must I feel, John, when Mr. Haydon rejects so many young men who come to him with letters of recommendation, and who have offered him large sums of money—one young man came recommended from Edinburgh. Mr. Haydon (as he says) soon found out what he was, and recommended him to begin immediately with portraits.'

This was in the spring of 1817. What he did for Bewick he did for others too.

Six years later, on 19 May 1823, Bewick writes to his brother: 'I am all anxiety and misery. Mr. Haydon's affairs are in confusion, and I am uncertain how far I am involved, and how to proceed.'

Haydon gives his version of what had happened:

'During Jerusalem Lord de Tabley gave me a commission. I begged him to transfer it to Bewick, as he was a young man of promise. He did so; and he was paid sixty guineas for his first picture. His second, Sir William Chater bought, and during his third his landlord refused to let him proceed unless I became security for his rent. I did so. In the meantime, I was becoming rapidly involved, and having helped Bewick in his difficulties I thoughtlessly asked him to help me by the usual iniquities of a struggling man, namely accommodation bills; Bewick and Harvey both did so. Those were not accommodation bills to raise money on, but accommodation bills to get time extended for money already owing. When in the hands of a lawyer, if I wanted time, "Get another name", was the reply. As I wished for secrecy, I asked these young men, into whose hands I had put the means of getting a living without charging a farthing. As the father of a family I see now the indelicacy and weakness of this conduct. But at the time I was young, a bachelor and at the head of a forlorn hope, and I relied on the honour and enthusiasm of my pupils. I had reduced Bewick's liabilities from £236 to £146, and Harvey's from £284 to £184, and whilst in the act of extricating them, I got through the "Lazarus" and was ruined. There is no excuse for my inducing my pupils to lend their names as security for bills, but I was in such a state of desperation that I wonder at nothing.'

This was written some twenty years after, about 1843. To return to Bewick's account, he writes on 12 June 1823, 'You will think it strange that Harvey and I can be losers by him, but so it is, as well as all his best friends. His most staunch friends, those who have stuck by him through thick and thin, through good report and evil report, are the greatest sufferers. Harvey's case is settled, but mine is not, which makes me anxious and uncomfortable.' Bewick soon cleared himself and had a happy and prosperous life. Much of his success he owed to the start that Haydon had given him.

He wrote years later:

'I should not like to reflect upon the memory of one who seems to
have had everybody upon him, who like most other men, was not
quite perfection, but had many fine qualities, and very great genius and
intellectual power. . . . As it was, under all the unfavourable circumstances, he earned, by his industry and talent, at the rate of £500 per
annum, or more; yet he could not keep the bailiffs out of the house!
Some years he cleared from a thousand to two thousand.'

In 1840 when he was very much pressed himself Haydon
wrote to a poor pupil, 'As I passed my word to your landlord to
pay your rent if you could not . . . I will undoubtedly pay it, so
make your mind easy, and don't let it press on you as a debt.
I release you from it entirely.'

Chatfield ends a letter to Haydon (1819), 'I remain, dear sir,
your devoted son (for you have ever been a father to me).' The
débâcle happened in 1823.

If his contemporaries blamed Haydon most for his behaviour
to his pupils, posterity has blamed him most for his behaviour
to Keats. Again, what exactly did he do?

To begin with he did not do what he has always been accused
of: he did not ask Keats for a loan; Keats offered him one.
Offered him one, and then (through no fault of his own) found
he could not lend the money without very great difficulty.
Pressed by Haydon, who had been counting on this loan, Keats
paid it; and within a month wanted it back. Haydon could not
return it and was off-hand in his refusal to do so.

The result was a coolness, though not a break. Both were
annoyed. Thirty pieces of gold, and the gilt off their friendship!
Keats's genius as against Haydon's pretensions to it, has influenced judgement on the matter. Keats appears in an even more
amiable light, from his generous eagerness to help, and Haydon
in a less unamiable one than has generally been admitted.

This partiality is well exemplified in Sir Sidney Colvin's version of the matter in his *John Keats*, he quotes from a letter:

'Believe me Haydon I have that sort of fire in my heart that would
sacrifice everything I have to your service—I speak without any reserve
—I know you would do so for me—I open my heart to you in a few
words. I will do this sooner than you shall be distressed: but let me be
the last stay—ask the rich lovers of Art first—I'll tell you why—I have
a little money which may enable me to study and to travel for three or

four years. I never expect to get anything by my books; and moreover I wish to avoid publishing—I admire Human Nature but I do not like Men. I should like to compose things honourable to Man—but not fingerable over by men. So I am anxious to exist without troubling the printer's devil or drawing upon Men's or Women's admiration—in which great solitude I hope God will give me strength to rejoice. Try the long purses—but do not sell your drawings or I shall consider it a breach of friendship.'

This letter is dated 23 December 1818. Anyone reading it would feel certain that this was an answer to a request for money from Haydon, 'I will do this sooner than you shall be distressed, but let me be the last stay—ask the rich lovers of Art first.'

And this is just the conclusion that Colvin does draw from his curtailed version. He says, 'This [a tiresome interruption which befell Keats] was a request for money from the insatiable Haydon. The correspondence on the matter cannot be read without anger against the elder man and admiring affection for the generous lad—yet not foolishly or recklessly generous—on whom he sponged.'

But Colvin has omitted the previous sentence in Keats's letter which gives an entirely different colour to the whole thing. After talking of quite other matters, he writes, '. . . Yet here I am sinning—so I will turn to a thing I have thought on more— I mean your means till your picture is finished: not only now but for this year and a half have I thought of it. Believe me Haydon I have that sort of fire in my heart' etc.

No one in answering a request for money would say in reference to it he would turn to a thing (*a* thing), which he had been thinking about *for a year and a half*.

This *offer*, which so soon after he would have liked to withdraw, while enhancing one's admiration for Keat's generosity, does not, as the event proved, quite bear out Colvin's statement that it was neither foolish nor reckless.

XI. SELF-ADVERTISEMENT

Say, what blinds us, that we claim the glory
Of possessing powers not our share?
MATTHEW ARNOLD

ONE evening,' says Haydon, 'just after the sun had gone down in its gold and crimson glory, as I was lying in my arm chair lost in meditation on my day's labour, my past uproar and my future success, dreaming of Raphael and the Greeks, the door opened without the least ceremony and like a vision there stood Maria Foote. She had been shopping with a young friend, had stayed later than usual, and called to beg I would protect them home. As we were on terms of family intimacy I was delighted at the request, and marched forth. Not far from my house she requested me to stop a moment whilst she left a letter with a lady who was going into Devonshire. I waited; a servant came down, and requested I would walk up. I walked up into a neat, small drawing-room, and in one instant the loveliest face that was ever created since God made Eve smiled gently at my approach. The effect of her beauty was instantaneous.

'On the sofa lay a dying man, and a boy about two years old by his side. What did it mean? We shortly took leave. I never spoke a word, and on seeing Maria home, returned to the house and stood outside in hopes she would appear at the windows.

'I went home, and for the first time in my life was really, heartily, thoroughly, passionately over head and ears and heart in love. I hated my pictures. I hated the Elgin Marbles. I hated books. I could not eat, or sleep, or think, or write, or talk. I got up early, examined the premises and street, and gave a man half a crown to let me sit concealed and watch for her coming out.

'Day after day I grew more and more inextricably enraptured till resistance was relinquished with a glorious defiance of restraint. Her conduct to her dying husband, her gentle reproof of my impassioned and unrestrained air, rivetted my being. But I must not anticipate. Sufficient for the present purpose, O reader, is to tell thee that B. R. Haydon is and for ever will be in love with that woman, and that she is his wife.'

As a proof of Haydon's constancy it should be remembered that this was written twenty-six years after. Perhaps his *Journals* will tell us more of this mysterious love affair that began at sight, and advanced so far on its passionate course while the dying husband was not yet dead, but that is all that Tom Taylor has chosen to say (Mary Haydon was still alive when he published), and the rest remains unknown with the fiery emotions that characterized it. Mary Hyman was at this time twenty-three. Nothing is known of her previous life or her origin, except that she was a pure Jewess and married to a Jew, and we hear very little about her till her second marriage. The engagement lasted four years as Haydon was too poor to marry, and during most of that time she was in Devonshire with her two little boys. Here she spent her time 'educating herself', living on the small income left her by her husband. That Mary Haydon was very lovely there can be no doubt. Miss Mitford called her 'a most beautiful woman, who quite realized the beauty of the Rebecca of Ivanhoe'. When she went to see Haydon's *Lazarus* she could hardly take her eyes off his wife to look at his picture. Hazlitt makes the same comparison between Mrs. Haydon and Rebecca. Her delicate and classic profile can still be admired among the crowd in *Lazarus*, high up on the right. The head is hooded, and the lovely face with its lowered lids looks down in an attitude that rounds still more the nobly rounded chin. Haydon said that of all the portraits he made from her this was 'the most like her beauty'. But there is nothing in the picture to suggest her dazzling colouring: the brilliant complexion, contrasting with the darkest eyes and hair. This Clytie-like head, moreover surmounted a figure of equal beauty. That she must have been robust and healthy is evident, since she went through so much without losing her strength or her cheerfulness. There was equal agreement about the sweetness of her disposition, and her devotion to her husband was unfailing. Like Blake, Haydon had the compensation of great married happiness for an unsuccessful career. Their love for each other seems to have sprung into life full-grown and never to have wavered. That there were, however, occasional dangers seems clear from Haydon's own showing. He told Elizabeth Barrett in strict confidence that the beautiful and celebrated Mrs. Norton (the original of Meredith's 'Diana') made overtures to him, and that his children out of loyalty to their mother smashed in pieces a bust of the poetess that stood in his studio. No doubt he had his own case in mind, when, years after, he told his audience at a lecture, that 'all the most eminent and celebrated lovers have been distinguished by mutual beauty of face and figure, and instant infatuation'. He told Miss Mitford many years after that he might have married a fortune, but chose love, and had never ceased to thank God that he had.

This was the laziest period of Haydon's life, when he took six years over one picture which Hazlitt criticized as being more in the nature of a sketch than a finished work. His health was less good now than at any other time, the strain of *Solomon* had affected his heart and his digestion, and it was some years before he recovered, while trouble with his eyes often prevented his working. He was more inclined to rest on his laurels, and to bask in the tropical heat of his infatuation for Mary than to be wholehearted in his asceticism.

Christ's Triumphal Entry into Jerusalem, so far as one can judge from a photograph, is perhaps his best historical picture among those that remain. There is a good reproduction of it in the Keats Museum at Hampstead, and examining this from the point of view of an age that accepted its chiaroscuric, post-Sebastiano-del-Piombo-like convention, one can understand its success. Look at it as Sir George Beaumont looked at it, and as Haydon meant it to be looked at, and there is something stirring about that vast crowd stretching away into the distance between the city buildings, whitened by an unearthly light, while every face turns towards the central figure; and the donkey is almost worthy to rank with that in Tintoretto's *Flight into Egypt*. Though how he managed to take six years over the picture it is hard to say. Haydon was, as Bewick said, much sought after and courted, and he was getting within what must have seemed to him measurable distance of 'that lonely position, isolated and grand' he so coveted. He admits that he began to be a very important person in his own eyes and thought of growing moustachios, 'but', he adds, 'that passed off'. It was his vainest, and probably his happiest period; he really was sought after by 'rank, beauty, and fashion', not as a protégé of any great person, but on his own account; he was enjoying a successful and passionate love-affair with a woman of surpassing loveliness; he was intimate with some of the most distinguished literary men of the day, and believed by them to rank as a genius; he was painting a picture that he himself knew to be the greatest masterpiece any Englishman had ever produced; no wonder he brooded over it, and caressed it, and took his time; no wonder he entertained and went out incessantly, and dreamt of Mary, and refused five-hundred-guinea commissions for the honour of his 'glorious Art' and his great Creator. And no wonder, when he looked back on this Elysium, he was a little muddled about it all, and thought those magic days really had been of sufficient length to allow him his ten or twelve working hours over and above the twenty-two he spent in eating, sleeping, entertaining, love-making and love-dreaming.

It was now that he began to form his school. His first pupil, Charles Eastlake, had come as early as 1809, but he was now abroad, and no others had succeeded him. In 1816 the three Landseers started, followed by William Harvey, Edward Chatfield, George Lance, and William Bewick. All these he took without fees, though why he did so is not clear; the Landseers could well have afforded to pay (apparently Lance and Chatfield did so after his ruin). From this beginning the school grew, and he charged a premium of £200 for three years to those who could afford it; if they could not, and he thought well of them, he allowed them to come without fee; if he did not think well of them he would not have them at any price. Pupils continued to be a source of income to him for the rest of his life; as late as 1845, the year before his death, he had three. His method was to give them, every Monday, work for the week, and to take them to the collections. 'I guide them,' he told a prospective pupil at that date, 'but not with the bit in their mouths.' They did not live with him in the house but were under his control 'morally and absolutely'. 'After paying me this money,' he continues, 'he has to *live*—I lived on £60 a year till I maintained myself[1]—*now* (1845) it could be done on £50, or perhaps £40 —till he paints. One good room would do—he could dine at a chop-house—for 8d. or 9d.—breakfast and tea at home. But a pupil of three years must have no anxiety about domestic affairs. The prospects of an historical painter and (now and then a portrait) are better than 40 years ago—a living may be got by combining History, Portrait and Decoration.'

Haydon had qualities which well fitted him to teach, and he won (before his catastrophe) the love and admiration of his pupils, all of whom, with the exception of Edwin Landseer, expressed in after life their gratitude and indebtedness to him. The school had not long been in existence when he conceived

---

[1] This is a fiction; he never did anything of the sort.

and carried out a plan, of which he remained inordinately proud
for the rest of his life. Through his friend Seguier he got the
permission of the Prince Regent to have two of Raphael's
Cartoons at Hampton Court brought up to London for his
pupils to copy. Cylinders were made, and up came *The Miracu-
lous Draught of Fishes* and *Paul at Athens*. Haydon moved in at
once and drew full size all the heads and the figure of St. Paul.
Then his pupils began, and 'made such studies and cartoons as
had never been seen in England before'. He says the excitement
was tremendous, and when the whole collection was hung up
at the end of the season with his Paul in the centre and his
pupils work round it 'the nobility were all highly delighted'.

This affair provoked the jealousy of his enemies, the school
was attacked in the Press (which, as Bewick said, only advertised
it) and there was published a caricature by John Bailey, in which
the students are shown making their copies. In this Bewick,
working away with dramatic intensity, has the centre place, his
fellow pupils round him, each before an immense stretcher,
while Haydon in the form of an owl wearing spectacles flies
above, blowing a trumpet. Bailey, who had been allowed to
visit the gallery while the copies were in progress and had seen
some of the students using compasses, made this the basis of his
attack. Under his caricature is the quotation from Sir Joshua
Reynolds: 'A Painter who relies on his compass, leans on a prop
which will not support him.' In the foreground one of the pupils,
Christmas, very down at heel, is so represented. Haydon's
friend, Elmes, who published this attack in the *Annals of the
Fine Arts*, says they did not use compasses, or if they did it was
against the rules of the school. Another caricature shows St.
James's Street on the private day of the exhibition, 30 January
1819. Haydon, with eagle-nose, straddles in the foreground, with
a pupil beside him, watching a confusion of coaches. Behind
him is a hissing goose, having a label attached to its neck with
the initials 'W.C.', and below a piece of paper bearing the
words, 'Quack Artist. Play. W.C. Weather Cock'. This probably refers to William Carey, the art critic, of whom more later.

Nothing will give a better idea of Haydon's importance, his
social position and his advertising ability than the names of some
of those who attended this exhibition of his pupils' work. There
were present the Duke of Argyll, the Marquess of Lansdowne,
the Swedish Minister, the Prussian Minister, the Saxon Minister,

M. Wagner, Chargé d'Affaires for Würtemberg, S. T. Coleridge, and J. M. W. Turner. During the public days H.R.H.
Archduke Maximilian came with M. de Neumann, Chargé
d'Affaires for Austria, and was received by Haydon. And then
there was nothing to be seen but eight chalk copies by Haydon's
pupils. So much had been achieved by the reputation of a single
picture, *Solomon*, and by his personality and social gifts.

All this, and the fact that he had not won a single vote when
he sent in his name for election to the Academy, together with
the recent excitement over the Elgin Marbles and the sense of
victory, combined to stir him up to a state of madness. He thirsted
for Academic blood. James Elmes had just started his periodical,
the *Annals of the Fine Arts,* and, being a great admirer of Haydon, gave him almost unlimited control, with the result, says
Haydon, that 'the Art was soon in an uproar, and the quarterly
appearance of the *Annals* was waited for with the same sort of
anxiety as a shell in the air during a siege. . . . Every weapon
of attack was resorted to—ridicule, sarcasm, allegory, and in-
sinuation—with such success that a member said, "By and by a
man will be afraid to become an Academician".' The *Annals* is
interesting as being the first paper of its sort to appear in England. It has articles on a wide range of subjects connected with
art, and its editor had the generosity to print hostile contributions. Haydon's spirit informs this quarterly; poems about him
and articles by him appear in almost every number. He asserts
that his *Dreams of Somniator* had a great success and sent up the
sales so much that both he and Elmes were afraid that the serious
intention of the paper would be overlooked. These dreams once
passed for wit. In one 'Somniator' sees *The River of Time* in
which Academicians are attempting to swim, only to get covered
with the mud of the banks. Suddenly with great uproar 'H-yd-n'
appears, recognizable by his 'eager energy and spectacles'. Like
Achilles, shouting horribly, he rushes into the front of the river
and offers to assist the Academicians and to show them how to
'co-rival greatness' and be worthy to float on the surface instead
of sinking to the bottom. In reply they throw mud at him, not
a bit of which sticks, but, rebounding upon themselves, makes
them dirtier than before. Then after more uproar all sink beneath the surface. Presently one Academician after another, almost unrecognizable with mud, comes up and scrambles on to
a plank, when 'H-yd-n', rising with such elasticity that he shoots

several feet into the air, lands triumphantly on a large plank 'well fitted to the buffettings of the boisterous river'. As he floats along Fame blows 'the trumpet's regal sound', and crowns him with the laurel and the oak—civic and heroic honours. A ray of sunshine bursting through the clouds strikes on Wilkie and 'H-yd-n' far in advance of all, preceded by Fame.

In another dream 'Somniator' enters the Academy where a deputation from the French Academy has come to try to discover the principles on which the Greeks executed their figures. Among others the venerable President, Benjamin West (Nestor), speaks as follows:

'Phidias you see, Sir, studied nater, on the—on the principles I painted my great picters—yes Sir, I painted my great picters—of Christ Rejected, and Christ Healing the Sick. Yes Sir Phidias and I, Sir, you see Sir, looked at natur Sir, with the same eye you see gentlemen. There is but two eras of art in the world, gentlemen, you see Sir—Phidias was one of 'em—gentlemen—you see Sir, and—and, and I—I—this here—here age, as you see this here era, that is, you see *my* era, is gentlemen, another—you see Sir, and now gentlemen, you see Sir—I would advise 'ee when you draw 'em, that is gentlemen, you see, the Elgin Marbles, that is, you see, the works of Phidias—not to make accurate finished drawings, as H-yd-n did, from 'em, that all their hidden excellence might be investigated; but to make compositions from 'em, as I did, without studying their hidden excellence at all, you see, Sir.

'Sir Th-m-s L-wr-nce arose, and said, "Exactly so!"'

The spirit of Michael Angelo appears, to rate the Academicians for encouraging only portrait painters in their exhibitions. He casts a spell transforming for one year each member into the shape most expressive of his qualities. Wilkie is ordered to depart from the Academy and join his friend 'H-yd-n' with Michael Angelo's best wishes—'tell him he will succeed in all his views and plans'—Fuseli is congratulated in that 'a brighter constellation of students' came to the Academy when he was Keeper than ever before or since. He is informed that 'The rising geniuses of England will ever acknowledge the sublimity and terror' of his ideas, 'without being led astray by the falsehood and absurdity' of his mode of expressing them. 'You are destined', says Michael Angelo 'not to be transformed, but to be translated to a place fit for your conceptions'—in a moment the whole place was in darkness, 'and I found myself', observes the Dreamer 'the next instant—*in Hell.*'

In another letter, the Ghost of Barry addressing the Dilettante Society criticizes the Academy, and exhorts it to purify itself. One can little wonder if 'the Art was in an uproar' on the appearance of these polemics. 'All this', says Haydon, 'told perniciously on my interests, though it fed my revenge on the Academy. . . . On the other hand, the combined fury, ridicule, sarcasm, and truth of my writing, understanding the subject as I did, indisputably turned the public mind in favour of High Art and laid the foundation of the great move that afterwards took place. I may have sacrificed my interests, and I did; but I kept the art in motion; I prevented stagnation, I laid open the pretences of a set of men who were masking their real views by the grossest hypocrisy, and prepared the people and the Government for what was their duty, if they wished the country to take its proper rank. The Academy never recovered this just exposure, and it never will.'

'But', he cries indignantly, 'such was the animosity generated by my terrific truths about the Academy that the good which was really in the work was rendered nugatory by the violence and injustice of those it skinned.'

In 1820 a short 'life' appeared in the *Annals,* in which Elmes claims that Haydon's 'appearance in the art will certainly form an era in its history'. The attitude throughout is that Haydon is a gentle innocent man persecuted by malignant enemies. An honour to his country, he has been thwarted and ruined, though he has 'done nothing to offend any human creature'.

Haydon's claim that the *Dreams* are the best things in the paper sets the reader turning the pages without much enthusiasm; so it is with a thrill that he suddenly comes upon the immortal words, 'My heart aches, and a drowsy numbness pains My sense'. The *Ode to a Nightingale* and the *Ode on a Grecian Urn* first appeared in the *Annals,* without, it would seem, arousing any particular attention; though they are cheek by jowl with poems of 'an almost indescribable insignificance'. Haydon, indeed, did write to Miss Mitford many years after, 'As we were one day walking in the Kilburn Meadows he repeated it (the *Ode to a Nightingale*) to me, before he put it to paper, in a low tremulous undertone which affected me extremely.'

This period of the *Annals,* which lasted from 1816 to 1820, and the year following it, when he exhibited *Jerusalem,* coincide with the highest point of Haydon's prestige. There was

enough truth in his tirades against the Academy for its mercen-
ary adherence to popular portraiture, and its indifference as a
body (at that time) to any art worthy of the name, to establish
him in the eyes of many as the champion of all that was worth
fighting for. His passionate pleading for the Elgin Marbles and
his spirited attack on Payne Knight aroused admiration, while
his supposed wrongs excited sympathy, so that it is not altogether surprising to find the young and ardent Keats writing
of 'that glorious Haydon and all his works', and speaking with
a thrill of the prospect of meeting him. This he did in 1816 at
Leigh Hunt's, and acquaintance ripened almost immediately into
friendship. Keats visited Haydon's studio 'at all times, and at all
times was welcome'. This friendship during its brief perfection
was a thing of beauty; for a time Haydon was an inspiration to
Keats, and Professor Garrod has the interesting theory that his
influence may in part account for Keats's obsession with the long
poem—the counterpart of his own obsession for the large picture. It will be remembered that Keats refers to *Lamia* (700
lines) as a short poem.

Haydon was quick to recognize Keats's genius, indeed it is
much to the credit of several of Keats's friends how quickly they
did so, considering his not always too promising beginnings. 'I
read one or two of his sonnets,' says Haydon, 'and formed a
very high idea of his genius.' After 'a most eager interchange
of thoughts', Keats sent Haydon the well-known sonnet:

> Great spirits now on earth are sojourning;
>   He of the cloud, the cataract, the lake,
>   Who on Helvellyn's summit, wide awake,
> Catches his freshness from Archangel's wing:
> He of the rose, the violet, the spring,
>   The social smile, the chain for freedom's sake:
>   And lo!—whose steadfastness would never take
> A meaner sound than Raphael's whispering.
> And other spirits there are standing apart
>   Upon the forehead of the age to come;
> These, these will give the world another heart,
>   And other pulses. Hear ye not the hum
> Of mighty workings in some distant mart?
>   Listen awhile ye nations and be dumb.

On Haydon's suggestion the penultimate line was cut to read:
'Of mighty workings?' and it is sometimes so printed.

He wrote to thank Keats, who replied, 'Your letter has filled me with a proud pleasure, and shall be kept by me as a stimulus to exertion. I begin to fix my eye on the horizon.' Haydon wrote of him, 'Keats was the only man I ever met who seemed and looked conscious of a high calling, except Wordsworth. Byron and Shelley were always sophisticating about their verses. Keats sophisticated about nothing. He had made up his mind to do great things. . . .' Describing his appearance he continues, 'He was below the middle size, with a low forehead, and an eye that had an inward look, perfectly divine, like a Delphian priestess who saw visions.' Few things have injured Haydon's reputation more than his quarrel with Keats and the remarks he made about him after his death. In the first case he has been blamed a little unjustly, in the second the generous things he said somewhat mitigate the ungenerous ones, and are less often quoted. Like most of Keats's friends he tried to make him out a much weaker man than he was in pretending that he was bowled over by hostile criticisms, but the additional accusation that he sought relief in dissipation and was once scarcely sober for six weeks must surely be one of Haydon's inventions. He gives himself away completely in telling the story about Keats's covering his tongue and throat as far as he could reach with cayenne pepper in order to appreciate 'the delicious coldness of claret in all its glory' as an instance of what a man will do to gratify his appetites when they get the better of him. At the worst, and if true, it would have only been a perfectly harmless experiment. Disease and the miserable nature of his wasting love for Fanny Brawne are strangely left out of account by Haydon in his elderbrotherly head-shakings over Keats's failure at the end, 'Latterly he grew irritated', Haydon writes, 'because I would shake my head at his irregularities and tell him he would destroy himself. The last time I ever saw him was at Hampstead, lying in a white bed with a book, hectic and on his back, irritable at his weakness and wounded at the way he had been used. . . . I told him to be calm, but he muttered that if he did not soon get better he would destroy himself. I tried to reason against such violence, but it was no use; he grew angry, and I went away deeply affected.

'Poor dear Keats! Had nature but given you firmness as well as fineness of nerve, you would have been glorious in your maturity as great in your promise.' But he also says, 'He was the most unselfish of human creatures: unadapted to this world, he cared not for himself, and put himself to any inconvenience for the sake of his friends. He was haughty, and had a fierce hatred of rank; but he had a kind gentle heart, and would have shared his fortune with any man who wanted it.' This well-known lament over his dead friend throws some light on Keats but perhaps more on Haydon. Generosity with a lacing of spitefulness is common enough; nor are Haydon's remarks so very far from the truth, 'A genius more purely poetical never existed!' 'He had no decision of character, and having no object upon which to direct his great powers was at the mercy of every petty theory ——'s ingenuity might start. One day he was full of an epic poem; the next day epic poems were splendid impositions on the world. Never for two days did he know his own intentions.' The statement is of course exaggerated, but Keats's dissatisfaction with what he did perfectly, and his uneasy hankering to attempt what he showed no signs of being able to do well give some colour to it. When Haydon wrote Keats was not recognized for the great poet he was, and seemed almost half a failure.

By the beginning of 1817 Haydon's health was suffering from the foul air of the small painting-room in which he worked and slept, and a move seemed desirable, and when 'many people of fashion' persuaded him to find better lodgings the matter became urgent.

He would need £300 to pay his landlord and establish himself afresh, and needless to say he had not got £300. In this dilemma Horace Smith suggested an application to a Mr. Harman, a wealthy man whom Haydon had met, and who had a reputation for generosity. Haydon wrote, was invited to see him, and came away with £300, offering his picture for security, which Harman apparently declined. This was by no means the last time he received help from Harman, who is said to have given him in all about a thousand pounds. He now, 'with affectionate regret', said good-bye to his old landlord and most kind friend, Perkins, who had trusted him so long for his rent, and whom even now he appears to have left in his debt, since, in referring later to his generosity, he added, 'Though he suffered in the end.' Most people did who had anything to do with Haydon. He had found comfortable and pleasant quarters in a house in Lisson Grove belonging to Rossi, the Academician. Leslie, the R.A., who succeeded him there, describes it as 'a small house with the convenience of a large painting-room attached to it'. Rossi made alterations in the building to suit Haydon, and was paid a quarter's rent (£60) in advance. The change was most beneficial, and his health began at once to improve. It was here soon after he was settled that there took place the celebrated dinner at which Keats first met Wordsworth. There were present in addition Charles Lamb and Monkhouse; 'and a very pleasant party we had', says Haydon. Haydon's *Dreams of Somniator* and suchlike, of which he was so proud, are poor fustian compared with the rich material of such descriptions as this; so in fairness to his best gift this famous account must be quoted again.

He had written to Lamb to tell him that the address was '22 Lisson Grove, North, at Rossi's, half-way up, right-hand corner', and received this in reply:

MY DEAR HAYDON,
I will come with pleasure to 22 Lisson Grove, North, at Rossi's half-way up, right-hand side, if I can find it.

Yours,
C. LAMB.

20, Russel Court,
    Covent Garden East,
        half-way up, next the corner,
            left hand side.

The 'immortal dinner' took place on 28 December.

'Wordsworth', Haydon writes, 'was in fine cue, and we had a glorious set-to—on Homer, Shakespeare, Milton and Virgil. Lamb got exceedingly merry and exquisitely witty; and his fun in the midst of Wordsworth's solemn intonations of oratory was like the sarcasm and wit of the fool in the intervals of Lear's passion. He made a speech and voted me absent, and made them drink my health. "Now", said Lamb, "you old lake poet, you rascally poet, why do you call Voltaire dull?" We all defended Wordsworth, and affirmed there was a state of mind when Voltaire would be dull. "Well," said Lamb, "here's Voltaire—the Messiah of the French nation, and a very proper one too."

'He then, in a strain of humour beyond description, abused me for putting Newton's head into my picture; "a fellow", said he, "who believed nothing unless it was as clear as the three sides of a triangle". And then he and Keats agreed he had destroyed all the poetry of the rainbow by reducing it to the prismatic colours. It was impossible to resist him and we all drank "Newton's health and confusion to mathematics". It was delightful to see the good humour of Wordsworth in giving in to all our frolics without affectation and laughing as heartily as the best of us.'

Other friends came in, among them Ritchie, who was going to penetrate by Fezzan to Timbuctoo. In the morning of this day a stranger had called saying he was a comptroller of stamps who had often corresponded with Wordsworth, and would like an introduction. Haydon said he might come. When they retired to tea they found him. Haydon continues:

'In introducing him to Wordsworth I forgot to say who he was. After a little time the comptroller looked down, looked up and said to Wordsworth: "Don't you think, sir, Milton was a great genius?" Keats looked at me, Wordsworth looked at the comptroller. Lamb who was dozing by the fire turned round and said: "Pray sir, did you say Milton was a great genius?" "No, sir, I asked Mr. Wordsworth if he were not." "Oh," said Lamb, "then you are a silly fellow." "Charles! my dear Charles!" said Wordsworth, but Lamb, perfectly innocent of the confusion he had created, was off again by the fire.

'After an awful pause the comptroller said: "Don't you think Newton a great genius?" I could not stand it any longer. Keats put his head into my books. Ritchie squeezed in a laugh. Wordsworth seemed asking himself: "Who is this?" Lamb got up, and taking a candle, said: "Sir, will you allow me to look at your phrenological development?" He then turned his back on the poor man, and at every question of the comptroller he chaunted:

> Diddle, diddle, dumpling, my son John
> Went to bed with his breeches on.

'The man in office finding Wordsworth did not know who he was, said in a spasmodic and half-chuckling anticipation of assured victory: "I have had the honour of some correspondence with you, Mr. Wordsworth." "With me, sir?" said Wordsworth, "not that I remember." "Don't you sir? I am a comptroller of stamps." There was a dead silence, the comptroller evidently thinking that was enough. While we were waiting for Wordsworth's reply, Lamb sung out:

> Hey diddle diddle,
> The cat and the fiddle.

"My dear Charles!" said Wordsworth.

> Diddle diddle dumpling, my son John,

chaunted Lamb, and then rising, exclaimed: "Do let me have another look at that gentleman's organs." Keats and I hurried Lamb into the painting-room, shut the door and gave way to inextinguishable laughter. Monkhouse followed and tried to get Lamb away. We went back but the comptroller was irreconcilable. We soothed and smiled and asked him to supper. He stayed though his dignity was sorely affected. However being a good-natured man, we parted all in good humour, and no ill-effects followed.

'All the while, until Monkhouse succeeded, we could hear Lamb struggling in the painting-room and calling at intervals: "Who is that fellow? Allow me to see his organs once more."

'It was indeed an immortal evening. Wordsworth's fine intonation as he quoted Milton and Virgil, Keats' eager inspired look, Lamb's quaint sparkle of lambent humour, so speeded the stream of conversation, that in my life I never passed a more delightful time . . . and my solemn Jerusalem flashing up by the flame of the fire, with Christ hanging over us like a vision, all made up a picture which will long glow upon that inward eye

Which is the bliss of solitude.'

As amusing in its way is his account of his first meeting with Shelley at Leigh Hunt's:

'I went', says he, 'a little after the time, and seated myself in the place kept for me at the table [this expanding table is now in the Keats' Museum] right opposite Shelley himself, as I was told after, for I did not then know what hectic, spare, weakly, yet intellectual-looking creature it was carving a bit of brocoli or cabbage on his plate, as if it had been the substantial wing of a chicken. Hunt and his wife and her sister, Keats, Horace Smith, and myself made up the party. In a few minutes Shelley opened the conversation by saying in a most feminine and gentle voice, "As to that detestable religion, the Christian . . . " I looked astounded, but casting a glance round the table easily saw by Hunt's expression of ecstacy and the women's simper, I was to be set at that evening *vi et armis*. No reply, however, was made to this sally during dinner, but when the dessert came and the servant was gone, to it we went like fiends. —— and —— were deists. I felt exactly like a stag at bay and resolved to gore without mercy. Shelley said the Mosaic and Christian dispensations were inconsistent. I swore they were not, and that the Ten Commandments had been the foundation of all the codes of law in the earth. Shelley denied it. —— backed him. I affirmed they were . . . neither of us using an atom of logic. . . . Neither ——, Keats nor —— said a word to this; but still Shelley, —— and —— kept at it till, finding I was a match for them in argument, they became personal, and so did I. We said unpleasant things to each other, and when I retired to the other room for a moment I overheard them say, "Haydon is fierce." "Yes," said Hunt; "the question always irritates him." As the women were dressing to go, —— said to me with a look of nervous fear, "Are these creatures to be damned Haydon?" "Good Heaven," said I, "what a morbid view of Christianity." The assertion of Hunt that these sort of discussions irritated me is perfectly true; but it was not so much the question as their manner of treating it. I never heard any sceptic but Hazlitt discuss the matter with the gravity such a question demanded. The eternity of the human soul is not a joke, as ―― was always inclined to make of it, not in reality—for the thought wrenched his being to the very midriff—but apparently that he might conceal his frightful apprehension. . . . My irritation proceeded not from my fear of them, but from my being unable to command my feelings when I heard Voltaire almost worshipped in the very same breath that had called St. Paul, Mr. Paul, and when, with a smile of uneffable superiority, it was intimated that he was a cunning fellow. I used to say, "Let us go on without appelations of that kind. I detest them." "Oh, the question irritates you?" was the reply. "And always will when so conducted," was my answer. . . . Often, when all discussion had ceased, and the wine had gone freely round—when long talk of poetry and painting had, as it were, opened our hearts ―― would suddenly (touching my arm with the most friendly pressure) show me a passage in the Bible and Testament, and say, as if appealing to my superiority of understanding, "Haydon do you believe this?" "Yes," I would answer instantly, with a look he will remember. He would then get up, close the book, and ejaculate, "By Heavens, is it possible!" This was another mode of appeal to my vanity. He would then look out of the window with an affected indifference, as if he pitied my shallow mind; and going jauntily to the piano, strike up "Cosi fan tutti", or "Addio il mio cuore", with a "Ring the bell for tea". After this I made up my mind to subject myself no more to the chance of those discussions, but gradually to withdraw from the whole party.'

XII. CHARACTERISTICS

What a race the young Haydons would have been with the blood of Michael Angelo mingled with mine!—B. R. HAYDON (*Letter to Kirkup* 1844)

HAYDON was now thirty-two. One glimpse of someone we have never seen would tell us more than pages of description, and the next best thing is a good portrait. There are several portraits of Haydon but they vary so much that it is difficult to form a clear idea of him. His appearance was a valuable asset, not only did he believe himself to be a genius, he looked like one. The future Lady Eastlake cannot have been alone in her 'childish delight' over the delicately cut and romantic profile in Phillips's drawing (now lost) if it at all resembled the drawing of Haydon as a young man by Harlow, in the Witt Collection. That this is a good likeness seems proved by its striking resemblance to his own self-portrait, as an elderly man, in the National Portrait Gallery. But the strange thing about these profiles is their utter dissimilarity to the full-face portraits; one can hardly believe they were done from the same man. In Harlow's drawing the face is sensitive and refined, though conceit is evident enough; it would be a face one would notice anywhere and wonder what future lay before its owner. In his own self-portrait we see the same man, old, bald, and disillusioned. To turn from these to the full-face drawings he made of himself, or to the engraving by W. Harvey, is to receive a shock. It would be difficult to imagine anything more square and bull-necked, more good-humouredly pugnacious and truculent than the first of these. It might be a picture of Hercules. Miss Mitford had noticed the similarity when she wrote, 'You, a sort of lesser Hercules,' and the same quality is apparent in a less degree in Miss Zornlin's portrait in the National Portrait Gallery. Besides these, the drawing for the head of *Solomon* in the Tate Gallery is almost certainly a self-portrait, so like is it to Miss Zornlin's head, though about fifteen years separates them. Elizabeth Barrett seems to imply no less when she writes, 'But, Mr. Haydon . . . *you* are Marcus Curtius . . . to say nothing of your being Solomon.' More than any of the other self-portraits it suggests Haydon's idea of himself—conscious worth, royal in its calm assumption of superiority to other men. Wilkie's two portraits suggest a different man, or different men, for neither bears the least resemblance to the other or to any other picture of him, and the same may be said of Haydon's portrait of himself in the *Reform Banquet*; while the figure bearing his name in Archer's picture of a group of artists among the Elgin Marbles, is, like the last mentioned, in profile, but differs from it in having the large aquiline nose with its delicately moulded droop at the end; a characteristic which fails to make its presence felt in any of the full-face portraits. The whole aspect is different in the two views, the belligerent expression of the full-face giving place to something much less strong and determined in the profile. Not only the features but the character seem changed. This duality is borne out by something in the *Journals*, it is as if he confronted the world with the qualities that show in the full-face, while the weakness and misery to which he sometimes gave way in private are implied in the profile.

Borrow's description of Haydon in *Lavengro* is vivid though a little unkind, 'The painter might be about thirty-five years old; he had a clever intelligent countenance, with a sharp grey eye—his hair was dark brown, and cut á-la-Rafael, as I was subsequently told, that is, there was little before and much behind—he did not wear a neckcloth; but in its stead, a black riband, so that his neck, which was rather fine, was somewhat exposed—he had a broad muscular breast, and I make no doubt that he would have been a very fine figure, but unfortunately his legs and thighs were somewhat short.' There must have been something remarkable about Haydon's eyes, Miss Mitford speaks of his 'tremendous eyes', and declares that she feels as afraid as a schoolboy of the rod, at the thought of them, when she sits down to write to their owner. Frederic thus describes his father as he remembered him in his fifty-third year—'a handsome, fresh-coloured, robust, little man, with a big bald head, small ears, aquiline features, a peculiarly short upper lip, and a keen, restless, azure-grey eye, the pupil of which contracted and expanded, rose and fell as he talked, just as if some inner light and fire was playing on his brain. He was a very active man; motion was his repose. In fact he lived in a hurricane, and fattened on anxiety and care. He carried himself uprightly and stamped his little feet upon the ground, as if he revelled in the consciousness of existence.'

Haydon put as much energy into misery as into self-assertiveness, or into any other form of activity. The stricken being who spent a day walking about the streets till he was exhausted because he was so full of grief that he could not have concealed it from his family, in another mood, as for instance when he approached the door of a well-filled drawing-room before dinner, would, 'like a comic hero in a farce . . . throw back his coat-collar on either shoulder . . . inflate his chest, and even beat his bosom to raise his spirits', while he lifted his chin high in the air. He had an unusual capacity for both happiness and grief, for hopefulness and despair; but in the latter case nothing depressed him long; and, as with Dr. Johnson's friend who tried to be a philosopher, 'cheerfulness would keep breaking in'. His son saw him as a man of many generous virtues and a few not ungenerous faults, which, had it not been for his vanity, was probably not far from the truth. But when his vanity was in action it would not allow him to be either generous or honest. He was kind to many of his pupils, and most generous in the assistance he gave to Lough, the young sculptor from Northumberland, whom he found practically starving, and of whose genius he thought highly; but directly he scented a rival he became mean, ill-natured and ill-mannered. No one must paint 'history' but himself, or under his instruction. Hilton, an old fellow-student, who had shown him kindness when he was in trouble, died in 1840, while Haydon was on a lecturing tour. An Academician, and an historical painter, he was not to be forgiven his greater success. Haydon writes to his wife: 'Poor Hilton is gone. All my life they puffed the poor fellow against me, and what has he done? . . . There is nothing mean men take such delight in as pretending great admiration for an inferior man in order to run down a man whose talents they cannot disprove. . . . In my second picture I opposed him at the British Gallery for the hundred guinea prize, and I beat both Hilton and Howard, who by the way hung this very picture, "Dentatus", out of sight in the ante-room at the Royal Academy.' This letter was written in 1840, nineteen years after his marriage. One wonders how many times Mary had heard about *Dentatus*; how often she had been told that it had been hung in the ante-room, and had then won the hundred-guinea prize.

Haydon also wrote to Lord Melbourne, 'Your lordship will see Hilton is dead, the historical painter; a good man, but not a

great artist. In early life his merits were overrated by the Royal
Academy in order to pit him against me, but I beat him wherever
we met. I first beat him with my second picture for the hundred
guinea prize at the British Institution in 1810. . . . He pilfered
from all. . . . His best work is in the Chelsea Church, though
without one original thought.'

Haydon's professional jealousy was disastrous to him, because
through it he made enemies of many people who were disposed
to be his friends. William Carey, the art-critic, wrote an article
in which he praised highly West's *Death on the Pale Horse*; this
was more than Haydon could bear. Through Elmes he launched
an attack on Carey in the *Annals*. In this West is accused of
having admitted Carey into his painting-room, and of having
'flattered and duly tutored' him to put forth his criticism to the
world 'with an unjust view to lower and trample on' Haydon.
Carey had championed Haydon, praising his work and supporting his pleas for art-education and State-patronage, and had been
warmly thanked for so doing. This useful friend became, owing
to Haydon's unwarrantable assertions, a bitter enemy. His
counter-attack took the form of a book of over 350 pages
written in a state of indignation bordering on frenzy. It throws
light on Haydon's publicity methods and on literary warfare in
those days. Not content with mere words Carey enforces his
meaning by underlining, and uses capitals of immense size to
add weight to his rage and contempt. On some pages hardly a
word is in ordinary type. Whatever Elmes wrote in the *Annals*
was written with Haydon's approval, if not with his actual col-
laboration. Carey begins by declaring Elmes's and Haydon's
accusations to be a 'false, envious, malignant calumny . . . a base
concert and conspiracy designed to injure West's and his own
moral character'. He quotes a passage from *Liber Falsitatis*, as he
dubs the *Annals*, the words being Elmes's but the type Carey's own:

'In the first place, Sir, will not HAYDON's FIRST PICTURE; *in
colour, drawing, expression, light and shadow, bear comparison with* ANY OF
RAFFAELE'S, *painted at the same age*? I am SURE IT WILL. . . . Did RAFFAELE
AT TWENTY put forth *a more powerful picture than* DENTATUS?
I have no hesitation in saying NO! *and that in the essential qualities of
heroic form, the figure of Dentatus alone will bear comparison with* ANY
FIGURE RAFFAELE EVER EXECUTED *in the heroic style* . . . *in the Judgement
of Solomon is not Haydon's* DECIDEDLY SUPERIOR to RAFFAELE'S? *and
I am convinced* RAFFAELE HIMSELF WOULD HAVE OWNED IT!'

After this quotation one has the impression that for Carey words almost cease to have any value as a means of expression; while Elmes, in his reply, remarks that he considers Carey one of the greatest pests in English art, adding that he does not know a greater misfortune to an artist than to be praised by him. Such a comparison with Raphael appearing in a magazine in which Haydon was known to have a predominating influence may have amused the public, but cannot have failed to tell 'perniciously upon his interests' with other artists and with the connoisseurs.

When the *Art Union* began its career in 1839 it showed itself well disposed to Haydon and printed a note from him, saying of himself that he is everywhere 'considered the most interesting lecturer and the greatest painter the world ever saw . . . all of which', he continues, 'I most powerfully and potently believe, have believed and ever shall believe . . .'. The editor's comment was friendly, he called Haydon, 'this accomplished artist but eccentric man of genius'. Not long after this the *Art Union* published extracts from the *Hull Times* protesting against lectures in which Haydon abused the Academy, saying, 'Mr. Haydon's venom has defeated his purpose; his lectures will be repeated in very few of the provincial towns', and adding that these lectures 'were full of the unfounded and unmeaning nonsense about grand art and himself of which he has long since sickened the London newspapers'. Whereupon Haydon accused the *Art Union* of 'being *established* by the Royal Academy to destroy his prospects opened in the provinces'. To which the editor retorted, 'I consider Mr. Haydon to be a quack of the worst order . . . the pen of Mr. Haydon has obtained for him a notoriety his pencil has failed to achieve, and for thirty years he has been writing himself up and painting himself down. He has two execrable pictures now in Suffolk Street.'

In a post-war period, when the new rich were thrusting themselves into notice by every device of ostentation and publicity, Haydon's self-advertising was by no means exceptional; nevertheless he came to feel it had done him harm. He was later to lose almost all his influence with the Press; John Scott, of the *Champion*, died in 1821, Hazlitt in 1830; with Barnes, of *The Times*, he quarrelled (owing to his refusal to allow Mrs. Haydon to visit Barnes's house); Elmes had given up the *Annals*, and Leigh Hunt the *Examiner*, so Haydon was left with only Lockhart to give him a helping hand in the *Quarterly*. At the end of his life the *Journals* are full of complaints of attacks in the Press, and, this state of things having come about, he expressed regret for his early writings and boastings. 'Ah, Keats,' he once wrote, '... the truest thing you ever said of mortal man was that I had a touch of Alexander in me! I have, I know it, and the world shall know it.' Bell Scott said of Haydon that his vanity was 'intellectual and personal, which made it impossible for him to regard any other man as of the same species with himself, and must have endangered his reason'. 'So you admit', Haydon wrote to a friend, 'if it were not for my vanity I should be a great man. Delightful! what more could you say of Alexander or Napoleon?' He expected everyone to think him a genius, and openly showed surprise if they did not. There must have been something disarming about his vanity or he would not have had so many friends; we have Bewick's word for it that 'he was courted by the greatest in the land', and he certainly got on well with a surprising variety of people, and made friends wherever he went. Their range is remarkable. He knew four Prime Ministers: Grey, Wellington, Peel and Melbourne, and the last found him sufficiently amusing to give him an interview apparently whenever he asked for one. He knew and corresponded with the Dukes of Bedford and Sutherland, and the Duchess of Sutherland drove to his house to welcome him when he came out of prison. She came a day too early, and he wrote to ask when she came again to do so in state, which she did, and often after sent her state carriage to wait outside his house to gain him credit with the tradespeople. Palmerston thought him one of the best after-dinner conversationalists he knew; Cobden liked and admired him. Wordsworth was a life-long friend, and told Frederic after Haydon's death that his father had 'a fine, frank, generous nature'. There was a warmth and vigour about him that won Keats's heart immediately, if it did cool later. He was intimate with Sidney Smith and Horace Smith, and friendly with D'Orsay and Lady Blessington, whose portrait he painted. Sir Walter Scott liked him and helped him when he was in difficulties. He pleased the business-men in the northern manufacturing towns; and his late landlord, Newton, was fond enough of him to let him owe rent and to take his pictures in place of it to the extent of thousands of pounds, though he is described as a poor man. A sitter for the *Reform Banquet* picture, of a completely different type, a sort of 'Squire Western', who came for an hour, shook him warmly by the hand at parting and expressed a wish to see more of him. The King's Bench after his first visit became full of friends. Frederic says that to his servants and all about him he was habitually kind and indulgent, and that he possessed 'in a rare degree, and in spite of a hasty temper and a rather dangerous candour, the power of winning and preserving the love and respect of all who knew him well'. He describes him at another time as being irritable and imperious, and habitually taciturn at home, but this did not prevent his wife and children from loving and admiring him to the end of his life.

Haydon spent much of his time alone, in a darkened room.

'Sometimes', he wrote, 'when I come to dinner my dear Mary says I have been a great deal alone. Such a sensation never enters my head, I never feel alone. With visions of ancient heroes, pictures of Christ, principles of ancient Art, humourous subjects, deductions, sarcasms against the Academy, piercing remembrance of my dear children all crowding upon me, I paint, write, conceive and fall asleep, start up refreshed, eat my lunch with the fierceness of a Polyphemus, return to my room, go on till near dinner, walk, dine, read the paper, return to my study, complete what I have been doing, or muse till dusk, then to bed, lamenting my mortality at being fatigued. I never rest, I talk all night in my sleep, start up; I scarce know whether I did not relish ruin, as a source of increased activity. "Rest, rest, perturbed spirit!" '

He must have been an uncomfortable table-companion; after he had bolted his food, as he habitually did, he read while Mary finished. She can have had little amusement in her life. Days spent as described above cannot have left much time for his wife's companionship, and even the nights were not hers, for Frederic says his father always slept in a separate room for about a year after each new baby had arrived, and this happened every eighteen months or so. She seems not to have gone with him to most of his evening entertainments, and £60 a year as the dress allowance of the entire family would hardly have afforded her suitable clothes. As head of the family he was evidently something of a disciplinarian, though rather by fits and starts. But that the children stood in no awe of him is shown by Frederic's testimony to his good-tempered forbearance when they hallooed about the house, and thumped at his painting-room door in passing, or burst it open and rushed in while he was working—a thing he loathed.

Some he attracted and some repelled; Hazlitt said it was impossible to resist him, so long as you kept on terms with him, 'any difference of opinion or reluctance on your part made no impression on him, and unless you quarrelled with him downright, you must do as he wished you'. How uncertain Hazlitt was of his own opinion is shown in such a criticism as the following, if it is compared with his high praise at other times; parts of it are manifestly unfair: 'He should', he said, 'have been a boatswain on a man-of-war, he has no other idea of glory than those which belong to a naval victory, or vulgar noise and insolence. . . . I never heard him speak with enthusiasm of any painter or work of merit, or show any love of art except as a puffing machine for him to get up into to blow a trumpet in his own praise.' But he liked his company nevertheless, 'One enjoys his hearty joyous laugh; it sets one on one's legs as it were better than a glass of champagne, for one is delighted to meet such a cheery spirit in the saddening depression that broods over the hypocrisy and depression of the world. His laugh rings in my ears like merry bells.' Miss Mitford, so enthusiastic in those early days, wrote to a friend, 'Oh! how you would like him! He is a creature of air and fire; the frankest truest man breathing; so absolutely free from pretence or trickery!' And again, comparing him with Serjeant Talfourd, 'I do not mean that Talfourd wrote as Haydon painted: the resemblance is rather in conversation, in enthusiasm, that powerful engine of genius, so fresh: there is such age in his knowledge, and such youth in his fancy, you would be charmed with him. . . . But he is not Haydon, he wants his noble and open simplicity, that charm of charms.'

XIII. THE PRIVATE DAY

Rank, beauty, and fashion.
HAYDON (*passim*)

AT last, in the early months of 1820, Haydon's large picture of *Christ's Triumphal Entry into Jerusalem* was finished. His two benefactors, Coutts and Harman, had kept him going through these long profitless years; what was to be their, and his, reward? He engaged the great room at the Egyptian Hall from 1 March for a year. He rented it for £300 without a shilling in his pocket; but Bullock, like most of the landlords of this remarkable painter, was 'a fine fellow, and loved the game of ruin or success—Westminster Abbey or victory'—as well as Haydon himself. By the end of January, only the final glazings remained to be done. The picture was already well known; it had been visited by Canova, Cuvier, Horace Vernet, the Grand Duke Michael (the younger brother of Nicholas), indeed by most of the distinguished foreigners who came to this country during its progress.

What was going to happen? Haydon trembled, but hoped and was confident. His debts he did not dare to think of, his Mary he thought of all the time he gazed at his picture. On it too much depended.

It had taken him six years. It might be considered a solitary effort.

The time came for rolling and moving this work, which had, he says, been visited by 'fashion, beauty, and rank; by genius, and by royalty'.

The head of Christ was his great anxiety. He had departed from the traditional head.

'Allow me to say,' he wrote to William Jerdan, 'that no other eyes or brows would have done for my principal figure. Dark eyes and forcible brows gave Him at once the look of a being liable to appetite and passions. The great thing to give Him was the look of power without the appearance as if its exercise was an effort. I painted the head seven times and tried every variety of human feature.'

He was still not satisfied. As was his custom he printed a long description of the picture in the sixpenny catalogue; in this he tells of his difficulties over this head, and describes how it was his intention to bring out the look of power combined with that of tenderness, then he bursts out:

'How does he feel the miserable incompetency of his own imagination, who struggles to see that face in which all that is visible of the deity is reflected!—Pure!—Serene!—Smiling awfully and sweet!—Bland! Benignant!—Lovely!—Sublime in its beauty!—Compassionate in its grandeur!—Quivering with sensibility!—Terrible in its composure!— Omnipotent in its sedateness!'

The picture (rolled) was carried on the shoulders of three life-guardsmen (Colonel Barton having given leave to Haydon to employ them). The frame weighed 600 pounds, and at the first attempt to hang it it snapped an iron ring, strong enough they had thought to carry anything.

The powerful soldiers were as nervous as infants, but finally they lifted it by machinery and pitched it without accident on its proper support.

The picture was 'tipped and ready for glazing', when Haydon found he had not a penny left.

Sir George had sent him £30, but that had all gone. The room was full of workmen ready to put the hangings on the walls, the invitation cards had been sent out, the picture was up, 'and looking gloriously'; Haydon, with his palette set, longing to get to it, the landlord popping in now and then as if half-suspicious, when there was a halt. There was nothing to buy the hangings with, or to pay the men.

This was one of those forlorn hopes which Haydon was so eminently fitted to meet. He went straight down to Coutts's and saw Sir E. Antrobus and Mr. Marjoribanks and said, 'I am going to exhibit a picture, which has taken six years to paint.' They stared, 'Six years over a picture?' 'Yes, sir.' 'Well what do you want?' 'Why, I am ashamed to say I have no money left, and am overdrawn.' 'How much do you want?' 'Why, £50 would do.' 'You shall have it,' said both; 'give us your note.'

Haydon rushed out for a stamp to a stationer's close by and never wrote 'I promise to pay' with such inspired fury before. He was back again in two minutes, had the note signed in two more, and in another five took out his £50. He hurried off to a wholesale house, bought all the fittings wanted (of a purple brown colour), and rushed back to the Hall. The huge Sammons (his servant) was like a child in a fright. Everyone had been alarmed and work was at a standstill, but Haydon's appearance with his 'mouth clenched five times fiercer than ever', the arrival of the fittings, his 'stamping walk and thundering voice, put fire into all'. The hive was in full buzz once more, when Haydon, mounting a ladder, let fly at his picture, and before dark had toned richly one-third of it. His pupils had been writing and addressing the tickets (800 in all) which Haydon signed in the evenings. 'All the ministers and their ladies, all the foreign ambassadors, all the bishops, all the beauties in high life, the officers on guard at the palace, all the geniuses in town, and everybody of any note was invited to come.'

He got through the glazing in three days; covered up the picture, and finished the room by Friday night, recklessly promising the men a guinea for drinks.

The Private Day. The longed-for and dreaded day, Saturday, 25 March, has come at last. Haydon, in a fever of anxiety, waits over the way at Hatchett's coffee room, with his eyes straying to the clock every minute. Unable to keep still he goes over to the Hall before the time fixed; there he finds everything ready, the servants at their posts, the chairs all in rows, and the table by the door piled with catalogues. At the end of the room hangs the work on which everything depends: fame, success, marriage, freedom from debt, escape from prison; while on the other walls are all the important pictures he has painted up to this time, *Solomon, Dentatus, Macbeth, The Flight into Egypt, Romeo and Juliet* (painted after *Solomon*), and the drawings for *Jerusalem*. No one has come; it is true it is not twelve o'clock (the time on the invitation cards) still one would have thought!—perhaps no one will come. He can't stay in that room with Sammons and the rest watching in uneasy silence, or talking under their breath, so he drifts back to Hatchett's, where he fidgets at the bar. At half-past twelve he steals over again; Sammons looks knowing. 'Anybody come?' 'Yes, sir, Sir William Scott is just gone in.' 'That will do, he always goes to every exhibition on earth, and brings everybody.' Much relieved Haydon goes away, eats a good lunch, drinks a couple of glasses of sherry, and sallies forth again at half-past three ready for anything. As he turns his eyes in the direction of the Hall he sees a crowd of carriages blocking Piccadilly. Bounding over, he finds the whole place full of servants, and 'all the bustle and chat, noise and hallooing of coachmen, of a regular rout at noonday!' He pushes through the throng, nodding at acquaintances right and left, everyone makes way for him. The room itself cannot hold the people, the queue blocks the stair and stretches out into the street like the crowd at a pit door. Some of these are the greatest persons in the land. Sammons is 'seven feet high, there is no speaking to him'. Haydon squeezes in and the buzz of talk directs itself towards him; in a corner are Keats and Hazlitt 'really rejoicing'. At this moment there is a stir and commotion, a passage is made and in comes the Persian Ambassador and his suite. His fine, manly person, black beard and resplendent dress make a prodigious show. There is a lull in the talk as he walks up to the picture, and says in a loud voice and in good English, 'I like the elbow of soldier.'

By five all is enthusiasm, especially amongst the women— 'pretty dears! when were their hearts ever shut against enterprise, pathos, or passion?' But Christ's head is not successful. Everything else is admired; the penitent girl, blushing and hiding her face; the Samaritan woman and the Centurion spreading their garments in the road; Wordsworth's bowing head; Newton and Voltaire; the pressing, shouting crowd, and the action of the principal figure. Christ's head startles people; it is not the type, not the traditional head. Everyone seems afraid, when in walks 'with all the dignity of her majestic presence, Mrs. Siddons, like a Ceres, or a Juno'. A dead silence falls on the room, the people crowd back on each others' feet as she approaches the picture, and having halted at a proper distance remains in the attitude for deep thought. There is not a sound for a full minute, when Sir George Beaumont, who is extremely anxious, says in a most delicate voice, 'How do you like the Christ?' Everyone listens for her reply. There is a pregnant pause, then, 'in a deep loud, tragic tone,' she says, 'It is completely successful.'

Haydon is then presented 'with all the ceremonies of a levee', and 'in an awful tone' is invited to her house. Mrs. Siddons then expresses her 'high admiration' for the way he has 'so variously modified the same expression. The paleness of your Christ', says she, 'gives it a supernatural look.' The word instantly catches on —his *Christ* is supernatural, and everything is explained.

Lady Murray says, 'Why, you have a complete rout.' Lord Mulgrave is at the top of the room receiving congratulations from everybody. Wilkie tries to be enthusiastic; Jackson is startled. Prince Hoare is here, all the world of rank, beauty, and fashion is here. The spring evening falls, the pictures grow dim, the room gradually empties, and Haydon returns home overwhelmed by a flood of sensations which exhaust him and make rest impossible. The mighty Sammons, devoted servant, breaks down and fairly sobs.

Looking back more than twenty years later upon the glamour of that spring evening when the colours were fading from the sky, and the departing ladies were casting friendly or curious glances at the handsome painter, Haydon is to be excused for believing that his picture had been considered a national triumph. Perhaps he was right. Nearly thirty-one thousand people visited it in London alone; sixteen hundred going in two days during the second week. It had been a day of triumph in his life; one of those occasions for which he lived: a long struggle against difficulties that would have broken most men's spirits, culminating in the thrilling publicity he craved for. When he thought of the distinguished men who had filled the great rooms (in which he himself was the principal figure), of the fashionable women, is it surprising if he felt dazed and drunk with success?

Two letters:

St. John's Wood Place,
March 27th 1820.

MADAM

I hope I may be pardoned for venturing to express again my gratitude for your unhesitating decision on Saturday.

I have ever estimated you, Madam, as the great high-priestess at the shrine of Nature; as the only being living who had ever been, or who was worthy to be admitted within the veil of her temple; as one whose immortality was long since decided. You will then judge of my feelings at having been so fortunate as to touch the sensibilities of so gifted a being. The whole evening I could not avoid believing I had held converse with a spirit of my own imagination, whom for years I had pictured in solitude as the organ of Nature herself, in whose immediate impressions I would place more confidence, and bow to them with more deference, than to the united reasoning of the rest of the world.

By this liberty I know I risk all prospect of any future notice from

you, yet I rely on your goodness to pardon the indelicacy as well a
rudeness of the intrusion.

I am, Madam,

With the most respectful admiration

Your faithful servant,

B. R. HAYDON.

Mrs. Siddons.

27 Upper Baker Street

Regent's Park.

SIR,

In answer to your very flattering note I can no otherwise reply thar
in the words of Hamlet, that 'the suffrage of one so great a geniu.
o'erweighs a whole theatre of others'.

Your time must of course be so completely devoted to your divine
art, that I can scarcely hope you will find leisure to gratify me by calling
here when it may not be out of your way to do me that favour; ye
I doubt; I will not despair, and I remain

With the utmost admiration

Your most obliged servant

S. SIDDONS.

He called and was gloriously received, 'It was', he says, 'like
speaking to the mother of the gods.'

The picture was a newspaper sensation. *The Times* called it
'a noble specimen of the highest class of art. . . . Some of the
heads', it continued, 'will remind connoisseurs of the best efforts
of the old masters.' The *Observer* gave it three whole columns,
and quoted Haydon's own description of it in his catalogue in
full and with high approval. Especially did it like his defence of
the introduction of the sneering Voltaire beside the reverent
Newton, for which he had been savagely attacked by the Deists.
'If Newton be wrong,' says Haydon, 'as the Deists think him,
Voltaire will be, as he ought to be reverenced. If, as Christians
believe him Newton be right, Voltaire will be, as he ought to
be, ridiculous. Where then is the injustice?' 'Such', comments
the *Observer*, 'is the language of this intelligent man. . . .' Both
The Times and the *Observer* bow before Mrs. Siddons, as 'the
most perfect existing judge of the human countenance' (*Observer*), in her approval of the head of Christ, and accept her word
'supernatural' as explaining satisfactorily what they were never-
theless evidently a little disturbed by. 'The artist has at once
attained the triumph of the history painter,' says the *Observer*,

in reference to his masterly telling of the story and, success with the facial expressions, 'The colouring is superb. He has here attained the second triumph. No living colourist has thrown upon the canvas a richer and more powerful depth of tint, the picture glows with living splendour . . . the passing of a century will not diminish its gorgeous beauty, nor perhaps produce its superior.'

The great success of the picture, and the crowds that went to see it had the unfortunate result of rousing Haydon's creditors to action. They smelt money, and what he describes as 'a base appetite' was awakened. Money kept pouring in, and he kept paying out, and though up to this time he had never had a penny of law costs, because he was poor, now, directly it was clear that things were changed, instead of relying on his honour, his creditors loaded him with lawyers' letters.

The picture did not sell. An offer of £1,000 made in Haydon's absence, was refused by Sammons. Sir George Beaumont first tried to get it bought for a church, then, when that fell through, started a subscription, but foolishly put a ten-pound limit; £200 was subscribed and lay at Coutts's where it was useless to creditors, and effectively stopped the purchase by individuals or bodies. Haydon wound up the exhibition with a total receipt (for entrances and catalogues) of £1,760, and a clear profit of £1,298. Every shilling was paid away as soon as it came in. His creditors considered it a case of now or never; the least delay was followed by a lawyer's letter.

When the exhibition in London closed he decided to take the picture up to Edinburgh. From his friendship with Leigh Hunt and the 'Cockney School' Haydon had come in for his share of mauling by *Blackwood*, and he thought it would be a fine thing to attack the enemy in his very camp. One of the first people he met when he arrived was Lockhart, who had assaulted him in the press. They made friends at once and he treated Haydon then and ever after as a man he had unwittingly injured. To make amends he wrote in *Blackwood* (1820):

'It is probable that the absurd style of language in which this picture has been lauded by the critics of Cockayne may have inspired many of our readers, as we confess it had ourselves, with many doubts and suspicions; but in order to do away with these we are quite sure nothing more can be necessary than a single glance at the wonderful performance itself. . . . It is quite evident that Mr. Haydon is already by far the greatest historical painter that England has yet produced. In time those that have observed this masterpiece can have no doubt he will take his place by the side of the greatest painters of Italy.'

The *Blackwood* set, not entirely satisfied that Haydon was not a cockney, thought to test him with a gallop. Bred up in Devonshire to ride 'all sorts of horses at all sorts of leaps, saddle or no saddle', he gloried inwardly at the proposal.

One of them lent him a fine spirited horse, expecting a tumble. Off they went and they soon found Haydon was not to be beaten. They raced once or twice and he won, because they did not want to heat their horses. He had a 'tremulous sort of hint' not to push the mare too much lest she should throw him. Then they came to the hills. The 'Blackwoods' cut capers and sprang up and down, Haydon after them, swearing to himself that wherever they went he would follow. Then he took the lead and bidding them follow him, which none dared do, he pushed his horse up the face of a rock, and there sat on his mare, 'who stood firmly planted, nostrils open, her eye brilliant, on a narrow pinnacle, breathing and glorying in defiance'. He leapt down and galloped off, his friends roaring, 'Haydon, you'll kill the mare!' 'Ha, ha! my friend,' thought he, 'what has become of the Cockney?'

Receipts of about £500 in Edinburgh, and £400 in Glasgow, brought his total to nearly £3,000. The picture made a great impression in the North. One day in Glasgow he came in to see how things were going, with his hat on. A venerable Scotchman came over and said, 'I think you should take your hat off in sic' an awfu' presence.' A year after, when a friend of his was sketching in the Highlands, a poor woman crept out of a mud hut and asked, 'Are ye fond of pectures?' 'Yes,' said he. 'Did ye see a pecture at Edinburgh of Christ coming into Jerusalem?' 'I did.' 'Yon *was* a pecture; when I saw a' the lads and lasses with their hats off, I jist sat me doon and grat.'

XIV. MARRIAGE

Creditors? Devils!
TIMON OF ATHENS

I got out early to-day and escaped all my duns.
SWIFT

AT this point in the five-act tragedy of *Haydon*, we can assume that we have just seen the conclusion of the third, which has brought the hero to the pinnacle of his worldly success. The interval is over, the lights have been lowered, and we settle ourselves in our seats as the curtain rises for the ominous fourth act, to find Nemesis alone for a moment on the stage, gathering together and docketing for future use all the acts of folly we have watched with growing uneasiness as the play advanced. Our hero has been bold and dashing and rather thrillingly reckless, a sort of D'Artagnan, with his back to a wall, his rapier flashing in a whirl of light around him, while he calls on his enemies to advance. Now, with certain low mutterings of thunder (off stage), the horizon grows dim, and we are preparing to see a more tragic figure, with a white face, who will show despair, and terror, as the storm breaks upon him. But it would be a poor end to the play, if that were all. There have been heroes who seem not to have known what fear is, but Haydon knew collapse and bitterness—and if only the hero of his own *Autobiography*, in his self-dramatizing way, weak with self-pity and clamouring for attention, he kept up for twenty-three years a struggle that would have crushed most men in one. The full-face and the profile alternate as he is on or off stage—before the world his aggressive truculence shows pretty much as before, but in the solitude of his painting-room when he sits down to his desk and begins to write we see a very different man —one racked with desire and disillusionment, despairing yet undaunted, seeing dawn in the blackest of the night—and wonder at the remarkable resilience with which nature had endowed him.

Haydon was not at first conscious of how sinister were the signs of the approaching storm; we find him (on what was to him a most important occasion) looking over prints at the British Museum; he has just taken up one of the *Raising of Lazarus*, with a blank space where the head of Lazarus should be, he is looking at it, when suddenly his imagination fills this space with a conception so awful that he trembles at the thought. He hurries home, sketches it, and determines to make it his largest and grandest work. He orders a canvas 19 feet long by 15 feet high, which fills his painting-room from floor to ceiling. When he has roughed it out, the figure of Christ is nine feet high. 'This was a size and subject', he says, 'which I loved to my very marrow, but how should I get through it? "Go on," said the inward voice I had heard from my youth: "work and trust"; and trust and work I did.' Here he was, up to his ears in debt, beginning a picture that would take two years to finish, and which was too large to sell; and, moreover, meaning to marry a young widow with two small boys. The fact is that he had become used to being in debt, and so far nothing much had happened; 'I now see difficulties are my lot in pecuniary matters,' he writes, 'and my plan must be to make up my mind to meet them, and fag as I can; to lose no single moment but seize on time that is free from disturbance and make the most of it. If I can float and keep alive through another picture, I will reach the shore. I am now clearly in sight of it, and I will yet land to the sound of trumpets and the shouts of my friends.'

It is conceivable that he might have landed had he not taken on board a woman and children; with this added weight the ship foundered. He did not marry at once when he began *Lazarus* but, seeing the madness of the step, he waited—in idleness! He felt he could not marry for want of money, and felt he could not work for want of marriage. So he mooned about and did nothing. And yet that is not quite true, he did what he could do better than anything else, he observed life and wrote down his impressions. The descriptions he has left of things he saw in this period of idleness are among the best he wrote, and while he is waiting to get married it will be a good opportunity to quote some of them.

This is how he immortalizes an evening party at Mrs. Siddons's, when she reads *Macbeth*:

'She acts Macbeth herself,' he writes, 'better than either Kemble or Kean. It is extraordinary the awe this wonderful woman inspires. After her first reading the men retired to tea. While we were all eating toast and tingling cups and saucers, she began again. It was like the effect of a mass bell at Madrid. All noise ceased; we slunk to our seats like boors, two or three of the most distinguished men of the day, with the very toast in their mouths, afraid to bite. It was curious to see Lawrence in this predicament, to hear him bite by degrees, and then stop for fear of making too much crackle, his eyes full of water from the constraint; and at the same time to hear Mrs. Siddons' "eye of newt and toe of frog!" and then to see Lawrence give a sly bite, and then look awed and pretend to be listening. I went away highly gratified, and as I stood on the landing-place to get cool I overheard my own servant in the hall say: "What! is that the old lady making such a noise?" "Yes." "Why, she makes as much noise as ever!" "Yes," was the answer; "she tunes her pipes as well as ever she did."'

Equally good in its way is this account of the coronation of George IV in Westminster Hall, on which that 'elderly Adonis' had spent so vast an amount of thought and money.

Haydon writes:

'19th [July 1821]—I only got my ticket on Wednesday at two, and dearest Mary [she had just returned to London] and I drove about to get all that was wanted. Sir George Beaumont lent me ruffles and frill, another friend a blue velvet coat, a third a sword, I bought buckles, and the rest I had. I went to bed at ten and arose at twelve, not having slept a wink. I dressed, breakfasted, and was at the hall door at half past one. Three ladies were before me. The doors opened about four, and I got a front place in the Chamberlain's box, between the door and the throne and saw the whole room distinctly. Many of the doorkeepers were tipsy, quarrels took place. The sun began to light up the old Gothic windows, the peers to stroll in, and other company of all descriptions to crowd to their places. Some took seats they had not any right to occupy, and were obliged to leave them after sturdy disputes. Others lost their tickets. The Hall occasionally echoed with the hollow roar of voices at the great door, till at last the galleries were filled; the Hall began to get crowded below. Every movement, as the time approached for the King's appearance, was pregnant with interest. The appearance of a monarch has something in it like the rising of a sun. There are indications which announce the luminary's approach; a streak of light—the tipping of a cloud—the singing of the lark—the brilliance of the sky, till the cloud edges get brighter and brighter, and he rides majestically in the heavens. So with a king's advance. A whisper of mystery turns all eyes to the throne. Suddenly two or three rise; others fall back; some talk, direct, hurry, stand still, or disappear. Then three or four of high rank appear from behind the throne; an interval is left; the crowds scarce breathe. Something rustles, and a being buried in satin, feathers, and diamonds rolls gracefully into his seat. The room rises with a sort of feathered, silken thunder. Plumes wave, eyes sparkle, glasses are out, mouths smile, and one man becomes the prime object of attraction to thousands. The way in which the King bowed was really royal. As he looked towards the peeresses and foreign ambassadors, he showed like some gorgeous bird of the East. After all the ceremonies he arose, the procession was arranged, the music played, and the lines began to move. All this was exceedingly imposing. After two or three hours waiting, during which the attempt of the Queen agitated the Hall, the doors opened, and the flower-girls entered strewing flowers. The grace of their action, their slow movement, their white dressses were indescribably touching; their light milky colour contrasted with the dark shadow of the archway, which though dark, was full of rich crimson dresses that gave the shadow a tone as of deep blood; the shadow again relieved by a peep of the crowd, shining in sunlight beyond the gates, and between the shoulders of the guard that crossed the platform. The distant trumpets and shouts of the people, the slow march, and at last the appearance of the King crowned and under a gold canopy, and the universal burst of the assembly at seeing him, affected everybody. As we were all huzzahing, and the King smiling I could not help thinking this would be too much for any human being if a drop of poison were not dropped into the cup before you tasted it. A man would go mad if mortality did not occasionally hold up the mirror. The Queen was to him the death's head at this stately feast. My imagination got so intoxicated that I came out with a great contempt for the plebs; and as I walked by with my sword I indulged myself in an "*odi profanum*". I got home quite well, and thought sacred subjects insipid things. How soon should I be ruined in luxurious society.'

In the *Journals* is a story about Wordsworth and Canova's group, which is so characteristic that it deserves quoting, but here is the version in a letter to Miss Mitford where it is told rather better:

'I dislike his selfish Quakerism,' Haydon writes, 'his affectation of superior virtue; his utter insensibility to the frailties—the beautiful frailties of passion. I was walking with him in Pall Mall; we darted into Christie's. A copy of the "Transfiguration" was at the head of the room, and in the corner a beautiful copy of the "Cupid and Psyche" (statues) kissing.... You remember this exquisite group?.... Catching sight of the Cupid ... Wordsworth's face reddened, he showed his teeth, and then said in a loud voice, "THE DEV-V-V-VILS!" There's a mind! Ought not this exquisite group to have roused his "Shapes of

Beauty", and have softened his heart as much as his old grey-mossed rocks, his withered thorn, and his dribbling mountain streams?'

In another letter to Miss Mitford (1825) there is an account of a party at Sir John Soane's, to see the sarcophagus by lamplight.

'The first person I met after seventeen years', writes Haydon, 'was Coleridge, silver-haired! He looked at my bald front, and I at his hair, with mutual looks of sympathy and mutual head-shaking. It affected me very much, and so it seemed to affect him. I did not know what to say, nor did he; and then in his chanting way, half-poetical, half-inspired, half-idiotic, he began to console me by trying to prove that the only way for a man of genius to be happy was just to put forth no more power than was sufficient for the purposes of the age in which he lived, as if genius was a power one could fold up like a parasol! . . . I was pushed against Turner, the landscape painter, with his red face and white waistcoat, and . . . was carried off my legs, and irretrievably bustled to where the sarcophagus lay. Soane's house is a perfect labyrinth; curious narrow staircases, landing places, balconies, spring doors, and little rooms filled with fragments to the very ceiling. It was the finest fun imaginable to see the people come into the library after wandering about below, amidst tombs and capitals, and shafts, and noseless heads, with a sort of expression of delighted relief at finding themselves again among the living, and with coffee and cake! . . . Fancy delicate ladies of fashion dipping their pretty heads into an old mouldy, fusty, hierogliphicked coffin, blessing their stars at its age, wondering whom it contained, and whispering that it was mentioned in Pliny. You can imagine the associations connected with such contrasts. Just as I was beginning to meditate, the Duke of Sussex, with a star on his breast, and an asthma inside it, came squeezing and wheezing along the narrow passage, driving all the women before him like a Blue-Beard, and putting his royal head into the coffin, added his wonder to the wonder of the rest.'

Passing from the gay to the grave, Haydon's account of John Scott's funeral may be given, not for any particular merit in the writing, but for the light it throws on his own character. He had quarrelled with Scott, and now Scott had been killed in a duel.

'For a fortnight before his burial,' Haydon says, 'I exhibited a fine instance of wounded pride struggling to keep down the urgings of former affection. I held out to the hour before his funeral, and then a sudden blaze of light on my brain showed me his body, stretched out dead. My old affections burst in like a torrent and bore down all my

petty feelings of irritation. I hurried on my clothes and drove down to
his door. As the room began to fill I felt my heart heave up and down;
my feelings were too strong to be restrained. I hung back and suffered
everyone to go before me; my very nature was altered! I, who was
always panting for distinction, even at a funeral (for I felt angry at
Opie's that I wasn't in the first coach) now slunk away from observation with my lips quivering, my eyes filling, and my mind struggling
to subdue its emotions into a stern feeling of painful sorrow. Nature
would not be commanded; when I got into the coach I hid my face
in my cloak and cried like a child.'

About this time there occurs in the *Journals* the first hint of
Haydon's preoccupation with the idea of suicide, which crops
up from time to time. He writes, 'Suppose in that humour I had
shot myself? Would a superior being have destroyed my soul,
because my brain being irritated by an indigestion, I had in a
state of perturbation put an end to a painful existence? Surely
not!' A few days after he continues, 'I am sorry to say that I am
not so convinced of the wickedness of suicide as I am of its
folly.' The two things that press on his mind more than anything
else are the passing of time and the growing of children. 'As to
"Time",' he writes, 'nothing is such a stimulus or such an
eternal haunter of my conscience. I have got into such a habit
of thinking of this, that resting a moment makes me start up as
if I heard Time's eternal waterfall tumbling into the gulf below!
I bustle myself into action and get rid of the roar.' Sir Walter
Scott considered this description of time the finest he had ever
read.

On 22 June 1821, Haydon was arrested for debt. At last the
dragons' teeth he had sown were coming up in the form of men
armed with the law. This was the first of the crop; how familiar
with them was he soon to become! It upset him badly and
frightened him, but the incident contained one of those picturesque contrasts which flattered his vanity, and were, he felt,
characteristic of his destiny. The officer called, Haydon said he
must shave and asked the man to wait in the painting-room.
When he came down he found the little fellow in a state of
agitation before *Lazarus*, 'Oh my God, sir! I won't take you.
Give me your word to meet me at twelve at the attorney's, and
I will take it.' At the attorney's Haydon postponed matters, and

the officer said he'd 'be damned if he did not see him through it'. The evening was appointed for a final arrangement. 'But you must remain in the officer's custody,' said the attorney. 'Not he,' said the officer, 'let him give me his word and I'll take it, though I am liable to pay the debt.' At night he settled everything, the expenses being eleven pounds. Haydon walked straight from the bailiff's to a party at Lord Grosvenor's, 'where', he says, 'my mind was extremely affected after the insult I had just received, on entering a room of lovely women, splendid furniture, exquisite pictures; all was gay, breathing animated voluptuousness. I strolled about amidst sparkling eyes, musing in the midst.'

So Haydon experienced his first arrest; he was still a bachelor, but marriage followed so soon after that the two things seem connected, and with marriage his troubles really began. Mary Hyman had returned to London in the summer, and on 10 October 1821, the wedding took place. His wife brought him happiness. Weighed against the evils of debt increased by the burden of an ever growing family are to be set the love and the perfect companionship she gave him, suiting herself to his difficult disposition, and the still more difficult circumstances in which it perpetually placed her. On the last day of the year he wrote:

'I don't know how it is but I get less reflective as I get older. I seem to take things as they come without much care. In early life, everything being new excites thought. As nothing is new when a man is thirty-five, one thinks less. Or perhaps being married to my dearest Mary, and having no longer anything to hope in love, I get more content with my lot, which, God knows is rapturous beyond imagination. Here I sit sketching with the loveliest face before me, smiling and laughing, and "solitude is not". Marriage has increased my happiness beyond expression. In the intervals of study a few minutes' conversation with a creature one loves is the greatest of all reliefs. God bless us both! My pecuniary difficulties are still great, but my love is intense, my ambition intense, and my hope in God's protection cheering! . . . I am really and truly in love, and without affectation, I can talk, write, or think of nothing else.'

He felt the softening influence of his wife in taming his aggressive pugnacity, and comments on the changed expression of his face. 'I look on women', he wrote to Miss Mitford, 'as angels sent from heaven to temper the fire and direct the furious energy of men into gentler paths, and for more amiable purposes than their own inherent fierceness would otherwise induce them to pursue.' In another letter he says, 'The finest sight on earth to me—even before a sunrise—is to see her wake and watch the gradual lovely stealings of consciousness over her divine face. If her eyes meet mine watching, the smile that follows is that of an angel after a sunny dream. I wish no other face to welcome me to heaven, and I should think heaven without it a perpetual twilight.'

Writing to Thomas Moore about ten years later he gives us an insight into one of the secrets of Mary's charm for him, 'When a man of great genius marries a woman who is perfectly content with the reflection of his splendour, and is willing to be informed by him alone, who watches his moments of abstraction, and never intrudes, though lovely as an angel, into his solitude, but when she sees he wishes for solitude no longer, such a wife would have softened and subdued and not lost Byron....' Mary seems indeed to have been unselfishness personified. Wordsworth asked her some ten years later what was her husband's chief delight; she replied, with complete amiability, 'Feeding on his own thoughts.' Well might so beautiful a woman have expected her own 'divine face', as Haydon put it, 'to have claimed his chief attention'.

After his marriage for a short time all went well, and he would have been ecstatically happy but for the bugbear of debt. But even so he came back from battling with moneylenders, lawyers, and creditors to his wife and his picture as a bird blown by the gale finds its nest. After a vain application for money to his patron, Sir George Philips:

'I left the house', he writes, 'braced to an intensity of feeling I have not felt for years. I called immediately on some turbulent creditors, and laid open the hopeless nature of my situation, having relieved my mind I walked furiously home, borne along on the wings of my own ardent aspirations. I never felt happier, more elevated, more confident. I walked in to my dear wife, kissed her, and then to my picture, which looked awful and grand. "Good God," I thought, "can the painter of that face tremble? Can he be in difficulty?" It looked like a delusion. The figures seemed all so busy, and so interested in their employments. When I look at a figure that is complete, and remember from what difficulties it has issued, I am astonished! But so it is with me. I am born to be the sport of fortune; to be put up in one freak and bowled down in another, to astonish everybody by being put up again. God grant me a spirit that will never flag—a mind not to be changed by time or

place. I shall yet have a day of glory to which all my other glories shall
be dull!'

'I write this', he adds, 'without a shilling in the world—with
a large picture before me not half done, yet with a soul aspiring,
ardent, confident—trusting on God for protection and support.'
Then after an interval, 'I shall read this again with delight and
others will read it with wonder.'

But now arrests began to come thick and fast—on one dramatic occasion three in one day, the day when he painted the
head and figure of the once celebrated Lazarus, generally agreed
to be his finest achievement. Bewick has left an account of that
memorable sitting, when he posed for the face and hands,
seated 'upon a box, upon a chair, upon a table, mounted up as
high as the head in the picture—and a very tottering, insecure
seat it was', he says, 'and painful to be pinned to a confined spot
so many hours'. Just as Haydon was beginning came the first
arrest; he arranged the affair as rapidly as he could, and then set
to work again. For a few minutes his mind, 'hurt and wounded,
struggled to regain its power. At last, in scrawling about the
brush, he gave an expression to the eye of Lazarus; he instantly
got interested. He soon became absorbed in his subject and forgot his arrest in the intensity of the effort to create so extraordinary an embodiment.' He worked on, when there came a
knock at the door, a short conversation in the hall, a request that
he would come out, and again he was arrested, and again postponed the matter. Once more he set to work, and once more
was stopped. 'I think I see the painter before me,' Bewick wrote
thirty years later, 'his palette and brushes in his left hand—returning from the sheriff's officer in the adjoining room—pale,
calm, and serious; no agitation—mounting his high steps and
continuing his arduous task; and as he looked round to his pallid
model, half-breathingly whispering, "Egad, Bewick! I have just
been arrested: that is the third time; if they come again I shall
not be able to go on." After he had worked in the head he stood
aghast before it exclaiming, "I've hit it now!—I've hit it!"' By
the time the two hands and figure were completed he was
exhausted; and 'For myself', writes Bewick, "I seemed as dead
as Lazarus was—no circulation, stiff as death. He laughed and
joked, and helped me down from my "high estate"; and a cup
of warm tea refreshed and resuscitated as cadaverous a Lazarus
as the painter could have wished for.' This was one of the three

occasions on which Haydon had brought off the best he had in him under great difficulties. The first, when he painted what he considered his best figure—a man climbing up in *Solomon*, just after hearing of his father's death; the second, the painting of *Solomon* itself, without any money, and in ill health; and now the figure of Lazarus. But such things need youth, and a freedom from a sense of responsibility to others, or the strain is too great. This was his last achievement of its order, but it was the best.

The figure of Lazarus made an immense impression. The story of how it was painted, says Tom Taylor, 'may give it an interest to those who have not yet felt one, and will increase the interest of those who, with me, see in it the most awful presentation of death ever put upon canvas'. Sir Walter Scott told Bewick that it was a perfect realization of what he had himself imagined when reading the account in the Bible.

By the end of May the picture was half finished, but the clouds were coming up ominously. Haydon was harassed by letters asking for money every hour, and alarmed by threats of an execution from Rossi, his landlord. His attitude to this is typical, 'Rossi is a man with a large family,' he writes, 'and I feel for his wants; but he ought to have a little sympathy with me, as I was always regular for the first four years.' A week, or even a day clear of money interruption was a thing to be thankful for, 'Out all day to pacify, put off, and arrange; came home nearly clear for the week. By God's blessing at work to-morrow, and then for a head. O God! have mercy on me, and bring me gloriously through, and after that enable me to begin and go more gloriously through the Crucifixion.' Another entry, 'I have now only three heads left. Huzza! Huzza! Huzza! Dearest Mary is by and laughing.'

They both laughed a good deal in spite of their anxieties; and a trip to Windsor, where they spent a night and returned the following day, not only illustrates Haydon's happy-go-lucky temperament, but shows also how well fitted Mary was to be the wife of an impecunious artist.

'16th and 17th Sept.—Dearest Mary and I were so set agog by Richmond, that I said, as we awoke, "Let us go to Windsor." She agreed, and away we went with barely money enough, but full of spirits. We got there, at six dined at the White Swan, evidently the remains of an ancient inn, and sallied forth to the Castle, so full of spirits that we laughed at an odd-shaped stone or anything that would excuse a jest.

The White Swan became so full and noisy, we went to the White Hart—a clean neat inn, and were in comfort. We walked to Eton, and sat and lounged in the shade of its classical playground. Our money lasted well, but unfortunately, a barber who shaved me, as he was lathering, so praised his Windsor soap, that I, victim as I was, took six cakes, spent four shillings out of the regular course, and thus crippled our resources. The great thing now was whether we should pay the inn bill, or pay our fare to town, and leave part of the bill to be sent. Mary was for paying the bill, and part of the fare, and paying the rest when we arrived. We did this, and I was reduced to sixpence when we took our places on the top. Before the coach set off I took out the sixpence, as if I had £50 in my pocket, and said: "Porter, here's sixpence for you"; flinging it so that it rang on the pavement. The porter unused to such a present for looking after luggage, bowed and thanked me so much that all the passengers saw it, and without sixpence in my pocket I got as much respect all the way home as if I had £100.'

But the constant strain began to tell; he seems to have felt it more than his wife, 'God be praised,' he writes, 'my dearest Mary's spirits are unaltered—this is a great blessing.' As for his own, there are records of many days spent in shivering before the fire, when he felt too worried to work. There are intimate scenes of heartbreak, when after being out all day struggling to avoid arrest, he would come home fagged to death, and Mary would cling to him, 'as if she grew on his form', sobbing with relief at having him back. 'I declare to God,' cries he, 'no lovers can know the depth of their passion unless they have had such checks and anxieties as these.'

Early in December *Lazarus* was finished, and on 12 December his first child, Frank Scott Haydon, was born. Haydon was delighted with his son, and for a short time was very happy; he began his next work, the enormous picture of the *Crucifixion*, in a mood of high ambition. This would have been the largest painting of the subject in the world, except Tintoretto's, but he was fated never to finish it. Haydon was forever drawing parallels between his own situation and that of world-famous conquerors, 'Cortez', he writes, 'was perhaps as remarkable an instance of decision of character as ever existed, always relieving himself from apparent ruin, by attempts which would have been more ruinous, if unsuccessful, than the situations he got out of by their success. This is the true nerve so essential to the completion of all schemes where great decision and energy and self-will are requisite.' This passage and many like it explain his behaviour from the beginning of his career until he found that what succeeded with Cortez did not necessarily do so with him. His mind was that of a schoolboy fired by a first reading of Horatius' defence of the bridge, or some other deed of heroism, and determined to apply similar heroics to the affairs of everyday life. And all the time a sword-of-Damocles hung over his head, while the thread slowly frazzled out.

In January he again took the great room at the Egyptian Hall for his exhibition. There seems something suitable about this room for Haydon and his pictures: in it were shown at different times, the Siamese Twins, a family of Laplanders (in 1822, just before *Lazarus*), the model of the field of Waterloo, and General Tom Thumb. Pictures that are painted to appeal primarily to 'rank, beauty and fashion', and secondarily to 'honest John Bull', should be shown in rooms of popular entertainment. Since it was the public he wished to catch, in order to appeal to its love of sensation he ought to have exhibited his pictures by artificial light, to be looked at through a peep-hole, in the same spirit in which his rival, John Martin, repeated his *Belshazzar's Feast* on plate-glass, and had it inserted in a wall, so that the light was really transmitted through the awful handwriting with startling effect.

When after many vicissitudes, Haydon saw *Lazarus* a year later, he wrote, 'If God in His mercy spare that picture my posthumous reputation is secured. O, God! grant it may reach the National Gallery in a few years, and be placed in fair competition with Sebastiano del Piombo. I ask no more to obtain justice from the world.'

At last all was ready, and he fell on his knees:

'Grant, O God, that nothing untoward may happen, and that all may turn out gloriously and triumphantly. O God, Thou who hast brought me to the point, bring me through that point. Grant during the exhibition, nothing may happen to dull its success, but that it may go on in one continual stream of success, to the last instant. O God, Thou knowest I am in the clutches of a villain; grant me the power entirely to get out of them, for Jesus Christ's sake, Amen. And subdue the evil dispositions of that villain, so that I may extricate myself from his power, without getting further into it. Grant this for Jesus Christ's sake. Amen, with all my soul.'

The private day came and was successful. He says, 'No picture I ever painted has been so universally approved of . . . it has not had the sudden burst the other did, but it will grow.' Then later, 'The impression grows, and the receipts increase. Thank God!'

The receipts compared favourably with those of *Jerusalem*, about £30 a day (a drop in the ocean of his debts). The Press was warm in praise; the *Observer* gave three columns to a description of the picture and illustrated it with a small line engraving, which, in eliminating the Rembrandtesque chiaroscuro, makes more apparent than ever the influence of Raphael. The writer urges the Government to buy the picture. To us who read it in the knowledge of later events this article is significant chiefly for a very startling and sinister prophecy. After speaking of the lack of patronage from which the history painter suffers, and his dependence on the man who pays his shilling and thinks he has as much right to criticize as the greatest connoisseur, the writer continues:

'But still his success is a matter of speculation; a cow with two heads, or a giant without one are very likely to divide the attention of his patrons; and we will venture to say, if any man were this week to arrive from abroad with a bit of the North Pole, or the very stone with which David killed Goliath . . . Lazarus might soon glare unnoticed at the drugget and chairs. . . . So far Mr. Haydon is safe. No wonder greater than his own has sprung up to divide the attention of the town; and in spite of the Wapeti below stairs, and the serpents eating live rabbits above, the visitors give Lazarus the preference.'

Immersed in difficulties Haydon began the Crucifixion, but soon came to a stop, 'totally unable from continued pressure to proceed. . . .' His *Journals*, Taylor says, were 'filled with sketches, sometimes of groups, often of the entire composition, with extracts from lawyers' letters, and complicated entries of figures, as if he were trying to calculate ways and means'. At last he decided on the strange expedient of presenting a petition to the House of Commons, backed by Brougham. Brougham showed great interest and appeared to give him hope. But before this could be tried an execution on *Lazarus* was put in on the thirteenth of April, and the steady stream of gate money was stopped.

On 21 April Haydon found himself in the King's Bench prison. He gave his own version of what had happened in a letter to Sir Walter Scott. A rich pupil, much given to wild speculation, on seeing Haydon pressed for money, generously offered help, and procured from a house in the city £900. The *Entry into Jerusalem* was made over as security. The pupil in a very short time lost all his fortune, leaving himself in the debt of this firm. They then sent for the *Entry into Jerusalem*, which Haydon packed up and sent; the moment they got it, without any warning, they put an execution in on *Lazarus*, which was bringing in £18, and £20 a day. Haydon had sent them £100, all he had left. Three executions followed in his house, besides three or four arrests.

He was taken out of his bed, escaped home again, barricaded the door, and arranged all his private papers.

'Such scenes in the house, my dear Sir Walter!' he cries, 'reptiles, intoxicated with tobacco and beer, rolling about under the *Illissus* and jesting on its naked beauty! My painting room where none but rank and talent had ever trod, was stenched with the sleeping heat of low-lived beasts, slumbering in blankets! At the foot of the Crucifixion, which I had just rubbed in! They drank my wine; they plundered the property they were protecting; they quarrelled with my servants! My blood was boiling half the day, and I declare solemnly, one night infuriated by anxiety and agony at seeing the state of my wife and the pining look of my infant because of its mother's condition, had I met either of the parties, I would have strangled him like a rabbit. I set out to look for them, and lucky for myself I met none! I really would have done it. I would have crushed him like paper....

'My property was all sold. What cost me (and it was all paid for) 2300£, fetched 600£! My picture *The Entry*, which had produced nearly 3000(£) in shillings, was bought by this very pupil for 220(£)! And *Lazarus*, for which I refused 1000(£) shortly after it opened, for 350(£) to my own Upholsterer! I assure you, Sir Walter, my home was the happiest on Earth. . . . Though harassed by difficulties . . . I lived in a comparative Paradise!'

His entry of 22 April 1823, is dated 'King's Bench'. 'And am I to be ruined,' he cries passionately, 'and all my glorious delusions and visions! O God spare me the agonizing disgrace of taking shelter under the law.'

'Well I am in prison,' he writes, 'so were Bacon, Raleigh, and Cervantes. Vanity! Vanity! Here's a consolation! I started up from sleep repeatedly during the night, from the songs and roarings of the other prisoners. "Their songs divide the night, and lift our thoughts"—not to heaven!'

His wife soon came to him, and often spent whole days cheering and comforting him against the depression of which there are abundant traces in the *Journals*. But it was not his nature to mope for long: Miss Mitford wrote to a friend while Haydon was in prison. 'I hear from him two or three times a week, and I assure you, my dear friend, his letters are full of feeling though his indestructible buoyancy will break out. His wife has behaved like an angel.'

It was while he was in prison that he got this anonymous letter, one of many received during his life:

HAYDON

I am glad to find you are so comfortable, and have made so good a sale of your property. Your present quarters are nicely adapted for study. All who know you say you are a low coxcomb, and a rotten hearted scoundrel.

YOUR HATER.

The novelty of his surroundings interested him. 'Prisoners of all descriptions', he writes, 'seem to get a marked look; neglect of person is the first characteristic, and a sly, cunning air, as if they were ready to take advantage of you.' It must have been a terrible change from his spacious painting-room at Lisson Grove. The King's Bench prison, which sometimes contained as many as 500 prisoners, had 225 rooms, none of which exceeded nine feet in length.

A meeting of creditors was called for 28 May.

His friends expressed their sympathy, both with their efforts and their money. Lord Mulgrave, Sir Edward Codrington, Mr. Brougham, Sir Walter Scott, Barnes (of *The Times*) and Miss Mitford at once came to his help.

The last wrote, '. . . I have no words to say how deeply we feel your situation. Oh! it is a dishonour to the age and to the country, as well as a grief to you and to those who love you. . . . It is terrible to think of you amongst these men, bearing, as you say, "the mark on their countenance". It is like an imprisoned antelope—a caged eagle. . . . The direction is heartbreaking!' (The direction was 'B. R. Haydon, Esq., Historical Painter, King's Bench Prison'.)

Dr. Darling, his friend and physician, with Sir George Beaumont, Wilkie and others, bought at the sale many of his casts, prints, and painting materials, that he might have a nucleus for beginning work with on coming out of prison.

On opposite pages of his *Journals* are a King's Bench day-rule, with the words, 'Diploma of merit for English Historical Painters', and a letter from M. Smirnove, informing him of his election as a member of the Imperial Academy of Russia!

His petition to the House of Commons was now presented by Brougham, 'The humble petition of Benjamin Robert Haydon, Historical Painter, late of Lisson Grove, North, now in the King's Bench Prison': the petition first reminds the House that the committee appointed to consider the question of the purchase of the Elgin Marbles seven years before had insisted on the importance of the encouragement of fine art; yet no further notice had been taken of the subject. It suggests the purchase of pictures for the adornment of churches and public halls, and the employment of artists of distinguished reputation to produce them. It points out that large sums of public money had been spent on sculpture but none on painting, and claims that in justice this should be remedied. It states that historical pictures, the full size of life, were the only ones that had given countries their fame where art had flourished, and asks that, as the production of such works is too costly for artists to embark on unassisted, the Government should set aside a small part of the public wealth to employ them. Then the petition turns to the petitioner's own case, showing how he has devoted nineteen years to the study of historical painting; that his productions have been visited by thousands in England and Scotland; that he has received signs of regard and estimation from many of the most celebrated men of Europe; that the day after he was imprisoned he was awarded a high honour from a foreign academy, but that in spite of all this he has been overwhelmed by the immense expense of his undertakings. 'That he has been torn from his home and his studies; that all the materials of his art, collected with the greatest care from all parts of the world, the savings and accumulations of his life, have been seized. That he is now in the King's Bench, separated from his family and his habits of employment, and will have to begin life again, with his prospects blighted, and the means by which alone he could pursue his art scattered and destroyed.' The petition ends by asking for such a committee as was appointed for the Elgin Marbles to be formed now to discuss the best method of encouraging historical painting, and for preventing, by moderate and judicious patronage, those who devote their lives to it from ending their days in prison and in disgrace.

Sir Charles Long (Paymaster-General, afterwards Lord Farn-borough), who met all Haydon's applications with a most diplomatic chilliness, insisted on some practical suggestion; Haydon thereupon laid before Brougham his plan for ornamenting the great room at the Admiralty with representations of naval actions, and busts and portraits of naval commanders. This scheme ultimately took shape in the decorations of the new Houses of Parliament, about twenty years later.

This is the first of the long series of petitions with which Haydon wearied every government for the next twenty years; continuing with a persistence that so plagued everyone that to mention his name in official circles became 'an offence'. That is a danger which all reformers have to risk, but in the end what he wanted came about, though the failure to reap any reward himself was the chief disaster of his life.

Tom Taylor says that were it decorous to publish the whole of the correspondence between Haydon and various ministers on this matter, it would be a dangerous encouragement to all men possessed of an idea for which they wish to win access to official minds. 'One would say,' he adds, 'after reading the correspondence on both sides, that never was anything so hopeless as these appeals.' Undeterred by indifference or hostility Haydon kept pouring in page after page of argument and exhortation to meet with nothing but refusals. He went on utterly regardless of his unsuccess, and in the end his plan went through and the Houses of Parliament got their decorations. It was his one hope if he was to go on painting large historical pictures.

We are so used now to the idea that art is of importance, and that public money should be spent on its instruction and encouragement, that it is not easy to realize what apathy, indifference, and ignorance existed in Haydon's time. Taylor writing in 1853, says '. . . it is difficult now to rate too highly the courage of Haydon's persistence, because we can hardly rate too low the conception then prevalent, even among men who held the first place as lovers of art, of what worthy patronage of Art really was. The best of them do not seem to have understood by it anything beyond buying pictures, and thus encouraging the painters whose works they especially admired. I cannot find from anything in these *Journals*, that Art was by any of the great patrons of that day seriously considered as an element of national education, or a source of national glory. It cannot, I think, be

denied to Haydon that his perpetual pressing of a nobler estimate of the relations of artists and people have done something
to create the feeling which has at length expressed itself, however imperfectly, in the plans for decorating our new Houses
of Parliament.' And since then the seeds which were planted by
Haydon have continued increasingly to bring forth fruit.

All attempts at an arrangement with his creditors having
failed Haydon had to face the Insolvency Court on 22 July. Only
one man 'That villain T——' entered his name as an opponent,
but withdrew it at the last moment. 'Never shall I forget his
withered air,' writes Haydon. He was oppressed and impressed
by the proceedings. 'The grave, good look of the robed judges,
the pertinacious ferreting air of the counsel, the eager listening
faces of the spectators, the prisoner standing up like a soul in
Purgatory.'

At last his name was called, 'Benjamin Robert Haydon! Does
anyone appear? Benjamin Robert Haydon!'

'Nobody came, and I mounted. My heart beat violently, I put my
clenched hand on the platform where the judges sat, and hung the
other over my hat. There was a dead silence: . . . I feared to look about.
. . . Startled a little I turned, and caught both judges with their glasses
off, darting their eyes with a sort of interest. I felt extremely agitated.
My heart swelled. My chest hove up, and I gave a sigh from my very
soul. I was honourably acquitted, bowed low and retired.'

On the 25th he was released, not one out of a hundred and
fifty creditors had opposed him.

'I am now free to begin life again,' he wrote, 'God protect me
and grant that I may yet accomplish my great object,' but that
was not to be. The gates of his strange Eden, in whose charmed
gardens he had painted vast pictures 'without one shilling of
legitimate resource' were closed to him for ever. No longer
could he pace his solitary painting-room and see the work he
was engaged on looming up above his head lit by the light of a
single candle. 'Adieu,' he cries, 'days of pure unadulterated enthusiasm. May your impressions go with me to the grave, and
attend me at the resurrection! I shall ever look on that part of
my life as a dream of unrivalled heaven.'

XV. HAYDON'S PLACE IN BRITISH ART

A good painter has two chief objects to paint—Man and the intention of his soul.
                                                            LEONARDO DA VINCI

*In a real history-painter, the same knowledge, the same study, and views, are
required, as in a real poet.*—LORD SHAFTESBURY (1711)

HAS Haydon a right to serious consideration as a painter, was he a man who mistook his profession, what is his place in British Art?

The answer to these questions would have been different at different times; for twenty years or so Haydon's work aroused high hopes and admiration among those of his contemporaries best qualified to judge. These hopes were not realized, denigration set in, to be followed by a long period of contemptuous dismissal. A reconsideration is due, indeed seems to have begun; Mr. Collins Baker considers him a master *manqué*, with warm praise for *Punch*, and Mr. A. C. Sewter, in an article in the *Art Quarterly*, 'A Revaluation of Haydon', rates his best work highly, while centenary notices show a renewal of interest and appreciation.

Haydon takes his place towards the end of a line of British historical painters beginning with Sir James Thornhill, Hogarth's father-in-law, and ending with Watts and Alfred Stevens; a period of about 150 years. Broadly speaking, they shared one influence in common—that of full Renaissance or post-Renaissance Italian art. It would be true to say that during this period the 'quality of Raphael', as the *Morning Post* (1843) called it, was the one most admired—'that poetical power over expression whose capacity of elevation was unshared even by the Greeks'. This poetical power was considered the highest gift of the artist —the ultimate achievement for the attainment of which all other qualities: draughtsmanship, craftsmanship, colour and design, should be called into play. It followed that portrait-painting, *genre*, landscape and still-life were thought to be lower forms.

Jonathan Richardson, whose *Theory of Painting* (1715) at once became a standard work, held 'history-painting' to be the only style worth serious study. The history-painter needed qualities so varied that they would have fitted him for distinction in almost any walk of life:

'As to paint a history,' writes Richardson, 'a man ought to have the main qualities of a good historian, and something more; he must go yet higher, and have the talents necessary to a good poet . . . and as his business is not to compose one Iliad only . . . but perhaps many, he must be furnished with a vast stock of poetical, as well as historical learning.

'Besides all this it is absolutely necessary to a history painter that he understand anatomy, osteology, geometry, perspective, architecture and many other sciences which the historian, or poet, has no occasion to know. . . .

'But all this is not sufficient for him, he must moreover know the forms of arms, the habits, customs, buildings, &c. of the age, and country, in which the things were transacted. . . . And as his business is not to write the history of few years, or of one age, or country, but all ages, and all nations, as occasion offers, he must have a proportionable fund of ancient and modern learning of all kinds. Over and above all this he must study thoroughly the works of the most excellent masters in painting and sculpture ancient and modern.'

It was also his business to raise nature and form a model of perfection in his own mind, not to be found in reality. Particularly with respect to mankind, he must 'raise the whole species, and give them all imaginable beauty and grace . . . every several character, whether it be good or bad, amiable or detestable, must be stronger and more perfect. . . . A brave man . . . must be imagined more brave. . . . A villain must be conceived to have something more diabolical than is to be found amongst us; a gentleman more so, and a peasant have more of the gentleman . . . with such as these an artist must people his pictures.'

Burke in his *Essay on the Sublime and the Beautiful* (1761), laid it down that 'when a work seems to have required immense force and labour to effect it, the idea is grand'. He considered that the ideas were opposed: that sublime things could not be beautiful, nor beautiful things sublime. For beauty smallness was necessary, and smoothness—especially smoothness; he could not recollect ever to have seen anything beautiful that was not smooth. For sublimity ruggedness was necessary, and terror, and nothing rugged could be beautiful. So the history painter had to choose between smooth small beauty, and terrible rugged sublimity.

Haydon, with vaulting ambition, did not hesitate, he chose the latter.

No more need be said in explanation of the interest he aroused when he arrived in London with the professed intention of reviving this admittedly high yet neglected form of art; for to the connoisseurs of that time such men as West and Haydon did seem to have caught something of the 'sublimity' and 'elevation' of the great Italians. It seemed clear to them that nothing grander or more perfect than Raphael's pictures existed, unless it were Michael Angelo's, whose style was more exclusively suited to grand mural decorations. It followed that what Raphael did was right, and by that standard 'historical pictures' were judged. There is considerable eclecticism about Raphael, therefore it was 'correct' to be eclectic, which opened up a multitude of unsuspected pitfalls. 'Let every youth look on all moderns with suspicion,' Haydon wrote in the *Annals of the Fine Arts*, 'The only certain beacons are Raphael and Michael Angelo: collect everything they did, dwell on them, muse on them, dream on them, in conjunction with nature. Raphael for expression, composition, purity of taste; Michael Angelo for devotion and grandeur; Titian for colour and dignity of portraits; Correggio for the divine momentary beauties of simple expression. . . . Paolo Veronese and Rubens for handling and management, colour, light and shadow; Rembrandt for surface and body. Make these your constant stimulators to perfect your divine Art, in union with Nature.' Such a precept of pure eclecticism is exactly what one would have expected from his pictures. So far as 'heroic art' was concerned, Nature meant to him paid models and studio accessories. He came at a time when the authority of the few was giving way to the taste of the many. The new patrons, who were often men of great wealth and small cultivation, cared nothing for 'the Art' as Haydon understood it, but regarded a picture as a means of arousing pleasing emotions by its story. To Haydon 'story' meant always something 'elevated', something noble enough to condition a noble design; to them it meant something mildly pathetic, familiar, or humorous, but at all events trivial. Haydon had little enough of his own to add, but he at least stood for art uncontaminated by commercialism, and for ideals for which he was prepared to starve. He missed for the most part in his own work the nobility he so desired, but it is to his credit that he did desire it; and with adequate backing he might have left a series of decorations that would have been interesting as bearing the stamp of its period impressed upon the last phase of a great tradition.

His 'beloved art' was the cause of his greatest happiness as well as of his greatest misery and his most powerful emotions, lifting him up above the world and affording him his chief solace in distress. On the eve of his first imprisonment he sketched on a page of his *Journals* a pencil and porte-crayon saltire-wise, with the motto, 'Balm of hurt minds'. While at work on *Jerusalem* he wrote, 'This week has really been a week of great delight. Never have I had such irresistible and perpetual urgings of future greatness. I have been like a man with air-balloons under his armpits, and ether in his soul. While I was painting, walking, or thinking, beaming flashes of energy flowed in and impressed me. O God! grant they be not presumptuous feelings. Grant they may be fiery anticipations of a great soul born to realize them. They came over me, and shot across me, and shook me, till I lifted up my heart and thanked God.' This passage is perhaps the most revealing of all Haydon's writing about himself. It expresses the hallucination that underlay all his actions in life. When doubt at last broke in the shock was mortal.

It is not to be denied that Haydon did some execrable work, that in many, perhaps most, of his pictures there is no fresh point of view or new way of seeing, no original thought or any indication of that renewal of art which must be present to justify the work of every period. His faults are easy to see, but I suggest that as a painter he had the germ of something good and even fine in him, that he could at his best rise to impressiveness, and was capable of subtle and delicate perception. His temperament was too excitable and restless for him often to attain unity, even if his taste had been better, so the number of his historical pictures worth serious consideration is small, perhaps three in all. As a history painter, to judge by what remains, he ceased to count after his first imprisonment, and to study his development would be waste of time; his reputation must stand or fall on *Christ's Triumphal Entry into Jerusalem* and *The Raising of Lazarus*. His humorous pictures, on the other hand, were all done after his first imprisonment, and can be considered separately.

It is unfortunate that *Solomon* is lost; it seems to have been without many of his worst faults. In his long article on this picture in the *Examiner* (1 May 1814) already referred to, Leigh Hunt gives it his unqualified approval:

'As the unity and richness of the colour, light and shade, resemble and indeed equal the lustre of the Venetian School, so the regular simplicity of composition has a striking similarity to the style of Raphael, so distinguished for composition. In these respects the invention of our young painter—young in years, but old in genius and study —is justly classed on a level with the great masters of Art. We will not scruple to add, that not even Raphael surpassed him in the grand object of Art—the portraiture of the heart, or, as it is commonly termed, expression.'

There follows a detailed description of the picture; he continues:

'The entire picture presents a mass of colour more perfect, in our estimation, than any specimen of it yet exhibited in this country, and equal to that of any foreign work that has come under our notice, for it is richly glowing, without any gaudiness, and is in entire unity throughout, while the individual parts have mostly their suitable hue. . . . To sum up our description; this extraordinary Picture is among the very few performances which are devoid of *manner*. Nature is in every part appealed to. Our hearts as well as our imaginations, and never merely our eyes, are addressed. We look at it with awakened and intense sensibilities, and the more we look, the more pleasantly are we rivetted to its beauties. In a word, the subject is accurately and vigourously told, and we receive all the pleasure from it of which art is capable. The intellectual feast is complete. The other pictures in this exhibition next week.'

It is impossible after reading this to feel surprise that a vain man like Haydon should believe himself indeed a genius; but we realize also what he is now up against: a complete change of fashion. He receives highest praise for the very qualities now considered irrelevant, or even worse, 'This extraordinary picture is among the very few performances which are devoid of *manner*. Nature is in every part appealed to' 'not even Raphael surpassed him in the grand object of Art—the portraiture of the heart' 'the subject is most accurately and vigorously told.'

Somewhere between the praise of Leigh Hunt, Hazlitt and Wilkie and modern indifference or contempt, comes the considered opinion of G. F. Watts, who writes to Tom Taylor:

'. . . the fact is I find it very difficult to arrive at a definite conclusion. . . . His art is defective in principle and wanting in attractiveness. . . . The characteristics appear to be great determination, and power, knowledge and effrontery. I cannot find that he strikes upon any chord that is the basis of true harmony. . . . Haydon seems to me to have succeeded as often as he displays any real anxiety to do so; but one is struck by the extraordinary discrepancy of different parts of his work, as though, by a fixed attention that had taken him out of himself, yet highly applauding the result, he had daubed and scrawled his brush about in a sort of intoxication of self-glory. Indeed his pictures are himself, and failed as he failed. . . . His pictures are themselves auto-biographical notes of the most interesting kind; but their want of beauty repels, and their want of modesty exasperates. . . . Pathos is also lacking. . . .

'To particularize—I should say that . . . his general effect is much less good than one would expect from the goodness of the parts, which I think arises principally from the coarseness of handling; that his ex-pressions of anatomy and general principles of form are the best by far that can be found in the English School; and I feel even a direction towards something that can only be found in Phidias. . . .

'I have pointed out all the things that strike me as errors, because I know that you fully appreciate the great qualities as I do. . . . His first great work, the Solomon, appears to me to be, beyond all comparison, his best. It is far more equal than anything else I have seen, very power-ful in execution and fine in colour. . . . Too much praise cannot, I think, be bestowed on the head of Lazarus; and in the absence of such important evidence as the Entry into Jerusalem would afford, it is hardly fair to pass judgement.'

Tom Taylor continues:

'I believe that this criticism points out, fairly and accurately, the defects of Haydon's art, taking for granted, rather than expressing, the countervailing beauties. These appear to me, besides the general power in drawing and action, to be a fine feeling for colour in draperies and backgrounds, vigorous and pregnant conception, both in single heads, figures and groups, great occasional truth of expression, such as I have noticed in the Punch, and such as is strikingly exhibited in particular parts of the Mock Election . . . and, in the earlier pictures at least, a large and noble arrangement of the composition. Besides these merits, there is a lower one even more distinctly shown, that of a great power of truthful imitation. The still life in Haydon's pictures is admirable, wherever he gave himself the trouble to elaborate it; so excellent, indeed, as to make even more apparent his unaccountable carelessness in parts of greater importance. This carelessness I attribute to the joint in-toxication of an impetuous conception and an inordinate vanity. Physical defects of sight may also have had much to do with this inequality.'

Mr. Sewter says of him that he was 'a battlefield in which the

principles of classicism were incessantly at war with the urgings
of romanticism'; and if we add that he was also one in which the
desire to emulate the highest achievements of Raphael and
Pheidias was incessantly at war with the desire to please 'rank,
beauty and fashion' and 'honest John Bull' we may get some
insight into one at least of the causes of his inequality. In other
words he was only half sincere, but it was not so much that he
mixed the two halves as that he alternated between them. He
had his moods when he was single-minded in his enthusiasm for
great work and in his determination to emulate it, but he also
had moods when he craved for the admiration of mere numbers
and of the powerful and wealthy. I see in most of the passages
of his work that I dislike the wish to catch the *profanum vulgus,*
his own phrase. He was, in present day parlance, both a high-
brow and a low-brow, a degrader, in his worse moments, of the
art he worshipped. My interpretation of the success of *Solomon*
is that it was painted at a time of loneliness and bitterness, when
he had temporarily turned against rank and fashion in a fury
of self-pity. He was determined to prove that he was the great
painter he had always claimed to be; so he shut himself up and
worked night and day for two years, the most truly, in fact the
only really dedicated years of his life. In them, I believe, he forgot everything but his art and was doing his very best, which
was at least good enough to create an immense impression on his
contemporaries. After his success with *Solomon* he plunged back
into the world, but until his first imprisonment for debt nine
years later he still had periods of high and legitimate ambition.

So in default of *Solomon,* which is lost, and of *Christ's Entry,*
which is in Ohio, the *Raising of Lazarus* must be taken as an
example of Haydon's 'grand manner'. It is in the cellars of the
National Gallery and can be seen only by artificial light.[1] It was
on this picture that Haydon prayed to be judged, and he wished
that it might be placed beside the picture of the same subject by
Sebastiano del Piombo, also in the National Gallery. Mr. Sewter
says, 'The comparison . . . which Haydon challenged, could it
be made in proper conditions, would probably lead to a close
finish, with Haydon perhaps leading by a head. . . .'

To form a just opinion of the picture the fact of fashion must
be taken into account. It is impossible to assess it fairly with our
minds full of such forms of art as are implied in the phrase

[1] It has now been transferred to the Tate Gallery.

'Après Cézanne'; to attempt to do so is irrelevant and quite unfair to a painter who lived and worked in an age having completely different values. Cézanne has his powerful message for us, just as Raphael had for the painters of Haydon's day. It was to Raphael that painters then looked for their highest inspiration, and it was on Raphael's practice they might, without the accusation of plagiarism, found the corner stones of their edifices. *Lazarus* is an original work, based broadly on the principles then thought 'correct', the enduring validity of which seemed established beyond all doubt. Looked at from this point of view, it becomes better worth considering than recent criticism has admitted. It is an example of the errors and excesses that may be tolerated, or even encouraged, by fashion, and this applies pretty equally to all periods. But it is not only that, for, as I hope to show, it has many merits and much real beauty. The figure of Christ may be written off at once; there is scarcely anything to be said for it, it is a very great blemish in the picture, and if only it could be imagined away the whole would gain, I feel sure, to an astonishing degree. It has no life, no magnetism, no authority. The raised arm and hand give the impression of having been suspended by a cord while Haydon painted them, and appear to hang rather than to be raised; it is the same with the drapery, which looks as if it had been carefully arranged and pulled about till the clumsy insignificant folds we see had been obtained. Mary and Martha, who kneel one on each side of Christ, are equally uninspired, and the terror of the running grave digger is not happily expressed. The rest of the picture, and there is quite a lot of it, seems to me to be almost masterly—if you accept the convention. Lazarus himself only needs that sympathy and attention which every artist has a right to expect to appear overwhelmingly impressive and awful. This terrible figure with its grave impassive face, swaying backward a little as it rises from the darkness, is haunting in its intensity, and expresses in a way as restrained as it is convincing the as yet almost solely physical response to the call of the Master, wherein we can see the first dull, dim, and still unaware reawakening of the mind. It is a veritable triumph of expressiveness, of which a great master might have been proud, and a prolonged contemplation of it in the original can arouse an almost hypnotic fascination. The feelings of awe and astonishment which Haydon meant to convey are well shown in the faces and gestures of all the background figures, especially in the remarkable head of the apostle nearest Lazarus—in a quiet way almost as great an achievement as Lazarus himself, and possibly comparable in its direct truth and simplicity to the dramatic figures of Rembrandt's early or middle periods. From these heights we sink for a moment to the spirit of Fra Bartolommeo, in the nun-like and emotional figure next to the right, but to the right again, behind the figure of Christ, the influences of Raphael and Rembrandt come once more into their own. Head after head is conceived with all the solemnity and reserve of the true grand manner to fit the role required of it, till another climax is reached in the really magnificent head of the old woman who turns towards the lovely profile of Haydon's young wife a glance as stern in its gravity and power as those that contemplate the figure of Anti-Christ in Signorelli's great fresco at Orvieto.

It is probable that Haydon had Raphael's *Transfiguration* in his mind while designing and carrying out this picture. He had seen the original, which was then in the Louvre, when he visited Paris in 1814. In each something of profound significance is taking place before a number of people; but while in the Raphael their interest is divided between Christ on the Mount and the idiot boy in the foreground, in Haydon's picture the attention of all, unless it be that of St. John, is focused on Lazarus alone. It seems to me that in this he has been happier than either Raphael or Sebastiano, in whose rendering the attention is so dispersed that our eyes are caught from point to point till we lose interest in the main event. St. John in Haydon's picture is very beautifully conceived—his eyes are raised in adoration to his Master, who stands between himself and Lazarus, so that he looks in the same direction as everyone else, and there is no disturbing duality of interest as in the *Transfiguration*. With the exception of the running grave digger this effect of concentration is achieved with greater economy of means in Haydon's picture than in Raphael's, where there is far more gesticulation, half the figures holding their arms out, sometimes rather meaninglessly, and where the heads turn in so many different directions. The sense of consternation and amazement is not only quite as fully realized in the Haydon, but it has been achieved throughout the whole group of figures in the background with greater solemnity and grandeur of effect. It was not sheer blindness and folly that made Hazlitt and Leigh Hunt talk of him as they did.

When we come to the figure of Christ the temperature drops from something near boiling point to something below zero. I personally regret the running grave digger less than Christ and the two women; these three ruin what came near to being—according to its lights—a great picture. This grave digger is perhaps worth some analysis, for he represents a point of view once accepted but now regarded with intolerance. The Italians are a gesticulating people, and in fully-blown Italian art gesture plays a very important and conspicuous part. In judging such pictures as *Lazarus* the quotation at the head of this chapter should be steadily borne in mind, 'A good painter has two chief objects to paint—Man and the intention of his soul.' It was a perfectly legitimate aim, a very fine one, and it was taken seriously and without question throughout the whole course of Christian art since Cimabue and Giotto until the violent reaction against it in the latter part of the nineteenth century. Since the whole gamut of human emotion was the end, and facial expression the means, the extreme range from impassivity to contortion became permissible and even necessary. Raphael allowed himself great violence when the occasion seemed to require it. The much admired *Expulsion of Heliodorus from The Temple*, painted when he had only just passed the peak of his achievement, contains examples of this, and a glance at the screaming soldier behind the prostrate figure of Heliodorus will show that for the violent expression of fear there is not much to choose between him and Haydon's grave digger, who seems less disturbing when the old convention is taken into account, and when one remembers that Raphael's soldier was an object of familiar admiration to all students of art. It may be that Haydon argued that to express gross fear in a subordinate character would enhance the dignity of the awe displayed by the nobler characters. If so, I think he was right in principle. Figures such as this were regarded as legitimate *tours de force*, and it was quite in the grand manner to introduce them, witness Titian's general who falls wounded from his horse in *The Battle of Cadore*. They corresponded to purple patches in literature and were felt to enhance the whole; when they came off they were often the most highly commended thing in the picture. I see nothing to object to in the other grave digger, who staggers back as the horrifying corpse comes to life. The cause was surely sufficient to excuse great violence of emotion. As parts of the design they fulfil a difficult requirement. Something was needed there, but something which was not to attract too much attention or come too high in the canvas, or it would conceal the more important things behind. The deep shadow in which Haydon has placed these figures solves one part of the problem, and their low, crouching attitudes partly solve the other. From the point of view of the composition they are satisfactory, but to meet the needs of the design the running man is made to crouch lower than would be compatible with his action of running, and it is this which gives rather an absurd impression. I can believe that Raphael himself might not have thought him amiss, there is an anatomical power about him which might have appealed to the designer of the Tapestries. And we must remember that the mere fact of fashion implies something unbalanced.

But the blemishes should not blind us to the merits. Is it too high praise to say of the group of some ten or a dozen figures in the background, so intensely stirred with a single emotion, together with the awe-inspiring cause of it as he rises from the pit of death to confront the presence of his Saviour, that according to its lights it is touched with greatness?

My interpretation of Haydon is that he was a man with vulgarity and the instinct of self-advertisement in his soul, who yet had a passion for beauty, and some periods of inner harmony when he was able to achieve it. These periods never lasted quite long enough to see him through any large painting except, perhaps, the *Solomon*. But while they lasted he did catch sparks of the divine fire. The figures I have referred to in *Lazarus* are not only finely conceived and painted, they are noble; they have the serious dignity and restraint of great work, and form, moreover, a beautiful pattern of glittering shapes set in a dark and sombre ground. But there, in the midst, stands that figure of Christ, catching the first attention of the beholder and causing him, by turning away his eyes, to miss these finer things.

His worst fault was that he cared too much about the impression his work would make on the wrong people. It was this, I suppose, that is chiefly responsible for the figure of Christ in *Lazarus*. He had painted a much better Christ in his *Entry into Jerusalem*, but this was, of course, the most criticized figure in the picture; it was considered 'unconventional', 'not the thing'. I feel sure he determined not to offend again in the same way, and contrived this stock figure, to the ruin of his picture.

When Haydon received the commission to paint a portrait of the *Duke of Wellington Musing on the Field of Waterloo* he wrote, 'Inspired by history I do not fear making it the grandest thing.' It is neither a very bad nor a very good picture, and the same may be said of *Earl Grey Musing by the Fire*. As has already been stressed, Haydon was not a gifted portrait painter, and he only came within measurable distance of the grandest thing once, even when inspired by history. This was in his portrait of *Wordsworth on Helvellyn* in the National Portrait Gallery. It is an impressive work and, to judge by other portraits of Wordsworth, an excellent likeness. But it is more than that, it is a portrait of the poet's inner as well as of his outer personality, of his poetic character; and it should satisfy lovers of his poetry as a worthy representation of its author. The composition is admirable—the figure looms up against a shadowy background of sky and mountain, the lights forming a diagonal from corner to corner, while all the attention goes to the pensive head, bowed as if under the weight of brooding thought. A truly fine work, one has only to imagine it in any modern exhibition of portraits to realize how outstanding in grandeur and sincerity it would appear. His portraits of himself and of Leigh Hunt in the same gallery are, in very different ways, excellent. The first is a rapid sketch, probably finished in one sitting; the touch is sure and delicate, and the whole is broadly seen, the least possible amount of shadow being used to convey the modelling, yet without sacrifice of solidity; it shows also a firm sense of selection, the accents being reserved exclusively for the eyes, eye-brows, and hair at the temple, giving a look of vitality and concentration.

The *Leigh Hunt* is as different as could be, yet equally good in its way. The paint is 'worked', scumbled and glazed, in the manner of Titian; though in the reduction of the light to a small area, the deep shadows on cheek and neck, and the intense gaze of the eyes out of the surrounding darkness, it has, perhaps, more general affinity with Tintoretto. The painting of the loose collar shows almost a master's hand. Many thousands of such, or similar, collars have been painted, showing every variety of overcarefulness or overlooseness, with accompanying lack of form. This seems to me a good example of how such things should be done—the shapes are beautiful and convincing and are seen in the largest manner, the mass of light is untroubled, the few shadows emphatic, and exactly where they should be to show the forms and to wed the light with the darkness. If Haydon had left no portraits but these three in the National Portrait Gallery, he would be considered a portrait painter of individuality and distinction. Yet there was evidently something odd about many of his portraits. He seems to have been incapable of being interested in or taking trouble over an ordinary commission portrait, forgetting that some of Raphael's finest pictures were portraits, and that most of Rembrandt's sitters were nonentities. He appears really to have thought portrait painting beneath his dignity. The head for its own sake, and unless it belonged to some famous man or personage in a historical picture, aroused in him no painter's enthusiasm; only when it held what he considered grander implications was his interest aroused and the needed stimulus supplied. An artist has a right to his own sources of inspiration, and what chiefly matters is that when they are present he should be able to produce something fine. I think he sometimes did. But there is astonishing inequality in his heads. All that can be said is that he held his equipment insecurely, that his taste was shaky, and that for him the step from the sublime to the ridiculous was an unusually short one.

It is perhaps in his humorous pictures that Haydon was least likely to make blunders. *Punch* and *The Mock Election* show great inequalities, but not so great as those in some of his historical works. As a design *The Mock Election* seems to me to have real power; but there is a want of sensibility in the details, and though much of the characterization is forcible it lacks subtlety.

Punch is, in my view, the better picture. The still-life throughout is excellent—in the painting, for instance, of such things as the wedding coaches and Punch's booth. As in *The Mock Election*, the characterization shows anything but a subtle mind, it is forceful, but crude and sometimes vulgar. But a true painter's eye and hand are at work in the broad atmospheric unity of the whole, the sense of open air and masterly handling and feeling for surface in many parts. Dr. Darling, the first owner of the picture, describes how David Wilkie passed his hand over the left portion, saying, 'How fine, how very fine that is! If that picture were in Italy, you would see it surrounded by students from all parts of Europe engaged in copying it.' There is a rich and harmonious variety of tone and colour throughout the foreground figures, but it is in the background of buildings and sky that the chief beauty lies. The buildings have a solidity and depth combined with an airy distance, the sky a movement and spaciousness that no one but a great painter, it seems to me, could have accomplished. That he seldom rose to such heights is true, but that he could do so on occasion proves his potential power.

Haydon's drawings, which can be seen in the British Museum, show the same kind of inequality as his paintings; they vary extremely both in manner and merit—from careful and rather timid copies of dull models to powerful anatomical studies, full of violence and not seldom of exaggeration. There are drawings conceived in terms of light and shade and even of atmosphere, and others in bold simple outline, and it is in these that he is generally at his best; for he had a fine line at his command on occasion, free, rhythmic and direct.

During Haydon's lifetime there were several accomplished artists who painted historical subjects in the 'grand manner' on a scale as large as Haydon's. Most of them, however, relied on other forms of art to make a living. Haydon never painted anything on so huge a scale as Sir Thomas Lawrence's *Satan Calling up his Legions*; West, Copley, Northcote, Fuseli, Etty, Hilton and, later, Maclise and Watts, all painted pictures on a scale similar to Haydon's. Etty's *Beniah*, which has only three figures, measures ten feet by thirteen; and Fuseli in his *Milton* series used canvases varying in size from ten feet by seven, to thirteen feet by twelve.

It is curious that Haydon's morbid jealousy seems never to have fixed on Etty as a rival. Etty was only a year his junior at the Academy Schools, yet in Tom Taylor's edition there is scarcely a mention of him. With John Martin he was on friendly terms, and all Haydon's rancour at the presumption of anyone else's painting historical pictures seems to have been reserved for West and Hilton. Hilton had more success than he, and, while a dull colourless artist, was at the time highly thought of. The really great painters then living in Britain were turning their attention to other branches of art—landscape and portraiture. When Haydon was beginning to exhibit Turner was already making his name, Constable, ten years older than Haydon, was still little known, but attracting intelligent notice here and there; Crome was over forty, Cotman four years older than Haydon; James Ward was elected A.R.A. the year after Haydon arrived in London; while the one great genius among the 'history' painters, William Blake, was working on a tiny scale in almost complete obscurity.

XVI. POT-BOILING

The portrait painter, doomed to trace
Each tenth transmitter's ugly face.
HORACE SMITH

HAYDON'S life as an artist divides itself very definitely into two parts; the first (nineteen years) ends with his first imprisonment. Till then he had lived roughly according to plan, that is he had spent his whole time painting historical pictures on a big scale. He came out of prison very much shattered; his self-respect had had a shock, and instead of subsisting 'entirely on the generosity of his friends', as hitherto, he now had to turn to the unpleasant task of making a living. To do this meant virtually abandoning all his cherished hopes as a painter. He could not work quickly on large pictures; when he tried he produced rubbish. He needed years of brooding to do himself justice. He could get through a great deal in one day sometimes, as in the case of the head and figure of Lazarus, but on the whole he was a slow worker. And he hated to work to order, even on commissions for historical paintings. He despised small pictures and did them badly. But there were limits to what even Haydon could extract from his friends, so he now attempted to live by portrait painting. No words could describe his detestation of this task. On 8 September 1823, he began what he called his portrait career. Before his sitter arrived he walked about the garden in sullen despair. The very thought of the man made him want to vomit. All his sitters induced this condition, and he regarded them with a malignancy that must have made a sympathetic likeness out of the question. Of one he writes, 'My breast swelled, my heart beat, and I nauseated this bit of miserable, feeble humanity!' One can respect his dislike of the commercial art of portrait painting as a means of making money; and though there is no reason a commissioned portrait should not be a work of art it did not become so in his hands. His expressions of abhorrence often cross the bounds of ordinary exaggeration and became ludicrous, 'My whole soul and body raise the gorge at portrait . . . as soon as the sitter is gone I turn from his resemblance with disgust.' It was of course his extreme un-success that so disgusted him. 'I really don't care about the half-tint of a cheek, I really do not. I would rather devour Aelian or search Strabo, and blaze with Homer—I really would—and give my imagination the reign for hours, than paint a cheek like Vandyke. This is the truth.' And again, 'Well, I have been all day at work, and what thoughts are the consequence?—how to work the tip of a nose, or the colour of a lip.' 'In portrait I lose that divine feeling of inspiration I always have in history. I feel as a common man; think as a common man; execute as the very commonest.' To him a hand in a portrait and a hand in a his-torical picture were different things. 'Worked hard but, alas! on what?—a hand and drapery round it.' 'Ah, my poor lay-figure!' he cries, 'He who bore the drapery of Christ and the grave-clothes of Lazarus, the cloak of the centurion and the gown of Newton, was to-day disgraced by a black coat and waistcoat.' It chanced about this time that Haydon met at a conversazione the distinguished editor (his name is unfortunately not revealed) of a leading Review, drunk, on the stairs; 'My dear fellow,' said the editor, 'I do hope you will get on, *paint their bloody faces.* Good night. God bless you!' and away he reeled. It is interesting to watch him striving to overcome his prejudice. He managed to persuade himself now and again that he was doing so, only to react with violence later. 'I am getting at last interested with portraits, and begin to feel eagerness for surface, tone, softness, likeness, effect and all the rich mockery of a head.' To this a note is added six months after, 'This was cant.' The prospect of a sitter made him get up with a nasty taste in his mouth, and in a state of 'dull foggy disgust'. 'This is very weak,' he says, 'but I cannot help it.' But worse was to come. The time arrived when these portraits had to be exhibited, and the critics fell on them like ravening wolves. Critics of those days allowed themselves great licence. 'The Daily Press', writes Mr. Oppé, 'had no com-punction in treating an artist who dared to exhibit a picture as a malefactor obtruding an outrage upon the public.' Their attacks took what Haydon called 'a new direction', and that the most damaging one possible for a portrait painter—the personal peculiarities of his sitters. Miss Mitford congratulated herself on her escape; her portrait had not been among those sent. 'Did you ever see or hear of Mr. Haydon's portrait of me?' she wrote, 'it was so exaggerated, both in size and colour, that none of my

friends could endure it. My father declared he would not have
it home, and I believe it is now quite demolished. We are not the
less good friends, for certainly he did not mean to produce a
caricature; for such I believe it is.' In another letter she refers to
it as 'the cook-maid thing of poor Mr. Haydon'. It was said of
Miss Mitford that 'she seldom had a good word for anyone who
did not flatter her continuously': and she herself wrote to Haydon about this very portrait, 'Miss James says . . . that it is . . .
"strikingly like and with an expression that none but you would
have known how to have given"—at once the truth and most
forcible!' To others than the victims his portraits were objects
of mirth. Haydon himself writes: 'H.' (Hamilton), 'laughed
heartily at my family picture, in which I joined most sincerely.'

Haydon's 'sublime' pictures sometimes have their comic side,
but he was on more dangerous ground still when he tried to
paint city merchants and their wives in the heroic style, and
larger than life. There was one occasion however when the
'heroic' was included in the terms of agreement, this was a
commission to which Borrow refers in *Lavengro*.

Borrow's brother, who lived in Norwich, had for a short time
been a pupil of Haydon's. He had been asked by a committee
of the townsfolk to paint a portrait of their mayor for £100.
This mayor was 'big and portly, with a voice like Boanerges';
Borrow, feeling himself unequal to the task, said it was a pity
that Crome was no longer alive. The spokesman of the committee,
a little hunchback, intimated that Crome would hardly have
been the man, 'He had no conception of the heroic, sir. We want
some person capable of representing our mayor striding under
the Norman arch out of the cathedral.' At the mention of the
heroic Borrow could but think of Haydon, and it was arranged
that he should get into touch with him.

He came up to town, and took his brother George to see
Haydon. They had a difficulty in being admitted, the servant
eyed them suspiciously, thinking they were duns. 'At length,'
says George Borrow, 'we were shown into the studio, where
we found the painter, with an easel and brush standing before a
huge piece of canvas, on which he had lately commenced painting a heroic picture. He recognized my brother and appeared
glad to see him.'

When the reason of the visit had been explained, Borrow
observed the painter's eyes to glisten. 'Really,' said he, 'it was

very kind to think of me. I am not very fond of painting portraits but a mayor is a mayor, and there is something grand in
that idea of a Norman arch. I'll go; moreover I am just at this
moment confoundedly in need of money, and when you
knocked at the door, I don't mind telling you, I thought it was
some dun . . . I'll go; when shall we set off?'

Borrow continues:

'We presently afterwards departed; my brother talked much about
the painter. "He is a noble fellow," said my brother, "but, like many
other noble fellows, has a great many enemies; he is hated by his
brethren of the brush—all the land and waterscape painters hate him—
but, above all, the race of portrait painters, who are ten times more
numerous than the other two sorts, detest him for his heroic tendencies.
It will be a kind of triumph to the last, I fear when they hear he has
condescended to paint a portrait; however, that Norman arch will
enable him to escape from their malice—that is a capital idea of the
watchmaker, that Norman arch. . . ." My brother departed with the
painter for the old town, and there the painter painted the mayor. I did
not see the picture for a great many years, when chancing to be at the
old town, I beheld it.

'The original mayor was a mighty, portly man, with a bull's head,
black hair, body like that of a dray-horse, and legs and thighs corresponding; a man six foot high at the least. To his bull's head, black
hair, and body the painter had done justice; there was one point however, in which the portrait did not correspond with the original—the
legs were disproportionably short, the painter having substituted his
own legs for those of the mayor. . . . Short legs in a heroic picture will
never do; and, upon the whole I think the painter's attempt at the
heroic in painting the mayor of the old town a decided failure. If I am
now asked whether the picture would have been a heroic one provided
the painter had not substituted his own legs for those of the mayor—
I must say, I am afraid not. I have no idea of making heroic pictures
out of English mayors, even with the assistance of Norman arches. . . .'

Besides his portraits Haydon had begun at last to paint small
pictures. This to him meant little less than deflation means to a
balloon. His spirit wilted and sank. One may feel amusement or
contempt for his obsession about size, but in whatever way it is
regarded it went deep into his being, so that his happiness did
literally depend on it. When, as sometimes happened, he carried
out the same design both on a small and a large scale, he could
hardly bear to look at the small one. There were several reasons
for it; one certainly was that on a small scale his pictures

suffered in comparison with those of many other painters; whereas a huge canvas was a sort of bludgeon with which he could batter his rivals into insignificances. Moreover, achievement on a small scale would have been failure for such a giant as he believed himself to be. Another very urgent reason was his craving for advertisement; obscurity was unendurable, not to be doing something that made people talk was unendurable. 'With sublime subjects,' he writes, 'you muse and have high thoughts, and think of death and destiny, of God and resurrection, and retire to rest above the world—prepared for its littlenesses.' We are familiar with his states of elation and ambition when he is engaged on a huge picture, and have seen how he could throw off despair with its help; let us hear him when not so supported:

'I am utterly abroad in mind, occupied with a continuity of daily trifles; in the evening I have no abstract idea or expression of character to muse on till the next day. I leave off wearied, and commence in disgust. I candidly confess I find my glorious art a bore. I cannot with pleasure paint any individual head for the mere purpose of domestic gratification. I must have a great subject to excite public feeling. I must be supported with all sorts of anticipatory hopes, fears and feelings. Velasquez used to paint fruit, vegetables, still-life, and all life, again and again, to get facility. I would willingly do this, and have done it, could it end in anything worthy; but what worthy thing will happen to me? Alas! I have no object in life now but my wife and children, and almost wish I had not them, that I might sit still and meditate on human ambition and human grandeur till I died. I really am heartily weary of life. I have known and tasted all the glories of fame, and distinction and triumph; all the raptures of love and affection, all the sweet feelings of a parent. And what then? The heart, as I have said before, sinks inwardly, and longs for a pleasure calm and eternal, majestic, unchangeable. I am not yet forty and can tell of a destiny, melancholy and rapturous, bitter beyond all bitterness, afflicting beyond all affliction, cursed, heart-burning, heart-breaking, maddening. Merciful God, that Thou should'st permit a being with thought and feeling to be so racked! But I dare not write now. The melancholy demon has grappled my heart, and crushed its turbulent beatings in his black, bony, clammy, clenching fingers. I stop till an opening of reason dawns again on my blurred head.'

This depression, dangerous at times, could be kept at bay only by a great canvas, for with that support, he might be harried half out of his wits, but was never despairing. He had steadily increased the scale of his pictures, beginning with the six-foot

Flight into Egypt, and ending with the enormous *Crucifixion.* If he had had any success he certainly would never have stopped till he had painted the largest picture in the world, and had beaten Tintoretto's *Paradise.* And he was encouraged in these absurdities. The critics flattered his vanity by talking of his falling from his high estate when he reduced his scale, so that he thought of himself more than ever as a fallen Titan. The *Morning Chronicle,* speaking of the pictures he exhibited in 1830 says, 'These considerations and experiences have brought him to descend from the pinnacle of art—grand historical pictures on a large scale for churches and public buildings—to pieces of smaller dimensions fitted for private collections—shrunk in size, like the fallen host in Milton, they still are spirits of a noble origin.'

Hazlitt too did his best to encourage his mania:

'We have said', he writes, 'that we regard the present performance [*Christ's Agony in the Garden*], as a comparative failure; and our reasons are briefly and plainly these following: First, this picture is inferior in size to those that Mr. Haydon has of late years painted, and is so far a falling-off. It does not occupy one side of a great room. It is the Iliad in a nutshell. . . . One of the great merits of Mr. Haydon's pictures is their size. Reduce him within narrow limits, and you cut off half his resources. His genius is gigantic. He is of the race of Brobdignag, and not of Lilliput. He can manage a group better than a single figure: he can manage ten groups better than one. He bestrides his art like a Colossus. The more you give him to do the better he does it. Arduous energy, boundless ambition, are the categories of his mind, the springs of his enterprises.'

Is it surprising that he felt deflated when circumstances forced him to paint small pictures? The old Haydon has gone and in his place we have a man who is keeping up his spirits artificially. He did occasionally do large pictures, but not so large, and he did them in a comparative hurry. No longer did rank, beauty, and fashion crowd his studio to watch the progress of his work. Gone were the days when, he says, 'I used to kneel down regularly before my picture, and pray to God for support through it, and then retire to rest after striding through my solemn and solitary painting-room, with the St. Paul of Raffaele gleaming through the dim light at one end, the Galatea at the other, the Jupiter of the Capitol over the chimney-piece, and behind all my Lazarus! What pleasure have I enjoyed in that study! In it have talked Walter Scott, Wordsworth, Keats, Procter, Belzoni, Campbell,

Canova, Cuvier, Lamb, Knowles, Hazlitt, Wilkie, and other spirits of the time. And above all thy sweet and sacred face, my Mary, was its chief grace, its ornament, its sunbeam.'

He confessed later that he would have liked to return to his empty studio at Lisson Grove and to go on with the *Crucifixion*, but his wife shrank from it and he loved her too much to press her. Not a quarter of the huge canvas could have been got into any of his subsequent painting-rooms, and the picture had to be abandoned. 'And here am I,' he cries, 'at this moment ready to do anything, to the portrait of a cat, for the means of an honest livelihood, without employment, or the notice of a patron in the country.' One day he writes, 'obliged to sally forth to get money, in consequence of the bullying insolence of a short, wicked-eyed, wrinkled, waddling, gin-drinking, dirty-ruffled landlady—poor old bit of asthmatic humanity! As I was finishing the foot in she bounced, and demanded the four pounds, with the air of a demirep duchess. I irritated her by my smile, and turned her out. I sat down quietly and finished my feet. Fielding should have seen the old devil.'

He left these lodgings and took a lease of 58 Connaught Terrace, and had only just moved in with the few belongings salvaged for him by his friends, when on the 24th came another execution. This time it was only for £4 10s., the remainder of the rent owing to the demirep duchess, £46 of which he had already paid. There had been frequent words with this lady, and one learns with interest that she and the gentle Mary never met but to exchange broadsides in which Haydon took his wife's part and flew at the old woman 'like a tiger'. On this occasion Mary was frightened, and being near her time suffered for an hour or two. Haydon was roused, set to work, and told his new landlord the situation. The latter immediately ordered men to get the house ready, 'and there were we', says Haydon, 'without a plate or a teacup, but with a great deal of experience'. This little jar upset him badly, he felt that this execution might hurt him more than the one that ruined him, it revived all the tortures of the previous year, and agitated his mind with pangs he thought had passed.

But help came from an unexpected quarter just when everything seemed most black. Haydon's legal adviser, a Mr. Kearsey, came forward. His kind and lengthy letter is an example of how galling generosity may be when it is too conscious of itself. The days were gone when Haydon defied Sir George Beaumont, and enlarged his canvas; now he must paint exactly to the scale Mr. Kearsey lays down, and do as he is told in half a dozen other ways if he wishes to live. With mixed feelings must he have read:

'October 25th, 1824.

'. . . I cannot forget that on your introduction to me (now a year since or so), you came to me driven by the pitiless storm which was then about to annihilate you. The storm was doubtless in no small degree of your own raising. I carried your bark through it, but miserably despoiled, it's true, of tackle and stores. You was, however, then pushed off the shore and afloat; but I found you on the crisis of my late attack in May last (which through a providence to you as well as to me I survived), with your bark aground, and as helpless, if not more helpless than ever . . . then, and ever since then, I carried and have carried you through the surge, and you are floating again on the wave. I have reason to think you are, and have been tolerably industrious since the first great week, and that your state of depression may with a helping hand at the critical moment be dispelled for ever, provided industry, economy and every good habit is in exercise by you. Therefore, although I have actually gone beyond my poor means already, yet I am resolved that if it is in my power your talents shall not be sacrificed to rapacity, greediness or avarice. . . . Your necessities must not and shall not compel your genius to go crippled, or on all fours, seeking for and picking up crumbs. You doubtless from the former class of your studies have something yet to attain in portrait-painting, more especially female portraits, and you must make, as you ought, for some time, a sacrifice in the price of portraits; . . . a whole length at this moment should not be done by you under seventy-five guineas, a three-quarter, fifty guineas, a half, thirty to thirty-five guineas; and in order to prevent your being obliged to take less than these sums, I have resolved, for one year, from 1st January 1825 to 1st January 1826, to come forward at intervals (provided there is need, and I have reason to think you deserve it) with a sum of £300, secured to me as I shall by and by state. Thus you will have a year clear before you, if you do not gain a farthing, and the year (free and well employed) will give you the command, I trust, of a better fate. . . . But mark well, while I do this, the following with others I may think of, of a similar nature, will be *sine qua nons*. And I am obliged to be precise, because in what I am thus uncalled for proposing to do for you, a stranger, I shall (if I am called on to do it) be doing more than, in justice to my family, as is the vulgar excuse, I ought to do for anyone not allied by ties of friendship, blood or other relationship.

'You will paint portraits to your best skill at the above prices when they offer, and you will try to get them.

'You will paint no portrait at less price unless I assent under penalty this [sic].

'While not engaged in painting portraits, you must be actively engaged in painting historic or compositions of fancy, of a small, and at most not larger than a saleable cabinet size, consulting me. I wish to know what you are doing or about to do, more for any aid I can give then any interest to be presumed by me.

'If I advance money, I must be repaid out of the produce of the first portraits, historic or other paintings, as paid for or sold, with interest at four per cent. I say this interest, because I will not have any earthly advantage of the smallest kind. All I propose or can have is to father on myself more anxieties and trouble.

'The historic and other paintings must be as security for my advances till sold.

'If the year's advance does not answer my or your expectations in giving you a command in portrait-painting, your honour must be pledged not to make any further request to me, so that I shall have a proper virtue exercised by you, and my feelings not harrowed. That you may not be tempted to depart from the prices I state, you shall, if I require, make a statement on oath of what you have done, and you shall communicate to me instantly on all work engaged for.

'My advances are to be secured by your bond and a life insurance. I add this latter, more especially because it will be a benefit to your family, and what as a professional man you must do to a considerable extent, as your means will admit by and by, for if you live and have employ, your works will support your family, but dying your works must close, and your life assurance will aid them. Think well on this.'

This offer was accepted. A better fortune dawned on him, and in spite of regrets for the glorious days that were passed, he found life more tolerable than he had expected now that he was not in daily and hourly anxiety. Another child at this time made Kearsey's help more than ever valuable, especially as the last picture, *Silenus* (which had taken six months to do) did not sell. But there was a price to pay in the temporary loss of all his enthusiasm. 'With respect to the great object of my former ambition,' he says, 'I candidly confess myself cooled. . . . In art I can be of little more utility. The vigour of my life has only made a cranny in the heavy wall of ignorance through which, it may be, a star of light shines; whether any other will batter a breach in it time only can prove. I think on the whole I have sunk, or am sinking into a sluggish apathy, perhaps despair. The end of the next year will show.'

Never did the schoolboy of tradition go to his work with more leaden feet than Haydon went to his painting-room for a sitting. He writes at this time, 'Ought to have painted a portrait; looked at my historical picture; thought I might as well set and arrange my drapery. I did so. There could be no harm in painting that bit! So I painted it. Then it looked so well there could be no harm in painting the other bit, and then the whole would be complete; so I did it and dinner was announced before I was aware. Delightful art! . . . When I painted poetry, night and day my mind and soul were occupied. . . . Would I could hit on some mode of putting forth sublime ideas which would provide me the means of existence.' So the battle raged within him; on the one side Kearsey's bond and a wife and four children, and on the other his historical subjects and every instinct in his nature.

At last he received a commission for his *Pharaoh*, and this picture occupied him in the intervals of portrait painting for the rest of the year. All his enthusiasm returned immediately. He got into his 'old delightful habits of study' again; his mind 'calm, happy, and conceiving'. 'The mixture of literature and painting I really think the perfection of human happiness. I paint a head, revel in colour, hit an expression, sit down fatigued, take up a poet or historian, write my own thoughts or muse on thoughts of others, and hours and troubles and the tortures of disappointed ambition, pass and are forgotten. I wake up from a dream to the drowsy, foggy world with sorrow and disgust.'

One piece of good fortune followed another; his last portrait was cancelled. His sitter, a rich city man, had grown suspicious over a long delay during which Haydon had put the picture aside to dry, and had hinted that he thought the painter was trying to cheat him. 'So much for his knowledge,' said the painter.

This weight off his mind, he went on with his *Pharaoh* in 'the greatest delight', and arrived at the following deep principle, 'If anything is too hot, put something hotter, and it becomes cool. If anything is too yellow, put something by it much yellower, and it becomes white. So of red, blue, black, etc. So of everything; lines, colour, expression. This is a deep principle, and cannot be too often remembered.' This truly Haydonian principle came in usefully soon after: when in his picture of *Alexander Taming Bucephalus* he found he had made his hero too middle-aged, by adding a figure far older still he gave Alexander a look of youth by sheer contrast, so very old was the other figure. There must have been something too yellow or too pale in *Pharaoh*, or perhaps he overdid the principle, because he thought it looked sickly and flat when it was exhibited; 'though', he adds characteristically, 'I ought to be satisfied with the look of my picture'. Here is his first conception of this heroic work: 'On the ground', he says, 'I would have had Pharaoh's queen in an agony of maternal hope, placing her hand on the heart of her boy, and listening for the beat of it in racking anxiety; the sisters, one exclaiming in affliction, the other, while supporting her dead brother, looking round to Moses with an enquiring horror; behind the queen, Pharaoh, the subdued monarch bending with majesty, and dismissing the lawgiver and his brother in waving, disdainful yet vanquished pride; Moses right opposite to him pointing to the dead child, and to heaven, as if saying, "I do this by superior direction"; and in the background the people in rebellion, dashing up their dead children, and roaring like the sea for the dismissal of the Jewish leaders while the guards press them back lest they burst into the palace. A sphinx or two, a pyramid or so, dark and awful, with the front groups lighted by torches, would make this subject terrific and affecting. It combines pathos and sublimity.'

'My eyes filled with tears', he wrote later, 'when I painted the mother, and so have the eyes of others now it is done. . . .' Still more convincing to him was the unconscious praise of his daughter (aged two), who on seeing the weeping mother, said, 'Poor! poor!' 'Depend upon it,' Haydon remarked, in telling Miss Mitford this incident, 'it will do.' So the less flattering judgement of George Borrow, who, though no artist, was on a higher level of intelligence than this, would probably, even if he had known it, have weighed lightly in the balance against that of Georgiana Haydon. When Borrow and his brother called on Haydon about the Mayor's portrait, they found him at work on *Pharaoh*:

'They began to talk about art,' says Borrow. "I'll stick to the heroic," said the painter; "I now and then dabble in the comic, but what I do gives me no pleasure, the comic is so low, there is nothing like the heroic. I am engaged here on a heroic picture," said he, pointing to the canvas, "the subject is 'Pharaoh dismissing Moses from Egypt', after the last plague—the death of the first-born—it is not far advanced—

that finished figure is Moses." They both looked at the canvas, and I, standing behind, took a modest peep. The picture, as the painter said, was not far advanced, the Pharaoh was merely in outline; my eye was, of course, attracted by the finished figure, or rather what the painter had called the finished figure; but, as I gazed upon it, it appeared to me that there was something defective—something unsatisfactory in the figure. I concluded, however, that the painter, notwithstanding what he had said, had omitted to give it the finishing touch. "I intend this to be my best picture," said the painter; "what I want now is a face for Pharaoh; I have long been meditating on a face for Pharaoh." Here, chancing to cast his eye upon my countenance, of whom he had scarcely taken any manner of notice, he remained with his mouth open for some time. "Who is this?" said he at last. "Oh, this is my brother, I forgot to introduce him——" On leaving they discussed the picture; "By the bye," said Borrow's brother, "do you not think the figure of Moses somewhat short?" "And then it appeared to me that I had thought the figure of Moses somewhat short, and I told my brother so. "Ah!" said my brother.

'I spent a happy day with my brother,' continues Borrow. 'On the morrow he went again to the painter, with whom he dined; I did not go with him. On his return he said, "The painter has been asking a great many questions about you, and expressed a wish that you would sit to him as Pharaoh; he thinks you would make a capital Pharaoh." "I have no wish to appear on canvas," said I; "moreover he can find much better Pharaohs than myself. . . ." As we know, Borrow had not admired the portrait of the mayor whose legs were disproportionably short, "which when I perceived," said he, "I rejoiced that I had not consented to be painted as Pharaoh, for, if I had, the chances are that he would have served me in exactly a similar way as he had served Moses and the mayor." '

Let us now stand behind as Borrow did when he looked at *Pharaoh*, and take a 'modest peep' at *him*:

DEAR SIR,

I should feel extremely obliged if you would allow me to sit to you as soon as possible. I am going to the south of France in little better than a fortnight, and I would sooner lose a thousand pounds than not have the honour of appearing in the picture.

Yours sincerely,
GEORGE BORROW.

The year 1826 was one of great commercial convulsion, and Haydon's patron was unable to pay him his money, £500. This was a terrible blow and he was at once plunged in the old difficulties.

XVII. LIGHTS AND SHADES

Words were insufficient for the elevation of his feelings.
JANE AUSTEN (*Pride and Prejudice*)

VERY far away were the days when 'H-yd-n' bounded on to his plank in the River of Time, and was carried along (in advance of the Academicians), crowned by Fame; now it is he, not they, who is trying to wipe off the mud from the banks of that river, the mud that he himself has thrown; and, worst humiliation of all, he must ask their help. He was beginning bitterly to regret his feud with the Academy, and would have liked to make it up, but pride rebelled. His friends advised him to send his picture of *Venus and Anchises* (commissioned by Sir John Leycester), to the Academy; it was indeed the only place, 'but I really cannot', he cries. 'After having said what I have said, and written what I have written, it could not be consistent. . . . Willingly I would shake hands and forget all, but I must be met half-way. The Academy is certainly modified, but still John Bull never pardons an appearance of renegadism.' There was a severe struggle, but as there was no alternative, there could be only one result; he yielded and sent. 'Perhaps after all,' he wrote, 'I do this on the same principle on which Alcibiades cut off his dog's tail, to make people talk—and talk they will.' Haydon did everything on that principle, it was one of the chief reasons for his failure. Never till it was too late did he realize the mistakes which his friends realized while he was making them. Wilkie, of course, had been right in preaching moderation; what he thought is made clear from a conversation with Bewick about this time (1826). Earnestly, and drawing a long breath, he said, 'You see, Haydon ought to have entered the Academy. Ay, he ought to have got in, he would have been a great acquisition; what a professor of painting he would have made! What powerful lectures we might have had! How the school of painting would have been extended and improved! But then, ha! he must have had all his own way, or we might have had poor Barry over again, and that would never have done in our days. No, no. However we might hope for better things, for he has great tact.'

Where Wilkie with only one talent had succeeded, Haydon with many had failed. He explained it in a way not unflattering to himself, 'Wilkie's system', said he, 'was Wellington's: principle and prudence the groundwork of risk. Mine that of Napoleon: audacity, with defiance of principle, if principle was in the way. I got into prison, Napoleon died in St. Helena. Wellington is living and honoured, and Wilkie has had a public dinner given him in Rome, the seat of art and genius, and has secured a competence, while I am as poor and necessitous as ever. Let no man use evil as a means for the success of any scheme, however grand. Evil that good may come is the prerogative of the Deity alone, and should never be ventured on by mortals.'

So now, hat in hand, poor Haydon tried to make up for his folly. He decided on a step which he ever after felt to be one of the most humiliating in his career—because it was unsuccessful. He called on most of the Academicians with a view to election.

'I shall call on all those whose feelings I have hurt,' he says, 'and I hurt the feelings of some of whom I had no right to complain, but as they were of the body corporate. This was wanton, and gives me pain —great pain. Surely there can be no degradation in trying to heal up wounds one has inflicted, without thought at thirty.'

This pain only became really acute when he discovered that the injury he had done was after all entirely to himself. The Academicians received him courteously, and all seemed glad to bury the hatchet.

'I cannot expect to be received with open arms at once,' he wrote, 'after the severity with which I have treated these men. But I see they are pleased with my present frame of mind. . . . I see they have a high opinion of me. But no concession; d—— me if I make any concession. I'll be patient and give them three years. If at the end of that time I am trifled with, then to hostilities again.'

This attempt was not successful, and when he put his name down for election he did not get a single vote. No doubt the Academicians shrank from having such a firebrand among them, even those of them who were ready to forgive Haydon's attacks. Such a man could have been a member of no corporate body without causing dissension. Having failed with the

Academy he tried soon after to win back lost ground with the British Institution. As a young man under the patronage of Lord Mulgrave and Sir George Beaumont he had been 'much amongst' the members of this important society of patrons and connoisseurs. This was a privilege shared by no other artist—it had been intimated even to West, who had been instrumental in founding the society, that it would cause misunderstandings if one practising painter only were admitted. But Haydon, so he tells Miss Mitford, was often admitted to their consultations. However, as one would have expected, he had much with which to find fault:

'I soon perceived', he writes, 'that if I wished to do anything in Art before I was thirty, I must depend on myself. When they asked my advice, I opposed their narrow views, I argued with them, I tried to persuade them, I pointed out what ought to be their objects, what their aim in their system of encouragement, and I said, in the presence of a large party of nobility and Dilettanti, that if they did not pursue some such course High Art would be in a worse condition in twenty-five years than when they first took it up. Not relishing these independent opinions, I was set adrift on the stream of my own independence.'

But too much independence has its disadvantages, later (1830) he was to write:

'Mr. Haydon presents his respects to the noblemen and gentlemen who compose the committee of the British Gallery, and begs to appeal to them in his present struggling condition, with eight children and nothing on earth left him in property but what he is clothed with, after twenty-six years of intense and ardent devotion to painting, after leaving a capital property and handsome income from pure devotion to historical Art.

'Mr. Haydon is well aware that more discretion in his early life would probably have placed him in a very different condition, and had he borne what he conceived injustice on the part of the Royal Academy with more temper such bitter ruin as he has been afflicted with would certainly never have happened, but still he was never actuated by any mean motive: his love of Art more than a just regard for his own personal interests he can conscientiously affirm was his great inducement.

'Perhaps the Directors of the British Gallery will not think too severely of his endeavouring by an appeal to their feelings to avert further calamities from his family.

'The kindness of Lord Stafford in lately giving him a small commission has saved them from wanting the commonest necessaries; and if the Committee would aid him by a moderate, though not unimportant, sum to finish his Xenophon, it would perhaps enable him to keep out of debt for the rest of his life. . . .

'Mr. Haydon anxiously apologizes for this intrusion, and hopes he may be so happy as to receive an answer which may reanimate his labours.'

The answer was a cheque for £50.

Haydon always believed he was beloved by the people—'honest John Bull'. His chief reason for this was the thirty thousand who visited the gallery to see *Jerusalem*. Most of his subsequent exhibitions were failures.

He now writes, 'I have tried the people and was nobly supported. I have tried the Ministers, and was coolly sympathized with. I have tried the Academy and was cruelly persecuted. But the people could do nothing. Time—time—time!' He was, however, fortunate in finding a patron in Lord Egremont, who could do something. This princely patron of the arts became known to him through his next picture—*Alexander Taming Bucephalus*, for it was through him that Haydon got permission to use the Guards' riding-school, where the finest man in the regiment, mounted naked on the finest horse, rode about, charged and reined-up for his benefit. Then the Colonel galloped a grey mare, pulled in, and Haydon sketched the nostrils of the mare while breathing hard, to get the shape and character. The man and horse were taken to a meadow behind his house, and the horse raced till it was exhausted, and at full speed pulled up suddenly. Afterwards they went inside Haydon's house and stood in the parlour for six hours, while he made an oil sketch. Never again did Haydon allow a horse to enter the parlour. Frederic says explicitly that all subsequent horses which came to the house had to remain in the hall.

Haydon, driven by want, had written to ask Lord Egremont's assistance; he came, saw the picture, and commissioned it. But though his worst anxieties were thus relieved he had to live in the meantime, and to do so began disposing of property of all descriptions; lay-figures, books, spoons and forks, went where so much had gone before. He looked at his Vasari, Lanzi, Homer, Tasso and Shakespeare—hesitated—but his heart was firm. He kept them. At last his difficulties had, he says, driven him 'up in a corner', and in spite of warnings he decided to appeal again to Lord Egremont. 'I begged him to pardon my laying open my circumstances to him. I was warned against applying for money to him by others. It ruined Rossi with him; but Rossi I suppose, applied in the style of a butcher. Oh, what anxiety dearest Mary and I suffered last night! "It will succeed", she said, "or ruin you." '

They had been warned of his arrival, and next day when they saw him coming they were walking on the leads, but agreed it would not be right to look too happy, being without sixpence; so they came in, he to the parlour to peep through the blinds, and she to the nursery. Lord Egremont arrived and walked up; he was not offended and advanced £100. 'My lord, that's salvation.' Lord Egremont smiled and put five twenties on a chair. He then walked about the plaster-room, Haydon following. 'Take up your money,' said he; Haydon did so. 'I wish to make Alexander an aspiring youth,' said Haydon. Lord Egremont nodded. 'Don't make the queen damned ugly.' He walked about and 'turned on his heel, as if he now had a right to be familiar'.

This money enabled Haydon to take his family to Brighton for a much-needed change in the beginning of November. While there he was invited to Petworth. The cup of his gratification brimmed and ran over during the visit itself, and in the remembrance of it he could not find words to express the bliss that reigned at Petworth:

'Nov. 13th.—Set off for Petworth, where I arrived at half-past three. Lord Egremont's reception was frank and noble. The party was quite a family one. All was frank good-humour and benevolence. Lord Egremont presided and helped, laughed and joked, and let others do the same.

'15th.—. . . I really never saw such a character as Lord Egremont. "Live and let live" seems to be his motto. He has placed me in one of the most magnificent bedrooms I ever saw. It speaks more for what he thinks of my talents than anything that ever happened to me. On the left of the bed hangs a portrait of William, Lord Marquis of Hertford, created knight of the garter 1649, and by Act of Parliament restored Duke of Somerset 1660. Over the chimney is a nobleman kneeling. A lady of high rank to the right. Opposite, Queen Mary. Over the door, a head. On the right of the cabinet, Sir Somebody. And over the entrance door, another head. The bed-curtains are of different coloured velvets let in on white satin. The walls, sofas, easy-chairs, green damask, and a beautiful view of the park out of the high windows.'

It was on this first evening at Petworth that Haydon repaid

some of Lord Egremont's hospitality by providing him with a good story: Frederic Haydon says that love of fresh air was his father's hobby, as well as his suspicion of a damp bed. Whenever he visited he always did two things: he opened all the windows and, summer or winter, lighting his bedroom fire, he aired his sheets and mattress. Lord Egremont used to tell a story of his first night at Petworth. Dinner was announced, and Haydon, who had been in the library, had disappeared. Search was made for him, and he was found in his bedroom with his evening coat carefully taken off, and his great coat buttoned round him, pulling his bed to pieces, hauling out blankets, sheets, mattresses, and pillows, and spreading them over the backs of chairs before the huge fire he had lighted.

'There is something peculiarly interesting', Haydon writes, 'in inhabiting these apartments, sacred to antiquity, which have contained a long list of deceased and illustrious ancestors. As I lay in my magnificent bed, and saw the old portraits trembling in a sort of twilight, I almost fancied I heard them breathe, and almost expected they would move out and shake my curtains. What a destiny is mine! One year in the Bench, the companion of gamblers and scoundrels—sleeping in wretchedness and dirt, on a flock bed low and filthy, with black worms crawling over my hands—another reposing in down and velvet, in a splendid apartment, in a splendid house, the guest of rank, and fashion and beauty! As I laid my head on my down pillow the first night I was deeply affected, and could hardly sleep. God in heaven grant my fortune may now be steady. At anyrate a nobleman has taken me by the hand, whose friendship generally increases in proportion to the necessity of its continuance. Such is Lord Egremont. Literally like the sun. The very flies at Petworth seem to know there is room for their existence, that the windows are theirs. Dogs, horses, cows, deer and pigs, peasantry and servants, guests and family, children and parents, all alike share his bounty and opulence and luxuries.

'At breakfast, after the guests have all breakfasted, in walks Lord Egremont; first comes a grandchild whom he sends away happy. Outside the window moan a dozen black spaniels, who are let in, and to them he distributes cakes and comfits, giving all equal shares. After chatting with one guest, and proposing some scheme of pleasure for others, his leathern gaiters are buttoned on, and away he walks, leaving everybody to take care of themselves, with all that opulence and generosity can place at their disposal entirely within their reach. At dinner he meets everybody and then are recounted the feats of the day. All principal dishes he helps, never minding the trouble of carving; he eats heartily and helps liberally. There is plenty but not absurd profusion;

good wines, but not extravagant waste. Everything solid, liberal, rich
and English. At seventy-four he still shoots daily, comes home wet
through and is as active and looks as well as many men of fifty. The
meanest insect at Petworth feels a ray of his lordship's fire in the justice
of distribution.

'I never saw such a character, or such a man, nor were there ever
many.

'18th.—I left Petworth to-day, and arrived safely at Brighton, where
I found my dear children and dearest Mary well.'

Mr. Collins himself was not more impressed by the splendours
of *Rosings*, and Haydon remarks:

'Before leaving that princely seat of magnificent hospitality, I wrote,
when I retired to my bedroom last night, the following letter:
MY LORD,
I cannot leave Petworth without intruding my gratitude for the
princely manner in which I have been treated during my stay; and
in earnestly hoping your lordship may live long, I only add my voice
to the voices of thousands, who never utter your lordship's name
without a blessing,
I am, my lord,
Your lordship's humble and grateful servant,
B. R. HAYDON.'

It is significant that Haydon was never asked again. Lord
Egremont (who lived some ten years longer) took great pleasure
in entertaining artists and often asked them with their families;
Turner, as is well known, had rooms and a studio always at his
disposal. It may have been something abject in Haydon's enjoyment that displeased; but, though no hint is given of anything
of the sort, it is more probable that he began begging, and this
as he tells us himself, was a habit Lord Egremont would not
forgive. He had commissioned Haydon's *Alexander*, but a fortnight's delay in the balance owing (£200) cost the poor painter
another execution and nearly another imprisonment. The money
came eventually on 16 January. Owing to this short delay, he
had no less than three warrants of attorney, three cognovits and
three actions. He was flying from one to another. One man,
after Haydon had paid him £10 out of £16, ran him to £18
expenses for the £6 left.

'And this is the way I am served if I am behind-hand for a
moment,' he cries. But directly his mind was relieved from these

agonizing pressures it began conceiving subjects as he walked along the streets with 'a sort of relishing delight'.

When *Alexander* was finished Haydon asked Lord Egremont's advice: would it not be a good thing to consult the Duke of Bedford, the Duke of Devonshire, the Marquesses of Lansdowne and Stafford, Lord Aberdeen and Lord Farnborough, and to get their criticisms on the picture? To which Egremont replied, 'I would not give a farthing for the opinions of all these persons; but the object now is to make the best use of this picture to get other orders, and more employment for yourself, and if you think that consulting all these persons will conduce to this object, as I think it may, I should advise you to do so.'[1]

But dukes and noble lords did not avail to keep Haydon out of prison, and before the end of June he was again in the King's Bench. He only remained there a month, but it was then that he saw the mock election. He thus described the incident to the Duke of Bedford:

'In the midst of this dreadful scene of affliction up sprung the masquerade election—a scene which, contrasted as it was with sorrow and prison walls, beggars all description. Distracted as I was, I was perpetually drawn to the windows by the boisterous merriment of the unfortunate happy beneath me. Rabelais or Cervantes alone could do it justice with their pens. Never was such an exquisite burlesque. Baronets and bankers, authors and merchants, young fellows of fashion and elegance; insanity, idiotism, poverty and bitter affliction, all for a moment forgetting their sorrows at the humour, the wit, the absurdity of what was before them.

'I saw the whole from beginning to end. I was resolved to paint it, for I thought it the finest subject for humour and pathos on earth.'

He once more appealed to the public through the press and to Parliament by petition. Brougham presented the petition and the newspapers printed the letters. These public appeals were in vain, but private applications met with immediate response. Sir Walter Scott sent £100; Lockhart suggested a subscription to buy one of Haydon's pictures; Joseph Strutt of Derby sent £100 on account for a picture to be painted later; the Duke of Bedford, Lady de Tabley and Chauncey Hare Townshend also sent money.

A public meeting was held, with Lord Francis Leveson Gower

---

[1] The picture was exhibited at the Academy. The *Morning Post* criticized it as being 'ill-grouped, ill-drawn, ill-coloured and extremely vulgar'.

in the chair, 'For the purpose of raising a subscription to restore Mr. Haydon to his family and pursuits, he having been imprisoned one month in consequence of embarrassments arising from an over-eagerness to pay off old debts, from which he was exonerated, and the want of employment for eight months.'

His debts amounted to £1,767, and his single asset was the picture of *Eucles*, which when finished might fetch five hundred guineas. It was resolved that he was entitled to public sympathy, and an account was opened with Coutts for a subscription for *Eucles*.

Release came at the end of July, and immediately he began rubbing in *The Mock Election*. He took delight in this picture, and spent many days at the prison making studies. 'Put in the gallant colonel exquisitely,' he says, 'from the remembrance of the principles of an idiot's head.' He enjoyed the contrast between this 'rag-fair' scene and the 'calm beauty' of *Eucles*. Wanting a model for the official who swears-in the members he bethought him of Hart senior, a man of peculiar ugliness, and wrote to his son, S. A. Hart the Academician, who was a friend of his, to ask if his father would sit. Solomon Hart, who was devoted to his father and very sensitive about his appearance, refused indignantly. Haydon wrote a long repentant letter and asked old Hart to come to breakfast as a proof of his forgiveness. The old man went with a heart overflowing. But no sooner had he started than the son, who knew Haydon, felt an uneasy suspicion. He argued that such a betrayal was impossible, yet his uneasiness could not be allayed, and he set out for the prison, where he discovered Haydon just finishing a wonderful likeness of his father swearing-in a dandy on a piece of burnt stick.

The picture was finished and exhibited before the end of the year, but though the exhibition did moderately the picture did not sell. He began the new year (1828) in 'apathy and indifference. No prayer, no thanksgiving, no reflection, no thought.' Frank, the eldest boy, was dangerously ill; it was then, while watching by his bed, sobbing quietly, in bitter grief, and resolving, if he died, 'to glory in letting his faculties rot over his blasted hopes', that Punch, as the subject of a picture, darted into his mind, and he composed it, quite lost to everything else, till Frank's feeble voice recalled him. 'This involuntary power it is which has always saved me,' he writes. 'To God I offer my gratitude for its possession.' In this mood of depression he began his second King's Bench picture—*Chairing the Member*—which represents a scene acted on a water-butt one evening in the prison as a 'dress rehearsal' for a grand performance next day. The Marshall, who feared a disturbance, had stopped the proceedings and, losing his head, had sent for the Guards. Haydon chose the moment of their entrance as the subject of his picture. It was while he was working at it that there came one of those strokes of good fortune which often came when things were at their worst: George IV bought his *Mock Election*.

This success Haydon probably owed to his friend Seguier.[1] The King had heard of the picture and asked that it might be sent to the palace. Seguier told Haydon the King was highly delighted, 'Come to me to-morrow,' said he. That was on Saturday; next day Haydon thought, 'Shall I go to church and pour forth my gratitude? Will it not be cant? Will it not be more in hopes of what is coming, than in gratitude of what is past? Yes. But my Creator is merciful. He knows the weakness of human nature. . . . I went. I laboured in prayer to vanquish my aspirations. I poured forth my gratitude, and felt the sweet assurance which prayer only brings.'

This was efficacious. On Monday he went to the British Gallery at half-past eleven; at twelve Seguier came, 'with a face bursting,' hurried up to Haydon, and said, 'Get a seven and sixpenny stamp.' 'My dear fellow I have only got 5s. in my pocket!' Seguier with a mischievously arch look lent him 2s. 6d. Off went Haydon for the stamp, 'Threepence more,' said the girl; back he ran, got the threepence, took the stamp, signed it, and received five hundred guineas.

Then Seguier did him another good turn: he dissuaded him from writing a letter of gratitude to the King. From this time there was no subject in the land more loyal than Haydon. The *Chairing* was exhibited with *Solomon*, *Jerusalem*, and the drawings for the two prison pictures. It was bought for £300. ('£225 less than its worth,' says he.) The net receipts from these two pictures, including the profits from the exhibition, and the sale of drawings, amounted to £1,396, a sum, as he observes, which in better circumstances, and with less expense, would have been a comfortable independence for the year.

[1] William Seguier: conservator of Royal Picture Galleries under George IV; William IV, and Queen Victoria; first keeper of National Gallery; superintendent of British Institution (b. 1771, d. 1843).

Punch was finished before the end of the following year and exhibited (March 1830) at the Western Bazaar with *Eucles*, the inevitable *Solomon* and *Jerusalem*, the unfinished picture of *Xenophon, Lady Macbeth on the Staircase, Uriel and Satan,* and *Napoleon at St. Helena.* It is interesting to know what was thought at the time of these pictures, and it may be said at once that they were greatly admired. There was a chorus of approval in the press. The *Court Journal* says of *Eucles* and *Punch*, '. . . why is it that an artist who can produce two such works as the above, each touching the highest point of merit in two opposite departments of his art, has hitherto remained an utter stranger to those honours which it is the chief object and duty of the Academy to bestow?'

The *Morning Post* calls the grouping of *Eucles* 'elegant and striking'. *The Times* is indignant, because, though on a former occasion when *Eucles* was shown in an unfinished state, it had criticized the principal figure, Haydon had not 'benefited' by this valuable advice, but had left it just as it was! 'These faults have been pointed out to Mr. Haydon,' says *The Times*, 'yet he has not thought fit to alter them.' The *Morning Chronicle* marvels exceedingly that such a painter should be excluded from the Academy. 'It would have surprised the world much less,' it says, 'and done them more honour, had they approached him cap in hand and requested him to number himself in their Association.'

Haydon's hopes were raised by receiving an order to send *Punch* to Windsor, but disappointment followed, for though his Majesty admired parts of the picture, he thought it crowded, and the chimney-sweeper like an opera dancer.

With the failure of this hope Haydon's position again became critical. He had paid off many debts from which he was legally freed, and the shadow of the King's Bench once more hung over him. To add to his troubles his wife lost her money (£50 a year) by the bankruptcy of the lawyer in, whose hands it was left by the trustees.

Then there took place one of those struggles between ambition and prudence, between the instincts of his nature and the demands of necessity. Ambition and instinct won, and he began *Xenophon* on a large scale. In such a way as this, we learn from the *Journals*, did it come about: God be praised! he had got a breathing space. His brain teemed with impressions; he saw his picture 'glowing and waving' in his mind's eye; the enthusiasm of Xenophon cheering on his men, with his helmet towering against the sky; a beautiful woman exhausted in her husband's arms hearing the shout of 'The sea, the sea!' languidly smiling and opening her lovely eyes. 'God!' he thought, 'what could I not do were I encouraged!' Such a whirl of images filled his mind as made him drunk, and confirmed, for the thousandth time, his conviction of his power: 'A wounded and sick soldier raising his pale head, and waving his thin arm and hand in answer to the cheer of his commander—horses, snorting and gallopping—soldiers cheering and huzzahing, all struggling to see the welcome sight.'

Resolutely abstracting his attention from what he was doing, he slipped on his painting-coat. No harm in just putting that large new canvas on the easel! He found he was humming a tune; he seemed to have a piece of chalk in his hand; might as well rough out the design to see how it looked! A brush and a little Vandyke brown would be quicker.

(Enter Mary on tip-toe.) 'Why do you not do it that size?' 'Shall I?' 'Yes, I know you are longing.'

Three days of hard work intervene.

Conscience speaks: 'For what purpose are you doing this? To die and leave your children starving, for that will be the end.'

Next day he went into his painting-room, and his heart swelled at the imposing look of his picture. 'An overwhelming whisper of the muse' urged him again and again to go on. This was the true Haydon, the Haydon who defied the world and painted *Solomon*, without any money 'because everyone said it was impossible'. That was eighteen years ago; he was still young and his powers greater than ever. This would be his best work. That woman now, so languid and exhausted, looking up with feeble joy—that was a grand idea, a conception of genius; but he would do better still, she should be a 'fine spirited creature, with sparkling eyes at the sound of the trumpet'. He would compete with Raphael, she should have a smooth bare shoulder and a lovely breast, and be 'such a one as would follow her lover through peril of land and water'. He would show them how to mould a knee, and her thigh should be like a pillar. The weight of the muscles below would narrow it when seen from the front, as she was in repose; when she began to get up the great muscles would tense and round the limb again. He knew it all, there was nothing he did not know. He heard the roar of the shouting, and sensed the sweat of the hurrying soldiers and the women. Hastily he set his palette; he was so happy, that all sense of time vanished and he came down that evening at nine o'clock with the old feelings of glory. He had been impelled to do this. God knows how! In Him he trusted, for ever, for ever!

'O God,' he cried, 'on my knees I humbly, humbly, humbly pray Thee to enable me to go through it. Let no difficulties obstruct me, no ill-health impede me, and let no sin displease Thee from its commencement to its conclusion. Oh save me from prison, on the confines of which I am hovering. I have no employment, no resources, a large family and no hope. In Thee alone I always trust. Oh, let me not now trust in vain. Grant O God, that the education of my children, my duties to my love and to society, may not be sacrificed in proceeding with this great work (it will be my greatest). Bless its commencement, its progression, its conclusion and its effect, for the sake of the intellectual elevation of my great and glorious country.'

The whole was nearly in, but there were money interruptions, cursed money interruptions; he looked over his picture with longing eyes. He had half an hour which he used before going to a lawyer for £10, and £6 expenses. He had £3 and wanted time. He left his dear picture, the lawyer gave him time, and away he ran with all the freshness of youth to his painting-room, and before dinner had rubbed in the whole.

'Would any man believe,' he says at this time in describing the 'leaden demon' that weighed on him while he was painting a portrait, that 'I often scrawled about with my brush, and did nothing, while studying *Xenophon* through the openings of my easel.' Before the end of October it was finished; noting this in his *Journals*, Haydon adds: 'Something extraordinary will happen with relation to *Xenophon*.' It did; it was exhibited at the Academy, and 'would any man believe', he asks later, 'that the whole body of Academicians have declared *Xenophon* a failure?'

But it was not a financial failure; it was eventually raffled, and the subscriptions amounted to £840. Here are some of the subscribers: King William IV, the Duchess of Kent, Princess Victoria, the Dukes of Bedford, Northumberland, Devonshire, Richmond, and Sutherland, the Marquesses of Lansdowne and Westminster, ten earls, six barons and Goethe. In his advertisement of the exhibition after mentioning the day of the opening, he announced that 'The Private View of the Nobility' would take place on the previous Saturday. In the descriptive catalogue he says: 'In bringing forward my work before the public, it is right the public should be told I labour under every disadvantage, for I have never had, as his late Majesty said, "Fair Play".' This he attributes to 'the personal animosity of forty men'. One newspaper complains of 'the quackery, conceit and bombast' of this catalogue.

Against the date 30 August 1830 in his *Journals*, is a note 'Out all day about my print. What a bore business is.' This refers to an engraving of a small picture of Napoleon musing at St. Helena, and little did he think that he was to live to paint some forty versions of this subject, and that it was to be a sort of widow's cruse in times of need. It began with a commission from Sir Robert Peel, who saw the print and gave Haydon an order for a large version of the subject. In Haydon's hands this led to a quarrel. Asked what his terms were for a full length, Haydon said 100 guineas, which Peel assumed to be the price for *Napoleon*. Nothing more was said at the time, but when the picture was finished and Haydon got his money, he demanded a higher price. Peel was naturally annoyed, but sent £30 more. To say that this was a grievance in the Haydon family is an understatement. Never was it forgotten. Years after he wrote from the King's Bench to Peel implying that he would not have been there but for his meanness over *Napoleon*, and that all his troubles since that time arose from the embarrassment this caused. Peel on several occasions had been very kind to him, but this 'injustice' became a legend in the family, and forty-six years later Frederic Haydon, referring to Peel's generosity to Mary—after her husband's death—pretended to regard it only as part payment of a long outstanding debt to his father for *Napoleon*, adding that Peel 'had helped to ruin him'.

Macaulay, who had a contempt for Haydon and all his works, said, not entirely without grounds, that 'whether you struck him or stroked him, starved him or fed him, he snapped at your hand in just the same way'. He added: 'He would beg you in piteous accents to buy an acre and a half of canvas he had spoiled; some good-natured Lord asks the price; Haydon demands a hundred guineas. His Lordship gives the money out of mere charity, and is rewarded by some such entry as this in Haydon's *Journals*: 'A hundred guineas for such a work! I expected that for very shame he would have made it a thousand. But he is a mean, sordid wretch.'"

Haydon himself admitted later that he had behaved with folly. The term 'full-length' usually applies to portraits, but it was entirely his own fault if he did not make himself clear. 'Such a picture as Napoleon' would legitimately be more highly priced than a portrait, as the background is not merely a setting but an important feature of the whole, and there is a great deal of it. The trouble was that it became celebrated. When Queen Victoria went to Drayton Manor in 1843 she was so delighted with *Napoleon* that she could not take her eyes off it to eat her dinner. Haydon's ideas of its value rose accordingly, and kept on rising as was their way.

Wordsworth wrote a sonnet on the picture, and Haydon again fancied himself 'the greatest of men', and indulged in 'anticipations of posthumous fame'. Need one seek further for an explanation of the demand for a higher price? 'The treatment of Peel,' he says a year or so later, '. . . to tell the truth has sunk deep into me; but it was my own fault, though he might have behaved more nobly. Only 130 guineas for such a picture as Napoleon! I expected from his fortune an ample reward.'

It is pleasant to turn from this to the cheerful *Waiting for the Times*, which he painted at this time, and which amused Princess Victoria so much when she went to see it with the Duchess of Kent that she laughed aloud. Another humorous work of the same date was a commission from Kearsey—a fulfilment of a bond and therefore a bore. The full title was—'*The first Child of a Young Couple—very Like Papa about the Nose and Mama about the Eyes*', and how humiliated must 'the painter of *Lazarus*' have felt at producing such a work! However a second version of it sold, as did one of *Waiting for the Times*, and two other small pictures: *The Sabbath evening of a Christian*, and *The First Start in Life, or Take Care, my Darling!* The critic of the *Gentleman's Magazine* says that all the men in them were like the painter himself, and all remarkable for the Dutchman-like proportions of their trousers. *The First Child* was painted in two days; 'I never painted a picture so quick in all my life,' he says. A picture painted in two days, with delight, may well be good, but of this he writes, 'It was my duty, but I could not get over a certain disgust.' So it is hardly surprising to find that Kearsey ('one of the most infernal self-willed devils (except myself) that ever lived)' Haydon writes, 'was not pleased'.

'After working with intense anxiety, to keep my engagement with Kearsey,' said the indignant painter, 'and having succeeded, to my conviction, in producing a rapid and finished sketch with character, colour, handling, and chiaroscuro, I took it down, expecting praise. When he saw it, with that air of insolence money gives city people, he said, "I suppose this was done in three-quarters of an hour?" What was that to the purpose? were there not all the requisites of Art, and all the experience of my life?' asks Haydon, and confidently replies—'There were.'

To pass from the ridiculous to the 'sublime', *Christ's Entry into Jerusalem* was sold by its owner to Messrs. Childs and Inman, of Philadelphia. This was a heavy blow to Haydon. He had spent some of the happiest years of his life upon this picture, which was full of associations. He went to see it, and 'It was melancholy', he writes, 'thus to look, for the last time, at a work which had excited so great a sensation in England and Scotland; the progress of which had been watched by all the nobility, foreign ministers and people of fashion, and on the success of which all prospect for the historical art of the country appeared to hang.'

The picture is now in St. Mary's Seminary, Norwood, Ohio.

XVIII. BIRTHS AND DEATHS

For I have eaten ashes like bread and mingled my drink with weeping.—PSALM CII
(Motto for the 15th volume of Haydon's Journals, 1 March 1828)

WHEN one reads of the considerable sums of money Haydon made it comes as a surprise to find how perpetually he was in difficulties. He assumed the right to live in a style he could not afford, and needed a fair-sized house for his growing family, with several servants to run it. He had his own servant, who seems to have remained with him till his death, while in a letter to Miss Mitford (1825) he speaks of dismissing the under-nurse for eating the children's food; how many more there were does not appear, but with Sammons, two nurses, a cook, and (almost certainly) a housemaid, there cannot have been less than five. With servants' wages at £30 a year all told, one can sympathize with the under-nurse for her lapse. Haydon could not afford so large a family, but prudence, expediency, and expostulations from Miss Mitford, were all disregarded. 'You say you cannot account for the weakness of people having more children than they can maintain'; he tells her. 'Stay my dear lady till you marry someone you passionately love, and then you will understand the secret. . . . I differ from you, though I feel diffident of saying more to a lady on such a delicate subject. . . . No, no, God bids increase; who bids abstain but our arch enemy, foe to God and man? "Increase and multiply", so said One when lovely woman was handed to her mate, and no man *with a proper religious feeling* would be so wicked as to dissolve such an order coming from such good authority. Burn Malthus, read Milton, and Shakespeare, and believe that population and prosperity go together. Adieu!'

There were in all eight children (besides the two stepsons), five of whom died in childhood. Frank, born in 1822, was the eldest; of the other survivors, Frederic, born in 1827, was the fourth child, Mary born in 1829 the fifth. The last, Newton, born in 1835, died ten months later, by which time only three were left. These five children died in five and a half years, between November 1831 and May 1836, not one of them reaching the age of nine. The cause of death in each case was the same, suffusion of the brain, according to Haydon, or, according to the *Journal of Psychological Medicine* (1853) *hydrencephalus* (probably tubercular meningitis). They were buried in Paddington New Churchyard, 'in a most retired and sweet spot,' Haydon writes, 'two trees weep over the grave. No place could be more poetic and secluded.' There is now no tree that appears to weep over the place, but a fine beech tree that must have been large even then stands near Haydon's grave (which is close to that of Mrs. Siddons) in which two of the children are buried, of the other graves there is no trace.[1] Of the stepsons Orlando entered the Church after a creditable career at Oxford (Wadham), Haydon having half-crippled himself financially to keep him there. The other, Simon, entered the Navy and showed every sign of becoming an able and resourceful officer (he dealt with a minor mutiny among some of the men when he was alone in a prompt and determined fashion) but died when he was about twenty-one from the bite of a serpent. When Haydon sent him off he pasted a set of maxims in the lid of his sea-chest, many of which laid stress on the evils of borrowing, 'Never purchase an enjoyment if it cannot be procured without borrowing from others. Never borrow money. It is degrading. I do not say never lend, but never lend if by lending you render yourself unable to pay what you owe; but under any circumstances never borrow. . . .'

Haydon's eldest son, Frank, a sensitive retiring boy, was overwhelmed by his father 'with an eager interest which broke him down', as Haydon says. One day in the park, to the amusement of the nursemaids, Haydon played with him so violently that the child nearly died from excitement, and was ill for weeks after. On leaving Cambridge Frank Haydon obtained through Peel a post in the Record Office. Of the other two who survived childhood, Mary grew to be a girl lovely both in face and figure and of a charming disposition, and Frederic, closely resembling his father, developed a strange urge to attack all the most powerful people he came in contact with. He began early to see mistakes; as a midshipman he sent to the Admiralty (through his approving father) a plan for the better armouring of the warships engaged in the Paraguayan rivers. Later, owing to loss of health from the climate he transferred to the Home Office as

[1] The churchyard was later turned into a playing-ground and many tombstones were removed and placed round the outskirts.

sub-inspector of factories. Haydon was much concerned about the moral welfare of his children, 'Wilkie is the man', said he, 'I shall ever hold up in point of caution and integrity . . . for happiness in life they must not follow my example. I am of the Napoleon species.' With a competence, Haydon would have been a prototype of the traditional Victorian father, for this romantic schoolboy was severe and imperious at home. At morning prayers he would pray pointedly against any prevalent 'vice', eyeing the offender sternly the while, which, he says, cured the vice.

Mary and Frederic had powerful lungs; their mother devoted herself to train and check them, but it was of no use, they never passed the painting-room door without shouting 'Papa!' through the keyhole, and if their father's step was heard anywhere in the house he was assailed with a chorus of 'Papas' from the nursery stairs. One night, putting on a Satyr mask, when they were at tea, he walked in, smothered in drapery, and took his seat. 'The silence that ensued was ludicrous,' he says, 'but they soon penetrated the disguise, and the dress was demolished in a moment. . . . I fear I am not just. I excite a great deal of this familiar fun, and then I complain of it afterwards, when I am not in the humour. Thus it is ever with children, who are mostly treated with injustice, and are generally fretful or happy, according to the fretful or happy humours of their nurses.' The children sometimes went without 'winter stockings' and other requisites, but horses stabled in the hall for hours at a time would make up for a good deal.

In these bad years Haydon not only suffered what he certainly felt as the agonizing loss of his children, but was in perpetual embarrassment for want of money; and the more he worried the more feverish became his applications for State support for art. He knew that nothing but public employment could solve his difficulties, so he perseveringly sent in petition after petition, and pamphlet after pamphlet to men in office, and letter after letter to the Press. The Duke of Wellington being now Prime Minister, he wrote to him. His correspondence with the Duke, begun now and renewed from time to time, is rich in the light it throws on his character, the Duke being his well-known self. Haydon sends in a long, impassioned appeal, the Duke, however busy, answers in his own hand with a polite, unirritated, instant refusal. On and on they go, Haydon showing no sign of feeling snubbed or of wavering, the Duke no sign of irritation or of yielding. The Duke's answers are curt, prompt, emphatic and final. Haydon's letters—with intervals for breath—continue undamped, lengthy, hortative, and persistent. Here was an irresistible force coming up against an immovable object. 'December 13th—I wrote to the Duke, begging his leave to dedicate a pamphlet to him, on the causes which have obstructed the advance of High Art in England for the last seventy years. Here is his answer in his own immortal hand:

'London, 12th December, 1828.
'The Duke of Wellington presents his compliments to Mr. Haydon, and has to acknowledge the receipt of his letter. The Duke has long found himself under the necessity of declining to give his formal permission that any work whatever should be dedicated to him.

'The Duke regrets much therefore that he cannot comply with Mr. Haydon's desire.'

Thus encouraged Haydon returned to the charge:

'December 21st.—Wrote the Duke and stated the leading points of a system of public encouragement. God in heaven grant I may interest him. Ah, if I do!'

The Duke replied at once that he would 'readily peruse and attend' to what Mr. Haydon has to say, 'but he is much concerned to repeat that he must decline to give permission that any work should be dedicated to him'.

On the 25th Haydon again wrote setting out the main points of his scheme. 'I concluded a strong letter', he says, 'by pointing out all the causes of the failure of historical painting. . . . I finished by saying, "Encumbered by laurel as the Duke is, there is yet a wreath that would not be the least illustrious of his crown." As this was an extract and not addressed to him I apologized for the allusion.'

'But', he adds, 'I suspect the Duke is innately modest: he was not pleased, and sent the following cold official reply, so different from his other letters:

'The Duke of Wellington presents his compliments to Mr. Haydon, and begs leave to acknowledge the receipt of his letter of the 2th instant.'

'I know his character,' Haydon remarks, 'I questioned the

policy of saying it; but still after my explanation, I trusted he would have understood the nature of my mind and my eager enthusiasm. At any rate the truth has gone into him, and though he may be angry with my obliging him to see it, he can't forget it. I have put him in possession of the ground. Time will develop all.'

In the first month of 1829 Haydon's pamphlet (undedicated), set before the public his plans for the encouragement of High Art. His warmest friends agreed that his hopes were groundless. The Catholic question was now agitating the country, and the Duke was more than usually immersed in the business of his office, yet he immediately acknowledged, with his own hand, the receipt of the pamphlet.

The greatly admiring Haydon remarks on this, 'What an extraordinary man Wellington is! The day I sent my letter his head must have been full, morning, noon and night. Parliament opens on Thursday. The Catholic question is coming on. The Spitalfields weavers came in procession with a petition. There was a Council till six. The day before he was at Windsor. In addition to all this, consider the hundreds of letters, and petitions and immediate duties, and yet he found time to answer himself my request, with as much caution and presence of mind as if lounging in his drawing-room with nothing else to do.'

On the 30th, he wrote again 'to ask with all the respect due to his illustrious character', whether if his plan for raising a sum of money to encourage historical painting were brought forward in the House of Commons it would meet with any obstacle on the part of His Grace, or whether, if His Grace should be favourably disposed towards his prostrate style of Art, he would rather that any plan of that nature should emanate entirely from himself?

The Duke replied that he could give no opinion till he had seen Mr. Haydon's practical plan for such encouragement. So Haydon sent his practical plan. It was an eager appeal for money (£4,000 every two years for six years, as a trial) for the best historical artists to decorate public buildings. One military—the Chelsea Hospital; one naval—the great room at the Admiralty; one sacred—an altar-piece; one civil—a hall of justice.

'London, Dec. 26th, 1828.

'The Duke of Wellington presents his compliments to Mr. Haydon, and has the honour of receiving his letter.

'The Duke must again beg leave to decline to give an answer until the plan shall be brought regularly before him.

'The Duke must, however, in the first instance, object to the grant of any public money for the object.'

Haydon then saw Agar Ellis, and asked him if he had any chance by laying the plan before the Duke through the secretaries:

'Not in the least,' said he, 'last year the Directors of the Gallery applied to the Government for £3,000, offering £3,000 of their own money, for a piece of ground to extend the National Gallery. Lord Wellington [sic] would not listen to it.'

Ellis asked Haydon to continue his pamphlets every year, and whenever he saw a chance he would make the necessary motion.

Haydon next sent a copy of the engraving of his *Napoleon* to the Duke, who wrote the following day, 'The Duke of Wellington presents his compliments to Mr. Haydon. The Duke begs leave to return thanks to Mr. Haydon for his letter, and for sending the Duke a print.' Stimulated by this acknowledgement, Haydon wrote once more about the encouragement of historical painting, and was told that there were no funds at the disposal of Ministers for such a purpose. Poor Haydon wrote again:

'14th.—This perpetual pauperism will in the end destroy my mind. I look round for help with a feeling of despair that is quite dreadful. At this moment I have a sick house without a shilling for the common necessaries of life. This is no exaggeration. Indulged by my landlord, indulged by the Lords of the Treasury for my taxes, my want of employment and my want of means exhaust the patience of my dearest friends, and give me a feeling as if I were branded with a curse. For God's sake, for the sake of my family, for the sake of the art I have struggled to save, permit me, my Lord Duke, to say, employ me. I will honour your patronage with all my heart and all my soul!'

But for once the prompt, curt answer did not come. Nevertheless, with sleepless persistence, he wrote once more on the old subject, and the answer came, short and final as ever.

'The Duke of Wellington presents his compliments to Mr. Haydon and has received his letter of the 14th.

'The Duke is convinced that Mr. Haydon's own good sense will point out to him the impossibility of doing what he suggests.'

Haydon wrote on the receipt of this letter, 'Impossibility from Wellington's mouth, must be impossibility indeed. He can't answer my letter. It is evident, he is worried about finance. At any rate it is a high honour to hear from him in this way. And his letters this time show more thinking on the subject than the last. At it again at a future time.'

The last remark, coming as it does in face of such a blank wall of discouragement, is significant. His disposition was naturally optimistic, but though he bore his spiritual troubles secretly for the most part he lacked dignity in the way he advertised his material ones. He was forever appealing to popular sympathy, a habit in which he persisted against the advice of his friends.

This did him infinite harm, but he believed otherwise, 'By dunning all classes about my misfortunes,' he says, 'I have got all classes to lament that my style of art is not more supported.' In this case at all events the appeal failed and on 19 May he was again imprisoned.

Amongst others were considerable demands for arrears of taxes, for recovery of which proceedings had already been begun. In his desperation he wrote to Sir Robert Peel (this was before the *Napoleon* episode), begging him to stay these proceedings. The answer came at once:

Whitehall, 29th May, 1830.

SIR

Immediately on receipt of your letter of yesterday I wrote to Mr. Dawson, transmitting the letter to him to be laid before the Lords of the Treasury, and expressing a hope that every indulgence consistent with the public interest might be shown you under the unfortunate circumstances in which you are placed.

I send you the letter I have just received, and I shall be glad if you are enabled to pursue your professional studies, and if your wife and children can be allowed to remain unmolested. I write in great haste, and

I am, Sir, your obedient servant,

ROBERT PEEL.

I beg you will send the enclosed note for ten pounds to your wife, as she may be in immediate difficulty.

Haydon comments on this letter, 'Considering that he went to Windsor and he had a long conference with the King, considering, too, the enormous quantity of public business, this hasty snatch of time to alleviate my family's sorrows is good and feeling. Is this letter a proof of Peel's frozen heart, as the Radicals call it?'

Haydon had enough to worry him for Mary was near another confinement, but Peel's letter relieved his mind, 'My miseries have been great,' he writes, 'but I feel a lightness of heart I cannot get rid of, a sort of breaking in of light on my brain, like the influence of a superior spirit.' This third arrest did not upset him so much as the first two, and he was getting used to the King's Bench, which was by this time a sort of second home. He had, on this visit, at first moved his room to a higher story to be out of the racket, but he came down again that he might be better placed for observation.

His *Journals* contain portraits of some of his friends, a sailor who drank twenty-four glasses of grog a day, and had changed from a roaring bluff fellow to a wheezing, flabby one between two of Haydon's visits; a gallant colonel with 'a child's cheeks, woman's nose, age's lips and chin, and a fool's forehead'; another man that greatly impressed Haydon, a sort of fallen angel, a man of family, and a soldier, who had served with distinction in Spain—with a head 'between Byron and Napoleon', the 'most tremendous' Haydon had ever seen. He had sat through the hullabaloo of the mock election without a smile on his pale determined face—without an emotion; his fine, athletic form sprawled across his chair, while his devoted mistress, 'a beautiful, black-eyed, refined little devil, with her black hair tumbling over her lustrous eyes', kept close to him in the shindy.

Now he was dying. Haydon went to see him and, when no one answered his knock, walked in. 'C——' lay on the bed, sound asleep, 'his grand Satanic head grander than ever; his black matted hair tumbled about his white pillow; his cheeks hollow, his mouth firm as if half dreaming, while his teeth grated a little'. Haydon, too affected to speak, folded his arms and watched 'this grand heroic fellow fast sinking to the grave, the victim of pride and passion'.

The King, moved to pity by his splendid appearance in *The Mock Election* (he sits in front on the right and holds a wineglass) had sent begging him to state his services, and his wishes, and they should be gratified. He did not answer. 'Too conscious of his fallen state, he never replied.'

Such were some of the strangely assorted characters with whom Haydon was in daily contact. That he found a pleasure in it is shown by the astonishing statement—after walking on several occasions on the racquet-ground at night with Col. L—— and Major B—— (two 'high-bred and accomplished men')—that he had 'never passed pleasanter evenings'.

But most remarkable of all the odd characters was the chief turnkey, Colwell; a man with the face of Cerberus and the heart of a sister-of-mercy. He used to feed the poor prisoners from his own table; divinity and medicine were his passions. He claimed that he knew more than most doctors and parsons; he claimed that he could always cure the cholera—that he never lost a case, and in twenty-four hours they would be better. He did it all by 'harbs'.

He gathered his plants under the planets, and it was wonderful the cures he could perform. 'Why there is Lord Wynford,' said he, 'he is bent as an old oak, and if he'd listen to me I'd make him as straight as a poplar.' 'No, Mr. Colwell!' said Haydon, 'I would though,' cried Colwell, in a loud voice finding Haydon did not laugh. His wife believed in him, and he had cured her often. 'Sir! he had out-argued Taylor, the atheist, before the people.' He could prove that Joseph of Arimathea had landed at Glastonbury! Why shouldn't he? At that time the sea came right up. And he could prove that Abraham was circumcized the very day before Sodom and Gomorrah were burnt!

The dark globular eyes of this man, one of them hideously awry, had filled Haydon with horror on his first arrival at the prison.

While Haydon was in the King's Bench another blow fell; George IV died.

When the king had bought the *Mock Election* he had done more than buy a picture; he had, though he did not know it, become almost a personal friend of the painter, an enlightened prince, a great patron of Art, the chief hope for historical painting in England; 'I have lost in him my sincere admirer,' cries Haydon. It was pitiful! here had died a monarch who had proved his taste in spite of all that 'coiled snake', the Academy, could do; 'Had not his wishes been perpetually thwarted,' declares the indignant painter, 'he would have given me ample and adequate employment.'

So enlightened a prince made vice itself appear desirable and threw a glamour over it. 'The people the King liked about him,' writes Haydon, 'had all a spice of vice in their natures. This is true. There was a relishing sort of abandonment about them which marked them as a peculiar class; . . . certainly there is an interest about vice, when joined to beauty and grace.'

This piling up of misfortunes produced the usual result, and another petition found its way to the House of Commons. Once more were set out the claims of the historical painter and of historical painting in England. The theme is the same, the arguments are similar.

On 19 July Haydon was honourably acquitted, the Chief Commissioner saying, 'There is nothing passed this day which can reflect in the slightest degree on your character!'

On his return home he found all well, though he was himself in a dull stupor, unable to work, and all abroad. However, he had many kind friends, and his spirits revived on receiving three commissions: from his physician, Dr. Darling, for his portrait; from his grocer for his; and from his landlord, Newton, to finish *Mercury and Argus* for twenty guineas.

This is the first mention of this landlord in the *Journals*; he was Haydon's best friend, a man of such extreme kindness, generosity, and gentleness under provocation, that it seems as if fate, regretting the harsh treatment she had meted out to Haydon in other ways, had sent him Newton as a compensation.

How he could have lived without him it is hard to see. He and his family always had a house, and a good one, to live in, whether he paid his rent or not. In times of great stress Newton gave him commissions for large pictures which he can hardly have wanted. And when Haydon, after all this, behaved with unreasonable irritability and ingratitude, he answered him in the gentlest way and continued his friendship unaltered.

XIX. THE REFORM BANQUET

Learn to consider yourself alone. Make yourself a god; and you deem all who dispute your pretensions little better than blasphemous. BULWER *(Bulwer, A Pan-orama,* MICHAEL SADLEIR*)*

What various ills the Painter's life assail
Pride, Envy, Want, the Patron, and the Jail.
JOHNSON (altered by Haydon)

THE year 1832 opens with a picture of peace and comfort: the family sitting round the fire after a good dinner, chatting innocently and happily. But this was only a bright interval in the generally bad weather that was to continue for another five years. Through the whole of that time there is constant reference in the *Journals* to anxiety and distress, alleviated only when some important commission supplied a little ready money. Somehow food and clothing were provided and the children were educated, but there were times when funds were so low that Haydon had to pawn his clothes to buy bread. This anxiety-motif runs through the whole of these years, though during them he had commissions for four large pictures, and at no time of his life went out more. Routs, charades, and evening parties figure frequently in the *Journals*, together with accounts of desperate efforts to quieten creditors and to raise money for the necessities of life. With a new commission the sky lightens immediately, the family perhaps goes away for a change, the entries become cheerful, and a month after one reads again of nights spent in sleepless anxiety about some bill, or of insolent tradesmen who demand their money. On such occasions he would return home 'in a state not to be described', to find the children all fighting, Mary scolding, and the butcher refusing to leave the meat till his bill was paid. Off Haydon would go to Newton to ask for a loan, sure of not being refused, and find he had gone to the play. 'Damn the play!' he would think, 'what business has he to be giggling at some stuff in the pit while I am in danger of having no money?' Returning home, 'Sir,' says the maid, 'the man won't send the wood without the money.' 'Sir,' says Sammons, 'there is no water in the cistern, and has not been all day.' Sometimes these situations had their humorous side: once when a bailiff came Haydon asked him to pose for him, and the broker arrived to find his man, an old soldier, pointing in the attitude of Cassandra (said to be a portrait of Mrs. Norton), bracelet on wrist, upright and stately, as if on guard, and Haydon painting away 'in an agony not to be described'. From this the harassed artist would go on to some party where all was security and wealth.

There are incidents that are tragic enough: when Georgy died he had to pawn some of the other children's clothes to bury her. When Mary was screaming in labour he took down all his own drawings of the children in the parlour to raise £2. Everything of value was pawned even to one of his three necessary pairs of spectacles. When his lectures began he waited till the first was over and immediately pawned his dress suit, not being able to bring himself to ask Mary for her 'little jewelries'; 'but now if I am invited to dinner,' he says, 'I am without a dress to dine in'. He sent the tea-urn off the table and got ten shillings. 'The children', he writes, 'expect something, and are nervous. The servants lag. What an instinct there is in a house.' Uselessly would he go out, and come back fatigued to death. 'What a condition mine is!' he cries, 'no prints—no books—all gone as security for loans to support my family.'

Even when he began to make a little money by his lectures he was so near the borderline that the least thing toppled him over. By an oversight an expected advance of £50 did not come, and he was at once in difficulties. He raised £5 on his prints, and found himself with only nine shillings in his pocket, so out went his anatomical studies for the wants of the week. A few days later his dress suit followed, then his greatcoat—then the cheque arrived.

This undercurrent of distress runs through the whole period up till his fifty-first birthday, but there were bright intervals when his old optimism returned and he believed himself once more on the eve of great achievements. The first of these came about through an important commission to paint the Reform Banquet in Guildhall on 11 August 1832. He obtained this indirectly through the failure of another scheme to paint the Political Union Meeting at Newhall Hill, Birmingham.

Haydon asked Lord Grey for his patronage, which was refused. 'But I should be happy', said his Lordship, 'to subscribe to any other subject connected with Reform.'

'My lord, I should be happy to paint the great leaders—the Ministry.'

'Suppose you paint the great dinner in the city, where we shall be on the eleventh.' 'I should be delighted. Of course you'll sit to me.' 'Certainly.'

The Newhall Hill picture fell through, but on the eleventh Haydon went to Guildhall early in the morning and prepared his sketch. Of that memorable day he has left a description:

'I spent the day at Guildhall, and the evening was, as Paddy would say, the most splendid day of my life.

'I breakfasted and dined with the committee, who treated me with the greatest distinction, and assigned me the place I had chosen to paint from (under Lord Chatham's monument). The confusion of the day is not to be described; but what was that to the roar of the night?

'I painted all the morning, and got in the room and window, amidst gasmen and waiters, and by night the instant the room filled I dashed away. It was a lesson in colour I shall never forget. The nobility treated me with great distinction. The Duke of Argyll sent to take wine, and so did others. I was obliged to sip, or I should have been more inspired than was requisite. It was a splendid sight—a glorious triumph, and a curious fact in my curious life that I should have been employed to paint it in the hall.'

On the 17th he called on Lord Grey with all his sketches, these were approved, and he received a commission to paint the picture for 500 guineas. Lord Grey showed the sketches to Lady Grey, saying, 'I mean this for Howick.' 'I glory in it,' said Haydon. 'You like your subject, I am sure.' 'Indeed I do.'

Haydon went for his first sitting from Lord Grey, who said, 'How long will you be?' 'Half an hour, my lord.' 'May I read?' 'If your lordship will hold your head high.' 'Where must I sit?' 'Opposite the window.' 'Ah!'

He took up his ministerial box, and came over, as if he thought it a great bore. Haydon sketched away like lightning.

Someone called and Lord Grey went out, leaving Haydon alone with the Ministerial boxes. He thought to himself, 'Now if I chose to be a villain, I might learn something.' But he went on chalking in the background. Presently Grey darted in, but finding all safe, sat down quietly.

The painting of this picture brought Haydon into that close contact with men of importance in which he revelled. There are nearly a hundred heads and for most of these he had sittings.

It was a blissful experience. 'I never, I think,' he writes soon after he had begun, 'passed a more interesting month. To be admitted, as I have been, on the most friendly terms to the secret recesses of Cabinet Ministers, left alone as I have been, with letters, dispatches, boxes, and trusted with perfect confidence, chatting with them on Art, and having the full confidence of them for an hour at a time, with no disturbance or interruption, is a very high distinction.'

The painting of this picture took a year and a half and Haydon enjoyed himself thoroughly. He pleased his sitters too; Lord Palmerston told him 'the aristocracy' considered him the pleasantest painter to sit to of any. He was not unobservant of their peculiarities, 'Lord Althorp,' he writes, 'who is a heavy man, stood up for the head that the engraver might touch it. The graceless way in which he stood was irresistible. I could paint a picture of such humour as would ruin me.' And again, 'Called on the Duke of Sussex, and saw him. It was quite a picture. There he sat in a little room, richly furnished, smoking, with a red Turkish cap, like Ali Pasha—his hands covered with rings—his voice loud, royal, and asthmatic.' The Duke came to the studio to sit. Haydon placed his sitters in three categories, 'Those noblemen' who came to him, those who obliged him to go to them, and those who did not sit at all. The Duke of Sussex exceeded all his sitters for patience and quiet. 'I never saw anything like it,' Haydon writes, 'there is literally as much difference between a royal person and a mere nobleman as between a nobleman and a mere plebeian.' Of another sitter he says, 'He had a head like a vulgar eagle—a complete specimen of a species nowhere to be seen but in an English country town. . . . There he sat as if defying the devil. I thought to myself, "Is there such another specimen on earth?" "They said to me," said the squire in the course of their conversation, "Who is Col. Grey?" "Who is he?" said I, "when you buy a cock you ask who his father is. Well, if he is of a good breed you buy him. Never mind who Col. Grey is: we know his sire." '

Of all his sitters Haydon preferred Lord Melbourne, who evidently looked upon the artist as a source of amusement not to be missed. He hardly ever seems to have denied him an interview, when he would listen with mock gravity to his passionate appeals for State patronage of art. 'Lord Melbourne', writes Haydon, 'is the most delightful sitter of any, and I am always brilliant with him. He seems equally pleased with me. I feel at my ease. He is a shrewd man and is not satisfied with random reasons. I was talking about Art and he brought me to anchor for a minute, by asking me a question that required reflection to refute, and set me thinking when he was gone. I never had a pleasanter sitter, a delightful, frank, easy, unaffected man of fashion. He has a fine head, and looked refined and handsome.'

Haydon went one evening to see Lord Grey, whom he found sitting quietly by the fire, reading his papers, and looking the essence of mildness. He seemed disposed for a chat. 'In my eagerness', says he, 'to tell him all he wanted to know I sprang up off my chair, and began to explain, bending my fist to enforce my argument. Lord Grey looked at me with a mild peacefulness of expression, as if regarding a bit of gunpowder he had admitted to disturb his thoughts. Now I should have sat and chatted quietly, for that is what he wanted—to be relieved by gentle talk. . . . I came in like a shot, talked like a Congreve-rocket and was off like an arrow, leaving Lord Grey not quite sure for five minutes if it was all a dream. How delightfully he looked by the fire. What a fine subject he would make in his official occupation.' Soon afterwards Haydon received a commission to paint a life-size picture of the Prime Minister as he saw him that evening musing by the fire.

For the heads in the large picture he made a chalk drawing, and a sketch in oil; from these he copied the head into its position in the picture, and then had sittings to finish. From Melbourne he seems to have had six sittings of about two hours each. Lord Spencer bought eighty of these chalk studies when Haydon had done with them, and hung them in a corridor at Althorp. The picture contains ninety-seven portraits, not a single one of which Lord Jeffrey recognized. 'I really begin to get sick of sitters,' Haydon writes towards the end, 'and long to be at the general effect. The work is beginning to tire me.' When it was finished it was exhibited at a loss of £230, so that the net profits for a year and a half's work were £295. It did not enhance his reputation as a painter of portraits. The picture was shown at the Great Room, No. 26 St. James's St., and, says *The Examiner*, 'We have twice visited the abomination, and on both occasions found in the room a crowd of three; but they were unanimous —screaming with laughter at the absurdity of the painting and nearly dying of the same disorder while reading the illustrative book. Proceed we now to squash this Haydon, and spread him out over his own canvas like a piece of high beef over a nasty bit of bread, and make a kind of dirt sandwich of him.' And proceed *The Examiner* does to scourge the picture and the catalogue. There was some excuse; the catalogue is an interesting document, though it should surely cause amusement rather than spleen. A group in the left-hand corner of the picture is labelled: 'Those Noblemen who were invited but did not come.' The great evening is described, and Haydon tells us how, 'The visitors drew up at the usual entrance, and passed in through a dingy passage lined with beautiful shrubs, and came out into the Hall in a blaze of gaslight. What a scene it was!' he continues, 'the crowding of the waiters, the jostling of servants . . . the splendour of colour; the magnificence of the gas.'

The Hall was fitted up with the greatest taste: at one end the word REFORM in coloured gas, at the other 'a magnificent star in gas', were the most noticeable features; while down the sides of the hall were flags, and suits of armour between stars of gas.

'About eleven o'clock at night,' Haydon continues, 'when the gas was at its meridian its splendour visibly affected everybody in the hall. There was a whispering of applause, which nearly broke out into a roar of approbation. This was the most interesting period of the night. The whole scene was a glittering enchantment—a magnificent vision: was it a crime to think of myself? Let the egotism be what it may, if I had not felt pride, and exultation, and gratitude, I must have been above the weaknesses as well as the sensibilities of mortality. I observed while Lord Grey was speaking, the great simplicity of attitude of everybody at table. There was no cant of academical composition, no separation into affected groups; no twirlings, nor twistings, nor foreshortenings; but everybody leaned at his ease, and sat by his next neighbour, as if he had no thought of being painted or looked at.'

Haydon's interest in this picture of noblemen who neither twirled nor foreshortened themselves was throughout more political then aesthetic, though a staunch Tory he was an ardent Reformer and like many others had feared revolution.

On 12 October 1831, he met a friend in a bookseller's shop in Pall Mall who undervalued the exasperation of the people, and said it would be over in a week. 'I beg his pardon,' says Haydon, 'it is a much deeper feeling than he or any other of the borough-mongers imagine . . . what I fear is, that the people have been so trifled with that mere reform will not satisfy them, that they will look beyond.' Not only did Haydon believe that immortality was conferred on him by 'painting a picture connected with Reform', but he believed that he himself had his share in bringing Reform about by three letters in *The Times*, which, however, seem in no way deserving of any special attention, being the usual sort of thing that is written by excited people exhorting others to keep calm. 'Oh! how I glory that I contributed to the great result', he cries, 'by my three letters to *The Times*. When my colours have faded, my canvas decayed, and my body mingled with the earth these glorious letters, the best things I ever wrote, will awaken the enthusiasm of my countrymen. I thank God I live in such a time, and that he gifted me with talent to serve the great cause. I did serve it. Gratitude to Him!'

In reading such accounts as this of the Reform Banquet one can hardly fail to be conscious that a change has come over Haydon since he painted *Dentatus* and *Macbeth*; not with so obsequious a delight would that young man have expressed his feelings. Rather would he have been aware of the distinction conferred on the Reformers by his painting them. There was then a certain arrogant dignity which has been exchanged for something at times not a little ridiculous.

In July 1834 Lord Grey resigned. 'Let us see what I can now do with Lord Melbourne?' said Haydon. 'God help the Minister who meddles with art,' said Melbourne.

In the siege of the Duke of Wellington Haydon had found himself confronted with a difficult quality—complete rigidity; he was now to find instead, another quality, almost more disconcerting—infinite elasticity.

The Duke had always been polite; Lord Melbourne was always amiable, chortled when Haydon called, and rubbed his hands in a spirit of mischievous resistance. These visits were frequent, 'Lord M.' would receive him in his dressing gown, and Haydon would comment afterwards in his *Journals* on his handsome bare neck. 'Lord M.' would cock an eye at him as he came in and looked round with his arch face, as much as to say, 'What the devil are you come about? Art I suppose.' Then he would listen like an exemplary child while Haydon urged and exhorted, sprang up from his chair, was told to sit down again, did so, and was up again in a moment. He would appeal to all that was best and noblest in the Prime Minister. 'Now, Lord

Melbourne, at the bottom of that love of fun you know you have a mine of common sense. You know the beautiful letter you wrote me. Do let us have a regular conversation. The art will go out.' 'Who is there to paint pictures?' 'Myself, Hilton, and Etty.' 'Etty! why he paints old ——' 'Now my dear lord, do be serious about it.' 'I will,' Lord M. would reply, looking archly grave. 'Do you admit the necessity of State support?' 'I do not, there is private patronage enough to do all that is requisite.' 'That I deny.' 'Ha, ha!' (rubbing his hands). Then Lord Melbourne would stroll to the dressing table and begin combing his hair.

A long harangue would follow on art in ancient Greece and Rome, drifting into an appeal to his lordship's vanity, 'Burke said it would ultimately rest on a Minister. Have you no ambition to be that man? For God's sake, Lord Melbourne, do not let this slip; for the sake of Art—for your own sake—only say you won't forget Art.' No reply. 'The fact is you are corrupted, you know you are, since I first talked to you. Callcott after dinner at Lord Holland's has corrupted you, sneered you out of your right feelings over your wine.' At which Lord Melbourne would laugh hearily and admit there was a great deal of truth in it.

At last fate took a hand: the old Houses of Parliament were burnt (16 October 1834) and most of the tapestries so hated and despised by Haydon, which had concealed the coveted walls, went up with the rest. Now, he thought, they would have to do what he wanted; a new building would be built and would call for decoration. He redoubled his efforts and his eloquence; he had made the most of his opportunities during his sittings from the Reform leaders, and was soon to use the lecture platform as a more effective means still. This came about by a sort of accident. A committee had been appointed (1835) under the chairmanship of William Ewart—'to inquire into the best means of extending a knowledge of the arts and principles of design among the people (especially among the manufacturing population) of the country; also to inquire into the constitution of the Royal Academy, and the effects produced by it.' This appointment, for which Haydon may be considered largely responsible, roused hopes in him which were to be disappointed, as the terms of reference did not include pictorial design, but manufactured articles only. To assist in the inquiry he wrote to the papers, and decided to give lectures at the Mechanics' Institute, under the auspices of Dr. Birkbeck. Though the inquiry into the encouragement of art took no account of historical painting, that into the constitution of the Academy gave Haydon a chance of getting his own back. The members of Ewart's Committee seem to have started with a determined bias against the Academy, listening with sympathy to the bitter criticisms of Haydon and Martin, and catching up Sir Martin Archer Shee, P.R.A., whenever he became heated in his answers. On some occasions indeed, when Shee expressed himself in strong terms on the tactics of the anti-academic intrigue, the Committee instructed the shorthand writer not to take down the words. Shee was an able advocate, and gave as good as he got, but the Committee, according to his son, showed him 'studied and insolent discourtesy' throughout, while it treated the plaintiffs with favour. The account of the proceedings seems to justify this accusation. Leading questions were put, for instance, Haydon was asked, 'Do you think that it (the R.A.) is a system which involves undue patronage on the part of some, and induces self-abasement and dependence on the part of others?' The examination was under several heads: The House of Commons demanded a return of the amount of money raised on the exhibitions. (The R.A. denied its responsibility to the House claiming that it held direct from the King)—the Committee asked to know why only R.A.s and A.R.A.s had the privilege of entering the gallery on varnishing-days. There was inquiry into the value of the Academy Schools.

There were two petitions against the Academy. One was Haydon's, the other a petition of the London Artists with seven signatures. There were two petitions for the Academy—one was signed by 470 artists, not Academicians, and the other by 120 students of the Academy Schools. There are said to have been about 800 artists living in London at that time. The Academy gained its point about the returns of its profits from the exhibitions; the Academy Schools were generally approved of, even by Haydon (up to that time nearly 20,000 students had been educated free, at a cost of £300,000 to the R.A.), and lack of room was the alleged reason for the exclusiveness of the Academicians on varnishing-days (the chief grievance of the plaintiffs). Haydon's evidence is interesting. He calls the Academy a House of Lords without appeal. He exhibits the complete unreasonableness of a man suffering from persecution mania, the old grievance of *Dentatus* is brought up again, and all the misfortunes of his life are attributed to its having been hung 'in the dark', which injustice, he says, had been, and was intended to be, his destruction.

Ewart: 'Have you suffered in your reputations and emoluments by the injustice of the Academy?'

Haydon: 'I was ruined entirely by their injustice. . . . I have never been able to add a single principle of the construction of the form of man as a species, since that period when I was 22 years old, because I got them from the Elgin Marbles. . . . I thought, and the public think, I was deserving to be elected, in consequence of the certainty of the principles on which *Dentatus* was painted. . . . I think the moral character of English artists is dreadfully affected: twenty years ago they were in such a state of abject degradation that to mention an objection against the Academy would have ruined immediately any artist, as it ruined me. For though the artists all agreed with me in my assaults, they were so frightened, they set upon me to prove they had no connection. Wilkie was so frightened, he refused to be seen with me in the streets. They were the most abject slaves in Europe at that time.'

Throughout life *Dentatus* was Haydon's King Charles's head; so now, in this inquiry, he could not leave it alone:

'I will show the Committee the consequences,' he says. 'My employer, Lord Mulgrave, began by believing I had no talent: yet while I was painting the latter part of that picture, my room was crowded with people of fashion five or six deep. Directly the Academy put it in the dark, I never saw a patron or a person of fashion, rank or fortune for a year and a half near my room, and I am perfectly convinced that these Academicians knew the effect of putting a picture of that class in such a situation on my particular friends, who were all people of the highest rank, would be destruction to me; as it was. . . . The consequences were so dreadful that I lost all employment, and a handsome commission (Macbeth) was taken from me, and I never had another commission for sixteen years. That is one of the consequences of the present system, and I myself have been the victim. . . . Afterwards I put my name down for an Associate in 1820; I had not a single vote. I sent the same picture to the British Gallery the year after, and it beat one of the Committee in contesting for the premium, and won the great prize. The Academy refused me admission in 1810 and in 1812; I attacked it, so that the Committee will see that I did not begin, as is generally supposed, by a turbulent and violent attack on the authorities in art. I then tried to found a school, and produced Eastlake, Harvey,

Lance, Chatfield; but the Academy opposed me, and destroyed my school with calumny.'

He had written (1829), 'I only beg here to repeat . . . that there was an attempt to crush me before I had given cause of offence, that for twenty-one years there has not been an affection they have not lacerated—an ambition they have not thwarted—a hope they have not blasted—a calumny they have not propagated—a friendship they have not chilled, or a disposition to employ me they have not tampered with.'

This was the grievance that poisoned Haydon's life. He speaks on one occasion of having had a week of lovely summer weather 'murdered' by his hatred of the Academy. As for its justification there are probably few artists alive or dead who have not at some time or other felt indignation at the hanging of some favourite work; and it is absurd to suppose that the placing of one picture in a not very good position could wreck a man's chances in life. The statement that *Macbeth* (which was commissioned after the *Dentatus* episode) was taken from him owing to the way *Dentatus* was hung, is an instance of how incapable he was of retaining any contact with facts or reality when a grievance or the demands of his vanity were concerned.

As has been said one reason for the appointment of Ewart's Committee was to inquire into 'the best means of extending a knowledge of the arts . . . among the people'; it was to assist in this that Haydon began to lecture, and it was fortunate for him that he did, because lecturing soon became his one reliable source of income. He was a first-rate lecturer, and learnt to be completely at his ease before any audience however large; but on the first occasion at the Mechanics Institute he was nervous, 'All his distresses, humiliation, and ruin crowded into his mind as he came on to the platform,' says Frederic. 'There was a dead silence and he stood stock still, looking at the mass of heads before him. He did not notice it, but taking off his spectacles, wiped them carefully for some time, then held them up to the light to see if they were clear. This was finesse to enable him to recover his self-possession. Then he opened his book and began his lecture. In ten minutes he had got the ear of his audience.'

He received intense and keen attention. He was an object of great interest, everyone there knew of his triumphs and his ruins, most of them had seen his huge pictures, they had read his letters and pamphlets, had heard of his quarrels with the Academy and the connoisseurs, and had been told the items of his private expenditure, and of the births and deaths of his children.

His first lecture was received with enthusiasm, and within a few months he was overwhelmed with offers of engagements all over the country.

'He had an inimitable way', says his son, 'of leaning over his reading desk, and taking his audience into his confidence; he would throw out good stories, fresh from life, and then suddenly by a gesture impose a silence that would at times be almost painful as he appealed to their nobler qualities, condemning their defects, denouncing their worship of wealth, their idolatry of greed and gain, and telling them that they so sunk their nobler feelings in their struggle for gold, that intellect, character, and service in England were as nothing in comparison with wealth; and yet when they had got it, they had no knowledge how to apply it to nobler purposes than to try to make more. Then he . . . would entreat them to try to rise above this and to combine their thirst for wealth and power with a love of the Fine Arts, and to give encouragement and support to them in proportion to their means. His pride in old England, his passionate love of what was lofty and true, his contempt for everything low and mean, his ardent appeals to the higher self that is within all of us, and his intense belief in the power of self-improvement affected his hearers deeply, and there can be no doubt did incalculable good in our manufacturing towns. The temper of such a man harmonized with the temper of such a people in its energy and sublime self-confidence, as in its earnestness and patriotism, and he never flattered their prejudices. He appealed to their innate love of fair play, and from the mouth of so earnest and sincere a man this had a double effect.

'His manner was natural, his voice clear and musical, his delivery rapid and impassioned, and the evident sincerity with which he drove home what he called "the naked truth", completely carried his audience with him.'

The *Athenaeum* says, 'His style is careless and altogether impromptu, but it is spirit-stirring.'

Sometimes in the north of England the whole room would spring to its feet and cheer him to the echo. So great was the confidence he inspired that even in those days of rigid puritanism in the northern towns he was able to bring naked models on to the platform to demonstrate the anatomical beauty of their forms. He boldly began at his second lecture at the Mechanics'

Institute. 'I told them', he says, 'that if they did not get rid of every feeling of indelicacy in seeing the naked form and did not relish its abstract beauty taste for grand art would never be rooted amongst them. This was received with applause, and I broke the ice for ever.' Nowadays the claims of the body to serious attention, and its right to be admired are pretty universally recognized, but the storms of outraged protest which one would have expected then, especially in the north, do not seem ever to have arisen, and this can only be attributed to Haydon's personality, for nothing else could account for it. On one occasion when he had on the platform two wrestlers—'stripped above and below', as he puts it—part of his audience burst out laughing at a chance position, but he turned on them and damned them for fools, telling them to respect the loveliness of the works of God. Fully to appreciate the revolutionary character of his achievement (aided certainly by an advance in broadmindedness), the criticisms made at the end of the previous century against the Academy may be remembered. The visitors to the exhibitions at Somerset House had to pass through the antique-room where were casts of the Apollo Belvedere, the standing Discobolus and the Fighting Gladiator. Outraged propriety suddenly burst forth in a storm of protest against these abominations—'the terror of every decent woman'. So shocking were they it was said that 'many women rather than pass them by had sacrificed the pleasure of seeing the best exhibition'.

Again, Bewick's account of Darlington at about this time will give an idea of what Haydon had to contend with in the provinces. Bewick says that the love of making and accumulating money was the ruling passion, the man who was known to be making money was not only spoken of under the breath, with veneration, but as if he were more nearly approaching creative power than any other human being. The works of Shakespeare were banished from the Public Library, and the novels of Scott subsequently shared the same fate. Poetry was described as a false jingle of words, music a great waste of valuable time. 'To live there was to live in the very temple of Mammon, the worship of the beautiful and the good found no place there.'

Into such places Haydon brought the first rays of delight in beauty, the first intimation that such a thing was not a snare of the evil one, but a means of elevating the whole mind.

His success was unprecedented; he knew his subject inside out, and had a power of rapid drawing on the blackboard to illustrate his points which astonished and delighted his audience. Wherever he went he left a deep impression, so that in one town after another schools of art were opened, and people began to be aware that art was not a mere amusement of the rich, but a thing of national importance.

With regard to the subject matter of his lectures he laid great stress on the study of the mechanism of the body; advocating anatomical dissection. He disagreed with Reynolds, that, 'It is better to diversify in particulars from the broad general ideas of things, than vainly attempt to ascend from particulars to the great general ideas.' Haydon held the opposite view, and his opinion was more nearly in agreement with Blake's, 'To generalize is to be an idiot, to particularize is the great distinction of merit.'

No one troubles to read Haydon's lectures now, but there are in them some theories that it would be a pity to lose. For instance he discovered another 'deep principle' relating to no less a thing than the norm of beauty itself in all its varied manifestations. The *Lecture on Beauty* is headed with Burns's lines:

> Auld Nature swears the lovely dears
> Her noblest works she classes, O:
> Her 'prentice han' she tried on man,
> And then she made the lasses, O.

In it he says (quoting Lord Jeffrey):

' "The form of a tree is beautiful, and the form of a fine woman and a column—and a vase; but how can it be said the form of a woman has anything in common with the form of a tree?" "Simply, I reply," answers Haydon, "because the vase, the column, and the tree, can be proved to deserve the appellation of beautiful only as they each partake more or less of the form of a woman. Have you any sensation of beauty from the form of the knarled oak, with its knotty irregularities, and its patriarchal age? But have you not with the waving willow, and trembling ash? Surely you have! Because the willow and the ash do, and the knarled oak does not, partake of the form of the lovely creature, the basis of all beauty on earth." He concludes: "Nothing is beautiful, physically or intellectually, in thought or form, but what has a feminine tendency, and can be traced to the perfection in form and sympathies to woman. If my theory be the true one . . . there is nothing in the world beautiful, but the perfect face and figure of woman." [1]

This basic principle being discovered he was able to arrive at another law:

'Let your colour be exquisite,' he says, 'let your light and shadow be perfect, let your expression be touching, let your forms be heroic, let your lines be the very thing, and your subject be full of action—you will not have the sympathy of the world, you will interest little the hearts of mankind, if you do not lay it down as an irrefutable law, that no composition can be complete, or ever will be interesting or deserve to be praised, that has not a beautiful woman, except as a series. This was the secret of Raphael's and Correggio's magic over our hearts; and be assured it is the truest, deepest, most delightful principle, and one in which I defy refutation, for it applies to our convictions at once, that a picture without a beautiful woman is and must be in opposition to all the sympathies of mankind, especially in an art the object of which is to instruct by beauty.

'Another cunning and touching secret of Raphael's and Correggio's power over us, was that in every face of a beautiful woman they painted, they gave a tender air of sympathy and love. So that in most of Correggio's and Raphael's women, if you clear all the figures away but the women, you may without the least alteration of look whatever, put a lover declaring his passion on his knee, and you will find the expression of the woman's face do exactly.'

As an instance to prove the misapplication of the term 'beautiful' to such things as can have no relation to the form of woman he quotes a certain Colonel Wheeler, who, in describing the taking of a fort in Afghanistan, remarks, '. . . and carried the fort in beautiful style, bayonetting all within'.

This lecture on beauty, the last of its series, was delivered with great applause. And so popular had he become that when Mary and Frank came into the hall they were loudly clapped.

From this beginning his popularity grew till he was eagerly sought by most of the important provincial towns. He was received with warmth in the north, where he found virgin soil. It gratified him to discover that the wealthy manufacturers in Liverpool, Hull and Manchester thought for themselves, and were unimpressed by what London might think. He lectured in

---

[1] Smoothness as well as smallness, it will be remembered, had been Burke's requisite for beauty; while the *Observer* (30 March 1823) notes that 'Size in women destroys sentiment . . . a painter of human nature should attend to this.'

Edinburgh, where he was given a public dinner; brought out a naked model, was applauded; attacked the Academy, and was applauded. He was too fond of attacking the Academy in his lectures, it was a temptation he could not resist, and it sometimes gave offence. He lectured in Manchester, where he agitated for a school of design, which was founded the next year. Manchester was the first provincial town to adopt Haydon's advice, and its example was followed by other towns in Lancashire and Yorkshire. Cobden told Frederic Haydon that the schools of design in their foundation owed everything to his father, 'Without him', he said, 'we would have had no schools of design for another twenty years. He worked hard to get them established throughout the great manufacturing towns. I have no hesitation in saying that if he had his deserts he would have a statue of gold raised to him in every manufacturing town in this country for the good he did us. He sowed, others reaped.'

Haydon was an energetic sightseer, and spent his spare time on these tours in visiting everything of interest. He was impressed by Fairbairn's 'vast engine works. Boilers for 400 horse-power engines; iron melting by fire that would have astonished the devils, roaring like thunder, dark with brightness, red with heat and liquid like lava.' He was delighted with the 'superb rapidity of steam' that took him from London to Manchester in little more than ten hours. His thirst for information enabled him to spend with pleasure a morning with Miss Bankes of Leeds, looking over her collection of shells 'according to La Marque, in which' he says, 'I gained immense knowledge, as I went through every species from the earliest formation to the last. The people here think her cracked.'

By impressing his audiences and making friends Haydon obtained some important commissions on these tours. The first was for a large picture of *Christ Blessing Little Children*, for the church of the Hospital of the Blind in Liverpool. This with the fees for his lectures gave him a year fairly free from anxiety; but the crowning triumph was an invitation to lecture at Oxford. 'To lecture at Oxford', he told Wordsworth, 'has been one of the day-dreams of my earliest youth.' He was delighted with the town and with the people he met there. 'Thank God,' he says, 'at last I have made my way to a society where I am happy.' He had no payment but was treated with distinction by the University, being received by the Vice-Chancellor, Ashurst

Turner Gilbert, and Dr. Shuttleworth, Warden of New College. Oxford immensely affected his imagination, 'Such silence, and solitude, and poetry; such unquestionable antiquity, such learning, and means of acquiring it.' He lectured six times in the Ashmolean to increasingly large audiences, the Vice-Chancellor being present on one occasion, while by the last the attendance had quadrupled.

Haydon returned to London like a conquering hero, expecting applause and congratulations—to find Mary out! She had not expected him before dinner. Piqued, he changed and walked into town; when he returned she was home, and hurt that he did not wait. There followed 'mutual allusions, which were anything but loving or happy'.

By means of his writings and, still more, of his lectures, Haydon became accepted as an authority on matters of art, and wrote the article on 'Painting' in the seventh edition of the *Encyclopaedia Britannica*. It is long and shows considerable historical knowledge. Like most of Haydon's writings on art it is a curious mixture of sense and absurdity. It purports to be a short review of painting from its earliest beginnings, but there is no attempt to show the characteristics of the various schools. In his eyes there was one norm by which to judge everything— Greek painting, and, failing that, Italian painting as exemplified by Raphael. Haydon was a remarkably intelligent man, with an enthusiasm for ancient art and a knowledge above that of most connoisseurs of the time. Hazlitt, the Ruskin or Roger Fry of the period, wrote the article on 'The Fine Arts' in the same edition, and his contribution cuts less ice and is more merely rhetorical than Haydon's. But Haydon shows here, as in his lectures, the same limitation of appreciation and the same curious disposition to judge the value of a work of art by the beauty of the women represented. It would be interesting to get inside the mind of a connoisseur of that time, for it is puzzling to us when we attempt to do so to find that Haydon, for instance, considered the art of the Chinese from the earliest ages and ever since 'miserable and wretched'. We are surprised that he thought the Indians (with their wonderful appreciation of the sensual and rhythmic beauty of the body) utterly ignorant of the naked form. Egyptian art pleased him better, and for a very good reason. 'The Egyptian female heads', he writes, 'are far from displeasing, they have a sleepy voluptuous eye, a full pleasant mouth, high cheekbones, and there is something by no means displeasing in the silent lazy look of their expressions.'

Few things in the history of criticism are more remarkable than the enthusiasm of the eighteenth and early nineteenth centuries for the work of the great Greek painters—not a single example of which had they ever seen. Apelles was a name to conjure with and he was considered far to surpass Raphael. Haydon was no exception, he quotes with approval Poussin's dictum that as Raphael was 'an angel compared with other modern painters, he was a miserable beggar compared with the Greeks'. Haydon personally considered Polygnotus better than Apelles. What he judged by it is difficult to know, but he thought his conception of the demon Eurynome, whom he painted with a skin coloured like a blue-bottle, so terrific as to be above Apelles's mark, both in idea and observation. Then again according to Haydon's standard Polygnotus was more of an innovator, one who opened up fresh horizons, because 'he first clothed lovely women in light and flowing draperies, adorned their beautiful heads with rich turbans and thus advanced the art immensely'.

Mankind has always loved stories in which some great artist has done wonders with a single line, though just how one line could be so very wonderful it is hard to understand, it is by combinations of lines that great artists show their powers. Giotto's circle, which an engineer might have drawn as well, is a case in point. So Haydon tells a story of how Apelles called upon Protogenes, and, finding him out, drew a contour line of part of the body on a wax tablet which he found prepared in the studio. When Protogenes returned he at once recognized the line as the work of Apelles, was overwhelmed with admiration but immediately drew a better line of the same part of the body alongside it. Apelles called again, and found Protogenes still away from home. He was even more overwhelmed by Protogenes's line than Protogenes had been by his, but at once drew a far better line still beside that of Protogenes. Then at last they met, Protogenes generously admitting himself vanquished. These three lines became famous throughout Greece; their fame spread through the world; Michael Angelo discussed them and surmised that they might have represented the front of the torso from the pit of the neck to the bottom of the stomach. Even this did not end it, in the *Encyclopaedia Britannica* (1842) may be found the last word: Haydon has undertaken to show us what these lines might have been like, and has drawn three lines representing the above-mentioned part, each easily surpassing the last.

As a review of the contribution of the Greeks to the pictorial art of the world Haydon gives a list of the most celebrated painters, with a short account of what he imagined each did. It is the same with his account of Italian painting. Giotto, one is glad to find, receives high praise, but Haydon holds himself well in hand till he arrives at Raphael, to whom he gives the palm, adding, rather surprisingly, that he died of overwork and dissipation. 'Taking into consideration', he writes, 'all the great men in modern art, this young man . . . must be placed on the throne, till one arises who shall have what he had not, in addition to his own perfections; and that young man will probably arise in Britain.'

Turning to Flemish and Dutch art, his admiration of Rubens is a little damped by his 'miserable, pallid women', whose luxuriant charms one would have expected him to like; while as for Rembrandt! 'his bistre drawings', writes Haydon 'are exquisite, his etchings unrivalled; his colour, light and shadow and surface, solemn, deep, and without example; but in the naked form, male or female, he was an Esquimaux. His notions of the delicate form of women would have frightened an Arctic bear.'

XX. TASTE

All our affirmations are mere matters of chronology; and even our bad taste is nothing more than the bad taste of the age we live in.

LOGAN PEARSALL SMITH

HIS vogue as a lecturer once established Haydon got along fairly well for a time, but before that happened there was to be one more imprisonment—the last. All through the year 1835 he struggled with debt, painted small pictures for money, went to dinners, routs and charades, wrote begging letters, endured agonies of despair, went to the city in states of misery not to be described, trusted in God, felt inspired over his painting, got more and more careless, persuaded himself he was improving, and arrived at the end of the year somehow, still strong in health and determined to carry his object. 'Mary in an agony of mind,' he writes. 'All my Italian books, and some of my best historical designs, are gone to a pawnbroker's. She packed up her best gown and the children's, and I drove away with what cost me £40 and got £4. The state of degradation, humiliation and pain of mind in which I sat in the dingy hell of a backroom is not to be described. The Duke of Bedford sat in the morning. I was in the House of Lords last night, the companion of princes; to-day in a pawnbroker's parlour.'

Mary bore it like a heroine; 'I shall carry my great object', he says, 'and, glorious creature, she will suffer anything rather than that I should fail.' Again, as so often before, he pawned everything, even to one of his three necessary pairs of spectacles. He spent nights of misery when he was too worried to sleep, and it was after such a night that he laid his case before Newton, who went about with him to quieten creditors, saying, 'I hope I shall get you through.' 'An instance', writes Haydon, 'of this man's innate goodness of heart.' On one occasion he was so utterly weary that he left Newton to attend to it, and came home and painted. 'But I despair not,' he cries. 'A star is always shining in my brain, which has ever led me on and ever will.' On the last day of this harrowing year he records in his *Journals* his gratitude to God for raising him up such a friend as his 'dear landlord', who had helped him when the nobility forsook him. By the end of the next year he was grandly talking of leaving this landlord on account of a purely imaginary insult. He was now fifty, and this was to be the last bad year for some time, though it was one of the worst. The blow fell on 6 September 1836 while he was at breakfast.

'I remember the morning well,' writes Frederic, who was nine at the time, 'the timid ring, the affected unconcern; the balancing of his spoon on the edge of his cup; the whisper in the hall; and the servant coming in with, "If you please, sir, Mr. 'Smith' wishes to see you." I shall not forget the expression of pain that passed over his face as he rose and left the room, not venturing to look any of his children in the face. "Tell your mother I have gone out," he said, sadly; that was all. In a few minutes we saw him driven away in a hackney coach, accompanied by two men, one sitting on the box!'

Newton offered to buy him off, but he refused, and prepared for the Court directly. 'Rather than go out to endure the horror this Journal gives evidence of,' he writes, 'I'd stay here for ever.' His landlord 'took possession and moved away his brushes and the grinding-stone for his paints. Took the things at £133 10s., paid the difference and took the rest for his rent.' This financial transaction is obscure to me, but at all events Newton was be- having as thoughtfully as he always did, and apparently buying up Haydon's property at the sale to let him have it back when he came out of prison, which he did on 17 November. What took place after that is again not clear, but there seems to have been some delay in the return of the studio furnishings; so Haydon writes:

London, 21st December 1836.

MY DEAR NEWTON,
   Mary came home last night with the usual quantity of gossip and scandal, of which you possess so abundant a fund. It seems it is . . . who has told you that falsehood of my having given six lectures at the Milton and received 20 guineas, whereas I only gave three lectures and received 10 guineas, £10 of which I brought you next day, ex- plaining I had only received half, though given to understand it would be all—which £10 I borrowed of you again, £5 at a time.
   And this is the way to excuse your own abominable cruelty in doing your best to add to the weight of degradation and misery I have suffered by insinuating to my wife these abominable lies. I am ashamed to use so gross a word, but your forgetfulness, your confusion of mem-

ory, your jumbling one thing with another, your making me write notes when harassed with want, which I forget to reclaim, and then your bringing them forward again when it suits your convenience, provoke me to it.

Don't talk to me of your affection. Pooh! To let a friend come out of prison after ten weeks locking up—degraded in character—calumniated and tortured in mind—to let him come to what had hitherto been the solace of his distresses [his painting-room] stripped of all that rendered it delightful, and stripped, too, under the smiling pretences of friendship, and under the most solemn assurances that everything would be returned, and then, on the very morning that I came home, when one would have thought all beastly feelings of interest would have been buried in the pleasure of welcoming me back, at such a moment to break your word, and to add to my forlorn wretchedness, by refusing to keep it, is a disgrace to your heart and understanding, and will be even after you are dead, as well as while you are living. Had I known the extent of what you had been guilty of, I should have scorned to receive the balance of Sampson. It was only when I came home I saw what you had done.

However, Mrs. Haydon says if I will only say you shall not be a loser, the pictures and sketches shall come back directly. I told you so in prison, and I still tell you so now. You know that: but your delight is the delight of the tiger over his prey, not to kill at once, but to play with your victim. I tell you again you shall not be a loser. Now keep your word with Mrs. Haydon and send back the things. I did not intend to say a word more, but as this proposition to Mrs. Haydon is not unreasonable, to oblige her I say you shall not be a loser.

Put this among your collection and bind them up. Now you have made a step, and I have made a step. I'll be frank; a threat is always the last refuge of a coward. I do not threaten—but if the things (pictures and sketches) are not in my painting-room by Friday night (I allude only to those you took away with the last books you returned), without any asperity or any ungrateful impertinence, or any wish to wound a kind-hearted (at bottom) old friend, but solely still to retain our affection, on Saturday I shall be guilty of the violence to my own heart of giving notice to quit, according to the terms of our lease, at Midsummer next, but as soon as possible before.

I am dear Newton,

Yours truly and affectionately,

B. R. HAYDON.

That Newton (though he made a show of sending a notice on his part) did not jump at that suggestion of a notice to quit, is proof enough of his innate goodness of heart, considering that his tenant not only never paid his rent, but was perpetually borrowing money from him and seemed to assume that a mere assurance that he would not be a loser was identical with repayment. 'Sampson' is presumably a slip for Samson, and if so refers to Haydon's picture of that subject: one of the many pictures by the artist which Newton bought out of charity, and which must have considerably disfigured his house.

Newton wrote two notes in answer—'not with ink,' says Tom Taylor, 'but with the very milk of human kindness. Was ever reminder more gently conveyed, passion more effectually disarmed, or undeserved reproach more completely turned back upon the reproacher, than by these short replies?'

DEAR HAYDON,

I shall send the pictures and sketches to you to-day, if possible.

Mrs. Haydon spoke of the sketch of the Widow's Son as though it had been received with the last things brought away. I referred to your note that came with it, and others, to assure Mrs. Haydon how it came into my possession, and the only convenience your note can be of to me is to bring them forward to rectify any misunderstanding. This, and your promissory notes (stamped and unstamped) being unpleasant truths, I suppose you call scandal: of them I have an abundant fund.

I will write you about the lease.

Yours truly,

W. F. NEWTON.

22nd December, 1836.

DEAR HAYDON,

The old-fashion compliments of the season. A merry Christmas and a happy new year and many of them is my sincere wish to you and and yours, and I hope you are as free from ill-will to anyone as I am.

I have yet to learn what act of mine is considered an insult to yourself, but as I am certain I am incapable of offering one, I give myself little trouble about it.

Thanks for your good wishes, and the ticket for the lectures, of which I have omitted to acknowledge the receipt.

Yours truly,

W. F. NEWTON.

Not the least strange part of this affair is that Haydon should have kept Newton's letters and pinned them into his *Journals* together with a copy of his own. The magnanimity of this landlord was scarcely human. This is illustrated by the story of Lord Audley's commission: on 24 February of this same year 1836, Haydon writes:

'I dined with Lord Audley last night. He gave me two hand-some commissions.' (To which Taylor appends a footnote, 'Lord Audley was undoubtedly at this time insane.') One of these was for a picture of the Black Prince after the Battle of Poictiers, and with Taylor's warning we are not surprised to learn later that the thing fell through, so that the work was left on Haydon's hands. The end of the episode appears six years afterwards in another entry, '. . . my dear old landlord Newton took the Poictiers, and struck off £525 of debt, reducing my balance, so now I hope to get clear, and give him equivalents, so that in case of death he might not be a loser'.

At all events, to return to 1836, Haydon managed to forgive Newton's insults, withdrew his threat to leave, and remained in his house more or less rent free, dying there nine years later, £1,200 in his debt. One more entry, in 1840, does something to palliate Haydon's unattractive behaviour in this matter, 'Went to church with my dear old landlord, Newton. When we were in, I was affected at all the disputes, kindnesses and fights we had had. He has been to me and my family an everlasting friend, a pivot to work on, an anchor to trust to, such as I believe no other human being ever had before.'

Haydon's attitude to his friends is worth studying. Let us watch him soothing Wilkie who was incensed at a remark in his evidence before Ewart's Committee (that Wilkie had been frightened at being seen in the streets with him after his attack on the Academy). 'I explained to him', says Haydon, 'that I mentioned the fact to illustrate the condition of abjectness to which English art had been reduced by such a man as he being terrified by my attack.'

Since 1823 Haydon had been seven times arrested, four times imprisoned and ruined, and had lost five children. What about his 'Art', and the education of the taste of the English people he had undertaken at such a sacrifice? That taste, unfortunately, was moving in a direction away from the lines he had laid down for it. He had believed he was the apostle and prophet of a new era in art; instead, he was the rearguard at the end of a dying one. It was his boast that he had at the age of twenty-two painted a figure (*Dentatus*) on theories so immutable that he had never since been able to add a single principle. It was this imperviousness to new ideas that helped in his undoing. In every way the world in which he lived was changing rapidly; he was of the eighteenth century, and while the discoveries of science impressed him his mind remained closed to their reactions on thought. Intellectually he cared only for the past. In George IV's reign a new London was coming into existence: Nash had introduced stucco and white paint in place of the sombre brick of the eighteenth century. Street lamps and the new gin-palaces flared with gas. The new railways which were transforming England carried Haydon on his lecturing tours from town to town like magic; and it was on these tours that he met the men who were to provide the new type of art-patron. With the death of Sir George Beaumont in 1827 there passed away one of the last of the old type. Yet he, with the Duke of Bedford (who sold his old masters and bought only modern paintings when he found the two did not go well together) and Lord Egremont, had been conspicuous among the old aristocratic sort of patron for his encouragement of living artists. But with the large fortunes made in business, especially in the north, a new type of buyer came into existence: men with big empty houses to furnish, who wanted something more cheerful than the dark masters, and liked pictures they could understand. Very large pictures went quite out of any fashion they had ever had. The great noblemen used to cover their walls from floor to ceiling, and did not mind a few big pictures to break the monotony, but they took years to do it, and the manufacturer with a new house preferred to have fewer pictures and liked them small. As a concomitant of smallness high finish became more desired than ever. High finish led to an insistence on minute detail; and it was not long before everything Haydon stood for was out of fashion, and everything he despised and hated was in. The connoisseurs of the eighteenth century had discussed sublimity, breadth, chiaroscuro, impasto, elevation; the prospective purchaser of the nineteenth took his magnifying glass and peered into the detail and surface finish of a picture. Haydon objected to the new method of judging a picture 'by the forefinger'; he distinguished between the 'touchers' and the 'polishers'. 'The principle', he wrote, 'which ought to guide all critics in judging of the execution of works is easily explained: if at the exact point where you can best see the whole picture, and the whole of every figure from top to toe; the expression, the form, the colour, the light and shadow appear finished—the end is answered.' But the new kind of patron did not care to look at pictures in this way, he liked polish, and he wanted something that would go with the brighter colours that had come into fashion. Fussy wallpapers called for elaborate delineation of leaves and grass in the pictures that hung on them, and made with them a consistent whole. The pictures and their setting suited each other, and the change of taste in furnishing had its effect on painting, just as it is having now. One remembers Haydon's description of the Duke of Sussex, sitting in his small richly furnished room, in a red Turkish cap, his hands ablaze with gems, and can call up pictures of the many other richly furnished rooms he must have seen: drawing-rooms—a mass of small objects and a clatter of bright colours—fringed tablecloths of amber or purple velvet, chimneypieces draped in plush, mother-of-pearl boxes, tasselled curtains, damask-covered gilt chairs, ebony and gold cupboards, lacquer trays, cushions in patch-works of gaily coloured satins, daguerreotypes in ornamental brass frames, albums embossed with semi-precious stones set in brass filigree, crimson velvet bell-pulls. Something lively in the picture line would be needed to go with all this—something metallic, highly finished and full of detail, small, rich, and brightly coloured. There was no room for sublimity in such a clutter, so the huge and the rugged and the terrible went out with Haydon, and the small and the smooth and the jewelled came in with Dyce; while there was ushered in a new era in which Haydon's reeling figure of Macbeth that he had 'reared' aloft on the principles of Pheidias, could have no possible place.

Haydon considered the change of taste dated from the death of West in 1821 and the succession of Lawrence to the President's Chair; at that time 'High Art', says he, 'was the predominant topic of conversation in high life. . . . Lawrence came to the Chair, and his Circean ability and seductive powers of manner and art, turned the whole tide of public feeling into his own channel.' But there was no exact moment at which the change can be said to have taken place; West's reputation, and the prestige of 'history painting', in the eighteenth-century sense of the term, lingered on for a few more years. In his address to the Academy students in 1823, Lawrence spoke of West's compositions as 'far surpassing contemporary merit on the continent, and as unequalled at any period below the schools of the Carracci'. While the next President, Shee, said West was 'the great-est man since Domenichino, Rubens and Rembrandt inter-vening'. At the sale by auction of West's pictures in 1829, 181 works fetched 19,137 guineas; *Death on the Pale Horse* fetched 2,000 guineas, and *Christ Rejected* 3,000 guineas. But in 1840 his picture of the *Annunciation* for which he had received 800 guineas from the vestry of St. Marylebone was sold for £10. Haydon's criticism (not unbiased by professional jealousy) of West's pictures at the sale in 1829 anticipated the full (and final?) slump in West's reputation; he wrote, 'there was not one single picture of a quality to delight the taste, the imagination, or the heart. The block-machine at Portsmouth could be taught to paint as well. His Venuses looked as if they never had been naked before.'

Shee, who became President in 1830, wrote to Lord John Russell, 'What wonder if it [the Academy] address itself chiefly to the gratification of the portraiture taste of the day. . . ?' and congratulates himself (a mere portrait painter) and the other R.A.s on their generous efforts 'at different times' to obtain support for the 'nobler but less favoured branches of art'.[1] Coming from a man who did not practice them this admission is significant.

A Frenchman, Defauconpret, visiting London in 1825 criti-cizes English art very severely, chiefly on the ground that there is so little historical painting. 'But', he adds, 'a good historical painter exists in London though his works never appear at this kind of annual competition' (the Academy). There follows a short biography of Haydon bearing unmistakable signs of being directly inspired by that artist. 'It is remarkable', he concludes, 'that this Mr. Haydon is not rich, he has never been willing to descend to portrait painting.' The writer is misinformed, Hay-don's descent had already begun, though certainly not willingly.

The change that was on the way did not affect the high valua-tion accorded to subject pictures, but only that kind of subject picture implied by the term 'history painting'—the manneristic productions of the eighteenth century. I believe it true to say that the term went out with Haydon, and that no artist after him called himself a history painter. It suggests melodrama, deep chiaroscuro, 'elevated' form and expression.

[1] Between 1823 and 1833, 1,398 'poetical and historical' works were ex-hibited at the Academy, as against 5,093 portraits.

For in spite of Haydon and his education of the taste of the people the dark masters were going out of fashion. When the great wars came to an end there was a rush to the continent, and most painters became conscious of the early Italian pictures for the first time—to fall in love with them at once. Those who remained at home caught the fever; they found more pleasure in silvery brightness than in golden depth, the old dark shadows became odious to them and were replaced by brilliant colour and lightness throughout. 'I have no sympathy with the moderns,' wrote Haydon to Kirkup in 1844. '. . . You cannot hear accounts of British art bad enough. It is getting, it *must* get, it has got into inextricable absurdity. The great principles of light and shadow, colour management, a whole equally applicable to monumental altar-work or easel, are going entirely out.' Haydon's work depended on shadow; he planned his pictures as patterns of light relieved from darkness, and the ubiquitous areas of dark paint, which in his later work passed for shadow, held the whole together. When he tried (in the Cartoon Contest in 1843) to work in a lighter key he found he could not do it.

Only in one way was he still in sympathy with his time: in his insistence on the importance of subject. When he said, as he frequently did, that a child or an ignorant person will often be a better judge of a picture than all the artists or connoisseurs in the world, he meant that it is not necessary to understand the technical qualities in a picture to appreciate its psychological qualities. 'It is extraordinary', he says in one of his lectures, 'that in the highest qualities of "high art"—expression and telling a story—the instinctive feeling of the untutored multitude is to be preferred often to the delusion of mere artists themselves. . . .' It was a tenet of the period that though only artists and a few connoisseurs could appreciate the technical parts of a picture, laymen were quite as good judges of the things that really mattered—its meaning and poetry.

Haydon quotes Aristotle, 'The multitude is the secret judge of the productions of art.' Later, Ruskin was to talk in much the same way about the mere technical qualities—'the upholstery'—as opposed to the spiritual.

This idea of the separation of the two things was of long standing; the interest artists felt in the technical side was supposed to prevent them from appreciating the emotional qualities, which—if they had succeeded—they had put into their own pictures by accident, presumably. The painter, having finished, stood aside, the technical part of the business was over, and the connoisseur then took the matter up and explained or analysed the higher qualities expressed in the subject. On that he was the better qualified to judge from the very fact of his ignorance (often his boasted ignorance) of the craftsmanship.

Haydon was not always consistent. In his first attack on Payne Knight in the *Examiner* he had claimed that artists were the best judges of art, and not connoisseurs, nor yet, by inference, the man in the street. But perhaps he was really consistent; he probably meant, then as always, that one artist was the best judge. However that may be he raised up a champion for Payne Knight and a foe for himself in another connoisseur, one signing himself 'J.W.' This writer accuses Haydon of trying to re-establish the long-contested but long-exploded maxim that 'Artists are the best judges of Art'. He compares the practising artist to the private soldier with the bayonet, the mere executant of battle, and the connoisseur to Wellington, the great directing mind. 'In every given instance,' he says, 'the decided claim to superiority is clearly on the side of the man of science; and it is equally clear that the less he intermeddles with the manual and mechanical branch of art, the greater opportunity hath he of generalizing his ideas, and the less danger of deviating from the ways of truth, by becoming a bigot to his own method, or the methods of those by whom he might be instructed.'

No painter could fail to be interested in the technical part of his work, and Haydon at one time became enamoured of the rich impasto of the Venetians, and tried to acquire it, but his insistence on the importance of the judgement of 'honest John Bull' shows that he considered everything technical—using the word in its broadest sense, to cover design, unity, manipulation of the pigment, and all the rest of it—as subservient to the main object of telling a fine story well (which was all John Bull when he was being really honest cared about). So in this one way Haydon continued to be in sympathy with the spirit of the new age, which, so far from showing any signs of going back on this preoccupation with subject, carried it a little later, in the hands of Ruskin, to lengths which have since brought a violent reaction.

What roused Haydon's wrath was the Germanic origin of the

new enthusiasm for the primitives. 'Just as I had really brought
the whole country to see the value of the figure,' he writes,
'come those Gothic ferocities.' He detested all modern foreign-
ness, and thought the wars had been a godsend to English art in
preventing artists from going to the continent, and so saving
them from the 'contagion of David's brick-dust'. Certain young
German painters who had gone to Rome to study, became disgusted with the vapidity of modern art, and, throwing over the
traditions of the schools, went back to the early Italians for their
inspiration. Their influence spread, and was helped by the cele-
brity of the recently finished frescoes by Peter Cornelius at
Munich. This medium necessitated a light treatment, and was
chosen instead of oil for the decoration of the new Houses of
Parliament in 1841. Haydon was at first opposed to fresco, calling it a 'branch of the same upas-root [David's brick-dust]
grafted upon Albert Durer's hardness, Cimabue's Gothicism,
and the gilt inanity of the middle ages'. He afterwards turned
round and began to advocate its use for the decoration, but he
soon wavered, and it is clear it was not the medium for him.

By that time, 1841, when the terms for competitors in the
contest were laid down, he was completely out of fashion; his
spiritual age had passed and he had ceased to count among contemporary painters.

Strange it is to find that not only to Frith, who felt great respect for his genius, but to the young Pre-Raphaelites, Haydon
was an object of veneration; Holman Hunt wrote late in life,
'Let us do honour to his perennial worth.' One would have
thought that no two styles could have been more opposed, but
the Pre-Raphaelites were reacting from the painters who immediately preceded them, such as Horsley and Armitage, and
as Haydon reacted from everyone but himself, and as they themselves only began after his death, perhaps they felt united with
him in having a common foe. He could scarcely have liked their
work had he seen it, and why they liked his is a mystery. He was
essentially and to the marrow of his bones Post-Raphaelite.

As the fashion for carefulness and finish grew, Haydon, getting old and bored, became hastier and more careless. His
vanity attributed this to greater skill, 'Pictures that used to take
me years,' he wrote, 'I now do in months. Those which *now*
take me months, I hope soon will only take me days.' But people
did not want pictures that were painted in days; they liked pic-

tures that looked as if they had taken years to do, such as Dyce's *Pegwell Bay*, seen, both in foreground and distance, with the detail of a telescopic camera. Compare with this, Haydon, who expressed a wish to paint a picture as if it had been shot out of Perkin's steam-gun, that terrific weapon so deadly that it was expected to make warfare impossible, and which ended in smoke, rather as Haydon did.

It was this spirit that led him to produce such things as *The Lion Hunt*, another lost picture, but one of which Redgrave has left a description:

'The drawing', he says, 'of the principal figure, and of the horse on which he rides, is most careless and incorrect; the head of the man is far too big for his body, the arms too weak for the lower limbs, the horse much too small to carry the man, who sits quite on its neck, and is so evidently too heavy for the animal, that it is quite weighed down in the hind quarters, not by the attack of the lion, but by the weight of the warrior. Like its rider the horse has too big a head, which is moreover fitted on to a short neck that the lion-killer's face may not be hidden; it has opened its jaws so wide as to include nearly half the neck of the lion within its teeth, while, with the hind legs almost paralyzed, it stands firmly enough on one fore-leg to be able to twist the other over the lion's back and to place it on the opposite flank. Another rider comes up in such hot haste to the aid of the first, that he has either run his horse and himself against the trunk of a tree, or else Haydon thought he had had trouble enough with the heads of one warrior and one horse, and deliberately blotted out the other two by painting the trunk completely across them; added to this the whole work is heavy and coarse, without style and without execution.'

On the accession of Queen Victoria Haydon applied for the appointment of her historical painter. This was of course a most humiliating step to have to take, and he describes it thus, 'Felt degraded in my own estimation in condescending to ask the Duchess of Sutherland to interfere with the Queen to appoint me her historical painter, with an income like West [£1,000 a year]. If I succeed, what will become of my liberty? I do it for dear Mary's sake, as her health is feeble, and any more shocks would endanger her life. If the Queen were to say, "Will he promise to cease assaulting the Academy?" I would reply, "If her Majesty were to offer me the alternative of the block, or to cease assaulting, I would choose the block." *Nous verrons.* Nothing will come of it, and secretly I hope nothing may.' Nothing did.

XXI. THE DUKE

God bless your Grace.

'THE success of these lectures at Liverpool, and the success of the Asylum picture, and the victory of a public commission, are really so glorious that no gratitude to God can be great enough.' So writes Haydon at the end of his fifty-third year. The public commission was for a life-size picture of the Duke of Wellington Musing on the Field of Waterloo. 'I prayed sincerely for a successful end of this labour,' he adds, 'and it has ended successfully. Gratitude to Him, the Protector of all His creatures. I now pray to Him to bless this new commission of the Duke, that Liverpool may possess the best historical picture and my grandest effort of the pencil in portrait.'

A committee of gentlemen in Liverpool had commissioned Haydon to paint this subject—one that made his breast swell. Five years before he had been asked by Boys, the publisher, to paint a small picture of the Duke at Waterloo for the purpose of an engraving, but the Duke had so strongly opposed it that the scheme had fallen through. He objected to the subject of the picture, which he considered failed in history (he had never mused there), philosophy, politics, poetry, and taste. He could not prevent Haydon from painting the picture, he must do as he pleased; he himself would have nothing to say to it.

The ultimate fate of the picture is recorded in the *Journals.* Haydon wrote, 'At dawn had a flash of an Imperial Guard musing at Waterloo as a fitter companion for Napoleon. Finished it over the Duke. This is the first time an Imperial Guard extinguished the Duke.'

But a request from a body of gentlemen in Liverpool was a different matter, and the Duke professed himself much flattered at their desire to possess a picture of him by Mr. Haydon. Haydon's admiration amounted almost to idolatry, and the pains he took were in proportion to the thrilling nature of the subject. His inspiration tended to lead him to one extreme or the other— he liked a subject that gave him a chance either for 'daring foreshortenings and desperate actions', or for silent brooding over the past. As we know he himself was greatly given to musing; he had mused in the gardens at Fontainebleau, in Napoleon's private apartment, at Stratford-on-Avon, and was just preparing to muse at Sir John Soane's when he was unfortunately interrupted by the arrival of the Duke of Sussex. He had painted *Napoleon Musing at St. Helena*, once on a large scale, and was to produce nearly forty versions of the same theme; he had painted *Lord Grey Musing by Firelight*, and a smaller version called *A Statesman Musing by Firelight*; and now he was to paint the Duke musing at Waterloo; while probably the best portrait he ever did was of Wordsworth musing on Helvellyn. The age was pretty generally addicted to musing; innumerable are the prints of young ladies musing by tombstones beneath weeping willows, and one remembers the American who some years later missed by half an hour the sublimest sight on earth—Macaulay musing by the grave of Wordsworth. So these musing themes of Haydon's had a great success and earned him money. In this case he brought severe application to bear on it, making elaborate studies for all the details, from the head, hands and costume, down to the minutest parts of the trappings of Copenhagen.

But about this there was difficulty. The Duke had his peculiarities, and one was an aversion from lending his clothes or accoutrements to the artists who were painting his portrait. While painting the original picture for Boys, Haydon had unwisely let out that he had borrowed some of the Duke's clothes from his valet, and had been severely reprimanded for doing so. Now when he asked to borrow them again he met with a point blank refusal. This was a facer, he could not proceed, and in despair he went to Lord Fitzroy Somerset, who told him that the saddle, cloth and all, was eaten by moths. But he explained to him the nature of everything and authorized him to use his name at Whippey's. Whippey had made all his Grace's saddles, and promised to fit everything up as he had worn it at Waterloo, put it on a horse, and let Haydon paint from the real thing.

Needless to say much correspondence passed between the artist and his sitter, till at last, 'The Duke of Wellington presents his compliments to Mr. Haydon. He hopes that he will have some cessation of note-writing about pictures.' He would allow the picture to be painted, and, when he had leisure, he would sit for it, but beyond that he would have nothing to do with it,

'The Duke knows nothing about the picture Mr. Haydon proposes to paint.' And again:

'The Duke of Wellington presents his compliments to Mr. Haydon. He will, according to what he stated to the Committee at Liverpool, sit to Mr. Haydon for his picture.

'The composition of the picture is the business of the artist; of the committee of gentlemen who asked its execution; of the gentlemen for whom it is intended; of anybody excepting the person who is to sit for it.

'The Duke begs leave to decline not only being responsible for the composition, but even to have a knowledge of the subject. When he will be able to receive Mr. Haydon he will write to him, but he begs leave to be clearly understood as having no knowledge whatever of the composition or subject of the picture for which he is to sit, excepting that it is for the committee of gentlemen at Liverpool, who have desired that he should sit to Mr. Haydon.'

At last Haydon received an invitation to Walmer, when he might have sittings, and on 11 October 1839 he left London by steam for Ramsgate, where he dined, and then set off in a chaise.

He was heartily welcomed, asked how he had come down, and the conversation became general.

Haydon writes:

'I studied his fine head intensely. Arbuthnot had begun to doze. I was like a lamp newly trimmed, and could have listened all night. The Duke gave a tremendous yawn, and said: "It is time to go to bed." Candles were rung for. He took two, and lighted them himself. The rest lighted their own. The Duke took one and gave me (being the stranger) the other, and led the way. At an old view of Dover, in the hall, he stopped and explained about the encroachments of the sea. I studied him again—we all held up our candles. Sir Astley went to Mr. Pitt's bedroom, and said: "God bless your Grace." They dropped off—his Grace, I and the valet going on. I came to my room, and said: "God bless your Grace." I saw him go into his. When I got to bed I could not sleep. Good God, I thought, here am I tête-à-tête with the greatest man on earth, and the noblest—the conqueror of Napoleon—sitting with him, talking to him, sleeping near him! His mind is unimpaired; his conversation powerful, humorous, witty, argumentative, sound, moral. Would he throw his stories, fresh from nature, into his speeches the effect would be prodigious! . . . I am deeply interested, and passionately affected. God bless his Grace, I repeat.'

At breakfast next morning, six children came to the windows. 'Let them in,' said the Duke, and in they came, rushing over to

him, saying, 'How d'ye do, Duke? How d'ye do, Duke?' They
scrambled round him and tried to slop the tea over him. Then
they all rushed out on the leads, and the Duke romped with
them, and Haydon saw one of them give him the devil of a
thump!

The artist was then told to choose a room and get his light in
order, and at two o'clock was given a sitting of an hour and a
half.

'I hit his grand, upright, manly expression,' he writes. 'He looked like
an eagle of the Gods who had put on human shape, and had got silvery
with age and service.

'At first I was a little affected, but I hit his features, and all went off.
Riding hard had made him rosy and dozy. His colour was fresh. All
the portraits are too pale. I found that to imagine he could not go
through any duty raised the lion. "Does the light hurt your Grace's
eyes?" "Not at all." And he stared at the light as much as to say: "I'll
see if you shall make me give in, Signor Light."

' 'Twas a noble head, I saw nothing of that peculiar expression of
mouth the sculptors give him, bordering on simpering. His colour was
beautiful and fleshy, his lips compressed and energetic. I foolishly said:
"Don't let me fatigue your Grace." "Well, sir," he said, "I'll give you
an hour and a half. To-morrow is Sunday. Monday I'll sit again." I
was delighted to see him pay his duty to Sunday. Up he rose. I opened
the door, and hold this as the highest distinction of my life. He bowed
and said: "We dine at seven."

'At seven we dined. His Grace took half a glass of sherry and put it
in water. I drank three glasses, Mr. Arbuthnot one. We then went to
the drawing-room, where, putting a candle on each side of him, he
read the *Standard* whilst I talked to Mr. Arbuthnot. . . .

'I did not stay up to-night. I was tired, went to bed and slept heartily.
It was most interesting to see him reading away. I believe he read
every iota. . . .

'Thus ends the second immortal day.'

On Sunday, they all went to the village church. Haydon got
there first and sat down in the ducal pew, 'From the bare wain-
scot, the absence of curtains, the dirty green footstools, and
common chairs, I feared I was in the wrong pew, and very
quietly sat myself down in the Duke's place. Mr. Arbuthnot
squeezed my arm before it was too late, and I crossed in an
instant.

'The Duke pulled out his prayer-book, and followed the clergyman
in the simplest way. I got deeply affected.

'. . . Arthur Wellesley in the village church at Walmer this day was more interesting to me than at the last charge of the Guards at Waterloo, or in the glory and paraphernalia of his entry into Paris. I would not have missed seeing him, for this will be the germ of some interesting work of Art—perhaps his youth, his manhood and his age in a series.'

At half-past five next morning Haydon was up and getting the head in from the drawing. At nine the Duke came in, looking extremely worn; his skin drawn tight over his face; his eye watery and aged. A chair was put for him, he mumbled 'I'd as soon stand'. He took out his watch three times; at ten he went to breakfast; he had been impatient all the time. He sat again at three, after hunting; Lady Burghersh came in also, and kept him talking.

'He has done,' said she, 'and it's very fine.' 'Is it though?' said the Duke, 'I'm very glad.' 'And now', said she, 'you must stand.' So up he got, and Haydon sketched two views of his back, his hands, legs, etc., etc. 'I did him so instantaneously that his eagle eyes looked me right through several times, when he thought I was not looking. As it was a point of honour with him not to see any sketch connected with my picture, he never glanced that way. . . . He then retired, and appeared gay and better.'

At night Haydon took leave of the Duke.

When he got home Rogers (the poet) called, and was pleased with the portrait. He said it was the man and told Haydon he was a great poet.

Lady Burghersh, and Colonel Gurwood called and 'were much delighted'. Lady Burghersh authorized the painter to say the likeness of the Duke was admirable, and so said Arbuthnot. Indeed, to judge from the engraving, it looks an admirable likeness. The Duke stands with his back to the spectator so that the head is seen in a little less than profile.

But Haydon had got into difficulties over Copenhagen. Proportion was never his strong point, and he began by making him leggy, and too big in the body, which gave him a heavy look, compensated to some extent by a passionate fire in the eye. Count D'Orsay called while it was in this state and made several useful suggestions. 'I did them,' says Haydon, 'and he took my brush in his dandy gloves, which made my heart ache, and lowered the hind-quarters by bringing over a bit of the sky. Such a dress! White waistcoat, blue satin cravat, hair oiled and curling, hat of the primest curve and purest water, gloves scented with *eau-de-Cologne* or *eau-de-jasmin*, primrose in tint, skin in tightness. In this prime of dandysim he took up a nasty, oily, dirty, hog-tool, and immortalized Copenhagen by touching the sky.'

Haydon had of course studied the horses in the Parthenon frieze and the Metopes, and had admired the wonderful veins that run down the bellies and legs, giving a sense of vitality; taking the hint he introduced similar veins in Copenhagen in a way that precluded any possibility that they should be over-looked.

The picture was engraved, and on receipt of a copy as a present from the artist Wordsworth wrote a sonnet:

> By Art's bold privilege Warrior and War-horse stand
>   On ground yet strewn with their last battle's wreck;
> Let the Steed glory while his Master's hand
>   Lies fixed for ages on his conscious neck;
> But by the Chieftain's look, though at his side
>   Hangs that day's treasured sword, how firm a check
> Is given to triumph and all human pride!
>   Yon trophied Mound shrinks to a shadowy speck
> In his calm presence! Him the mighty deed
>   Elates not, brought far nearer the grave's rest
> As shows that time-worn face, for he such seed
>   Has sown as yields, we trust, the fruit of fame
>   In Heaven; hence no one blushes for thy name,
> Conqueror, 'mid some sad thoughts, divinely blest!

Soon after he had finished the Duke, Haydon received another important commission, to paint the Anti-Slavery Convention.

This picture, which hangs in the National Portrait Gallery, contains 138 heads, and took him eleven months to paint. He made his studies at enormous speed—fourteen portrait studies in chalk in one day, thirty in three days, fifty-two in five days. On one occasion he began at half-past seven and worked till ten at night, with half an hour for lunch, and two hours' reading including dinner. 'Had my eyes lasted,' he says, 'I could have gone on all night.' Such a canvas could hardly be attractive, and though Haydon has done his work creditably, considering the task, it is a picture no one would wish to see twice except for historical reference. The whole is conceived in the manner of the dying tradition he practised—a mass of shadow from which the forms are relieved as lights. Bad portrait painter as he was, the last course Haydon should have adopted was to run down other portrait painters and the craft itself, because when he tried his own hand at it he got as good as he gave. The critics, no less than other painters, jumped on him with delight. His conviction that all he did must be remarkable saved his vanity, but his indignation boiled, 'The criticism of this picture has been absurd,' he writes. 'Because it looks like mere nature, the critics think that art has been overlooked; whereas there is as much or more art, in this artless look than in many compositions of more profundity.'

XXII. THE STATE AND THE ARTIST

Iron tears and groans of lead
Bind around my aking head.

BLAKE

IN the *Journals* from this time, 1841, there is a change of
note. The atmosphere darkens ominously. There has been
misery enough on occasion before, but, though the victim
writhed under it, he faced it bravely and with wonderful cheerfulness.

What may be described as the fifth act opened with two blows,
one immediate and momentarily stunning, and the other a sinister rap, pregnant with warning of unbearable disappointment.
The news of Wilkie's death, which reached Haydon early in
May, struck at his happiness. Soon after this a committee was
set up to discuss the decoration of the new Houses of Parliament
and Haydon was not consulted.

The *Journals* leave a sense of confusion, of alternating success
and failure' (the latter predominating as the author grew older),
of an immense variety of contacts and interests which cloud the
main issues. But there is a distinguishable pattern to be made out
once the essentials of the design have been seized. The big canvas
about which he talks so incessantly as his sure help in times of
trouble, was the sail which, however bad the storm, enabled him
to navigate his ship. Without it she tossed helplessly. So Haydon
steered a straight course up to his first imprisonment, because,
whatever the weather, he was making for a definite port. When
he came out of prison and had to start afresh without the help
of large historical pictures he lost his bearings. Then followed
the long period of chaos which continued till this year, 1841. It
was not that he was painting no large pictures, but they were not
his special sort of picture, not highly dramatic events which put
him in direct contact with 'sublimity', enabled him 'to muse and
have high thoughts, and think of death and destiny, of God and
resurrection, and retire to rest above the world—prepared for
its restlessness'. Even the *Duke*—his 'grandest effort of the pencil
in portrait'—did not do that for him. But now he gets it back.

The competition that was opened for the decoration of the Houses of Parliament at last gave him the chance he had waited for all his life. Up goes the sail at once—made of paper (significantly) this time, not canvas, for the competitors are to make cartoons, not paintings—and off goes Haydon, the true Haydon, once more. Most of the old confidence has evaporated, he is more than doubtful of the result, but if his talents have suffered an eclipse his courage has not. Everything, and he glories in the thought in spite of his misery at the knowledge, is against him: his age, the change of taste, and prejudice in high places. But this again at last is 'history', it is huge and it is for a public building—*the* public building—and it is his own scheme.

He was not without hope. That he was the acknowledged leader in 'history', he believed; that he was a great genius, he knew; and that his merciful Protector had explicitly told him to 'go on', and meant to back him, he trusted. Of the 'Duke' he had written 'Inspired by history I fear not making it the grandest thing'. And here was 'history' in its very fount and essence: *Adam and Eve expelled from Eden*, for that was one of the subjects he had chosen. He was to fail, start again on his own 'foundation', fail again, and go on. 'This is B. R. Haydon'—he cries, 'the *real* man—may he live a thousand years!' The real man, with whom many will feel some sympathy, for whom almost all will feel some pity, and not a few some admiration, as he gets on to his own course, never to swerve from it again, sets his sail, fearful yet determined, and steers his barque with ever accelerating speed—straight at the rocks.

When Wilkie died Haydon realized how he had loved him. Wilkie was the only painter with whom he had been really intimate, and whose opinion he valued and relied on. They had been much separated of late years while Wilkie was travelling, but whenever they met they were reluctant to part, and each had that feeling for the other which arises from early intimacy. In Haydon's eyes Wilkie stood for the days of promise when he believed he would take the world by storm. He could not look back on that time without seeing it in the hues of romance. As he thought of his friend's body being lowered to its grave in the sea far away memories rushed across his mind: the poorly furnished painting-rooms in which they had visited almost daily each other's pictures to advise and criticize; evenings when Wilkie got his way and they had gone to see *Mother Goose* or something equally frivolous at Drury Lane, or when Haydon got his and they went to see *Hamlet* or *Macbeth* at the Lyceum; dinners at Lord Mulgrave's, when in their first evening suits and with *chapeaux bras* they had talked with ministers and peers; the marvellous day when Wilkie had really taken London by storm with his *Village Politicians*, and Haydon, rejoicing for his friend, had lost himself in dreams of his own future glory; and with the loss of that friend life seemed stripped of its meaning.

When Haydon read in the *Chronicle* 'Sir David Wilkie expired in the Bay of Gibraltar', a painful trembling seized him. Entry after entry in the *Journals* reverts to him, criticizing his faults, condemning his weakness and his abjectness, praising his gentleness and his reliability, worshipping his art, and longing for his presence:

'I dreamt I was sleeping in the tombs of the Kings at Jerusalem, and awoke in a wild confusion. . . . Poor Wilkie! he seemed to look at me and say, "Did I ever give you cause of offence? Did I not bear and forbear? Did I not assist you with money? Was not our friendship unalloyed till you tried to destroy the Institution in which you were brought up? Then did I leave you? Did I not enjoy your genius, bear testimony to your great talents? My character was different from yours. You have no right to reproach me for not being willing to go to the extremes of your hatred, and involve myself in suspicions which I did not deserve. No my dear Haydon, I loved you as much as, nay more than any man; and while we entertained the same views, saw each other daily, and pursued the same objects, nothing disturbed our happiness. When you did not fear ill-usage as I did; when worse treatment afflicted and nearly destroyed me, you ought not to blame me for wishing for that peace so natural to my nature." This passed through my imagination as I lay dozing; and I hugged my pillow and seemed to wish never again to wake.

' "But", I replied, "you were a slave to the great world. You feared to show regard for a man the world had deserted. You shrank from an ardent heart, whose only fault was an excess of affection. You were not a Christian where the applause of men was concerned, and fell a victim to a disappointment at Court, which you pursued with mean adulation, till you were driven from its precincts. I acknowledge you bore and forbore not from Christian duty, but because it was to your interests the less dangerous course of the two. You lent me money, but you talked of it with gross want of delicacy. When the world complained you abused me. You ridiculed the school I formed. You envied me all my great successes—Jerusalem, Lazarus, Mock Election, pupils, drawings, lectures; and at all times tried to prove they were not successes, with a pale face and quivering lip—more pale and more quivering than usual. There was no occasion to join in the cry to prove you had no connection with me; our friendship would have induced my bitterest enemies to pardon in you a delicate and affectionate silence.

' "These were frailties. Your virtues were great, your love of art a passion, your industry unexampled, your decorum deserving imitation; but you might have had virtues, you might have loved your art, you might have been industrious, you might have been decorous, and yet not have deserted your sincere and affectionate old friend in the time of his sorrow—sorrow brought on by his disgust at your treatment by men *you* tried to conciliate, afterwards, by calumniating the man who defended you." '

The wildness of many of these assertions hardly needs comment.

The pretence that his attack on the Academy had been partly made in defence of Wilkie, who had suffered nothing whatever at its hands, who liked the Academy, and ardently wished not to offend it, and was only enraged by Haydon's interference, is so preposterous that it is difficult to realize that he actually believed it.

The entries relating to Wilkie continue almost daily for months. Again and again come the words, 'Poor Wilkie! Poor fellow!' and then follows a record of his faults and his virtues; his loss to 'the Art', his loss to Haydon himself as he looks over his prints and remembers how his friend delighted in them too, or as he studies his picture and remembers the sound advice of his old fellow-student.

'Poor Wilkie! Poor fellow! Could one have imagined he would have been flung in the depths of the ocean! . . . My only regret is that the thirty-nine Academicians were not flung in after him. Poor Wilkie! I don't feel my heart beat so much to-day; I was frightened at its continuance yesterday, and last night but now it's gone. Let me think of his virtues, and forget all his abject slavery to the world.

'It is extraordinary the impression the man has made on my mind. His presence haunts me. I hear his voice fifty times a day. . . . Yet taking him as a man, he was not worthy of such interest.'

So it goes on, the left hand taking away what the right has just given without detracting from the impression of his devotion or the absorption of his mind. But death and the sense of loss did not affect the play of Haydon's egotism: he would not sign the address to Wilkie's mother, because it was inaugurated by the Academy. 'This was cunning,' he writes, 'they thought my feelings would hurry me away to sign it without reflection or reading, and then they would have turned round and said, "See! he acknowledges our authority." '

He appears to have thought that the thirty-nine members laid a plot to catch him out; much as another history painter, Barry, in the previous century, had seriously believed that his fellow Academicians used to meet at dead of night to make plots for stopping up his latch-key with dust, and for breaking into his painting-room to steal his designs.

The pang caused by Wilkie's death was to be softened by time, but the pain of the other blow was only to be deepened. It was cruel indeed. Haydon had been the first to conceive the idea of decorating the old House of Lords with pictures, and for twenty years had pressed it, in season and out of season. In his opinion he stood for large mural painting, for public patronage, and for this particular venture; and now the thing was going to be done and he was ignored. Why this was it is difficult to say; that he had wearied everyone—sickened would be nearer the mark—with his talk and his petitions is clear; he had intruded, he had clamoured and boasted and made enemies, but, even so, not to have included him among those consulted seems too hard a treatment. It would have been a mere act of courtesy, and his views, if not his work, were sound.

If Wilkie's death for a time broke his happiness, this affair in its beginning and its end completed the embittering of his already embittered soul. He bore it bravely and tried to resign himself to feeling that he was rewarded sufficiently by the coming-to-pass of his life's dream, even if he should be allowed no share in it. But his spirit had been wounded, and at this point a change of feeling must come over many readers of the *Journals*. All his life he had advertised his martyrdom, without, so far as one can see, having real cause for complaint, but there can be hardly a question that now he was badly used. Tom Taylor spared his readers when he edited the *Journals* by giving samples only (a sufficient number at that, in all conscience) of the incessant struggles and agonies endured by its author in his endeavour to make ends meet. He says that to read the original manuscript was to be wearied almost till one lost sympathy, and became callous through the sheer monotony of suffering. But in spite of the squalor of bills and debts and shameless begging a quality of true drama at last emerges from the turbid stream of ink of this highly self-dramatizing autobiographer. The plot has deepened and the end begins to be in sight. Inevitably one's attention sharpens as one becomes conscious of a new note, a discord of opposites, a curious blend of courage and determination with a sort of low broken whimpering of the soul that had been struck a mortal blow. This arrant boaster suddenly becomes moving, as in terrible pain he keeps calling on his courage to 'go on', keeps calling on that god of his to let him triumph and to bring him through at last. The visions of glory show only in glimpses now through the smoke of this awful battle that will not end. There is a mixture of weakness and strength, of knowing that he is beaten and refusing to give in, of furious tears and passionate determination to have his way, like the spoilt child he was and always had been. And Fate played her part as cruelly as if she had made up her mind to punish without mercy his faults and his follies. The slight of not being examined by the Committee was the first horrible taste of an unexpected poison that he instantly realized might be going to fill the cup of his destiny to the brim. He at once set about calling up his reserves; he tried to arm himself in advance against what he saw might be coming; he pleaded his own cause to himself, and, like a Roman general, showed his wounds, asking for justice and reward.

This drama of human suffering is no less interesting, for being based on a completely false assumption. Haydon assumed that he was a great artist because he wished to be one. But as a young man, as a boy almost, he fell in love, head over ears, with greatness. It was admirable, pathetic, or merely ridiculous, as you choose to look at it. His young friend Keats, who at first so admired him, did much the same thing. That 'cliff of poetry' at which he looked and felt sick at the thought of not climbing, corresponded with Haydon's cliff of 'Art' which he felt quite confident of climbing. Keats thought Haydon far more likely to succeed than himself. And who could have told at that time? Considering the character of most of Keats's early efforts Leigh Hunt made a creditable guess that he would be a great poet; but he guessed as confidently that Haydon would be, was in fact, a great painter.

So much may be said in excuse for him; and the agonies of his spirit are no less real for their association with misconceptions. To him, diseased with vanity, failure was death. The last scenes of this tragedy were enacted in a confusion of sordid worries so that their significance is often lost; but beneath the surface of daily occurrences the deep rhythms of his spirit were pulsing towards what seems to have been their appointed end.

Haydon began his *Autobiography* in 1841, soon after the slight of his non-inclusion among the artists examined by the Fine Arts Commission, and he makes it clear that he wrote it to lay his case before the world. 'Every man', he says in his Author's Introduction, 'who has suffered for a principle and would lose his life for its success—who in his early days had been oppressed without ever giving the slightest grounds for oppression, and persecuted to ruin because his oppression was unmerited—who has incurred the hatred of his enemies exactly in proportion as they became convinced they were wrong—every man who, like me, has eaten the bitter crust of poverty, and endured the penalties of vice and wickedness where he merited the rewards of virtue and industry—should write his own life.' He claims veracity for all he says, 'When a man writes a life of himself or others the principle of truth should be the basis of his work . . . a biography derives its sole interest or utility from its EXACT TRUTH.' As has been said, he continued to write for about two years, carrying his story up to the beginning of *Lazarus*, in 1820, when it abruptly breaks off. He wished his style to be left unaltered, slips, redundancies and all, and it is lively enough to the end. Why he stopped is not explained, but it may well have been the second blow, his failure in the cartoon contest, that broke his spirit and made it impossible for him to go on.

So in the first instance it was the bitterness of failure in a project which could never have brought him immortality that drove him to the retaliation that has been the means of giving it him. In the second the failure was so bitter as to cripple him, though the *Journals* carry the story on to the end, and become, as the tragedy deepens, the better medium of expression.

'These journals', says Taylor, 'are curious volumes, twenty-six in number, bulky parchment-bound, ledger-like folios. He has recorded in them the incidents of his days, his deductions from books he has read or pictures he has seen, and such passing thoughts as seemed to have been worth arresting and fixing in this way. By their help one may follow the progress of all his pictures from the first conception— often the best—through all the alterations in composition, the trials of effects in light and shade, studies of groups, single figures, and parts of figures. All these drawings are dashed in with pen and ink, careless and hasty, but almost always spirited and instinct with characteristic action. Under sketches of the same subject in different arrangements are often written the reasons why one is better than another; and so with draperies hands and feet. From these may be determined with tolerable precision the time each picture was in hand from first to last.'

From the time when he heard that his old pupil, Eastlake, had been examined while he had not the *Journals* become full of angry complaints and self-pity. He was told that he had no chance of employment in either House, that if he had gone twenty years ago to Italy it would have made all the difference.

'Where did Shakespeare go?' he cries, 'Where Raffaele, Phidias, Michael Angelo? What absurdity!

'These Journals show I first proposed in the House schools of design. I petitioned the Committee to adorn the House. . . . And now at the instigation of the Academy, Eastlake, my pupil, is to be chosen, because, being my pupil it may be mortifying to my feelings. Good God! Such is irritated power. However they know not the resting-place of my mind.

'. . . I have sacrificed myself always for the art and this is my reward. Thou, O Lord, knowest my heart, and that rather than the thing should not be done, I would grind the colours of others.

'. . . I am prepared for every disgrace, and bow humbly to that Creator who seems to think I am not yet endowed with humility sufficient.' (Haydon's attitude to his god was changing.)

And again, 'Read prayers, but I am not content. I feel as if I had been slighted. After so many years of devotion as these *Journals* exhibit, never to be thought of in the examination, or given any status by official consultation, pains my heart.'

He could not keep his mind off the rankling misery of his ill-usage as fresh aspects of the injustice struck him:

'After thirty-eight years of bitter suffering, perpetual struggle, incessant industry, undaunted perseverance, four imprisonments, three ruins, and five petitions to the House—never letting the subject of State support rest, day or night, in prison or out; turning everything before the public, and hanging it on this necessity—the wants of his family the agonies of his wife, the oppression of the Academy, directing all to the great cause—it is curious to see that the man who has got hold of the public heart, who is listened to and hailed by the masses . . . it is curious as a bit of human justice, to find chairmen, committee, witnesses, pupils, avoid throughout the whole inquiry any thought, word, or deed, which could convey to a foreign nation or a native artist, a noble lord, or an honourable member, that there was such a creature as Haydon on earth!

'And do they suppose that their unjust omission of me will make the British public forget me? No, no. I defy them. I am too deep in the hearts of the public, and the very omission will in all reason bring me more ardently to their minds.

'In truth I have been much hurt that my services have not been acknowledged in the evidence, or otherwise. But I have recovered the balance of my mind again, and feel I am born for whatever is arduous, and that I must be actuated by higher feelings than trust in human gratitude. People are never charitable enough to think of my neglect of my own interests.

'Engaged a model for to-morrow, and at it again. Huzza!'

Many years before this he had written to Miss Mitford, 'I like to see a fellow who has not committed murder die like a gentleman! There is something self-willed and grand about that defiance of an unknown hereafter.' And now dark thoughts return to his mind, 'It may be laid down', he writes, 'that self-destruction is the physical mode of relieving a disordered brain, because the first impression on a brain diseased, or diseased for a time, is the necessity for this horrid crime. There is no doubt of it.'

In this mood of misery and resentment Haydon called on Eastlake and discussed the probable ornament. Eastlake spoke of his evidence, and Haydon told him that if he were not consulted by the Commission he would come out as on the Elgin Marbles question.

A word of this Royal Commission, appointed by Peel in 1841, to decide on the best way to encourage English art, with special reference to the new Houses of Parliament. It was composed (with the Prince Consort at the head and Eastlake as secretary) of twenty-nine members, all important men, whose names dazzled the country, all men accustomed to direct in their various spheres, not a single one of whom (Eastlake, and possibly Prince Albert, excepted) knew anything whatever of the subject. Its activities, occupying some twenty years, were marked by a combination of indecision, procrastination, self-distrust, and futility which it would be hard to parallel. Competitions were opened, premiums (small ones, considering the amount of work the artists had to do) were awarded, a certain number of candidates were chosen as suitable, and then told that they must all compete again, in open competition, with another set of tests. These tests comprised huge pictures averaging a hundred square feet, for which the poor artists had to hire large studios, and to give up all lucrative work. The second competition proving that most of the previous winners had justified their selection, and had 'satisfied' the Commission, the six winners were told to furnish designs, colour-sketches, and specimens of fresco painting, for certain subjects chosen by the Commission, which however did not bind itself, even now, to employ them, and in fact did not. Moreover, so anxious was it to consider safety first, these twice-successful candidates had still to compete in this new test with all comers. On and on it went, the painters expended their time and money over and over again, and over and over again the highly distinguished members of the Commission were 'satisfied'.

It is true, as Mr. Oppé points out, that four years were needed for the walls to dry before they would be ready for painting on, and there is that much to be said in excuse, but the fact remains that after five years only one fresco (by Dyce) had been finished, and three commissioned, as the result of all these competitions, the Commissioners stating that it was not advisable to continue with more at the present time. This long period of necessary waiting was occasioned by the Commissioners' choice of fresco as the medium; oil pictures could have been temporarily stretched free from the wall with less delay. In making this choice they started off with a mistake, it was found later that fresco was unsuited to this climate, and it was abandoned after most of the work had been done in it. As is generally known, fresco consists in applying the colours to a wall newly plastered, into which they are absorbed by the chemical action of the lime while drying; only so much space being prepared each morning as can be covered and finished by the artist in one day. Not only is the method difficult in itself, as the colours dry lighter and great knowledge and experience is needed to allow for this, but for artists trained in oil the whole approach and outlook is different. The painter in oil (then at anyrate) generally rubbed in the whole straight away, often in monochrome, and worked anywhere he felt inclined afterwards, while the fresco painter has to make a patchwork, finishing as he goes.

Eastlake, who as secretary had no vote, and who was the only artist among the Commissioners, strongly advocated oil, saying that fresco was unsuited both to the climate and to the painters. The Commissioners were probably influenced by the prevailing preference for lightness of tone, the question being more a choice between lightness and darkness than between fresco and oil. One evening, when Lord Melbourne appeared to be half asleep after dinner while the matter was being discussed, he woke up enough to ask which was the lighter, and on being told that fresco was, said, 'Then I'm for fresco.'

Meanwhile the fourth competition (for oil paintings) had been held to which 103 artists contributed. The pictures averaged over a hundred square feet in size, and the Commissioners stated that pictures combining appropriate subjects with a high degree of merit should be considered eligible for purchase by the nation. Redgrave estimates that the artists must in mere outlay have spent in this competition alone about £7,500 (a most moderate estimate) while the Commissioners awarded £3,000 in premiums and made purchases to the amount of £1,300. That was absolutely all. But there was irony even in that; the £1,300 was the gate money which the artists themselves had earned by the exhibition of their works, which the Government graciously consented to set aside for their reward and the general encouragement of art. The huge pictures were all useless except for the competition; young painters had been encouraged to spend years in hope of a reward which was constantly snatched from even the winners, and were finally told that the Commissioners 'proposed to consider a scheme in which the possible great events of the future might be commemorated by artists of another generation'. It is fair to say what may be said for the Commissioners; Mr. Oppé writes, 'It was also recognized from the first that a school of designers would have to be trained before a commission for all time was undertaken.' But who were they going to be trained by, who was there who could have pretended to train them? And how would the Commissioners, who knew nothing whatever about painting, have known when the training had been sufficient? The best of the competitors were themselves, of all the talent then available, the best suited to teach—themselves! At all events a system of one disheartening competition after another was not a good way to train them.

After seven years of deliberations three more frescoes were finished, making four altogether, and two of the painters were commissioned to do an additional two. Four more artists were instructed to begin frescoes in the Upper Waiting Hall. In their tenth report after thirteen years the Commissioners announced the completion of eight frescoes in the Upper Waiting Hall. They were hardly finished when decay set in and a general mildew spread over the whole, while the ground itself blistered and disintegrated. The Commissioners terminated their own existence after twenty-one years of muddle, and since then in 1864 Maclise painted his huge picture of *Wellington and Blucher at Waterloo*, not in fresco, but in the water-glass method, the picture being a water-colour with a silica surface spread over it by a fine syringe.

This was State patronage of art for which Haydon had spent his life in struggling. It began with a flourish of trumpets, under Royal patronage and with Royal participation, and everyone believed a new era in art had arrived. It encouraged hopes almost all of which were disappointed; it produced a few pictures, which for the most part had better not have been painted: it rewarded Watts with a premium for his *Caractacus*, but did not commission him to execute it; of Madox-Brown's *Justice* (which both Haydon and the young Rossetti greatly admired), it took no notice; it called away young artists from work on which they would have been more happily and far more profitably employed to waste their time and money on work for which they were not suited, in a medium which anyhow would have defeated their best efforts, and incidentally, by its cold neglect of his claims, it broke the heart of the man who above all others had brought the thing to pass.

'Shame on you', he writes in his *Journals*, 'to trample down and desert, and calumniate, and ridicule a nature that "loved not wisely, but too well". Shame on you! And now you will reap the reward of your folly. To whom do I owe my salvation? To the people, who believed in my truth, sympathized with my sufferings, and gave my genius that fair play, which you, with mortified pride refused.

'We shall all meet hereafter stripped and without disguise. May you be able in the presence of your God to say you have done your duty as I have done mine.'

Haydon explained to Bell Scott (who detested him) and others at dinner one night, that the proper way to carry out the decorations was for one master mind, meaning himself, to have the entire control, and produce sketches which younger men should execute under his directions. Haydon turned the laugh on Scott (who claims that he had 'proved the notion ridiculous'), and Scott revenged himself in a sonnet of a highly unflattering nature after Haydon's death. 'We had all thought', adds Scott, 'he had made up his mind that the whole work was to be placed in his hands.'

'As to the state of Art,' Haydon writes in his *Journals*, 'it is dangerous. A great moment is come; and I do not believe anyone so capable of wielding it as myself, when from circumstances, and the prejudices of all men, I have the least chance of any. Because:

'1st. I have loved my Art always better than myself.

'2nd. I dissected and drew two years before I painted.

'3rd. My pictures of Solomon, Jerusalem and Lazarus are indisputable evidences of genius.

'4th. I educated Eastlake, the Landseers, Harvey, Bewick, Chatfield, Lance, and founded a school, the shattered fragments of which have reformed Art in England. Therefore I have no claim.

'5th. I stood forth and defended the Elgin Marbles and demolished Knight.

'6th. I have been imprisoned four times for persevering to improve the people.

'7th. I first proposed to adorn the House of Lords.

'8th. I have had a plan before every Ministry for twenty-five years.

'9th. I first petitioned the House by Lord Brougham, 1823; by Lord Durham, 1824; by Lord Colborne, 1826; by Lord Dover, 1827; by Lord Morpeth, 1833 or '34, in favour of High Art, and the Building Committee in specific favour of this very object—the decoration of the House of Lords.

'I have lost all my property; have been refused the honours of my country; have had my talents denied, my character defamed, my property dissipated, my health injured, my mind distracted, for my invincible devotion to the great object now about to be carried. And therefore I cannot, ought not to be, and have not any right to hope to be rewarded by having a share in its emolument, its honour, or its glory.

'But still I trust my merciful Creator will not let me leave this world without an opportunity to put forth, to the full extent of their capability, the talents with which he has blessed me, to promote by Art the cause of virtue, morality, patriotism, or religion. In Him I trust, as I always have done, and am sure these Journals, which have so often recorded his mercies, will not cease continuance till I have recorded in them the realization, under his merciful blessing, of the great object of my being.

'I feel I shall realize this instinct in gratitude and shouts.

'O Lord, let not this be the presumption of imbecility, but the just confidence of anticipating inspiration.'

On 25 April 1842, appeared the notice of the Fine Arts Commission, with conditions for the cartoon competition,[1] which was to be the qualifying test for candidates for the decoration of the new Houses of Parliament. Haydon, indignant at not being consulted, had considered that he ought to be employed in any case for the decoration, as the acknowledged leader in historical art, and as the originator of the scheme, but when the Royal Commission published the terms he was overjoyed that what he had so long worked for was at last really going to happen. He was delighted that Eastlake was to be secretary, 'Here is my pupil, Eastlake,' he writes, 'whom I instructed, whose dissections I superintended, whose ambition I excited, whose principles of Art I formed—putting forth a code by my influence and the influence of his own sound understanding, which will entirely change the whole system of British Art. . . . O God! Bless me with life, and health, and intellect, and eyes to realize the wishes of the Commissioners.'

He was to discover later, when he began, that finished cartoons were not his line, and he was soon complaining that they would be the ruin of the art of the country, 'The modern Italian dwells for days, and months, and years over finished cartoons. There is nothing so delusive as this sleepy practice, and after all this "trouble", this "learned trouble", said Lawrence, "there comes a d——d bad picture".'

While all the other competitors were occupied with their cartoons, Haydon got busy on the art of fresco painting. The battle between the claims of oil and fresco was being fought in high places, and, determined not to be left out of anything that was going, he took lessons (only two apparently) from one Latilla, who painted a head to show him the method. It was disconcerting both to master and pupil that this head began to crack while Latilla was actually working on it, and by next morning was blistered to atoms. Then Haydon followed. 'I began fresco to-day', he writes on 30 August 1841, 'and have succeeded, and taken off all apprehensions as to the process. I'll take to it. God bless me in it. . . . It was interesting, I knelt down

---

[1] A cartoon is a drawing, usually in black and white on stout paper, as a preparatory design, full-size or not, to be carried out in some other medium.

yesterday morning and prayed God with all my heart to bless my beginning and progression in fresco with all the ardour with which I knelt down on my arrival in London in 1804.' Ardour was the word. He laid down two tons of lime in his garden to mature ready for use in case of need. A Mr. Hawes called and said, 'If they ask about fresco—there it is.' So Haydon wrote to him that night offering to give up his whole time to fresco for the next ten years for a certain income. Newton permitting, he pulled down half the wall in his painting-room (properly speaking the drawing-room of the house), prepared it, and painted in giant size a figure of Uriel, sublime but conventional, which he showed to all the members of the Commission, 'and now they are off into the country', he says, 'where they will spread it'. It was a little damping that when 'D——' called he 'saw and felt nothing of the poetry', only 'with the air of a master', pointing out something wrong with the colour of the lips. Still, 'Nothing could be better hit than the fresco,' cries Haydon.

But the fresco took the matter into its own hands and began to do disconcerting things, assuming a ghastly pallor. 'Anyone else', says Bell Scott, 'would have seriously studied the method of fresco abroad, but here was Haydon inviting visitors to inspect his faint specimen ... without ever having seen a fresco picture.'

'What I suffered at first', Haydon writes, 'lest some artist might get the start of me! My excitement has completely knocked me up—taken away my voice.' Soon after he describes how he went to the National Gallery, 'and came back disgusted with the horny, oily, heavy, dull look of the finest works after fresco.

'My soul begins to yearn for something else,' he continues, 'my attempt in fresco has opened my eyes so completely to a power I knew nothing of, that all Art here palls on my senses. Great and good and merciful Creator, spare me till I have realized what I now see I can do.

'If ever an artist was fit for fresco, I am.'

Then later, 'The obstructions in fresco do not deserve the name of difficulties. They are useless and petty annoyances. It is a nuisance to have a colour dry one thing when you mean it another. It is a nuisance to have a seam in the flesh and to have no depth in the shadow. It is a bore to copy your own cartoon when the fire of invention is over, and can never be recalled. . . .

But I do not see they entitle fresco to any superiority over oil.'

Then, 'Went to the National Gallery, and after dwelling on the rawness of fresco the tone of Titian went into my soul like the tone of an organ. How I gloried in the Bacchus and Ariadne! How I tasted the Ganymede with its fleshiness. . . . Nothing in fresco can equal these—their juicy richness, their delicious harmony. Oh I shall get sick of lime, but duty calls.'

Alas! the ardour of 1804 had a more consistent character, leading him on through much study of Albinus, nude models, and the Elgin Marbles, to produce 'such a picture' as *Dentatus*, with its 'standard figure' of the hero, his 'ponderous weight' and awful contempt. Now he varies between, 'No boy of eighteen is more eager to attain excellence than I am, or more alive to and desirous of discovering my own errors: I trust I shall always be the same till the day of my death.' And, 'I am very discontented all of a sudden, and cannot tell why. It is the agony of ungratified ambition; that is the reason.'

The Duke of Wellington said of habit that it is 'ten times nature'; in the intricate mechanism which is the mind of man, how much in the present instance was this hectic enthusiasm habit, how much an escape from despair? It is painful to watch its manifestations. One can almost see the hasty feverish incompetence with which he was now working, in reading his daily notes, 'I seized chalk all of a sudden as I was writing, and placed the leg and thigh of the Angel Gabriel rightly.'

In his cartoon of Adam and Eve he had made Adam's leg too short, and knew it, but would not alter it as it was nicely worked. Fortunately he had an accident and split some oil on the paper, so he had to paste a fresh piece over it and do it again; 'But for the oil splash,' he says, 'I should perhaps have sullenly risked disapprobation of a short leg.' His friends were aware of his negligence, Kirkup wrote, 'Let not your powers in form, and action be annulled by some *childish* neglect of proportion.' And Kirkup, who was in Florence, and had not seen his old master for twenty years or more, did not know of his great deterioration, which those who were near him saw clearly enough. He does not seem to have been conscious of it himself, or he would not admit it; his naïve trust in the infallible nature of the principles he believed he had acquired from the Elgin Marbles was such that he thought he could hardly go wrong, and if he did it did not matter, the principles were too deep, and would carry off any small errors. 'Good heavens!' he writes, 'when I think how my pictures are abused, and know the deep principles on which I arrange and paint every iota in them. The young men little know what they might learn if they would—as they will by and by—study them.' He was enraged at any criticism:

'I have only to show a work to set the whole press in an uproar of abuse,' he cries, 'and the general tone the students imbibed at the Academy, as a pupil told me, was to consider me a monster. . . . The last picture I exhibited was the Samson. All the sound principles of its composition, its colour, its story, its drawing, its light and shadow were utterly unnoticed, and the picture was held up as an abortion not to be tolerated. Had the student gone to it with modesty, and tried to find out what is good, his mind, his practice, and his hand would have been improved.'

As always when he needed encouragement the memory of *Solomon* came to his mind:

'O Almighty God! It is now thirty years since I commenced my picture of Solomon; though deserted by the world, my family, father, friends, Thou knowest well that I trusted in Thee; that Thou didst inspire my spirit with a fiery confidence; that Thou didst whisper to me to endure as seeing One who is invisible: Thou knowest I never doubted, though without money, though in debt, though oppressed. I prayed for Thy blessing on commencing my labours. Thou carried me through to victory, and triumph and exultation. I am at this moment going to begin a grand work of Alexander and the Lion; bless its commencement and progression, and conclusion, as Thou blessedst Solomon. Grant, in spite of whatever obstruction, I may bring it to a grand and triumphant conclusion. Spare my intellect, my eyes, my health, my head, my strength. Confirm my poetry, and grant O Lord, that this work may advance the feeling of my great country for high and moral Art, and that I may not be taken till Art be on a firm foundation, never to recede, and that I may realize all my imagination hoped in my early youth, for Jesus Christ's sake.

'Many years ago, on my knees, in an agony of pain, I prayed I might live to see the great principles of Art acknowledged—I cared not for tasting the fruits—and that I might not leave the world with the talents with which God had blessed me, cruelly ruined or wasted. Perhaps I shall be taken at my word.'

With the thought of *Solomon* came the determination to do again what he had done then, order a large canvas and succeed in spite of his enemies. 'There is nothing like a large canvas. Let me be penniless, helpless, hungry, thirsty, croaking or fierce, the blank, even space of a large canvas restores me to happiness, to anticipations of glory, difficulty, danger, ruin or victory. My heart expands and I stride my room like a Hercules. . . . I despair not. He who carried me through so many trials will carry me gloriously through this. I know it, I feel it and rejoice in the trial. I glory in being tried.' In his own eyes he occupied a position on the world's stage somewhere near the centre, 'Let me live in the hearts of my countrymen, like John Milton and William Shakespeare.' How many people have wished that, and how very, very few have said it!

'Good and merciful God,' he cries, 'am I not reserved for great things? Surely I am. Surely at fifty-six to be more active than at twenty-six is extraordinary. . . . Here was I with hardly any money for the week . . . seized at daybreak with an irresistible impulse—a whisper audible, loud, startling—to begin a great work. I rub in Curtius to-day. Oh God, bless me at beginning, progression, and conclusion.'

The inevitable reaction follows such forced and feverish enthusiasm, 'I feel disposed to stand still, think of nothing, do nothing, see nothing, speak nothing, hear nothing, and listen to nothing for hours. It is a sort of catelepsy of the brain.' But a few mornings after he—'awoke at four, with two sublime conceptions. One of Nebuchadnezzar walking on the terrace, and saying, "Is not this Great Babylon?" and the other of his spirit visiting the Euphrates now, "*Was* not this Great Babylon?" '

It is a little surprising that for all Haydon's excitement about the cartoon contest and his prayers that he might realize the wishes of the Commissioners, he let four months go by before he began. The fact is he was, as he had confessed to Borrow on a former occasion, 'confoundedly in need of money', and dared not embark on so large a piece of work with such doubtful prospects of success. Everything had been going wrong: three commissions amounting to £700 were deferred, and he found himself in want once more. His children's education was costing him a great deal; the eldest boy, Frank, was at Cambridge, and to pay his expenses Haydon had to sell the copyright of the engraving of his picture of the *Duke*, thus sacrificing, he believed, 'a trump that might have been a property for life'. Frederic was in the Navy, and Mary at school. Frank was doing well, 'How I am to manage the £25, or £56 3s. 8d., for Frank's college bill,' says his father, 'I know not. Lord Brougham has helped me for the last with half, £16 the balance of £87. Dear Mary raised £10 on her watch for Frank, and I £10 more, so we brought him clear home, crowned as first prizeman in mathematics at Jesus, first year, but were drained.'

The *Journals* at this time are full of accounts of desperate efforts to postpone bills, and to find money to pay his servants, so, being what he was, the soil was ready for the seed, and he only needed that whisper which generally came at such times to start him off. It happened in church. 'As I prayed,' he writes, 'I felt uneasy at risking labour on a cartoon, with the uncertainty of reward and with my family, however much my duty may involve my executing such a cartoon; when suddenly a ray of light seemed to pass into my heart and I felt inexpressible joy and encouragement to go on. Go on I will, and from this instant all doubt has vanished. I shall proceed with the certainty of success; reward and employment will follow, as surely as if it were announced.

'I put this impression down to judge of results, believing and trusting in God with all my heart.'

So his fate was sealed; but he was Haydon once more.

For a week or ten days before beginning he had had no time for painting:

'All has been begging friends for help,' he writes, 'dwelling in an agony (when my family thought I was sleeping) on the certainty of ruin at the end of my great cartoon, yet with that pertinacity which is characteristic of my whole life, ordering the paper, canvas, frame 13 feet by 10½ to begin as soon as possible, though ruin will follow.

'Huzza—Huzza—Huzza; and one cheer more!

'My cartoon is up, and makes my heart beat, as all large bare spaces do, and ever have done. Difficulties to conquer. Victories to win. Enemies to beat. The nation to please. The honour of England to be kept up. Huzza—huzza—huzza; and one cheer more! Good heavens! But I conscientiously believe, under the blessing of God, that all this row about art will be a working up of glory for me. I feel it, and know it. In Him I trust.'

Soon after: 'Completed Adam and Eve. Now for Satan on Monday, with only 1s. 6d. in my pocket. Huzza!' Eastlake and other friends became alarmed, wondering what madness he might commit, and implored him to be quiet. He had no sooner begun than he found he had only seven shillings in the house, four of which had been raised on one of his two remaining pairs of spectacles, without three of which he could not paint. Many bills were pressing. He borrowed £10 from an old pupil, now a successful butter merchant. 'I paid £7 out of the £10,' he explains, 'and borrowed £10 of the man I paid £7 to. . . . "Then they cried unto the Lord in their trouble, and He saved them out of their distresses." Most cordially do I believe it. . . . The moment a disappointment takes place, my mind springs to a new hope. It is this elasticity which supports me.'

So he proceeded with *Adam and Eve*, and during its progress went to see the pictures at the British Gallery, where being especially pleased with one of *Polly Peacham* (now in the South Kensington Museum) by an unknown young artist, W. P. Frith, he called to congratulate him. Frith was out, so Haydon left his card, explaining to the maid that she must tell her master that Mr. Haydon wanted to talk about the picture, 'which you must tell him I admired. Now you won't forget, there's a good girl.' Frith called the following Sunday. Haydon, who had forgotten all about it, was astonished to see a strange young man come into the studio, but, on being reminded of his call, recovered from his surprise, and was most kind, giving Frith some excellent technical advice, and prophesying a prosperous career. Frith thought *Adam and Eve* very fine, and said so. 'Glad you like it,' said Haydon. 'That's intended for Satan; do you think it like him?'

On one occasion at this time when he had been working 'in delicious and exquisite misery', he bursts out:

'The greatest curse that can befall a father in England is to have a son gifted with a passion and genius for High Art. Thank God with all my soul and all my nature, my children have witnessed the harassing agonies under which I have ever painted; and the very name of painting, the very name of High Art, the very thought of a picture, gives them a hideous and disgusting taste in their mouths. Thank God not one of my boys, nor my girl can draw a straight line, even with a ruler, much less without one. And I pray God, on my knees, with my forehead bent to the earth, and my lips to the dust, that He will, in His mercy, afflict them with every other passion, appetite, or misery, with wretchedness, disease, insanity, or gabbling idiotism, rather than a longing for painting—that scorned miserable art, that greater imposture than the human species it imitates.'

XXIII. THE CARTOON CONTEST

Never, Never, I return,
Still for victory I burn.

BLAKE

THAT hopeful disposition, which always saw the future in the roseate colours of success, that swelling anticipation of glory, which was Haydon's greatest strength and greatest weakness, which had kept him going up to this time through years of disappointment was now 'through a combination of circumstances', as he pathetically said in one of his letters from the King's Bench, to receive a mortal wound. A combination of circumstances: advancing years; failing powers; a financial crisis in the country; changes of fashion; debt, despair, and angry creditors; weary friends, who were sick of lending; the sadness of age that sees itself outstripped by youth; the loneliness of passing from the brightness of the stage into the darkness of the wings, and the bitterness of seeing that come to pass for which he had spent his life in struggling and of being himself left out.

Taylor says, 'The last two volumes of the *Journals* are little more than a record of desperate struggles, alternating with despondency and angry protestations; and I feel it due to the reader to be as brief, in my extracts . . . as I can be, consistently with distinctness.'

What has been left makes painful reading. To stand by, in actual fact, and watch a soul in torment would be unendurable, but there is something of the quality of a work of art about Haydon's life that has in it the saving note of beauty. It is present by reason of his perfect consistency; his life had been passed from the beginning in an imaginary world in which there were still *Stanze* to be decorated, in which princes commissioned huge altar-pieces, and in which there was a painter called Haydon who was the glory of his country, and almost as good an artist as Raphael. He would have been more reasonable and more ordinary if the compelling force of facts had made him revise these ideas early in life, but he would have been less like one of

those tragic figures of drama who pursues his course undevi-
atingly to the final catastrophe. As a work of art his whole life
demands the tragedy of its end. Almost his greatest gift was to
struggle spectacularly with misery before what he hoped was
an admiring world. The ultimate tragedy for him would have
been not to be noticed, and in the final resort to prevent that
humiliation he was prepared to throw his last terrific stake.
However absurd ill-founded claims to greatness may be they
cease to be laughable when they have been purged in the flames
of disaster. From youth to manhood, and from manhood to
age he followed the one star, no matter where it led him, and
when he felt the ground shelving away to the brink of the precipice he never altered his step.

The world has not often been given such an opportunity of
watching a fellow-being sowing the seeds, and reaping the har-
vest of calamity. Nemesis had observed Haydon's conjurings
with his god, whom by a species of self-deluding ventriloquism
he made to speak in a voice that, being only his own, nevertheless seemed to him to come direct from heaven. She had noticed
this god, his doll, settled on his knee while he worked, his right
hand not knowing what his left hand did. And while he worked
more and more flaggingly the left hand would creep for the
string that moved the mouth of the puppet, whose whole jaw
would open in the manner of its kind and the familiar words
would issue—words so stirring to the painter that they never
failed of their effect—'Go on!' And, 'Go on I will!' Haydon
would answer, never realizing that both remarks were his own.
Now from long use the doll's celestial robes are worn, and the
sinister mechanism that underlies its trappings of divinity begins
to appear, while the flames of adversity roar fiercer. A subtle
change in their relationship makes itself felt; Haydon's old confident reliance on his god is marred, sometimes by a note of
irritation or complaint, at others by a horrid doubt, 'Perhaps I
have presumed too much on the goodness of my Creator,
appealed to Him too often and too freely.'

The first months of the year 1843 were passed in anxiety about
the fate of his cartoons, and in trying to prepare for the blow he
felt was coming. All his friends expected it, however he might
delude himself that his powers were unimpaired. 'You ask if
my mind or eyes are affected?' he writes to Kirkup in Florence.
'My mind, my dear fellow, is more vigorous than ever. My

eyes have never been ill since I married, and my general health has never been so strong. I have not had one day's serious illness for twenty-three years. For any great public work I am more fit than when you knew me: tempered by misfortune and corrected by adversity, my mind I trust is more attuned.' Kirkup answered that he clearly foresaw a 'job' in the decorations, to which Haydon replied, 'I see and am convinced there exists the intention to leave me out, exactly as they are convinced I ought to be brought in.'

Worry and vanity had played their part. Herr Passavent, a German artist, had assessed Haydon's position six years earlier, 'B. R. Haydon has obtained a higher reputation as an artist in Germany by paragraphs in the German Gazette than the exhibition of his pictures has procured him in England. His earlier productions, such as *Christ's Entry into Jerusalem*, and *The Judgement of Solomon*, prove that he is not devoid of talent, but the high estimate he has formed of his own powers has so paralysed his efforts that his later works have no comparison with his earlier promise.'

How much the Decoration scheme meant to him appears in a letter to Eastlake:

'I appeal to the Royal Commission, to the First Lord, to you the secretary, to Barry the architect, if I ought not to be indulged in my hereditary right to do this, viz. that when the Houses are ready, cartoons done, colours mixed, and all at their posts, I shall be allowed, *employed* or not employed, to take the *first* brush and dip it into the *first* colour, and put the *first* touch on the *first* intonaco.

'If this is not granted, I'll haunt every noble Lord and you, till you join my disturbed spirit on the banks of the Styx.'

In February he sent his picture of *Curtius Leaping into the Gulf* to the British Institution, and a few days after was laid up with a burnt foot. He could not paint, so wrote his memoirs, often writing eight hours a day. Thinking without painting disturbed his mind, and there are some gloomy entries, '. . . suffered excruciating agony for want of money'.

'Went in great distress to raise £6 10s.'

'Awoke in the night, my heart beating and my head aching from my anxieties.'

Immediately following this last, comes relief, 'Now reader, whoever thou art, young and thoughtless, or old and reflecting, was I not right to trust in God? Was it vanity? Was it presumption? Was it weakness? To-day, this very day, I have sold my Curtius, when only yesterday I had no hope: and my heart beat, and my head whirled, and my hand shook in my distress. I had taken the butter-knife off the table to raise 3s.'

A pupil with £100, part of £200 premium, helped still further.

On 1 June he placed his cartoons in Westminster Hall, with the statement that it was a great day for his mind and soul. But he was terribly anxious about the result.

'Perhaps God may punish me, as he did Napoleon, as an example, for pursuing a great object with less regard to moral principle than became a Christian—that is, raising money to get through, careless of the means of repaying. . . . The decision will take place in a few days. What ought I to have done? Kept my cartoons, and showed them alone? It would have been a wiser plan but it would have been shrinking from a contest with my brothers, which might have turned to my disadvantage. It is my policy to go through without complaint all the steps degradation points to, to give them no excuse for not employing me, and what then? Shall I be employed? No, indeed: but have the door slammed in my face, while my enemies will chuckle at my degradation and submission. . . .

'I have made up my mind to a reverse. Though I trust in God with confidence, yet I am not sure I am yet sufficiently cleansed by adversity not to need more of it.'

The opening of the Cartoon Exhibition was fixed for 3 July. On 27 June Eastlake told him that his cartoons were not among those chosen for reward.[1] It was three days before he could tell Mary. When he did her face was a study. She said, 'We shall be ruined.' 'I am wounded,' he writes, 'and being ill from confinement it shook me.' The wound was mortal.

He went to see William Hamilton, his old friend who had backed him in his fight about the Marbles, and who now told him Peel was annoyed at his restless activity about the arts, and because he interfered in things he had no business to. Hamilton said, 'You wrote about the Arabesques, now we had settled to buy them before; and it was intrusion.' He said to mention Haydon's name was an insult. 'Good heavens!' cries Haydon,

[1] The judges were: Sir Robert Peel, Lord Lansdowne, Richard Cook, Richard Westmacott, Samuel Rogers and William Etty. Of these Haydon believed the first to be an enemy; but the last three were friends.

'no feeling for my enthusiasm for Art. . . . Hamilton had no objection to my *intrusion* on the Elgin Marble question, and gave me the motto. He said, "You should write to Sir Robert Peel."'

When the exhibition opened the excitement was tremendous, between twenty and thirty thousand people a day visited it; almost a million in the two months it was open; all the more painful were the wounds to Haydon's vanity. The full bitterness of his failure is to be found in the report of the Fine Arts Commission. There were three premiums of £300; three of £200; and five of £100 (for some hundred competitors). Later the Commission decided to give ten consolation awards of £100, yet Haydon got nothing. He who believed himself the acknowledged leader in historical art, without rivals, found a crowd of young men had grown up unknown to him, who were more academic, better draughtsmen, better designers. Even Bell Scott felt sorry for him when he saw him in Westminster Hall on the opening day.

'I saw all my acquaintance,' he writes, 'and among them one to whom it carried the warrant of death. I mean Haydon! . . . He was walking about like a man in a dream, now and then waking up, affecting an amused manner, then again collapsing. . . . The inflation was gone; he was suddenly changed into an aged man. Every competition', adds Scott, 'has its dark side: dark with the red light of the nether pit shining through it. . . . Youth can stand much . . . but this veteran on that day was one of the most melancholy spectacles.'

It happened that same day that John Thomas, who made the sculpture on the exterior of the Houses, was lunching at a restaurant nearby, when he noticed a man sitting at another table with a bottle of wine before him. He thought the figure familiar, but as the stranger was leaning forward with the upper part of his face covered by his hand he failed to identify him. Presently tears began trickling slowly down the man's face, and when a few minutes after he moved his hand Haydon was revealed.

Twenty-five years before a man in the prime of life, calling himself, not 'Somniator' this time, but 'Somnabulus' [sic], had a dream or vision of the future, in which he found himself wandering about St. Paul's Cathedral and looking at the effigies of famous men. Suddenly he came upon an energetic-looking statue—with head uplifted, a piercing eye and eagle nose, looking defiance, with a palette on his thumb—inscribed with the name of HAYDON. Attempts had been made to erase this name, but it was too deeply engraved. He dreamt how his friends and all those who love genius for itself would have cried out:

> Build him a pedestal and say, 'Stand there,
> And be our admiration and our praise.'

Thirty-nine years before a young man just arrived in London had fallen on his knees, and, having prayed that he might 'rescue the Art from that stigma of incapacity which was impressed upon it', rose up with 'a breathing assurance of spiritual aid, resolved to be a great painter'. And as Constable said 'if you rob an artist of his conceit you had better hang him up at once'.

Elizabeth Barrett wrote a few years after his death:

'Poor Haydon! Think what an agony life was to him, so constituted!—his own genius a clinging curse! the fire and clay in him seething and quenching one another!—the man seeing maniacally in all men the assassins of his fame! and, with the whole world against him, struggling for the thing which was his life, through night and day, in thoughts and dreams . . . struggling, stifling, breaking the hearts of the creatures dearest to him, in the conflict for which there was no victory, though he could not choose but fight it. Tell me if Laocoön's anguish was not as an infant's sleep, compared to his?'

'Be assured,' Haydon wrote to the Duke of Sutherland, 'I have broken a hard shell, and found more ashes than fruit? . . . I am now hard at work on Alexander killing a Lion, as the only subject likely to make me bear up under a cloud of tortures which make me wonder my faculties remain clear. I believe I am meant to try the experiment how much a human brain can bear without insanity, or a human constitution without death.'

In spite of what he felt to be the insult to himself he was generous in his praise of his rivals, 'There are cartoons equal to any school,' he writes. 'I am astonished at the power displayed.' He adds with characteristic vanity, 'My own looked grand, like the effusions of a master, soft and natural, but not hard and definite; too much shadow for fresco; fit for oil; but there were disproportions. I gained great knowledge.' To Wordsworth he wrote, '. . . the proportion of a boy in "Edward" shocked me, for I could not see its error in my own room. . . . I have learned an immense deal. I see clearly now the future grandeur of the British School, and I hope it will not be forgotten that I have been the basis of this mighty change.' Bell Scott says of Haydon's contributions, 'His two cartoons were laboured enough according to his method, that is to say, they were not careful studies of form and design, but of light and shade; they were costume subjects, but conventionally incorrect; they were a survival from the previous generation.' On the other hand John Lucas, the portrait painter, wrote 'rapturously' to Miss Mitford of Haydon's cartoons; while Lockhart wrote to Haydon himself, '. . . I have a perfect conviction that your own are among the works that should have been rewarded, nay, that they ought to have had some of the highest rewards. There could be no doubt whose they were: and I really cannot guess why they were passed over, unless the judges conceived them to be mainly pieces of plagiarism, in which guess, if they made it, I feel sure they were quite mistaken.' Nor are these the only favourable opinions. Redgrave says, 'His [Haydon's] powers of rapid execution, his aptitude to work on a large scale, and other qualities, fitted him for employment . . . and he had, also, claims on the Commissioners. Men with far less qualifications were selected, and we think that to him especially . . . the Commissioners did great injustice in sheltering themselves behind a competition, and then dexterously managing to evade responsibility with regard to the selection of artists of established reputation which they were bound to have assumed.'

A *Handbook Guide to the Cartoons* has a reference to Haydon's *Edward the Black Prince*, 'Mr. Haydon is an enthusiast as regards phrenological and physionomical beauty, and he even extends his principles to every limb—hence, all the noses are alike, and so are the hands and legs, &c., throughout the composition.'

The Exhibition as a whole did not get a very good press, 'The one thing wanting', says the *Spectator*, 'is grandeur of conception.' The *Morning Post* did not expect originality, and was therefore 'far from disappointed' when it found none. Particularly did it miss the quality of Raphael, 'We allude', it explains, 'to that poetical power over expression whose capacity of elevation was unshared even by the Greeks—that power which has only fully belonged to Rafaelle of Urbine. . . . Little enough, indeed, of this elevated beauty is there to be found on the walls of Westminster Hall at present. . . . This utter want of perception of the elevated', it says, 'is capable of disgracing the national mind.' But it was precisely in this quality that Haydon knew himself to excel, he had used the expression a thousand times since he had made up his mind at the very beginning of his career 'to elevate the taste of the people of England', 'to raise the Art' of his country. Here was further proof, if that were needed, of the injustice and prejudice of the press against him. 'My cartoons . . . it was clearly premeditated, were not to be rewarded', he cries, 'on the principle of authority being supported at all hazards.

'Every artist of any feeling saw, whatever merit there might be in my cartoons, 1st, that they were the cartoons of a painter who could execute them with the brush; 2nd, that no principle of Art had been neglected, as applicable in them; and 3rdly, that though there were two or three disproportions, from the smallness of the room in which they were executed, a day's labour would have remedied them: and because a shoulder might be a trifle too heavy, or a calf a trifle too large, to deny reward to works whose character, expression and knowledge of construction were self-evident, was unjust, tyrannical; particularly taking into consideration that they were known to be by a man who made the very first cartoon display ever made, and who wherever the art was in danger from any cause, has shown fight whatever were or might be the consequences.'

The blow of his failure paralysed him for a time, and the *Journals* bear witness to his state of mind:

'Worked but unhappily. I am ashamed to own how the attacks of the press wound me. . . . How cruel it is! What a pleasure they seem to have in preventing people from accomplishing the darling object of their existence.'

'Prayed, but felt harassed. One struggles still to trust in God, but I am afraid to do so any longer, from my own unworthiness.'

'If a child asked a father for food, would he give him a serpent?'

'I ask from my heart, Thou good Being, to be saved, with my family, from the fatal ruin which must overwhelm me and them without Thy interference, promising repentance sincere and intense.'

'It is indeed cruel of Sir Robert Peel to have sanctioned such decisions, and to have left out my cartoons, after the battle I have fought for so many years.'

Elizabeth Barrett wrote:

'And with regard to these cartoons, having seen nothing at all of them, I cannot, you know, be sure whether justice or unjustice has been done in the decision, however great may be my own regret and disappointment at it. You are a man of genius—but you may have failed

in the cartoons—in these particular cartoons; with all your genius—
and it is impossible for one who is most your friend to deny the
hypothesis of it. On the other hand, you may not have failed—your
cartoons may have deserved the first prizes; and you may be a cruelly
wronged man. Still *a mistake* may have wronged you, and not a
treachery—and you cannot deny the possibility of this. It is better and
happier to doubt of the knowledge of men than of their integrity—
and it is for your own sake that I press this consideration upon you.
Mr. Lucas called your cartoon of Adam and Eve "sublime work"—
I had never doubted for a moment your gaining one prize at least—and
I understand, I repeat, to the uttermost the anguish of the reaction of
your aspiration. But think—if you write violently! if you were to
speak violently to another besides me! . . . pause——'[1]

The *Journals*:

'O Haydon, Haydon! Your love of Art, and your willingness at
fifty-seven to think better than you knew of your species, got the better
of your common sense. I imagined at such a bright epoch all hearts
would unite, all hearts rejoice, all hearts forget and forgive. . . . What
was there to forgive? A too ardent zeal and over-anxious ardour for the
principles of High Art, offensive to the authorities who wished to
check it. Shocking, but true!

'Hankered after my divine art, but feel oppressed by my ill-treat-
ment. I hope in God I shall recover my enthusiasm, but at present I am
exceedingly shocked.

'Another day to go through. Stale, flat, and unprofitable are days
to me. . . . I am waiting for sitters I detest, and could vomit over. . . .
My sitters came, but I was so nervously disgusted I told them frankly
it was not my forte. I presented them with a drawing, and begged them
to let me off. They were so kind, they saw the propriety.'

He gave a lecture, and the audience, moved to pity by his
bad fortune, gave him the warmest welcome he had ever had.

Week after week the cries and complaints continue:

'Sept. 14th. Went and removed my cartoons. . . . I am deeply
wounded at the insult inflicted.'

'Awoke severely pained at the insult.'

'Awoke again physically depressed. I got up saying, "Is this Benjamin
Robert Haydon? I'll see if I'll be conquered by cartoons." '

Outwardly he kept up his spirits when the first shock had
passed, and began painting Napoleons at a great rate. Meeting
a friend in Pall Mall, he collared him, saying, 'Your life or a

[1] They never met.

Napoleon?' the friend burst out laughing, and said, 'A Napoleon, of course.' So Haydon went home and got it in before four. By March 1844 he had painted nineteen versions, one of which was bought by the King of Hanover the following year for 200 guineas. The Duke of Devonshire asking Haydon what subjects he would suggest for two windows at Chatsworth, he instantly replied, 'Napoleon musing at St. Helena, and the Duke at Waterloo.' 'Capital idea!' said his Grace. At the end of the year he finished one in two hours; the quickest he ever did—and the twenty-fifth.

After finishing another in three days, he writes, 'Put in the sea—a delicious tint. How exquisite is a bare canvas, sized alone, to paint on; how the colour drags over; how the slightest colour, thin as water, tells; how it glitters in body; how the brush flies, now here, now there; it seems as if face, hands, sky, thought, poetry and expression were hid in the handle, and streamed out as it touched the canvas. What magic! What fire! What unerring hand and eye! What fancy! What power! What a gift of God! I bow and am grateful!'

By means of *Napoleons* (at £5 or £6 apiece for the quick ones) and fees for lectures (he once gave twenty-three in sixteen days), he managed to get along; but he had heavy calls, and needed all he could make. Frank's education at Cambridge had cost £860, but he now, through Sir Robert Peel's recommendation, obtained a post as clerk in the Record Office with a salary of £80 a year. Frederic (in the Navy) sailed for South America at this time. So the money came, and went instantly. A new pupil arriving with a premium of £200, Haydon writes, 'It has really saved me. . . . The guardian said to me as if half frightened, "Will you believe I prayed to the Lord you might encourage him, if he ought to be encouraged?" How curious,' Haydon remarks, 'here was I, praying in the depths of midnight that no accident might prevent the youth coming to me, and here was the guardian praying I might think he had talent.'

A further piece of encouragement came in the form of a real success with a large picture, which he now sent to the Academy, where it obtained a flattering notice in *The Times*:

'There is one picture which makes us depart from our design of adhering to the great room exclusively on this occasion; that is Haydon's large painting of "Uriel and Satan" (605), which must arrest even those who are hastening to depart from the Exhibition as a most remarkable work. A striking contrast to the gaudy colouring on which the eye has been feasted, it appears with a subdued tone, reminding one of a fresco. The figure of the angel is drawn with a boldness which some might call exaggerated, but with the simplicity and anatomical effect of sculpture, every muscle looking hard and unyielding as iron. The face is noble and ideal, and a fine effect is produced by the golden colour of the hair. This huge commanding figure is backed by limitless space, represented by a very dark positive blue, and the whole conveys the impression of a simple vastness. There is a certain crudity about the picture, but the impress of genius is unmistakeable.'

Thackeray's criticism of this work, much less flattering than that of *The Times*, well expresses what many evidently felt about Haydon's pictures—a willingness to like what had cost so much labour and sacrifice, together with an incapacity to do so. Under the pseudonym of 'Michael Angelo Titmarsh', Thackeray writes:

'Among the heroic pictures of course Mr. Haydon's ranks first, its size and pretensions call for that place. It roars out to you as it were with a Titanic voice from among all the competition to public favour, "Come and look at me." A broad-shouldered, swaggering, hulking archangel, with those rolling eyes and distending nostrils, which belong to the species of sublime caricature, stands scowling on a sphere from which the devil is just descending bound earthwards. Planets, comets, and other astronomical phenomena roll and blaze round the pair and flame in the new blue sky. There is something burly and bold in this resolute genius which will attack only enormous subjects, which will deal in nothing but the epic, something respectable even in the defects of such characters . . . and so instead of laughing at Haydon, which you and I were just about to do, let us check our jocularity, and give him credit for his great earnestness of purpose. I begin to find the world growing more pathetic daily, and laugh less every year of my life. Why laugh at idle hopes, or vain purposes, or utter blundering self-confidence? Let us be gentle with them henceforth, who knows whether there may not be something of the sort *chez nous*? But I am wandering from Haydon and his big picture. Let us hope somebody will buy. Who I cannot tell; it will do for a chapel; it is too big for a house: I have it—it might answer to hang up in a caravan at a fair if a travelling orrery were exhibited inside.

'This may be sheer impertinence and error, the picture may suit some tastes, it does *The Times* for instance, which pronounces it to be a noble work of the highest art; whereas the *Post* won't believe a bit, and passes it by with scorn.'

The picture was bought, and its owner had a special room

made for it in his house. This was Haydon's last success, and his reaction to it was curious: he happened to be beginning another design of Satan and Uriel, and he felt great uneasiness in case he might 'excite admiration by encasing evil in beauty'. He dreaded lest he should make Satan so fascinating as to become a snare; 'O God,' he cries, 'if I deserve not to succeed—if danger to virtue would accrue from complete success . . . let me fail.'

In spite of his unsuccess in the Cartoon Competition Haydon retained considerable prestige; the Commission for building the Royal Exchange considered a series of frescoes to decorate the merchant's area, and Tite, the architect, wrote to Haydon for his ideas and an estimate of costs. Haydon answered that, without presuming the letter to have any reference to himself, he would be delighted to undertake the whole for £3,500. This figure staggered the Commissioners, who said no more. Another compliment was his being asked to act with Eastlake as judge in an open competition for an altar-piece in St. James's Church, Bermondsey; while the success of the first volume of his lectures, now published, added to his reputation. These things mitigated the pain of his humiliation, but could not heal the wound, and he looked back on the past as a golden age.

'The art with me is becoming a beastly vulgarity,' he wrote. 'The solitary grandeur of historical painting is gone. There was something grand, something poetical, something touching, something inspiring, something heroic, something mysterious, something awful, in pacing your quiet painting-room after midnight, with a work lifted up on a gigantic easel, glimmering by the trembling light of a solitary candle, "when the whole world seemed adverse to desert". There was something truly poetical in devoting yourself to what the vulgar dared not touch—holding converse with the great Spirit; your heart swelling, your imagination teeming, your being rising.'

This 'something' had to be won back at all costs; there was certainly not much solitary grandeur left in historical painting when Westminster Hall was filled with the work of a hundred historical painters; so it came about that he took his last fatal decision, and embarked on his last great undertaking. The plan was suggested, as usual, by his secret voice—'that sort of audible whisper Socrates, Columbus and Tasso heard'—and the question it asked was, 'Why do you not paint your own six designs for the House on your own foundation, and exhibit them?' Knowing what was to be the result, there is something sinister in this audible whisper, and in reading that:

'I knelt up in my bed and prayed heartily to accomplish them, whatever might be the obstruction. . . . I will begin them as my next great works; I feel as if they will be my last, and I think I shall then have done my duty. O God! bless the beginning, progression and conclusion of these six great designs. . . . Grant me health of mind and body, vigour perseverance and undaunted courage; let no difficulty or want obstruct me; but let me put forth to their full intensity the powers of mind with which Thou hast blessed me, to Thy glory, and elevation and the innocent pleasure of my country; and grant the moral duties due to my dear children and wife may not be neglected, whatever may be my ambition, my delight, my rapture in my art. . . .

'One of the most remarkable days and nights of my life,' he adds. 'I slept at the Adelphi last night, high up, and just at break of day I awoke, and felt as if a heavenly choir was leaving my slumbers as day dawned and had been hanging over and inspiring me as I slept. I had not dreamt, but heard the inspiration. When I awoke, I saw the creeping light. If this be delusion, so was Columbus's voice in the roaring of the Atlantic winds; but neither was, and under the blessing of God the result shall show it as to myself—but only under his blessing.'

With his instinct for self-advertisement he announced his decision in a lecture at the Mechanics' Institute, and was rewarded by roars of applause. So he had got back his solitary grandeur. It was an immense undertaking, to paint six great pictures, without commission, merely to show how he would decorate the House if he were given the chance.

He began with a picture of himself—in other words, *Aristides* (the just man) *Being Hooted by the Populace*. Most of his pictures were now of himself in various disguises—*Curtius Leaping into the Gulf*, *Napoleon* brooding over his past glories, *Alexander* strangling an enormous lion, *Uriel* frowning down Satan. He admits to using his own head for Curtius (it is quite a good likeness) and he painted the subject many times, running his *Napoleons* close. The subjects were not the same as those chosen for his cartoons, but were to represent just and unjust forms of government, the foil to *Aristides* being *Nero Harping while Rome Burned*. And now he was able to say again, 'My position is still solitary and glorious. In me the solitary sublimity of High Art is not gone. I still pursue my course, neglected, little employed, too happy if the approval of my own conscience is the only reward for my labours.'

'Strange the action of the faculty called genius!' he writes, '. . . I sketched Aristides, the populace hooting him. On Sunday I looked at it without thought or reflection. In flowed a brilliant flash of placing him in the middle; the gateways—the Acropolis —the Temple of Theseus—the expression of the Democrats, of Themistocles, of Aristides' wife, of his child! For five minutes I was lost to external objects; I saw the whole—never clearer— never stronger—never finer. Thank God! Thank God!'

'What a pity', he writes later, 'that a man of my order, sincerity, perhaps genius' (in the *Journals* he adds '*private*, not perhaps') 'is not employed. What honour, what distinction, would I not confer on my great country! However it is my destiny to perform great things, not in consequence of encouragement, but in spite of opposition, so let it be. In fact, God knows best, and He knows what suits every man He gives. He knows that luxury, even competence, would dull my mind.'

In all this one must not forget the refrain of money-worry that continues uninterrupted, never to cease till the end: 'O God! I am again without resource but in Thy mercy. Enable me to bear up, and vanquish, as I have done, all difficulties. Let nothing however desperate or overwhelming, stop me from the completion of my six designs. On these my country's honour rests, and my own fame on earth. Thou knowest how for forty years I have struggled and resisted. Enable me to do so to the last gasp of my life.'

Let it be noted once again that the impression of violent mental excitement, and emotional disturbance, conveyed so unmistakably by these entries, was, for the most part, not evident to the world. His death, when it came, astonished everyone who knew him, his wife most of all. Outwardly he was the same man, full of activity and enthusiasm, and the reader of his *Journals* sees something that his most intimate friends did not. He describes how his 'enemies', meeting him, would place their hands on his chest, asking 'What is the reason of this extraordinary stamina? Is it here?' 'Their air', says Haydon, 'was exactly as if they had been looking out for my death.'

He was writing constantly to the press, urging, in *The Times* and *Morning Chronicle*, the danger of an invasion of German art, and its probable pernicious influence on the Fine Arts Commission. It was characteristic of him that he began this attack just before the Cartoon Contest, thereby certainly not prejudicing the President of the Royal Commission in his favour. So much annoyance did it cause that when he wrote an article on fresco painting, and dedicated it to the Prince Consort, his presentation copy was returned. In this connection it is not improbable that his fatal habit of writing to the Press once again ruined his chances, and that the judges, fearing to displease the Prince, would not vote for his cartoons. There are doubts of Eastlake's loyalty. He had behaved throughout as Haydon's friend, but Bell Scott says, 'What chance had Haydon with Eastlake, his enemy, being President of the Royal Academy?'[1] And Charles Boner writes, 'Sir Charles Eastlake would not give Haydon's letters to him [Tom Taylor]. No wonder! The life had shown his base ingratitude already.' Haydon himself was suspicious, but Kirkup who knew Eastlake well, asks, 'Whom has he ever betrayed? His advice to me has always been the best.'

In spite of everything Haydon's vitality was still ready to obey every call; he made a flying visit to Rochester merely to see a picture from which Wilkie was said to have got his idea of the *Blind Fiddler*, and another to Plymouth to examine the private papers of Sir Joshua Reynolds with reference to his resignation from the Academy.

He was also actively interesting himself in the Government Schools of Design. The London School was split by the feud between those who, like Haydon, wished to make drawing from the figure the basis of the designer's training, and those who wished to make a sharp distinction between the instruction of the artist and the commercial designer. Haydon used all his energy to urge the former course, and was indefatigable in persuading the President of the Board of Trade, and the public by letters in the newspapers, that all decorative art not based on fine art must be unworthy of the name of art altogether.

In 1837 Haydon, in conjunction with Ewart and others, had started a school calling itself The Society for Promoting Practical Design. Mechanics were invited, and came in large numbers. Haydon and others lectured, a fine female model was engaged and the working-men set to draw from her. The school became immensely popular and soon filled.

The object was not to ruin, but, by example, to improve the Government School at Somerset House, and to show them, by drawing their students away, that if they wished to compete

[1] Eastlake was not at this time P.R.A., but became so in 1850.

with the Saville House School (Haydon's) they must adopt the same methods.

The Government-and-Academy party took the strange step of getting some of its members on to the board of Haydon's school to counteract his influence, but these ended by acting under him and adopting his ideas, which through them were extended to the school at Somerset House. The latter school even went one better, and engaged a nude male model as well as a female, which, according to Frederic Haydon, 'of course drew all the women students to Somerset House as well as the men'. This happy result having been achieved, and the nude model being accepted as the basis of all study for every form of art, the Saville House School closed down. Haydon's principles had triumphed.

On the last day but one of the year he had the shock of hearing of Colonel Gurwood's suicide, 'Good heavens! Gurwood has cut his throat. The man who headed the forlorn hope at Cuidad Rodrigo, the rigid soldier, the iron-nerved hero . . . where is the responsibility of a man with a mind so easily affected by body? Romilly, Castlereagh, and Gurwood!'

On 31 December he wrote:

'The end of 1845 is approaching rapidly; ten minutes after nine. I prayed at the end of 1844 that I might get through the great works in hand. I have accomplished (all but) Aristides and Nero of the six contemplated. O God! grant that no difficulty, however apparently insurmountable, may conquer my spirit, or prevent me from bringing to a triumphant conclusion my six works. . . . I prayed to accomplish Aristides and Nero; I have attained, by Thy blessing, my desire. I prayed for health; I have had it. I prayed for blessings on my family; they have been blessed. Can I feel grateful enough? Never.

'I now pray, O Almighty, surrounded by difficulties, and in great necessity, that I may accomplish two more of my six. . . . O Lord! let not this be presumption, but the just confidence inspired by Thee, O God! This year is closing rapidly. I almost hear the rush and roar of the mighty wave from eternity that will overwhelm it for ever!'

XXIV. FINIS

Sleep brings no wish to fret
My harassed heart beneath;
My only wish is to forget
In endless sleep of death.

EMILY BRONTË

Stretch me no longer on this rough world.

B. R. HAYDON (misquoted from *Lear*)

THE fatal year 1846 opened. One can picture Haydon in his painting-room, an elderly white-haired man, still retaining the delicate profile that in his youth had added beauty to his many gifts. The sensitive outline of the nose is hardly altered, and forty years have made surprisingly little difference in the short upper lip, the mouth and chin. But the youth and the beauty have gone, and the slightly truculent, half-heroic certainty of high destiny has been replaced by trembling doubt and anxiety as he writes on the morning of that first day of January, 'O God, bless the beginning, progression and conclusion of this year, for Jesus Christ's sake, my dear family, my art, and myself!'

The year began badly; on the first day he declared himself very uneasy; he owed about £3,000, and had paid away too rapidly, leaving himself bare. He was clinging like a drowning man to the thought of finishing his six designs as if his salvation depended on them, when no one but himself cared whether he finished them or not. He believed the moment propitious for exhibiting the first two, since there was to be no competition that year, and he hoped to enlist public sympathy before it was too late, and to show how unjust had been his exclusion. All his plans were ill-conceived now; he made one fatal decision after another, this last, through an unlucky accident, one of the most fatal of all. His family and friends tried to dissuade him, pointing out that he had lost large sums (nearly £250 in one case) by his recent exhibitions. But he would listen to no one, priding himself on the infallibility of his judgement, and refusing to believe he was not still 'deep in the hearts of the people'. So,

279

on 12 January, he took one of the rooms (not the great room this time, that was already engaged) at the Egyptian Hall for an exhibition to be held in April; and the die was cast. He published an advertisement setting forth his claims and appealing to the public to support the exhibition:

'HAYDON'S NEW PICTURES.—On Easter Monday next will open for exhibition, at the Egyptian Hall . . . two large pictures, viz. 1. "The Banishment of Aristides with His Wife and Children", to show the Injustice of Democracy. 2. "Nero playing his Lyre whilst Rome is burning", to prove the heartlessness of despotism. These works are part of a series of six designs, made thirty-four years ago for the old House of Lords, and laid before every Minister to the present day. . . . This exhibition will open in no spirit of opposition to the Government plan about to be put into force, but with a view of letting the public see that works endeavoured to be executed on the principle of the great masters of the British school, founded on those established by the greater men of other schools, are perfectly consistent with the decoration of any building. . . . He (Mr. Haydon) was the first to petition the House for State support to High Art—he was the first to petition for schools of design—he was the first to plan the decoration of the Old House of Lords, and to keep up the excitement till it was resolved to decorate the new—he has devoted forty-two years, without omission of a day, to simplify the principles of the art for the instruction of the people; and having been utterly neglected when all his plans have been adopted, he appeals to the public to support his exhibition, that he may be able to complete the series he has planned.'

Aristides was painted in four months and *Nero* in two; *Jerusalem* had taken six years. It was by no means the case that he had learnt to work more quickly as he seemed to think; but he could not possibly afford more time on large pictures and hurried, to their detriment. On his sixtieth birthday (25 January), he prayed, 'O God! continue my eyes and faculties to the last hour of existence. Bless me through my ensuing years. Grant I may live to accomplish my six great works.' There is evidence in the *Journals* at this time of much misery, a state all too familiar with him, but not of despair. The incessant struggle was telling severely, but any success would have saved him. He had none. He was hard pressed: he went out 'in misery' to raise money for a bill of £26. He tried Coutts's, and said to Mr. Marjoribanks, 'Sir, do help me.' Marjoribanks was humane, he begged Haydon to sit down, saying, 'You know it is against the rule.' Then with a trembling head and a shaking hand (he was fifty) he gave

Haydon the money. 'I declare I feel as young as ever,' says Haydon. 'These rich men always look older than we struggling men of genius.'

A few days after he was again in the greatest anxiety; accommodation in the City was out of the question, and the only cure for such a state of things was a new canvas, so he decided to order one at once and begin the third picture of his series— *Alfred and the First British Jury*. He allowed a day to pass without doing so, and on the following evening he cries 'O, O, O; I sat all day and looked into the fire. I must get up my third canvas, or I shall go cracked. . . . Perhaps this paralysis was nature's repose. I stared like a baby, and felt like one. A man who has had so many misfortunes as I have had gets frightened at leaving his family for a day.' By borrowing £10 from one friend, £10 from another and £5 10s. from his hatter he contrived to satisfy claims for £62, but notes, 'Next week I must be at it again.' The following day he got his new canvas and began the third picture, trusting that from trials inflicted his genius would only burn the brighter.

In February he gave a series of lectures in Edinburgh to crowded rooms. The future Lady Eastlake in her self-complacent way describes how she met him at Lord Jeffrey's, 'Not a very large gathering: Macready and Haydon the lions—the latter still preserving the outline of feature which Phillips drew to my childish delight, but otherwise fat and uninteresting.' 'Haydon,' said his host, 'you look fat and well, the sure signs of prosperity.' 'Ah!' thought Haydon, 'if you knew the trouble I have to pay my bills you would not say that.'

On his return to London he was busy with the preparations for the exhibition, but wished it were over, and felt excruciating pain of mind when not actually painting. Hearing that the fifth report of the Fine Arts Commission was to be published at the beginning and not at the end of the session, his distorting vanity at once connected the change of plan with himself, 'Are the secretary and his masters afraid of the probable consequences of Haydon's exhibition, with his two pictures? . . .'

At the end of March Mary went to Brighton for 'her dear health', the first time his 'dearest love' had left him for twenty-five years. They were touched as he tied up her trunk. In driving along the cab-horse fell, which annoyed him; the same thing had happened before the Cartoon Contest. Bad omens followed one another; in posting the letters for the private day he dropped three parts on the pavement, about 300. He hung the pictures on All-Fool's day, and had arranged for the public opening on the thirteenth. In putting up the portrait of Wordsworth he let it fall, knocking down that of Lord Althorp and breaking the frame.

The private day was wet, the rain never stopped and hardly anyone came; on the following days the receipts varied between £1 1s. 6d., and £1 8s. 6d.—in 1820, while he was showing *Jerusalem*, they had been as high as £50 a day. To stimulate interest he published an advertisement:

'Haydon's new pictures are now open at the Egyptian Hall . . . in these two magnificent pictures of the burning of Rome by Nero, and Banishment of Aristides, the "drawing is grand, and characters most felicitous, and we hope the artist will reap the reward he merits", says *The Times*, April 6th. "These are Haydon's best works," says the *Herald*, same day. N.B.—Visitors are requested to go up into the gallery of the room, in order to see the full effect of the flame of the burning city. Nero accused the Christians of this cruel act, covered hundreds of them with combustible materials, and burnt them for the amusement of the savage Romans. (See Tacitus.) Haydon has devoted forty-two years to improve the taste of the people; and let every Briton who has pluck in his bosom, and a shilling in his pocket crowd to his works during Easter week.'

'An advertisement of a finer description to catch the *profanum vulgus* could not be written,' he says on Easter Monday, 13 April, 'yet not a shilling was added to the receipts.'

Fate seems to have waited for this ill-omened day as if intending not only to strike the poor artist a deathblow but to overwhelm him with ridicule. That great room of Bullock's, the scene of so many fantastic exhibitions, in which Haydon himself had had his triumphs, had been pre-engaged by Barnum, who on Easter Monday produced before a delighted world his tremendous novelty, General Tom Thumb. The height of this dwarf was 31 inches, and over its abnormal deficiency London went mad. It may almost be said that restraint and decency were laid aside, while day after day peers and commoners, duchesses and coal-heavers, the young and the old in their hundreds and thousands pushed and fought and jostled, in at the door, up the stairs, and past the room where hung, unvisited and unwanted, the last dying efforts of eighteenth-century English Historical Art.[1]

[1] The first week Tom Thumb took £600; Haydon £7 13s.

The *Art Union* (18 May) said of *Nero*, 'It is perhaps the best picture which the artist ever painted.' But in a footnote it expresses 'extreme regret' at Haydon's advertisement, 'High Art—the Egyptian Hall, exquisite feeling of the English people for high Art—General Tom Thumb last week received 12,000 people, who paid him £600, B. R. Haydon, who has devoted 42 years to elevate their taste was honoured by the visits of 133½, producing £5 13s. 6d., being a reward for painting two of his finest works, *Aristides* and *Nero*. Horace Vernet, Delaroche, Ingrès [*sic*], Cornelius, Hess, Schnorr and Scheffer, hasten to this glorious country of fresco and patronage, and grand design if you have a tender fancy to end your days in a Whig Union. "Ingenuas dedicisse",'[1] &c.

To read the *Journals* from now on is like watching a play where we foresee and dread the end. All that has gone before takes on a dark significance in the shadow of what we know to be coming: Haydon's vanity and self-applause, his quarrelsome pugnacity, his reckless borrowing, his wearisome self-assertiveness and bad taste seem to crowd on to the stage like actors in the chorus of a Greek tragedy, as the hero staggers out for the last act. He was not without dignity; broken and despairing, he followed with proud consistency the path he had chosen to its end. The whispering voices that had called St. Joan and Columbus to achievement, called Haydon to destruction. Misled by their siren notes he had snatched the trumpet from the hand of Fame, and had tried to blow it with his own lips, but the sounds he produced were false and disturbed Nemesis in her sleep. He had gone through life to the strains of an incessant band, echoes of his imagination, that would sound in reality on his day of glory, and it was his belief in that day that had been the source of all his strength. Even now when he no longer hoped for it in his lifetime, he felt convinced that his very sufferings, which his *Journals* were to immortalize, would be the means of 'working up' that glory, and that posterity would honour him (he really came to believe it) as one who had suffered all for the good of his country.

Looking back in the light of our knowledge on those few weeks in the England of 1846 before the fatal 22 June, though

[1] According to the *Art Union* (1846, p. 236) Haydon was offered, within a few weeks of his death, 500 guineas for *Aristides*, which he indignantly refused as an insult.

the drama was being acted in secret, and the blaze of publicity only burst when the curtain fell, the battered figure of Haydon may almost be granted the centre of the stage, so immense was the sensation caused by his death.

By the middle of April there is another of those changes in the entries that mark his descent: a sense of real danger, an alarming oscillation of the mind, and the accounts of ordinary happenings cease. He clung to the finishing of his six designs as if it was his only hope in a tottering world:

'Bless my exertions, O Lord, now, bless the beginning, progression and conclusion, not only of Alfred but the remaining three; and grant I may accomplish the whole four remaining, with glory to thy gifts, honour to my country and blessing to my family. Grant all these things, for Jesus Christ's sake. Amen! Amen! Amen!

'How mysterious is the whisper which, in such anxieties, impels to paint, conceive and invent! How mysterious!'

For several days there will be little more than a short prayer for blessing:

'O God! bless me through the evils of this day.'
'I thank Thee. Thou hast done so. Amen.'

And again:

'Bless me, O God, through the evils of this day. Amen.'

And again, 'Bless me, O God, through the evils of this day. Amen!'

'God has blessed me. Thanks. Amen.'

There is something very moving about the sudden note of humility in these short prayers, so different from the confident demanding tone he generally adopted. A flicker of the old buoyancy shows now and again to die at once, as when he says he has advanced *Alfred* 'gloriously', though borne down at first by misery. Early in May he writes:

'Came home in excruciating anxiety, not being able to raise the money for my rent for the Hall, and found a notice from a broker, for a quarter's rent from Newton, my old landlord for twenty-two years. . . . For a moment my brain was confused. I had paid him half; and, therefore, there was only ten pounds left. I went into the painting-room in great misery of mind. That so old a friend should have chosen such a moment to do such a thing is painful. After an hour's dullness, my mind suddenly fired up with a new background for Alfred. I dashed at it, and at dinner it was enormously improved.

'6th. . . . I set my palette with a disgust, and yet under irresistible impulse. On coming into the parlour, the cook, whose wages I had not been able to pay, handed me a card from a broker, saying he called for a quarter's rent from Mr. Newton. I felt my heart sink, my brain confused, as I foresaw ruin, misery and a prison! It was hoisting the standard!

'This is temper. I went on with my palette in a giddy fidget. . . . I dined, expecting an execution every moment, and retired to rest in misery. I awoke continually; and this morning went off to Fairbairn of Leeds to ask him to pay me for his brother. He could not. I drove back, finding his brother was in town. He was out and I flew up to my landlord Newton. He was irritable, and in bad health. He said I was in a bad temper. I promised him payment this week. He promised to let me alone. Home I came and made a sketch; and this moment comes a cheque from my dear friend Kemp, which has really saved me for the time.

'This is historical painting in England!

'The struggle is severe; for myself I care not, but for her so dear to me I feel. It presses on her mind; and in a moment of pain she wrote the following simple bit of feeling to Frederic, who is in South America, on board the *Grecian*—a Middy. It shows the inmost state of her soul, and what she really feels as to the danger of our position.'

There follow seven verses written in a jingling metre but with genuine emotion: it begins:

> This is thy natal day, my child;
> And where art thou so dear?
> My heart is sad, and yet 'tis glad
> To know thou art not here.

After wishing she could join him 'in those bright isles' she asks:

> Should I sigh for this land of oppression and toil,
> Where each morn is expected with fear?

The exhibition had been a complete failure, and he closed it on 18 May with a loss of £111. 'Cleared out my exhibition,' he writes. 'Removed Aristides and Themistocles, and all my drawings. Next to a victory is a skilful retreat; and I marched out before General Tom Thumb, a beaten but not a conquered exhibitor.' His friends had been right, but he prided himself on never taking advice unless it coincided with his own intentions.

He had the fatal habit of thinking of such things as Nelson's putting the telescope to his blind eye whenever common prudence was in danger of getting the upper hand. Contemporary opinions differ about the effect on him of Tom Thumb's victory; his son, Frederic, discounts it, but he is not a reliable witness, as he was in South America and wrote thirty years after with a strong bias in favour of his father, whose dignity rather suffers from the opposite idea—that it was mortal. Talfourd and Elizabeth Barrett put Tom Thumb in a place of importance in Haydon's downfall; they agree in thinking that opposition, abuse, neglect even, could have been borne, but the sense of ridicule drove him to despair.

After Haydon's death, when Robert Browning, sheltering under a windy archway from the rain, was hurriedly skimming through a batch of letters from Haydon, which Elizabeth Barrett at parting had put into his hands, he came upon the sentence in which the writer speaks of the glory of being a painter if only for the neglect, and his heart, which had been hard with prejudice, was melted. It was no common mind that wrote those words. Haydon was alive to a certain beauty in failure. The soul aspires, the hand fumbles, the spirit receives a bitter wound, and the heart bears it bravely. Of how many artists, in every form, has not that been the history?

Tom Thumb was only one of the last straws that broke Haydon's courage, not the main cause. His position was hopeless, there was no future; everything had come together to crush him—the blow of the Cartoon Competition and the bitter humiliation of not being consulted by the committee, the endless anxiety about money, the failure of his exhibition, and the annihilation which that must have been of any hopes with regard to the remaining four pictures, and finally the cruel insult that the public and the world of fashion he so loved offered him through the poor dwarf, which associated him for ever with the latter as an object of pity. It was a painful contrast: the afternoon of that spring day when Sir George Beaumont led Mrs. Siddons before *Jerusalem*, while the grand assembly ceased its chatter to hear her verdict, with the empty dusty room where his last two works hung, and which would have been so silent but for the vulgar hullabaloo next door.

Talfourd says that until near the end Haydon's anxieties and sorrows did not destroy the buoyancy of his spirits, or spoil his conviviality, but that he struggled, and toiled, and laughed, and triumphed, and failed, and hoped on till age came upon him, and he found himself still in opposition to the world and as far from fortune as ever. But just at the end, and only the very end, in Talfourd's words, 'His mind was shattered to pieces—all distorted and broken—with only one feeling left entire, the perversion of which led to the deed, a hope to awaken sympathy in death for those whom living he could not shelter.'

A month before his death his old friend Samuel Prout showed him a drawing that Jackson had made of him forty-one years before, and which he had given to Prout. Haydon was moved at seeing again this drawing of himself at the age of nineteen, the occasion of which he well remembered. Jackson had come home with him from the Academy Schools, and Haydon suggested that they should sit up all night and draw each other. The result of this was that he received notice from his landlord on the following morning for the noise and disturbance that had prevented him and his wife from sleeping; but on being shown Jackson's excellent likeness they relented. Haydon now wrote on the back of it, 'Forty-one years ago it was done; I think myself and so does my wife, a better-looking man at 60 than at 19.' Not many days afterwards, indeed only fourteen days before his death, he made a drawing of himself from his own bust by Park. This drawing, which also has disappeared, was considered a spirited likeness; under it Haydon wrote μεγα θρονεων (meditating great things).

A few days after he writes, 'Awoke at three, in very great agony of mind; and lay awake till long after five, affected by my position. . . . I have done a great deal this week under all circumstances. . . . There lie Aristides and Nero, unasked for, unfelt for, rolled up; Aristides, a subject Raffaele would have praised and complimented me on! Good God! And £111 11s. 5d. loss by showing it.'

On 31 May he seemed to have a prevision of something to dread, but had evidently as yet no tragic intention in his mind, he writes, 'Alfred is well on, in spite of dreadful need. O Lord! carry me through the next and the dangerous month. Amen.'

And on 1 June, 'O God I begin this month, June, in fear and submission. Thy will not mine be done. Carry me through, in spite of all appearances and realities of danger, for Jesus Christ's sake; and enable me to keep my health in eyes and mind, and to

bear up and get through my six great works in spite of all difficulties, calamities or obstruction which ever afflicted humanity.'

Three days after he went to the Saltmarsh Collection, and saw
again a Rubens he had seen thirty years before at De la Hant's.
'I remember it used to be a wonder to me,' he writes, 'but I saw
through it at once now. . . . I felt every touch from experience.
I know what feelings he must have had when he touched so and
so.' Was this the *Chapeau de Poil* which he visited thirty years
before with John Martin (clothed gaily in a blue coat and prim-
rose-coloured vest) on the occasion when Bewick had been em-
barrassed by the strange snortings of his two companions, 'like
the sneezing of dumb animals', in the otherwise silent room?

The pressure of his debts gave him no rest; on the eleventh is
the entry:

'I have £15 to pay to-morrow, without a shilling. How I shall
manage to get seven hours' peace for work, and yet satisfy my creditors, Heaven only knows!

'£30 Newton, on the 25th. £31 17s. 6d. Newman, same day.
£26 10s. Coutts, on the 24th. £29 16s. 9d. Gillots, on the 29th.
£17 10s. 6d. to baker—in all £136 14s. 10d. this month, with only 18s.
in the house; nothing coming in, all received; one large picture painting
and three more getting ready, and Alfred's head to do. In God alone
I trust, in humility.'

On 13 June came the final blow from which there was no
recovery; he writes:

'Picture much advanced; but my necessities are dreadful, owing to
my failure at the Hall. In God alone I trust, to bring me through, and
extricate me safe and capable of paying my way. O God! It is hard,
this struggle of forty-two years; but Thy will, and not mine, be done,
if it save the art in the end. O God, bless me through my pictures, the
four remaining, and grant nothing on earth may stop the completion
of the six.'

But Frederic tells how his father that evening went to meet
an old friend who had promised to lend him £1,000. They
dined in the city, but after dinner his host broke the news that,
owing to the bad times, he was unable to advance the money.

Haydon drank deeply and came home drunk, the only time
his wife ever saw him so. The weather next day became intensely hot; he woke 'wrong in his head', and completely out of
health. He could not sleep, and gradually gave up working. This

loss of sleep was fatal; he used to say that he could face any
misfortune if he got his sleep.

He wrote on the 16th:

'I sat from two till five staring at my picture like an idiot. My brain
pressed down by anxiety and anxious looks of my dear Mary and
children, whom I was compelled to inform. I dined, after having raised
money on all our silver, to keep us from want in case of accidents. . . .
I came home and sat as I described. I had written to Sir R. Peel, Duke
of Beaufort and Lord Brougham, saying I had a heavy sum to pay. I
offered the Duke's study to the Duke of Beaufort for £50. Who answered first? Tormented by Disraeli, harassed by public business, up
came the following letter:

SIR,
    I am sorry to hear of your continual embarrassments. From a
limited fund which is at my disposal, I send as a contribution towards
your relief from those embarrassments the sum of £50.
                            I am, Sir,
                                Your obedient servant
                                    ROBERT PEEL.

'And this Peel is the man who has no heart!

'17th.—Dearest Mary, with woman's passion, wishes me at once to
stop payment, and close the whole thing. I will not. I will finish my six,
under the blessing of God; reduce my expenses; and hope his mercy
will not desert me, but bring me through in health and vigour, gratitude and grandeur of soul, to the end. In Him alone I trust.

'In the morning, fearing I should be involved, I took down books
I had not paid for to a young bookseller with a family, to return them.
As I drove along, I thought I might get money on them. I felt disgusted at such a thought, and stopped and told him I feared I was in
danger; and as I feared he might lose, I begged him to keep them for a
few days. He was grateful, and in the evening came this £50. *I know
what I believe.*'

It is significant that this £50 was found untouched after his
death. He spent an entire day burning vast quantities of letters
and documents in the courtyard of his house.

Every post brought angry demands for the settlement of bills,
threats of execution, and immediate prospects of arrest and
imprisonment.

On the 18th:

'Great anxiety. My landlord, Newton, called. I said, "I see a quarter's
rent in thy face; but none from me." I appointed to-morrow night to

see him, and lay before him every iota of my position. "Good-hearted Newton!" I said, "Don't put in an execution."

' "Nothing of the sort," he replied, half-hurt.

'I sent the Duke, Wordsworth, dear Fred's and Mary's heads, to Miss Barrett to protect.'

'21st.—Slept horribly. Prayed in sorrow, and got up in agitation.'

The stress of spirit is seen in the short prayers, and invocations which recur day after day:

'O God, how have I wearied Thy invisibility with entreaty!'
'O God, bless us all through the evils of this day.'
'My danger is great!'

And the ominous sentence,

'My situation is now of more extreme peril than even when I began Solomon thirty-three years ago.'

In the knowledge of what was so soon to happen these entries have a shocking significance; we seem to be intruding on a suffering too great for exposure, yet he wished the world to know what he felt, and in showing it has produced something unique in literature.

'I call on my Creator still to support me through trials severer than I have ever gone through, to the accomplishment of my remaining four. I call on Him who has led me through the wilderness for forty-two years, under every depression and excitement, to sixty years of age, not to desert me in this the eleventh hour.'

In the long course of his *Journals* we can follow him through varying fortunes, and see, as he could not, his many fatal mistakes. He had overestimated his gifts—that was the cause of all his failure; and how bitter must have been his thoughts when he remembered the heights he had set out to climb and felt the gulf between. He had seen himself as the equal of the greatest men. In his early twenties he nearly wrote to the Duke of Wellington that he clearly foresaw his triumph in Spain and his crossing of the French frontier, and had intended to add that if it turned out as he had said, he hoped he would be allowed to remind him of his prophecy in the hour of victory, as his views in Art were as grand as his lordship's in military matters. He never ceased to regret that he had not sent that letter. Almost as a child, as he walked by the sea, he had indulged in visions of greatness, and as a young man had wondered what the crowned heads of Europe would think of him; while, at Fontainebleau, he had fancied himself the next scourge of the world. His 'whole frame had convulsed at the thought of being a great painter', and when what he believed to be the divine spirit visited him he felt like a man 'with balloons under his armpits and ether in his soul'. He *knew* himself to be of the same order as Raphael and Michael Angelo. All his life, in every emergency, had he not acted with 'the fiery fury' of his own Dentatus, and with the courage of Curtius leaping into the gulf? He was the peer of these men, and knew their hearts. Caesar wept because Alexander was master of the world at the age of twenty-four; he himself was that order of being; he too had heard the roaring blast of the trumpet-voice of Ambition, and felt her hot breath take the hair at his temples, as his spirit raised its eyes aloft and his thought dared the topmost pinnacles of fame. Caesar and Alexander: Haydon and Tom Thumb!

'O God, not mine, but Thy will be done!'

He has told us without concealment of one pang all the sickness of his soul; can we venture, with the help of a description that was left of it, to look into his painting-room in some moment of silence during those last hours when the accumulated burdens of his difficulties had tipped the balance of his mind? The small room is crowded with canvases, some on easels, some leaning against the walls, while others, unstretched and rolled, are stacked in corners. The shutters are nearly closed to keep out the blazing sunlight, for this chiaroscuric artist prefers to paint in semi-darkness. In spite of its crowded condition everything is in its proper place, and the room, like its owner, is neat. A cupboard containing books of poetry in many languages hangs over a writing-table on which a much-thumbed Bible lies open, with markers between its leaves so that passages of special consolation can be turned to quickly. It is very still in the room, but from outside obtrudes the incessant clatter of the Edgware Road, a few houses off down Burwood Place. There are two french windows, and by one of these, so placed that the light falls from the painter's left, stands a large unfinished picture, while opposite this, on a small easel, is the portrait of a very beautiful woman in the full flush of her resplendent youth, who gazes out from the canvas with a smile of gentle contentment at the figure of an old man, very still, stooping forward over the writing-table with his head bowed between his arms. This is

'H-yd-n', who, as *Somniator*, had seen himself jumping in high fettle on his plank, crowned with civic and heroic honours, and whose knuckles now show white on his clenched fists, as he lies washed up on the muddy flats of the 'River of Time', where Fame (and the Academicians) have passed him by.

On Sunday 21 June he walked out with Frank to dine with a friend at Hampstead. The heat had been intense for days, and he complained much of it. On their way through Regent's Park he said that when lying awake the night before he had understood how it was people killed themselves; that he had dwelt with pleasure on the idea of throwing himself off the Monument and dashing his head to pieces. His son begged him not to think such things, and after a time he grew more calm. Frank left him at the Avenue Bridge Road to return home, and at parting Haydon said, 'Tell your mother not to be anxious about me.' Frank was so alarmed by this conversation that he wished to tell the family doctor, but Mrs. Haydon laughed at the idea of her husband's 'committing suicide', and begged him to dismiss such suspicions from his mind. Haydon himself came back about five, not having felt in sufficiently good spirits to stay at Hampstead. At dinner he got up from his chair and turned a glazed picture to the wall, saying his brain could not bear the reflected light. He looked flushed and haggard.

During the evening he seems to have recovered; he suggested that Mary should go next day to Brixton to visit a Mr. Coulton, who was an old friend (and one of the executors Haydon named that night in his will). Although this appeared rather a strange request she promised to go; and soon after her husband went to bed, apparently in his usual health and spirits.

They heard him walking about his room nearly all night, and it must have been then that he was making up his mind, and that he wrote Mary the letter found after his death:

'God bless thee, dearest Love! Pardon thy last pang! Many hast thou suffered from me! God bless thee in dear widowhood: I hope Sir Robert Peel will consider that I have earned a pension for thee. A thousand kisses—
'Thy dear husband—and love to the last

B. R. HAYDON.'

On Monday morning at 8.30 he rang for his servant and asked him to be in attendance at 1 o'clock to take a letter to the Duke of Sutherland. As his man was leaving the room Haydon told him not to wait for an answer. He then went out, before having breakfast, to Riviere, a gun-maker in Oxford Street, where he bought one of a pair of pistols. Returning at nine, he breakfasted alone, and then went to his painting-room, where he wrote letters to his children, his will, and 'last thoughts'. He had locked himself in as usual, and when Mary tried the door at about 10.30 he called out sharply, 'Who's there?' She replied that she was just going up to dress before going out, and he answered, 'Oh, very well. God bless you! I will see you presently.' A few minutes later he came up to her room, and kissed her fervently, then lingered as if he had something he wished to say, but thought better of it and returned to his own room. At 10.45 his wife and daughter heard a shot, but thought it was from troops exercising in the Park. Five minutes later a heavy fall was heard in the studio and they supposed he had dropped one of the large' canvases he was in the habit of moving. Mrs. Haydon started for Brixton, her daughter going a little way with her. On her return, thinking to comfort and console her father, she stole gently to his painting-room, and finding the door unlocked looked in. Not many years after, on her deathbed, she told her brother what she saw. At first, in the subdued light, she could see nothing clearly; the room seemed empty, but there was an awful silence that chilled her heart, broken only by the loud ticking of her father's watch, which lay on the table. She said it was as if some sorrow had passed into the air, and oppressed her. She looked for her father but he was not there, though his *Journals* lay open on the table as if he had just been writing, and there were some sealed letters, and a prayer book she herself had given him. She walked into the room and saw him lying on the floor. She thought he had thrown himself down to study the foreground of his picture, and called gently to him, but he did not answer. She came closer and softly called again. She looked steadily. He was all huddled up on the floor. A violent dread seized her; she stepped close and her foot slipped in what she thought was a pool of red paint. Then, as she bent over him, her heart stopped beating. He lay with his head half resting on his right arm, his face a greenish white, and across his neck in different directions were two frightful gashes. Her father had killed himself and she was standing in his blood.

Vehement to the last it was more a slaughter than a killing. It appeared from the traces of the blood that he had first fired the shot, and finding that death did not follow had loaded again; that he had then gone from before his picture (which was splashed with blood) to the door, where, with his right hand on the door handle, he inflicted a fearful gash on his throat with a razor from right to left, and then had returned to the easel and made a similar cut from left to right. By his side lay two razors, one in its case, the other on the floor; the latter was half opened and smeared with blood, while near it was a small pocket-pistol, which had been discharged and reloaded. He was dressed with great neatness, and everything in the room had been the subject of careful arrangement: opposite the huge canvas of *Alfred and the First British Jury* stood, on a small easel, the portrait of Mary as a young woman. His letters to his wife and children and the will lay on the writing-table beside the *Journals*, completed to the last few minutes of his life with the concluding words:

'God forgive me. Amen.
Finis
of
B. R. HAYDON
"Stretch me no longer on this rough world."

Lear.

End of Twenty-sixth Volume.'

EPILOGUE

The fathers have eaten sour grapes and the children's teeth are set on edge.
EZEKIEL

HAYDON'S uneven fate granted him one compensation for the insult of Tom Thumb: to close the fierce heat which had been the cause of many deaths, and which may have been a factor in his own, a terrific thunderstorm broke over the whole of England accompanied by torrents of rain—a fitting requiem to his stormy life. We are told that 'a wave of horror swept the country'. Haydon was found by a Coroner's Jury to have killed himself while of unsound mind, and was buried in Paddington New Churchyard among his many children, an enormous crowd following him to the grave. His tomb stands close to that of Mrs. Siddons, and bears the inscription, 'He devoted 42 years to the improvement of the taste of the English People in high art and died broken hearted from pecuniary distresses.'

In his last hour he wrote to Peel:

'June 22nd
'Life is insupportable. Accept my gratitude for *always* feeling for me in adversity. I hope I have earned for my dearest wife security from want. God bless you.'

This Peel endorsed, 'Last letter from Haydon. It must have been written a few minutes before he deprived himself of life. Observe the word "wife" had been originally written "widow", and been altered by him.'

This letter seems to prove that he killed himself to provide for his wife and family.

The question of Haydon's sanity must be considered, though until near the end there is no reason to regard him as of unsound mind, unless in his intemperate hatred of the Academicians. His 'Last Thoughts', written in the hour of his death, and bearing evidence of feverish excitement, consisted in a comparison between Wellington and Napoleon in which he seemed anxious to repair some supposed injustice to the former occasioned by his admiration of the latter. This puzzled everyone at the time. But it has been seen that he constantly repeated that he was of 'the Napoleon species', one born to bend facts to his will, and of sufficient power and genius to do evil (to borrow, perhaps?) that good might come; though he did subsequently admit that this was the special prerogative of the Deity and that his trespass thereon was presumption. Wellington and Napoleon represented for him opposing moral codes: the one—cautious, calm, self-contained, the servant of Duty, consolidating his position in advance—Wilkie, in fact; the other—bold unscrupulous ambitious, the servant of Genius, ready to dare everything and take all risks—himself, in fact. When these 'Last Thoughts' came out at the inquest, it was taken to be a proof of his madness that he should trouble himself about Wellington and Napoleon at so awful a moment. It was nothing of the sort, it was an act of repentance, a recantation, if it was not too late, of the principle on which he had conducted his whole life.

Within a week of his death he wrote three letters to Elizabeth Barrett, the first in so light a vein that the second followed to desire her not to attribute to him a want of feeling. Of the third she wrote:

'Never could he have meditated self-destruction while writing that note. He said he should write six sets of lectures more . . . six more Volumes. He said he was painting a new background to a picture, which made him "feel as if his soul had wings". . . . And then he hoped his brain would not turn. And he gloried in the naval dangers of his son at sea. And he repeated an old phrase of his, which I had heard from him often before . . . that he couldn't and wouldn't die. Strange and dreadful.'

Haydon had always been eccentric and at the last his stepson, Orlando Hyman, considered that he had become more so; while the post-mortem examination of his head disclosed, in the opinion of the two doctors who carried it out, the existence of disease in the brain. One of these doctors believed the appearances indicated long-standing irritation, the other that though the thickened state of the vessels of the brain was of long standing, the inflammation of the brain itself was comparatively recent. A writer in a medical Journal, in 1853, says that the condition of his brain was doubtless of an asthenic character from over-work and excitement. Bewick scoffs at the idea of insanity,

whereas J. F. Nisbet, writing in 1891, states boldly that he inherited 'a double strain of insanity, first from an eccentric father,
who in recording his (Haydon's) birth in a diary, added that the
wind at the time was W.S.W.; and secondly from a mother who
suffered from mental derangement, and who died of angina
pectoris'. If the only reason this writer can produce for throwing
suspicions on the elder Haydon's sanity is his habit of recording
each day the state of the wind, his opinion may be discounted;
while there is no hint anywhere else that I have discovered that
Haydon's mother was other than completely normal, nor is
angina pectoris generally considered either a cause or a result of
insanity. It may then be assumed that, until the last few weeks of
his life, Haydon, though eccentric, was perfectly sane, but that
anxiety and disappointment lasting over a period of some twenty
years did eventually upset the balance of his mind. If it be con-
tended that Haydon's vanity as an artist amounted to insanity
then it will have to be admitted that the condition among artists,
especially young artists, is fairly common. But Haydon had
some excuse; he was welcomed as a genius almost on his arrival in
London, and was petted as one by a large number of important
people. He was always being compared to Michael Angelo, and
treated as if the art of the country depended on him: in 1842
Kirkup, his old pupil, wrote, 'God bless you, and keep you from
those you admire—your mean, ignorant aristocracy—who with
one drop of their oceans of wealth, plunder, might have placed
your name on a level with Buonarrotti, for the honour of their
country.'

The *Art Union* in an obituary notice (July 1846) says, 'His
whole life, private and professional, proceeded under erroneous
views of human nature; he was always expecting too much and
surely obtained too little. . . . Whatever were his mistakes, Mr.
Haydon was a great movement in Art.'

A committee was formed and subscriptions raised for the
family, Sir Robert Peel (on the eve of his resignation, when he
might well have been entirely absorbed in the fate of his Ministry) giving £100, and Lady Peel £25 a year from a fund at
her disposal, while a civil-list pension of £50 a year was granted
to the widow. Four hundred pounds was subscribed on the first
day at Serjeant Talfourd's. The Academy gave £50, the Duke
of Sutherland £200. Frederic Haydon intended to repay all

this money, and many years later accumulated a large part of it when the bank in which it was deposited failed and the whole was lost.

Mary Haydon survived her husband by six years, dying in-testate at the age of sixty-one at Hensbridge Villas, St. John's Wood, leaving £300. Frederic, whose health had suffered in the Paraguayan rivers, left the Navy in 1854 and transferred to the Civil Service. In 1858 Disraeli, out of respect to his late father, offered him the further post of sub-inspector of fac-tories at Halifax, Yorks. But Frederic, with certain fine qualities, inherited also certain unfortunate ones from his father and, in tones strangely familiar to readers of the *Journals*, declares that in 1867 'without full or fair enquiry, and without just cause, Mr. Gaythorne Hardy deprived me of this post, and "declined" my "further services" because I had ventured to call attention to certain departmental irregularities'. His experience had shown him that officials were 'opposed to any change for the better, although it can be indisputably shown to be for the better . . . and are too apt to crush resentfully any active subordinate who ventures to expose negligence or abuse. I had', he says, 'com-mitted the error—officially speaking—of telling the plain truth plainly.' That plain truth was such a snare to the Haydon family, they saw it so clearly when no one else did. B. R. Haydon chose to be a painter, if he had gone instead into the Civil Service and had written his autobiography, should we not sooner or later have come upon some such entry as this of Frederic's?

'I had quite unintentionally made myself previously disagree-able to the Home Office, partly by correcting certain oversights in their Factory Bills, and partly by showing them that it was no part of their business to audit Factory accounts.' And as the son suggested to Mr. Walpole in 1866, might not the father in his turn have suggested, that it would have been better that the Factory Department be reconstructed and 'bodily transferred from the Home Office to the Board of Trade'? 'I heard after-wards', writes poor Frederic, 'that this exhibition of industry and observation on my part confirmed the displeasure, if it did not seal my doom.' At any rate his doom was sealed, and he wrote (1867) a letter to Gladstone entitled 'Our Officials at the Home Office' in much the same spirit as his father wrote his *Autobiography*.

Frederic published B. R. Haydon's life and correspondence

in 1876, and ten years later ended his well-meaning and troubled life in Bethlehem Hospital. Frank, the eldest, also following in another way too closely in his father's footsteps, committed suicide in 1887, leaving a grown-up daughter. As for Mary their sister, 'once', in the opinion of her devoted brother, 'one of the loveliest girls in England', she never recovered from the shock of her father's death, and died a few years after her mother. Haydon had loved her as he loved all his family; but there was something in this ill-fated man that made him dangerous to know, and, like so many others who came in contact with him, she too 'suffered in the end'.

So Benjamin Robert Haydon, who from his youth had fixed his eyes upon the stars, died by his own hand, having failed in all his intentions. Brilliant, vital, ambitious and determined, he set forth with no doubt of success; old, poor, bitter and out of fashion, he saw the glory that was the meaning of his existence shining as brightly as ever—as ever, out of reach. His *Solomon* has disappeared, the posthumous fame as a painter of which he felt so secure is a remote sound carrying with it what to his ears would have been a horror—the nightmare suspicion of mirth. The 'Art' he stood for has become more completely eclipsed than he would have conceived to be possible, and his own exercises in it (though wrongly) the very byword of absurdity. He killed himself for the sake of his wife and children, and his god to whom he prayed so often and so fervently, and who led him on only in mockery, could not grant even his last request: when in the closing sentence of his will, while begging forgiveness of those dear ones, he prayed that they might be happier and suffer less—released from the burden of his ambition.

AUTHORITIES

General Sources

The Autobiography and Memoirs of Benjamin Robert Haydon (1786-1846), edited by Tom Taylor. New Edition with an introduction by Aldous Huxley, 1926.

The Autobiography of Benjamin Robert Haydon (World's Classics). Foreword by Edmund Blunden.

Benjamin Robert Haydon, Correspondence and Table Talk, with Memoir by his Son, Frederic Wordsworth Haydon, 1876.

'B. R. Haydon', by Cosmo Monkhouse, in *Dictionary of National Biography.*

Chapter I

Lewis Einstein, *Divided Loyalties.* 1933. p. 319.

John Pye, *Patronage of British Art.* 1845. p. 302.

Letters of Robert Browning and Elizabeth Barrett, 1845-6. 1899. ii, 303.

Miss Mitford's Letters, ed. E. H. Chorley. 1872. 2nd Series. ii, 121.

James Elmes, 'Biography of B. R. Haydon', *Annals of the Fine Arts.* Vol. V. 1820. p. 337.

William T. Whitley, *Artists and their Friends in England.* Vol. I. pp. 220, 310, 339, 341.

Chapter II

The Private Letter Books of Sir Walter Scott, ed. Wilfred Partington. 1930. p. 173.

Notes and Queries. 4th Series. Vol. VII, pp. 55, 143, 144. Vol. VIII, p. 149. 5th Series. Vol. X, p. 370. Vol. XI, p. 111.

Illustrated London News: 4 July 1846.

Prince's Worthies of Devon, 1701 (another edition 1810). pp. 480-3.

Plymouth Guide Book, 1812.

Gentleman's Magazine, 1813. May 1813.

Advertisement in the *London Chronicle,* 23 July 1788. (Printed, Plymouth 2 July 1788).

Chapter IV

Quarterly Review, 1867. ii, 74.

Journal of Hellenic Studies. Vol. XXXVI. 1916. p. 302.

Edmund Blunden, *Leigh Hunt's Examiner Examined.* 1928. pp. 10-11.

Life and Letters of William Bewick, ed. Thomas Landseer. 1871. l. 266.

The Letters of Sir Walter Scott: ed. H. S. C. Grierson. 1934. 7 January 1821. Vol. VI. pp. 332-3.

Chapter V

Cyrus Redding, 'Haydon,' *Past Celebrities Whom I have Known.* 1866.
Edmund Blunden, *Leigh Hunt's Examiner Examined.* 1928, p. 28.
Lady Eastlake, *Sir Charles Lock Eastlake, Memoir.* 1870. p. 15.
Examiner, 25 January 1812; 2 February 1812.
Blackwood's Magazine, November 1853.
S. C. Hall, *Book of Memories.* 1871. p. 471.
James Elmes, 'Biography of B. R. Haydon', *The Annals of the Fine Arts.* Vol. V. 1820. p. 356.

Chapter VI

Miss Mitford's Letters. 1872. l. 220. 3 July 1846.

Chapter VIII

Additional MSS. (British Museum) 38108. ff. 169, 170.
Journal of Hellenic Studies. Vol. XXXVI. 1916. p. 333.

Chapter IX

Mrs. Laurence Binyon, *The Mind of the Artist.* 1909. p. 28.
Report from the Select Committee on the Earl of Elgin's Collection of Sculptured Marbles. 25 March 1816.
John Galt, *Life, Studies and Works of Benjamin West.* 1820. p. 51.
Journal of Hellenic Studies. Vol. XXXVI. 1916. pp. 297, 305, 306.
Byron, *The Curse of Minerva.*
B. R. Haydon, *Lectures on Painting and Design.* Vol. II. 1846. Lecture XIII.
Lady Eastlake, *Sir Charles Lock Eastlake: Memoir.* 1870. p. 147.
The Life of Sir Martin Archer Shee, by his Son. 1860. ii, 345.
Hansard, *Parliamentary Debates.* 1816. Vol. XXXII.

Chapter X

Miss Mitford's Letters, 2nd Series, ed. H. Chorley. 1872. p. 117.
Life and Letters of William Bewick, ed. Thomas Landseer. 1871. p. 268.
E. V. Lucas, *Works of Charles and Mary Lamb.* 1903. ii, pp. 23, 24, 25.
Spectator. 9 July 1853.
Letters of Robert Browning and Elizabeth Barrett. 1899. ii, 265.
Cyrus Redding, *Past Celebrities, etc.* 1860. ii, 254.
Henry Vizetelly, *Glances Back through Seventy Years.* 1893. i, 134.
James Manson, *Sir Edwin Landseer, R.A.* 1902. p. 165.
A. P. Oppé, 'Art', *Early Victorian England,* ed. G. M. Young. 1934. ii, 127.
Autobiography and Memoirs of B. R. Haydon, ed. Tom Taylor. New edition 1926. ii, 839 (Addenda).

The Hon. Andrew Shirley, 'Painting and Engraving', *Johnson's England*, ed. A. S. Turberville. 1933. ii, 58.

Crabb Robinson, *Diary, Reminiscences, and Correspondence*. 1869. ii, 162.

E. V. Rippingille, *The Late B. R. Haydon, Historical Painter* (Bentley's Miscellany, Vol. XX. 1846. p. 216).

Life and Letters of William Bewick. 1871. pp. 34–40.

Ibid., p. 151.

Ibid., ii, 173.

The Letters of John Keats: ed. M. Buxton Forman. Vol. II. 1931. pp. 295–6.

Sir Sidney Colvin, *John Keats*. 1917. p. 323.

Chapter XI

Miss Mitford's Letters. 1872. ii, 154–5.

Collected Works of William Hazlitt. Vol. VI. 1903. p. 399.

Journal of Psychological Medicine and Mental Pathology. Vol. VI. 1853. p. 523.

Additional MSS. (B.M.) 39168, ff. 104–8.

Annals of the Fine Arts. Part VII, 1817; Part VIII, 1818.

H. W. Garrod, *Keats*. 1926. pp. 65–6.

Autobiographical Recollections of Charles Robert Leslie, R.A., ed. Tom Taylor. 1860. i, 97.

Letters of Robert Browning and Elizabeth Barrett, 1845–6. 1899. pp. 309–310.

Annals of the Fine Arts. No. XII. p. 124, *et seq*.

Miss Mitford's Letters. 1872. (13 August 1842).

Chapter XII

Lady Eastlake, *Sir Charles Lock Eastlake: Memoir*. 1870. i, p. 361.

George Borrow, *Lavengro*. p. 217.

William Bell Scott, *Autobiographical Notes and Life*. 1892. i, p. 167.

William Carey, *Desultory Exposition of an Anti-British System of Incendiary Publication*, etc., etc. 1819.

William Bell Scott, op. cit., p. 167.

S. C. Hall, *Book of Memories*. 1871. p. 469.

Works of William Hazlitt. Vol. XI. 1903. p. 590.

Miss Mitford's Letters. 1872. ii, 186.

Morning Post, 6 July 1843.

Jonathan Richardson, *Works of*, 1773. pp. 10, 93, 94, 172.

Edmund Burke, *Philosophical Enquiry into the Origin of the Sublime and Beautiful*. 1761. pp. 58, 139, 212, 213, 237.

Letters of Elizabeth Barrett to B. R. Haydon: ed. Martha Hale Shackford. 1939. p. 26.

Chapter XIII

William Jerdan, *Autobiography*. 1850. iii, 131–2.
B. R. Haydon, *Description of Mr. Haydon's Picture of Christ's Triumphal Entry into Jerusalem*, etc.
James Elmes, *Annals of the Fine Arts*. 1820, Vol. V, p. 372.
Miss Mitford's Letters. 1872. 2nd Series. i, 87.
The Times, 27 March 1820.
Observer, 10 April 1820.
James Elmes, Biography of B. R. Haydon, *Annals of the Fine Arts*, Vol. V, 1820. p. 372.

Chapter XIV

Life and Letters of William Bewick. 1871. ii, 167–8.
Wheatley and Cunningham, *London Past and Present*. 1891. ii, 7–8.
Richard and Samuel Redgrave, *A Century of Painters*. 1866. ii, 429.
Observer, 30 March 1823.
The Private Letter Books of Sir Walter Scott, ed. Wilfred Partington. 1930. pp. 165–7.
B. R. Haydon, *Some Enquiries into the Causes which have obstructed the Advance of Historical Painting*, etc. 1829.
Miss Mitford's Letters. 1872. ii, 165.

Chapter XV

British Painting (1933), pp. 85, 204. By C. H. Collins Baker.
'A Revaluation of Haydon', *The Art Quarterly*, by A. C. Sewter. Autumn 1942.
The Burlington Magazine, July 1946.

Chapter XVI

A. P. Oppé, 'Art', *Early Victorian England*, ed. G. M. Young. 1934. ii, 120.
Miss Mitford's Letters. 1872. ii, 259.
Ibid., ii, 262.
Adrian H. Joline, *Meditations of an Autograph Collector*. 1902. 198–9.
George Borrow, *Lavengro*. Chap. XXXVIII.
Morning Chronicle, 1 March 1830.
Collected Works of William Hazlitt, Vol. XI, 481.

Chapter XVII

Life and Letters of William Bewick, ed. Thomas Landseer. 1871. i, 265 7.
William Whitley, *Art in England, 1821–1837*. 1928. p. 177.
Ibid., p. 140.

Court Journal, 6 March 1830.
Morning Post, 1 March 1830.
The Times, 5 March 1830.
Morning Chronicle, 1 March 1830.
Catalogue, *Haydon's Pictures of Xenophon, Mock Election, etc. at the Egyptian Hall*, 1836.
William Whitley, op. cit., p. 322.
Henry Vizetelly, *Glances back through Seventy Years*. 1893. i, 274.
W. P. Frith, *My Autobiography and Reminiscences*. 1887. i, p. 331.

Chapter XIX

Report of the Select Committee of Arts and Manufacturers, 1835.
Examiner, June 1834.
Description of Haydon's Picture of the Reform Banquet. 1834.
The Life of Sir Martin Archer Shee. 1860. ii, 200.
Athenaeum, 18 July 1846.
The Hon. Andrew Shirley, 'Painting and Engraving', *Johnson's England*, ed. A. S. Turberville. 1933. ii, 53.
Life and Letters of William Bewick, ed. Thomas Landseer. 1871. i, 4-5.
B. R. Haydon, *Lectures on Painting and Design*. Vol. I. 1844; Vol. II, 1846.
Encyclopaedia Britannica, 7th edn.

Chapter XX

Letters of Robert Browning and Elizabeth Barrett, 8 July 1846.
A. P. Oppé, 'Art', *Early Victorian England*, ed. G. M. Young. ii, 114.
'Benjamin West', by Cosmo Monkhouse, in *Dictionary of National Biography*.
E. Edwards, *A Letter to Sir Martin Shee on the Reform of the Royal Academy*. 1839. p. 41.
Ibid., p. 31.
A.-J.-B. Defauconpret, *Loudres en 1824*. 1825. pp. 72-3.
A. P. Oppé, op. cit. ii, 157.
Examiner, 17 March 1816.
Examiner, 7 April 1816.
A. P. Oppé, op. cit., ii, 157-8.
Report of the Commissioners on the Fine Arts. Vol. XXV. p. 113.
W. P. Frith, *My Autobiography and Reminiscences*. i, 83.
W. Holman Hunt, *Pre-Raphaelitism and the Pre-Raphaelite Brotherhood*. 1905.
Henry Vizetelly, *Glances back through Seventy Years*. 1893. i, 117.
R. and S. Redgrave, *A Century of Painters*. 1866. ii, 195.

Chapter XXII

Report of the Commissioners of the Fine Arts, 1842-3, etc.

R. and S. Redgrave, *A Century of Painters*. 1866. Chapter XV.
A. P. Oppé, *Victorian England*. ii, 111.
W. Bell Scott, *Autobiographical Notes*. 1892. i. 168.
W. P. Frith, *My Autobiography and Reminiscences*. 1887. i, 83–4.

Chapter XXIII

M. Passavent, *Tour of a German Artist in England*. 1836. ii, 254.
Report of the Commissioners of the Fine Arts, 24 June 1843. Vol. XXV, 66.
Lady Eastlake, *Sir Charles Lock Eastlake: Memoir*. 1870. p. 174.
W. Bell Scott, *Autobiographical Notes*. 1892. i, 171.
W. P. Frith, *My Autobiography and Reminiscences*. 1887. i, 334.
Letters of Robert Browning and Elizabeth Barrett. ii, 322. 10 July 1846.
R. and S. Redgrave, *A Century of Painters*. 1866. p. 197.
Spectator, 8 July. 15 July 1843.
Morning Post, 6 July 1843.
Illustrated London News, 8 July 1843.
Henry Green Clarke, *Critical Catalogue to the Cartoons at Westminster Hall,* 1843.
W. Bell Scott, op. cit., p. 168.
Charles Boner, *Memoirs and Letters*, p. 279.
The Works of Thackeray. 1911. Vol. XIX. p. 238.
Annals of the Fine Arts, Vol. V. 1820. p. 333.
Letters of Elizabeth Barrett to B. R. Haydon, ed. Martha Hale Shackford. 1939. p. 38.

Chapter XXIV

Lady Eastlake, *Sir Charles Lock Eastlake: Memoir*. 1870. i, 179.
Art Union, 1 December 1846.
Devonport Independent, 27 June 1846.
Examiner, July 1846.

Epilogue

Manchester Guardian, 27 June 1846.
Letters of Robert Browning and Elizabeth Barrett (postmark 23 June 1846). Ibid., ii, 265.
Sir Robert Peel, From His Private Correspondence, ed. C. S. Parker, M.P. 1891. iii, 449.
J. F. Nisbet, *The Insanity of Genius.* 1891. 182.
Probate Registry (Mary Haydon), Somerset House.
Frederick Boase, *Modern English Biography*. 1892. Mary, Frederic and Frank Haydon.
Frederic Haydon, *Our Officials at the Home Office*. 1867.

APPENDICES

Appendix I

Poems addressed to Haydon or to his pictures. Those marked with an asterisk are not given in the World's Classics edition of the *Autobiography*.

KEATS.—Sonnet: *Great spirits now on earth are sojourning;* (Published 1817.)
Sonnet: *Highmindedness, a jealousy for good,* (Published 1817.)
Sonnet (with the one following): *Haydon! forgive me that I cannot speak*
Sonnet on seeing the Elgin Marbles: *My spirit is too weak—mortality* (1817.)

WORDSWORTH.—Sonnet: *High is our calling Friend! Creative Art* (1816.)
Sonnet on 'Napoleon Musing at St. Helena': *Haydon! let worthier judges praise the skill* (1831.)
Sonnet on 'Wellington Musing at Waterloo': *By art's bold privilege warrior and war-horse stand* (Composed while ascending Helvellyn. Monday, 31 August 1840.)

ELIZABETH BARRETT.—Sonnet on Haydon's portrait of Wordsworth: *Wordsworth upon Helvellyn! Let the cloud* (1842.)

JOHN HAMILTON REYNOLDS.—Sonnet: *Haydon! Thou'rt born to immortality!* (*Champion*, 24 November 1816.)

LEIGH HUNT.—Sonnet: *Haydon, whom now the conquered toil confesses* (*Examiner*, 20 October 1816.)

MARY RUSSELL MITFORD.—Sonnet: *Haydon! this dull age and this northern clime* (1823.)
Sonnet on Haydon's picture 'A Study from Nature': *Tears in the eye, and on the lips a sigh!* (*Annals of the Fine Arts*, 1817.)

CHARLES LAMB.—Latin verses on Haydon's picture of 'Christ's Entry into Jerusalem': *Quid vult Iste Equitans? et quid velit ista virorum* (*Champion*, 1820.)
Translation: *What rider's that? and who those myriads bringing* (*Champion*, 1820).

WILLIAM BELL SCOTT.—Sonnet, on reading Haydon's Autobiography: *The coarse-voiced peacock spreads his starry tail* (*Poems*, 1854.)

GEORGE STANLEY.—*Sonnet, on seeing Haydon's portrait of Wordsworth: *Great intellect is here! whether it speak* (*Annals of the Fine Arts,* IX.)

*Poem, in seven verses, on reading Haydon's Letter in defence of the Elgin Marbles: *Spirit of Fire! Strong, lucid, and sublime* (*Annals,* 1816.)

ANONYMOUS.—*Sonnet in Italian: *L'Arte tua magica, e l'Armonia soave* (*Annals* IV, 1819.)

FRANCIS BENNOCK.—*Sonnet, on seeing Haydon's painting of 'Christ's Entry into Jerusalem': *What great magician of the earth art thou,* (*Poems, Lyrics and Sonnets,* 1877.)

CHARLES BONER.—*Poem in three verses on reading the account of Haydon's death, verse ii: *And well do I remember thy glad look* (*Verse,* 1834–1858, 1858.)

GEORGE CROLY.—*Poem in four verses on Haydon's 'Christ's Entry into Jerusalem': *The air is filled with shouts, and trumpets' sounding;* (*Poetical Works,* 1830.)

R. H. HORNE.—*Epicedium to the Memory of B. R. Haydon, by the author of 'Orion': *Mourn, fatal Voice, whom ancients called the Muse!*

Note to Appendix I

DAVID MACBETH MOIR ('Delta', 'the Scottish Dickens').—Sonnet to Haydon: *Genius immortal, industry untired* (*Blackwood's Magazine* ix, February 1821; printed in Olney, *Haydon,* p. 266).

DANIEL TERRY[1] (actor and playwright).—'Lines addressed to Haydon': *Thou has[t] a Spirit, of power and magnitude* (n.d.). 'A loud and everlasting Note of Fame' is prophesied if Haydon will 'Quit the pencil for the Pen', 'Fly from Self-Conceit', etc. Printed by Olney, pp. 268–9, from a holograph in the possession of Mr. Wilfrid Partington.

BENJAMIN BAILEY.—'On a female figure in Mr. Haydon's Picture of Christ entering Jerusalem': *Her arms are folded meekly on her breast.* She is Jairus's daughter, but Bailey takes her for the Penitent Girl. Transcribed by Bailey (dated 1815–16) in a letter to Monckton Milnes, 7 May 1849. A copy dated 1817 is in 'Poems by two Friends' (Bailey and J. H. Reynolds), a manuscript in the Keats Museum, Hampstead. *The Keats Circle* ii. 281–2.

D. T. Coulton's sonnet, 'The Painter's Daughter' (p. 356), is partly addressed to Haydon.

---

[1] It was through Terry that Haydon was introduced to Sir Walter Scott (Olney, pp. 108–9). He is not mentioned in the *Journals,* where the meeting is dated 30 March 1820. According to Olney, the dinner, at William Atkinson's, Scott's architect, was on 30 April. Cf. p. 325, n. 1.

Appendix II

HERE
LIETH THE BODY
OF
BENJAMIN ROBERT HAYDON

An English Historical Painter, who, in a struggle to make the People, the Legislature, the Nobility, and the Sovereign of England give due dignity and rank to the highest Art, which had ever languished, and, until the Government intervenes, ever will languish in England, fell a victim to his ardour and his love of country; an evidence that to seek the benefit of your Country by telling the Truth to Power, is a crime that can only be expiated by the ruin and destruction of the Man who is so Patriotic and so imprudent.

He was born at Plymouth, 26 January, 1786, and died on the (   ), 18   , believing in Christ as the Mediator and Advocate of Mankind:

'What various ills the Painter's life assail,
Pride, Envy, Want, the Patron and the Jail.'

This I wish written on my tombstone when my day comes.

B. R. HAYDON
Correspondence and Table Talk, 2, p. 484

Note to Appendix II

Frederic has taken this epitaph from the *Journal* entry of 10 October 1827, the sixth anniversary of Haydon's wedding.[1] His alterations doubtless reflect his own experience of truth-telling to Power. There are no capitals or heading to the entry, which begins 'Here lies . . .'. While Taylor deflates, Frederic inflates. Haydon: 'the people, Legislature & King'. Frederic: 'the People, the Legislature, the Nobility and the Sovereign of England'. After some minor variants; Haydon: 'his ardour & enthusiasm'. Frederic: 'his ardour and Love of Country'. Haydon: 'a crime that can finally be expiated by the destruction of its Victim'. Frederic: 'a crime that can only be expiated by the ruin and destruction of the Man who is so Patriotic and so imprudent.' The rest follows Haydon, except for 'the day' instead of Frederic's 'my day'.

[1] *Diary* iii. 226, 10 Oct. 1827.

Haydon wrote a second version, also without comment, appending it to his summary of the critical year 1841 ('as to the state of Art it is dangerous, a great moment is come . . .').

Here lies the body of B. R. Haydon, Historical Painter . . . [born and died as before]

He passed his life in a desperate struggle to make People, Legislature, & Sovereign give efficient support to the highest branch of Art, by public encouragement, which they had neglected to do since the establishment of the Protestant Religion.

He was a good Father, a faithful & tender Husband, and lived an indisputable evidence, if any was wanting, that no affliction is considered an adequate punishment for having told Truth to Power.

He died as he had always lived, an ardent & sincere believer in Jesus Christ, his only Mediator & Redeemer.[1]

He ends with the same adaptation of Johnson's lines, but omits the wish for a tombstone inscription.

Appendix III

PORTRAITS IN HAYDON'S PICTURES

In spite of Haydon's abhorrence of the commissioned portrait he was fond of introducing portraits of his friends into his historical pictures. These are not always easy to trace, but some are known and others may be guessed. Haydon himself was to be found in the lost picture of *Solomon*, and the study for the head of Solomon (see illustration) was almost certainly drawn from himself. *Curtius Leaping into the Gulf* is Haydon. I saw this picture when I was a child in Gatti's Restaurant, but it has since passed into limbo, to join so many others of Haydon's works. He is also to be seen looking out of a window in the top left-hand corner of *The Mock Election*; and, in profile, on the extreme right of *The Reform Banquet*. His own head is said to be included among the many portraits in *Christ's Entry into Jerusalem*; I cannot identify it. Keats appears in this picture immediately above the bowed head of Wordsworth (third from the right); the man in profile on the extreme right being, I suppose, Hazlitt with Voltaire between. Lamb is said to be there, and Newton, on Haydon's authority, but where, I don't know. The really charming figure in the picture, that of the girl who kneels in deep shadow below Christ's left hand, may have been done from Haydon's future wife; if so she inspired the best that was in him. Miss Webb, his favourite model at that time, was a less happy influence: she appears, largely, on the right; and, again, to mar his picture, as both

[1] *Diary*, v. 110, 31 Dec. 1841.

the Marys in *Lazarus*. For it was Haydon's too-great reliance on what he called 'the life', in other words, his fatal habit of painting direct from the model in what were intended to be imaginative works, that often introduced into them an element of falsity and discord. In *Lazarus* also Mrs. Haydon stands, in profile, on the extreme right. Keats, too, may be there; for there is a small figure in the background, high above and a little to the right of Christ, with his head leaning on his right hand. This strongly resembles, in reverse, the head and shoulders of Keats in Joseph Severn's miniature (National Portrait Gallery), from which it may well have been taken after Keats's death. Mrs. Norton is Cassandra, in *Cassandra Prophesying the Death of Hector*, of which there is a photograph in the British Museum.

In the British Museum there is an engraving of *The Reform Banquet* with a key to the portraits it contains. There is also a key to the *Anti-Slavery Convention* in the National Portrait Gallery. In the remarkable sketch for *The Meeting of the Unions on Newhall Hill*, in Birmingham, on 16 May 1832, the speaker is Thomas Attwood.

SUPPLEMENT
TO THE
SECOND EDITION

1. THE *AUTOBIOGRAPHY* AND THE JOURNALS

My Memoirs are to 1820, my journals will supply the rest. The style, the individuality of Richardson, which I wish not curtailed by an Editor. Correspondence & journals for the rest. Haydon's will, clause 13

SINCE this book was published the *Journals* have been printed at length, splendidly edited by Professor Pope, splendidly produced by the Harvard University Press,[1] subsidized by two learned foundations, on a scale that would have delighted Haydon, apart from some dismaying additions by his son Frank. We can now compare not only the full text with Taylor's abridgement, but Haydon's *Autobiography* with the *Journals* from 1808 to 1820, never before printed. As a feat of narrative and creative memory the comparison increases one's admiration for the book, especially considering the circumstances in which it was written— by fits and starts—on Sundays, and when unable to paint, and always under pressure of more urgent matters—averting ruin— and tortured by anxieties. One is Haydon chastened by adversity and influenced by Miss Barrett's good advice, the other is Haydon in his years of success, glorious self-confidence, and uninhibited vanity. And one sees what he means by the style of Richardson.

Though much shorter than the *Journals* for the corresponding years, the *Autobiography* has much that is new. While writing it Haydon was reading Vasari, and he asks, 'Why have the lives of English Painters never gone to a second Edition? Because all that is adventurous or anecdotal is left out.'[2] He was doubtless thinking of Cunningham's *Lives*, which he often denigrates, but he certainly applied the lesson to himself. He was determined that his book should be interesting as well as cautionary. Though it contains many quotations from the *Journals*—freely treated, re-arranged, and added to—the books are essentially different. I think there can be no doubt that the *Autobiography* is as Haydon wrote it, though there have been suggestions to the contrary. Taylor was

[1] *The Diary of Benjamin Robert Haydon*, ed. W. B. Pope, Harvard, 5 vols. (1960–3).

[2] *Diary* v. 282, 5 June 1843.

conscientious: Haydon's wishes were precise. Near the beginning, when Haydon omits part of a *Journal* quotation, Taylor adds it in a note. But he must soon have found that the discrepancies outran editorial comment. More important, a comparison of the alterations in the *Autobiography* with those made by Taylor to the text of the *Journals* leaves no doubt that in the former the alterations are the author's.

There is no manuscript of the *Autobiography*, but there is a rough draft called *Vita* belonging to Professor Pope which goes to 1823. Haydon finished what he called his second volume covering the year 1820 in June 1845. (His first 'volume' ended with 1812 and is almost exactly half the complete text.) After that the pressure of calamity and writing the second volume of his Lectures must have halted any further instalment of the 'Memoirs'. In March 1846 he was 'very fatigued', correcting proofs of the Lectures and the Catalogue of his disastrous last exhibition. Conceivably, the *Autobiography* was not intended to go beyond that watershed in his life, the first imprisonment in 1823. Lamenting the past, Haydon writes of a Sunday in March 1824: 'Ah how different to my former ones! walking about with my sweetest Mary . . . or, dining with Wilkie, Lamb, Hazlitt, Wordsworth, or Keats, and a grand picture blazing . . . in golden & glorious splendour. Passed! Passed! Passed! But if God spares my life these shall live by my pen.'[1] Was this the germ of the *Autobiography*? Neither in it nor in the *Journals* are his Sunday literary dinners mentioned.[2] In 1836, in a moment of triumph (as he thought) over the Academy—the Ewart Committee, he recorded, 'My Life has been a romance. God spare me to write it, & the aspiring youth shall hereafter hug it to his heart.'[3]

While the *Autobiography* is a narrative intended for immediate publication (Haydon sent a specimen first chapter to Murray in 1841,[4] but nothing came of this), the *Journals* are a blend of *journal intime*, sketch book, commonplace book, and a receptacle for letters and documents, intended for posterity, a product of

[1] *Diary* ii. 474, 25 Apr. 1824.

[2] On 11 Jan. 1817 Haydon invited Keats to start coming to dinner every Sunday at three: 'accept this engagement as long as we live'. W. J. Bate, *John Keats* (Harvard and O.U.P., 1963), p. 274.

[3] iv. 362, 16 July 1836.

[4] Haydon mentions beginning his life in 1839 and writing it in 1840, but these seem to have been false starts. Cf. his remark to Hunt, p. 321. These dates for the writing of the *Autobiography* correct those on p. 249.

inspiration, musing, and reading—the history of his mind, his art, his circumstances, and, he says once, of his passions. Facts one would expect to find are not there and events are often recorded not as they happen but in retrospect. The end of one volume and the beginning of the next became landmarks in his life, each headed by epigraphs, with a tragic climax in the 'Finis' of Volume XXVI. They were read, reread, mused over, sometimes annotated at different times with approval or dissent. They are far from 'pages which he scribbled without thought of Genius or Art or Posterity'.[1] His Art, his Genius, and what constitutes genius are leading themes, and they were written for posterity. 'It is time that all the obscurity about Genius should be dispersed, and that the belief that such men at once burst into full possession of their knowledge, when it is only that they have acquired it with the same progression, tho with infinitely more rapidity. On this principle it is I write my own life.'[2] And a little later he reflects: 'There is one disadvantage in writing your own memoirs. It sets at rest all conjecture as to your habits and knowledge. Had Shakespeare given us something of course we should not have had the numerous volumes about him.' This is Haydon at thirty-one, and at his most vain. Ironically, it is the *Journals* not the pictures that have elicited volumes about himself. 'This book', he writes in 1820, 'is a picture of human life, now full of arguments for religion, now advocating virtue, then drawn from chaste piety, & then melting from a bed of pleasure, idle & active, dissipated & temperate, voluptuous & holy! ready to blaze in a battalion when I read Homer! weeping at Rimini and at Othello, laughing & without sixpence, in boisterous spirits when I ought to be sad, & melancholy when I have every reason to be happy!—such are the elements of that mysterious, incomprehensible, singular bit of blood & genius, B. R. Haydon!'[3]

Ten years later he reached Volume XVII (April 1830): 'I begin my Volume of daily thought, sketching, & circumstances—in them is a curious private history of the Art for these 24 years!" (actually 22).[4] He ends the volume: 'I must this day conclude this Journal, and a curious record it is of my mind & sufferings. Strange & extraordinary events are recorded of the fate of Nations & many singular sufferings of myself as an individual. . . .'[5] (His reflections

[1] Virginia Woolf, *The Moment* (1964), p. 155.
[2] *Diary* ii. 4, 16 Jan. 1816.   [3] ii. 273, 8 July 1820.
[4] iii. 439, 12 Apr. 1830.   [5] iii. 565, 22 Oct. 1831.

on Reform and on the French Revolution of July, in which he was deeply interested.) 'Thus ends another Journal,' he wrote in August 1844 of his last volume but one, 'a record of feelings, thoughts, hopes, fears, & thanksgivings, as usual—anticipations, deductions, and denunciations.'[1] Near the end of his life, 'My Journal seems to have lost all its copiousness & Inspiration.'[2]

The *Journals* begin in July 1808 with an account of a visit to Dover, not mentioned in the *Autobiography*; Haydon records with panache his musing on Shakespeare's Cliff. By a strange coincidence they begin, as they end, with *Lear*, 'here perhaps, I said, Lear defied the Storm; there, as I looked towards the Castle, Cordelia died. . . .' A vision flashed into his mind of 'a Colossal Statue of Britannia with her Lion at her feet, surveying France with a lofty air. If this remained alone when England becomes a desart, how poetical would this and its White cliffs be. . . .' Some person . . . said . . . "Why it must be 20 feet high"— "20 feet! 150".'

To return to the *Autobiography* and its relation with the *Journals*. Since Haydon wrote it with Richardson in his mind, we may begin by comparing two allusions to *Clarissa Harlowe*. *Autobiography*: 'March 3rd [1813] . . . Except by *Clarissa Harlowe* I was never so moved by a work of genius as by *Othello*. I read seventeen hours a day at Clarissa, and held the book so long up leaning on my elbows in an armchair that I stopped the circulation and could not move. When Lovelace writes: "Dear Belton, it is all over, and Clarissa lives," I got up in a fury and wept like an infant, and cursed and d——d Lovelace till exhausted.' In the *Journal Clarissa* is not mentioned in the 3 March entry (which otherwise corresponds to the *Autobiography*). But in the previous entry, dated 20 February, there is an interesting comparison between *Tom Jones* and *Clarissa Harlowe* which ends: 'Fielding is the Hogarth of novelists & something higher, while Richardson may be called without exaggeration the Raphael of domestic life.' (Haydon was obsessed by the book. Shortly before his marriage he was haunted by Mary's 'dear image' as 'Clarissa's remembrance haunted Lovelace'.[3] And when, as he thought, Alfred, aged six, was dying, 'Good God, how affecting. It was like Clarissa Harlowe!')[4]

This contrast in approach between *Autobiography* and *Journal*

---

[1] *Diary*, v. 379, 2 Aug. 1844.   [2] v. 397, 6 Nov. 1844.
[3] ii. 325, 30 Apr. 1821.
[4] iii. 585, Nov. 1831. Alfred did not die till 17 May 1833.

comes out strikingly in the treatment of Haydon's triumph, the exhibition and sale of *Solomon*, so dramatically described in the *Autobiography*. There is nothing of this in the *Journal*, where the only reference to the exhibition is retrospective, on 4 May: 'O God Almighty, permit me on my knees to thank thee for thy mercies, the great work to which two years of serious study was devoted, is finished, exhibited, sold & has succeeded. O God, it has given that shock to Art that I prayed it might give at its commencement, it has roused the people, it has affected the Artists, it has excited the nobility. O God grant its effects may succeed beyond example. . . .' From later comments in the *Journals* we learn that he regarded it as a complete victory over the Academy and regretted that his campaign against them had not ended there.

The Paris visit in 1814 is based on the *Journal*, but written up and improved, with added detail, especially about Wilkie. There is nothing in the *Journal* about the pretty maidservant or the indelicate prints, or about Wilkie's illness. The conversation in the Louvre, when Wilkie said the English 'just look as if they had a balance at their bankers', is an addition. So is Haydon's race *en poste* with the postillion. By 1840 Haydon had become Francophobe as he was not in 1814 (or in 1830). In 1814 there is no comparison between Brighton and Dieppe, and the description of Dieppe is more favourable: ' . . . old, & Gothic & fine like Vanderheyden's views in Holland. A great proportion of Women. . . . Shops open & airy & every thing looking elegant.' He describes the journey to Rouen in very English French saying, '*J'aime la France*'. But, on landing at Dover, 'Oh how the honest simplicity of the English character affected me on entering England.' There are interesting passages in the *Journal* only. For instance, 'I do not wonder at the Nations of the Continent having a contempt for the English, when they only know them from external appearance. Of all Nations on Earth I think the air of the English is the most awkward, both in Men & Women; the Women with exquisite figures, plump bosoms, destroy the effect of both by a clodhopping clumsy role, as if they wished to be free from affectation, no doubt, but as if they were indifferent to appearance. The Men with the noblest chests and finest heads, have an unexpressive cut in comparison with the Nations of the Continent. . . . But O God, the qualities of England's soul are always in reserve for grand occasions, and ever veiled when they would be needless.'[1] Haydon

[1] *Diary* i. 381, July 1814.

must have seen the print-shop windows in Paris filled with prints of clumsy, ill-dressed English visitors—a reaction to defeat renewed after Waterloo.

The passages on the Hundred Days have remarkable differences. In the *Journal* the first mention is a newspaper cutting of Napoleon's proclamation on landing (1 March). Haydon's comment: 'The prospects of the World are at this moment dreadful. If there were any hope of his reformation or any prospect that adversity had calmed his passion for rule, I should be delighted to see such Genius at the—'; he breaks off.[1] Napoleon is not mentioned again till 23 June. There is nothing about the meeting with the messenger in Portman Square with news of victory, which is dated in the *Autobiography* 23 June—two days late. In both books Haydon reads the *Gazette* till he knows it by heart. The reflections on the victory differ, both are interesting. The Waterloo anecdotes which in the *Autobiography* are told by wounded privates shepherded by Sammons in August 1815, were in fact told to Haydon on two occasions in 1816, when he was visited by the only one of his models—Corporal Webster—to survive the battle.[2]

Three famous set pieces are based on the *Journals*, the christening party at Hazlitt's in 1815, the dinner at which Haydon first met Shelley, and the 'immortal dinner' in December 1817. They illustrate Haydon's treatment of his material most interestingly. Each has some telling phrase that the other has not got, but only in the 'immortal dinner' is the advantage on balance perhaps with the *Journal* (where it is not 'immortal'). Here is a passage from the *Journal*. 'There is no describing this scene adequately. There was not the restraint of refined company, nor the vulgar freedom of low, but a frank, natural license, such as one sees in an act of Shakespeare, every man expressing his natural emotions without fear.' Its deep impression on Haydon is attested by three successive notes. First, '. . . poor Ritchie is dead! . . .'. Second, 'Keats too is gone! How one ought to treasure such evenings when life gives us so few of them. 1823, Nov.' And last, 'Lamb too is gone! Monkhouse, the other Friend, is gone. Wordsworth & I alone remain. . . . If the Comptroller of Stamps lives I know not. Jany 24, 1837.'[3]

[1] *Diary* i. 418 (between 11 Feb. and 8 Apr.: the news was announced in England on 10 Mar.).

[2] ii. 8–10, 2 Mar. 1816 and 32–34, 8 June 1816. Corporal Webster was the model for Lazarus in *Christ's Entry*.   [3] ii. 173–6, 28 Dec. 1817.

It is in the Shelley dinner that the divergencies are truly remarkable. The account in the *Autobiography* is reconstructed from two entries, one in 1817, the other in 1822. In the *Journal* the dinner is not at Hunt's but at Horace Smith's. In the *Autobiography* it is in 1816, in the *Journal* on 20 January 1817. In both Haydon defends Christianity and Keats and Smith are silent. But in the *Autobiography* (where Hunt is '——') Shelley leads the conversation, in the *Journal*, Hunt. In both there are quotations and counterquotations from Shakespeare, but almost all the dialogue is different. The passage quoted on pp. 117–18 is new, except for Hunt's question, 'Are these creatures to be damned Haydon?' In the *Journal* Haydon makes no answer, but reflects—significantly, as we shall see—'Poor dear Hunt, he'll die like Cowper [insane]. He is like a moth who flutters about a candle & sophisticates himself into the midst of it.' The *Journal*: 20 January 1817, 'Dined at Horace Smith's. Met Hunt, Shelley & young Keats; became excessively irritable at Hunt's unfeeling, heartless and brutal ridicule of Christ and his divine doctrine. . . .' Changes in the *Autobiography* were probably due in part to Haydon's meeting Hunt in 1840, 'after years'. ' "Hunt" (said I) "I am going to write my Life, & I'll do you justice. You would have been burnt at the Stake for a principle, & would have feared to put your foot in the mud." '[1] But in the 1817 account of the dinner, 'This [is] a man who can scarcely talk of a principle he has not violated, of a promise he has not broken, of a vice that he does not sophisticate into a virtue, of a virtue he has not negatived into a vice.' With a great deal more. 'I write these faults in a passion, but it is a passion that in its heat pours forth truths which have for a long time been overlooked, like the moral axioms Shakespeare thunders forth in the rage of his characters.'[2] (Aspersions on Hunt are scattered through the *Journals*: Haydon is not mentioned in Hunt's *Autobiography*.)

The description of Shelley is taken and improved from a passage dated 3 August 1822. 'Called on John Hunt. Found him deeply affected at the loss of Shelley. . . . The first time I ever saw him was at dinner. I could not think what little, delicate, feeble creature it was, eating vegetable only, when suddenly I was roused by hearing him say, "as to that detestable religion, the Christian religion." ' A denigrating account of Shelley follows, ending: 'Pride was the foundation of his heart, I suspect, though I certainly saw very little of him.'[3]

[1] *Diary* iv. 603–4, 5 Feb. 1840.   [2] ii. 80–87.   [3] ii. 372.

The *Autobiography* ends with the triumphant exhibition of *Jerusalem* and the visit to Scotland to exhibit the picture there. The very lively account of the Private Day (pp. 127–33), written in 1845, is based on an outline in the *Journal* (where the picture is described in great detail): '. . . I sit down to record one of the most glorious triumphs of my life.' The only visitors mentioned are Sir William Scott and Mrs. Siddons, and of her he says only, 'A great many were wavering about Christ, when Mrs. Siddons in her solemn & sublime tone, said, "It is decidedly successful and its paleness gives it an awful & supernatural look." This was not said to me, but reported. I sent back my everlasting gratitude & was introduced.'[1] He added later, 'Mrs Siddons' suffrage settled my business with the unsophisticated; the public soon got hold of it, & in spite of the Artists, my Christ triumphed indeed.'[2] On her death he wrote, 'She said to me in a splendid room, 1820, "What astonished me, Mr Haydon, in your Jerusalem, is the infinite modification of the same expression." '[3]

None of the lively details in the account of the Scottish visit (pp. 133–4) is in the *Journal*, and the two accounts might be of different occasions on both of which Haydon dined with Sir Walter. But only in the *Journal* does he say that he visited Southey and Wordsworth in the Lakes on his return journey, and went on to Liverpool and Chester, 'Liverpool, a sort of beau ideal of Wapping'.[4]

There are some remarkable omissions in the early *Journals*. One is his father's death in 1813, occasionally touched on much later. For instance, 'My dear Father's birth day. He would have been 84, he died broken down from excess at 55.'[5] Another is the application for Associateship of the R.A., briefly mentioned in the *Autobiography*. There is nothing about the *Annals of the Fine Arts* and Haydon's contributions to it, so important in the *Autobiography* (pp. 109–11). Elmes appears only as an architect with whom Haydon walked to Dulwich in October 1816, and as a kind friend who went with him into the country when he was 'in a state of wretched debility & nervousness' in 1818.[6] This visit to Devonshire is not mentioned in the *Autobiography*.

---

[1] *Diary* ii. 265, 31 Mar. 1820. [2] ii. 267.
[3] iii. 520, 9 June 1831.
[4] ii. 294–7, Nov.–Dec. 1820. In 1838 Haydon writes of 'glorious Liverpool' (iv. 534). [5] v. 136, 8 Mar. 1842.
[6] ii. 204–6, 31 Aug. 1818. The visit is described in a letter to Keats.

But the most noteworthy omission from the *Journals* is Haydon's mysterious first meeting with his future wife (p. 104). The progress of this love affair and how it led to marriage is related, evasively, in the *Journals*, and is the chief omission from the *Autobiography*, where his relations with women are only touched on; in the early *Journals* they are a recurrent theme.

Among passages in the *Journals* omitted in the *Autobiography* are these two on Wordsworth. On 25 October 1816 Haydon wrote, with additions at a later date which are here given in brackets, 'If I ever loved any man (once) with a fullness of Soul, it was Leigh Hunt. If I ever reverenced a man, in which virtue, forbearance & principle were personified (now & formerly) it is *John*. If I ever adored another it is (not) Wordsworth.'[1] And in December 1817 (shortly before the immortal dinner), 'Wordsworth is in Town again & looks better than ever. He sat to me today for his head & I made a drawing of him. He read Milton & his Tintern Abbey, & the Happy Warrior, & some of his finest things. He is a most eloquent power. He looked like a spirit of Nature, pure & elementary. His head is like as if it was carved out of a mossy rock, created before the flood! It is grand & broad & persevering. That nose announces a wonder. He sees his road & his object vividly & clearly & intensely, and never turns aside. In moral grandeur of Soul and extension of scope, he is equal to Milton. He seems to me to be the organ of the Deity as to conduct & what ought to be cherished & what commended, to lead a Man to that immortal glory, endless & infinite!'[2]

[1] *Diary* ii. 63 (originally: 'it was Wordsworth').
[2] ii. 147–8, 2 Dec. 1817.

2. TOM TAYLOR'S TREATMENT OF THE *JOURNALS*

I hope that my journals, if ever they are thought worthy of publication, will give as much pleasure to others, as other journals have given delight to me. Autobiography[1]

THE first question is, what proportion of the original did Taylor print? After a page-by-page comparison I can only guess—a quarter? Possibly less. There is so much pruning as well as lopping, the paragraphing is so different, the connecting passages and summaries are threaded with quotations. Taylor adds letters and documents that Professor Pope omits. The principles of the abridgement are clear. Everything that could distress or embarrass the living or offend Victorian propriety. Much that is repetitive and dull—at least to the general reader. Disquisitions on the technique of painting, ancient and modern, with quotations from Latin, Italian, and French authorities. Haydon's 'denunciations', which are a feature of the *Journals*, sometimes with epitaphs for his enemies. Tirades against the Academy are long, varied, and not without interest, and are understandably omitted or curtailed. Politics are almost excluded; so are literary anecdotes and gossip and most of Haydon's musings on books. Religious musings, confessions of faith, questionings and doubts are usually omitted, and there are samples only of addresses to the Almighty. After 1820 there are few star descriptive passages, and these are given almost intact—notably the visits to Petworth and Walmer. Taylor had an eye for the telling phrase and significant comment, and when these are within his canon he usually prints them. Considering the limits of space and period the abridgement seems to deserve its reputation—the approval it was given in 1853. How he managed to do it, in the intervals of a busy life as civil servant, journalist, and playwright, remains a mystery.

[1] Haydon eagerly read autobiographies, biographies, memoirs—beginning with Boswell: 'there is no resisting this book'. Johnson's advice to Boswell was the starting-point of his own journalizing. Vasari, Cellini, Johnson's *Lives of the Poets*, Rousseau, Saint Augustine, Alfieri, Gibbon, 'Pepys Memoirs, a Dutch Picture of the Times', Tom Moore's *Sheridan* and *Byron*, Lockhart's *Scott*, Southey's *Nelson*, Fanny Burney's little volumes, *Memoirs of Lady Hester Stanhope* (1845), 'which made me melancholy', and, of course, everything he could get hold of relating to Napoleon.

When it comes to editing, it is slightly different. Taylor had little respect for his text as a text. Few passages of any length are exactly as Haydon wrote them, though the alterations may be minimal. Dates are confused (but when Haydon quotes in the *Autobiography* the confusion is greater).[1] Occasionally two entries are merged though there are intervening ones. The editorial pen tidied up loose ends, reversed inversions, altered the order of phrases, and made some meaningless verbal changes—'appears' for 'seems' and vice versa. Taylor shrank from terms of endearment, and these are many. When Haydon writes 'my lovely Mary', Taylor alters—though not invariably—to 'my dear Mary'. Haydon describes his return from a lecture tour: Taylor deletes 'after hugging my wife'. To counteract despair, Haydon counts his blessings: 'My wife faithful as far as women go, further.' Taylor condenses to 'my wife loving'. Haydon speaks of Byron's 'vices', Taylor, 'Italian dissipations'. His discretion was extreme. When Haydon was painting Lord Grey, he writes 'his brother came in'. Taylor: 'someone came in'.

The smallest alterations can mislead. Haydon wrote of his *Autobiography*, 'My object will be *not* [his italics] to paint ourselves *en beau*.' Taylor, 'My object will not be. . . .' Deeply anxious, Haydon writes, 'Frank is just recovered from a nervous fever.' Taylor, 'quite recovered'. 'The only bit of fresco fit to look at', writes Haydon, 'is by a Ford Brown.' Taylor deletes the 'a', implying that Haydon knew Ford Brown at least by repute. After one of the many petitions with which he bombarded Parliament, Haydon writes, 'I have made up my mind to interfere after this no more, except in my own way.' Taylor omits the last five words.

Alterations become progressively less as Taylor wearied or came to appreciate Haydon's style. The passage on the moment of vision in the Adelphi at Liverpool (p. 275) is intact. The famous description of George IV's coronation is sprinkled with minor changes and there are two deletions. A passage about Mary putting on Haydon's coat and sword 'with the playful, bewitching elegance of a beauty' was doubly inadmissible as it implies that she

[1] The most striking instance of this is in the first two mentions of Wordsworth (1815). In the *Journal* Haydon breakfasts with Wordsworth on 23 May; on 13 June Wordsworth breakfasts with Haydon, who has first superintended the taking of a life mask. In the *Autobiography* the entry for 23 May is the same, but the other entry is transferred from June to 13 April. *Diary* i. 446, 450; *Autobiography and Memoirs* (1926), pp. 209, 210. This is one of many indications that the *Journals* were sometimes written up after a lapse of time.

was living in his house three months before their marriage. He also omits 'elegant young men tripping along in silken grace with elegant girls trembling in feathers & diamonds, old peers & old peeresses, some in one dress some in another, many with swords, whose awkwardness in managing them shewed how unused their sides had been to the graceful encumbrance, and many with coats, velvet & satin, of all ages, all courts, & all times, bought or borrowed of Jews, because there was not time or they had not money to get the regular ones—of such were the company composed, all happy, eager, smiling & anticipating'. The much longer description of the visit to Walmer in 1839 is almost accurate. The only omission is Haydon's (short) admiring description of Lady Mahon. The most noteworthy alteration is a 'sir' inserted into the Duke's words to Haydon (p. 239). The *Journal*: 'Well, I'll give you 1 hour & ½.'

The most noteworthy mutilations are to the often-quoted description of Keats (pp. 113–14). It is impossible here to give every verbal variant. Haydon writes of Keats's 'glorious spirit', Taylor alters to 'kind and gentle', seemingly to avoid a repetition of glorious. Haydon, 'I was attached to Keats, he had great enthusiasm for me.' Taylor, 'I was much attached to Keats, and he had a fellow-feeling for me.' One deleted passage, describing Keats bowing to the portrait of Voltaire, has now been cited twice.[1] Another omission is 'Leigh Hunt was in my estimation the great unhinger of his best dispositions; latterly, poor dear fellow, he distrusted his guide. Keats saw through Hunt's weakness, but thinking him ill used, he would not cease to visit him, this shewed the goodness of his heart.'[2]

Here are two characteristic examples of alterations at their more extensive. One is the passage on suicide quoted on p. 140. What Haydon wrote was 'All this anxiety was owing to the non-digestion of a bit of almonds, which I imprudently eat. My stomach got heated & affected my brain. Suppose in that humour, I had shot myself? Would a superior being have punished my soul, because, my brain being irritated by the indigestion of almonds, [I] had in a state of perturbation & false imagination put an end to a painful existence? Surely not!'[3] Anticipating a propitiatory visit to Chantrey in 1826, Haydon writes, 'we shall see how he will take a wish on my part to recommence'. This

---

[1] W. J. Bate, *John Keats* (1963), p. 112; A. Ward, *John Keats* (1963), p. 98.
[2] *Diary* ii. 316–18, 29 Mar. 1821.   [3] ii. 326, 2 May 1821.

becomes, 'We shall see how he will take a visit to pave the way to reconciliation.'[1]

Many names and passages were, of course, inevitably omitted. We now know that the drunken editor (p. 178) was Lockhart. Taylor omits the whole incident. Here is the *Journal* version. 'Last night I was at a Conversazione, & while there the Editor of the Quarterly came in quite drunk. He walked steadily through the Rooms & then *out*. I walked after him & caught him on the stairs. He was quite affectionate & said, "My dear fellow, I hope you will get on. Paint their *blasted faces*. Goodnight" & away he reeled.'[2] The context of the famous anecdote of Wordsworth's reactions to Canova's *Cupid and Psyche* (pp. 138–9) was clearly unprintable. 'He was relating to me with great horror Hazlitt's licentious conduct to the girls of the Lake, & that no woman would walk after dark for "his Satyr & *beastly* appetites". Some girl called him a black-faced rascal, when Hazlitt enraged pushed her down, "& because, Sir," said Wordsworth, "she refused his abominable & devilish propensities," he lifted up her petticoats and smote her on the *bottom*.'[3] Long afterwards, ' "Pray", said I to Wordsworth, "what did you mean, many, many years ago, when I took you accidentally into Christie's . . . & we saw Cupid & Psyche kissing—what did you mean, after looking some time, by inwardly saying 'the Devils'." He laughed heartily, & replied, "*I cant tell*." '[4]

Haydon occasionally lapses into impromptu verse of varying kinds and extreme badness. Taylor never mentions this, though there are revealing lines here and there. The motive seems to be— sometimes at least—the expression of thoughts or moods too bizarre or extravagant for prose. One of the oddest instances is verse addressed to Wordsworth on his visit to Court in 1845 as Laureate, wearing Rogers's clothes. This made a great impression on Haydon. He first heard of it from Hallam (the historian), then there was more gossip at Talfourd's. The last is quoted by Taylor without the comments. One of these, 'Napoleon crowning himself & Wordsworth on his knees unable to rise before the Queen, after his early Democracy, are beautiful specimens of the consistency of Genius, and are everlasting tribute to the monarchical principle'. Fifty-six lines of verse follow, beginning 'O W' (O Wordsworth) and ending 'Farewell old Friend, no longer friend

---

[1] *Diary* iii. 119, 10 July 1826.   [2] iii. 338, 13 Feb. 1829.
[3] ii. 470, 29 Mar. 1824.   [4] v. 170, 17 June 1842.

of mine, / For thy betrayal of the great & sacred Cause / Of Intellectual independence of all / Authority & Royalty & power.
B. R. Haydon, May 14 1845.'[1] (Before the dinner at Talfourd's.)
On 22 May Haydon wrote to Wordsworth (one of the letters of
disapproval, admonition, or approval with which he bombarded
the Great and others): 'I wish you had not gone to court. . . . I
think of you as Nature's high priest. . . . I have not been able to sup-
press my feelings. Believe me ever your old friend, B. R. Haydon.'[2]
Haydon wrote about this incident to Miss Barrett, and amused her,
and she told Miss Mitford. But she added, 'And now only fancy
what harm Mr Haydon does himself by talking after this fashion
at Mr Serjt. Talfourd's and elsewhere—think how he kills *himself*
by it! And after all it isn't consistent doctrine for a man who talks
of the "divine right" by the hour,—now is it?'[3] A very puzzling
remark this last, especially as she and Haydon never met. Haydon
was—in his *Journals*—an enemy of divine right. As early as 1817
he had reconciled himself to the restoration of the Bourbons
'because their Divine right & stuff cannot last, & something purer
than either [Bourbon or Bonaparte] will yet start up for the
blessing of mankind'.[4] The anti-establishment outburst in 1845
probably reflects the bitterness of the cartoon disappointment.

[1] *Diary* v. 441–4, 15 and 16 May 1845.
[2] Haydon, *Autobiography and Memoirs* (1926), ii. 788.
[3] Betty Miller, *Elizabeth Barrett to Miss Mitford* (1954), p. 243.
[4] ii. 80, 19 Jan. 1817.

3. MARRIAGE

Hail Wedded Love! (*Paradise Lost*, often quoted by Haydon)

NOTABLE omissions by Taylor are all that Haydon has to say about sex and domestic stresses and strains. Haydon's own omissions are also noteworthy. In the *Autobiography* there is little about his love affairs. There is a 'very beautiful woman' who 'nearly drove me insane' in 1805, 'an infernal Woman' who tried to seduce him in 1812. And there is the country idyll of 1806 (p. 23). 'I was fervently alive to the beauty of woman', he writes of 1808, 'and though never vicious was always falling in love.' But in his *Journal* he annotated in 1816 a torn-out page for a day in September 1808: 'I remember my tremendous struggles against vice at this period with wonder—it was useless—I was totally unable to remit my burning appetites in spite of all my efforts.' Much later, his son Frank added a note to the stub of the torn-out page: 'Unchastity—broke his oath "never to touch a woman again" in two days.'[1] In 1831 Haydon compares himself with Byron, 'the same precocious feeling for love at 9 years old, but yet by a Religious feeling that kept me from Vice'.[2]

Haydon believed himself irresistible to women: 'It is extraordinary what an influence Genius & reputation have on Women. Without affectation, if I did not perpetually struggle against it, I might do nothing else but doze on lovely bosoms. . . .'[3] Women were irresistible to him—'dear, dear creatures'. 'As my object is to trace the progress of my mind', he wrote of his *Journals* in 1816, 'it is also with my passions, and really I cannot help saying that no human being can conceive their intensity unless he has felt them in the same degree. They are now more intense, more burning, more furious than ever. I cannot help writing this down because I have experienced a burst lately that has born down all that I ever before felt.' A passage follows about 'a little lovely plump ambling creature', who minced by him in the Strand, that irresistibly recalls Boswell's *London Journal*. He resisted, regretted it, tried desperately to find her. 'What are the passions of eighteen to these?

[1] *Diary* i. 20.   [2] iv. 385, 10 Nov. 1831.
[3] ii. 77–78, 5 Jan. 1817.

Is this a proof of superior or inferior capacity? God knows,'[1] This must have been written shortly before he first met Mary.

There is a good deal about the 'Infernal Woman'—married, with five children. It is of interest because it strangely anticipated the pattern (according to himself) of his relations with Mrs. Norton. There are pages of invective—'I have more respect for Messalina herself who disguised not her vices.' 'Attracted by her apparent innocence I became enamoured, & tho by a mere accident I escaped without vice, yet with my mind so shattered, my peace so disturbed, my health so affected, & my habits so ruined, that it was long, long, before I relapsed into tranquillity . . . still longer before I erased that impression she had burnt on my aking soul.'[2]

Haydon's affairs with women were numerous and various. In April 1815 he goes into raptures about the delight of 'declaring a passion which has long possessed one to a pure, delicious girl', and keeping it secret from her parents. Two sketches of Maria Foote, besides other indications, reveal the girl's identity.[3] Next December he was mourning the absence from his studio of 'sweet, dearest V——'. 'It seems as if an Angel had gone with all its brightness, and left the World in an huge eclipse.'[4] As for Maria, he wrote evasively in verse, in 1828, of this relationship (when she had become 'the public sneer'). 'Would she bewitching torment him [Haydon] she / Loved most, and by him was most purely, / Most ardently was loved. . . .' But she was distracted by 'The bauble of a Coronet.'[5]

Here are some characteristic reflections. 'Marriage is the only chance I have of attaining a composed deportment. I am now at the mercy of every sleepy and lustrous eye, of every bending & voluptuous hip. Sometimes, when I successfully contend & conquer, it is always at the expence of such agitations & agony that I am unnerved & reduced for a week.'[6] 'Tenderly directed, the passion for a woman becomes the greatest blessing of life; indecently & immorally gratified, it becomes the greatest curse. For

---

[1] *Diary* ii. 10–11, 2 Mar. 1816.

[2] i. 410, 5 Feb. 1815.

[3] i. 423–5, 16 Apr. 1815. Sketches of M. F. and her mother and details for *Christ's Entry* fill ten pages in November 1816 (ii. 71).

[4] i. 494, 30 Dec. 1815.

[5] iii. 290, 13 July 1828. The scandal was a breach of promise case in 1824 against a young man who had been informed of her liaison with Col. Berkeley. She married Lord Harrington in 1831.

[6] i. 278, 31 Dec. 1812.

my part, I cannot be happy the moment my Soul is left to itself
if it has been at the expence of innocence or duty; it is a great
happiness [that] I cannot & may I always feel so.'[1] This hardly
seems consistent with his appraisal of himself in 1830: 'I never
seduced innocence or corrupted virtue, and when women have
made advances I have guided them rightly to their duties &
resisted my own desires. On my conscience I have done this. . . .'[2]
'How singular it is that the same women who scorn any liberty by
day will shrink at nothing by night. . . . You then get up, dress,
& meet the same creature, demure, awful, lovely, & distant, who
was 6 hours ago hugging! amorous! melting! heated!—extraordinary!'[3] The next page is torn out.

After reflecting on the happiness of his marriage on the fifth
anniversary of his wedding, Haydon makes this strange statement.
'I never loved but once, though out of feeling I have been
induced to enter into engagements from duty, & then repent them,
break them off, & lacerate the hearts of three or four [sic] interesting girls. One only is married since. The others justly reproach me
by their looks when I meet them. This was wrong & cruel & the
only [thing] that pangs my conscience.'[4] And in 1833, writing of
one of Mrs. Norton's admirers: 'How a man can be such an ass
as to declare to any woman unless he was sure, it is to me extraordinary! I never was refused, but always accepted, and God knows
I proposed often enough—I had 4 on my hands at once. What a
heartless Shame!—one dear Girl is an old maid yet. I would never
propose to a dear Girl till I had kissed her lips, and not then till by
a little piquing I saw her getting ill.'[5] Nothing in the *Journals*
suggests the year of this embarrassing situation.

'My youth has been passed in Love, Study, Fame, & Fighting',
Haydon wrote in January 1818, '& now I am reaping the reward
of each; my constitution is shaken by the two first, & my mind
balmed by the two latter.'[6] By this time he was in love with
Mary. She, one supposes, was in Devonshire. At one time he had
decided not to marry. 'I have not time to gain the affections of a
woman', he wrote in 1811. 'I have no time to suffer the petty interruptions of love, to be harrassed by the caprices of my mistress, or
the jealousy of my own disposition—all this is delightful, no man

[1] *Diary*, ii. 79, 17 Jan. 1817. Professor Pope interprets '. . . happiness I cannot
[have]. . .'.   [2] iii. 470, 5 July 1830.
[3] ii. 273, 10 July 1820.   [4] iii. 158, 10 Oct. 1826.
[5] iv. 111, 10 July 1833.   [6] ii. 185, 27 Jan. 1818.

on earth would enjoy it more than myself, but all this distracts attention, and disturbs thought. I have not time to devote to it— and relinquish it I will. June 26th 1811.' He added a note: 'If I can. Note 1835, Mary's eyes settled this!'[1] In 1813 he mused on the great difficulty of finding 'a woman of exquisite susceptibility, curbed & directed by principle', a lovely woman who 'would encourage & participate in my efforts for grandeur . . . who would shrink with horror at cruelly trifling to prove one's affection . . . but rather feel agony at giving a moment's uneasiness. . . . Let me but find such a creature susceptible of the tenderest, the most exquisite trembling love, and the purest virtue, . . . [etc. etc.] and I am her slave, her devoted enraptured, impassioned admirer while existence lasts.' He adds, 'I begin to be weary, to be heartily weary, of vice'.[2] Surprisingly, within the limits of the possible, he found his ideal.

We know no more of the date of the mysterious first meeting than that it was in 1816. A rapturous evening at Richmond in June with '——' must surely have been with Mary. The long and ecstatic diary entry is dated 2 June 1816. 'The three summits of human happiness are first the consciousness of having done your duty & the pious purity that comes over your Soul. The next, success in great schemes, & the third is a lovely girl who loves you . . . sitting after dinner on your knee . . . while you are sufficiently heated to be passionately alive to the ectasy [sic] without having lost your sense from its excess. . . . I think I felt yesterday a new feeling for the beauties of the world. . . . So intensely do I feel yesterday's beauty, that the air yet perfumes my nostrils, the sunny mistiness haunts my inward eye. I pray God I may awake to the cool vigour of my accustomed thoughts, or I am lost! . . . It seemed one of nature's great days. . . . I felt for a moment as if the mortal film was removed from [my] eyes, & I saw all but the great Creator. I saw millions on millions of genii who guarded every shrub & flower. . . .'[3] Haydon wrote in 1822 of Richmond as 'the scene of our love and courtship'. Nothing else in the Journals approaches this rapture, though there was another moment of vision in the Adelphi, in Liverpool, in 1844 (p. 275). Next October, 'Oh the agonizing searchings of a heart which feels there is another that beats in secret—at a distance! in grief!'[4]

Mary's name first appears on a sketch of her face framed in soft

[1] *Diary* i. 204, 26 June 1811.   [2] i. 320–1, 26 Aug. 1813.
[3] ii. 21–24.   [4] ii. 48, 5 Oct. 1816.

curls: 'My lovely Mary when first I saw her', attached to the *Journal* for February 1817.[1] On it is written, folded under,

> O God that we had met in time
> Thy heart as fond, thy hand more free
> Then thou hads't loved without a crime
> And I'd been less unworthy thee.
>   B. R. Haydon.

Nothing more of Mary in the *Journals* till 21 September 1820. 'I have passed the most enchanting fortnight mortal creature ever passed on Earth.' Mary had suddenly arrived from Devonshire. ' "Good Heavens Mary!" I could not say more—it was the sweet creature with whom I had been on the Thames 3 years ago, to see the opening of Waterloo bridge! On that sunny lovely day, when we glided away up the glittering river & passed the evening in sunny shade & sweet conversation!' What an occasion that would have been for one of the set pieces. The second anniversary of Waterloo—an anniversary often mentioned by Haydon—the pageant on the sparkling river, when the Regent opened the bridge, the crowds on the banks. But in 1817 there are no diary entries between 18 May and 26 June. After a long description of the rapturous fortnight Haydon records all we hear of Mary's history. She had been a widow for perhaps not much more than two years, so that the husband was by no means on his deathbed in 1816. (He was Simon Hyman of Devenport, a jeweller.) 'Her private History is as affecting as her beauty is enchanting. At 16, she was such an exquisite girl & so persecuted by men of fortune, that her friends hurried her into a marriage with a man old enough to be her Father, because he was rich,—he was ruined and died. I knew her before, but she kept me at a distance, though I saw I had touched her heart. The way she did all her duties to this man doubled in my eyes the effect of her beauty. He had presentiment of our love, but in his confidence in her was justified by her virtue. . . . For two years, beautiful & pestered to death, uncertain of my real intentions, she suffered . . . a fascinating young man . . . to draw her from her privacy. . . . she had flirted too far to retreat.' It was to disentangle herself that she had come to Haydon: '& being now assured of my fixed resolution to marry her, laid open her situation to me. I advised her how to act, & she says she feels as if it will be her salvation. I believe so myself. I am to blame for leaving her so long without explanation. . . .'[2]

[1] *Diary* ii. 94–95.   [2] ii. 281–5.

Next year Haydon was less than ever in a position to marry. His first arrest for debt was in June. But, 'July 10. My dearest Mary came to town for a short time.' 'July 11. Omnia vincit &c', and on the 12th, 'Spent the most delightful day of my life at Richmond.' He describes it. 'She has the simplicity of a child, the passions of an Italian woman, joined to the wholesome tenderness & fidelity of an English one.'[1] Taylor renders this, 'Haydon was now very happy for his future wife had arrived in town.'

They married on 10 October. The first mention of this is on 4 December: 'I am married! Ah, what a crowd of feelings lie buried in that little word . . . Dearest dearest Mary—I cannot write.' He ends the customary summing up of the year on 31 December, 'I am really & truly in love, & without affectation, I can talk, write or think of nothing else. Amen.'[2] He does not mention that in November Mary returned to Devonshire 'to put the final close to some matters of business', and he went to Edinburgh to exhibit *Christ's Agony* with *Solomon* and *Dentatus* and some other pictures which were shown from 21 November to 16 February without success.[3]

What is one to make of the beginning of an ending to a rapturous description of Mary's visit to him in his first imprisonment? 'I who have never known any other woman but *thee* reverence the raptures of holy love as the sacred blessing of a merciful God, as the only pure, unadulterated relick of lost Paradise!'[4]

The picture of Haydon as a devoted husband and father remains. That of Mary as healthy and cheerful does not. As might be expected there were family stresses and strains. Haydon regretted the solitude of his painting room. In January 1825, 'I sat late up last night and enjoyed all the luxuries of solitude for two hours. The moment I am *alone* I seem to have all my old inspirations. Let them be delusions!—never mind! They are rapturous! glorious! inspiring! . . .'[5] But on a wedding anniversary, 'I have been married five years, and who on Earth would have suited me so entirely? Who would have given up Society, so beautiful, and so admired, and been content to shine in secret, domestic, & loving!'[6] Later entries suggest that Haydon kept his wife in an almost oriental seclusion.

'The occupations of a man with a large family', Haydon wrote

[1] *Diary* ii. 348.
[2] ii. 352, 354.
[3] ii. 352 n.
[4] ii. 420, 10 July 1823.
[5] iii. 5, 13 Jan. 1825.
[6] iii. 158, 10 Oct. 1825.

in 1829, 'are so distracting that Art & information are all buried & forgotten.'[1] Two years later:

I am not adapted for the World. I could live for ever in my own. I want no other. But, alas, with a large family, how often is my own World broken in on. I lose sight of it for days—illness, pleasure, worrit, the wants of a wife & 8 children, all take their forms of harrass, and make me weep when I lock myself into my painting room & gaze at my Zenophon! Why did I marry?—however, that delicious dream of rapture exceeded even my imagination. It was my ruin. It brought all the World at once on me, from the bare idea that no man in his senses would have done so, but with some property or other. Alas, they little knew me. I married because I loved, & for no other reason. It was a rash step, it brought misery on a lovely creature, and brought other lovely creatures into the World, who would have been happier not born, but it saved my life, & my health & certainly my intellects when trouble came. Yet it has cut up my habits.

I am melancholy—can I be otherwise? After 28 years of work & sincere devotion, not to have saved one guinea, or to know where to go for one in case of sudden illness, broken limbs or fever!—Not only not to have any prospects [? property] left, but to have lost all utterly I had ever saved, all the School books of my youth, all the accumulations of boyhood, youth & manhood, to lose impressions of languages for want of means of reference—to forget poets—to have Tasso slide from my mind & almost dear Shakespeare fade on my memory.[2]

A few weeks later he attributes his melancholy to ill health due to separation from Mary while she was nursing. Then, on his tenth wedding anniversary, he muses on marriage. 'Though we have suffered greatly, to my feelings the pleasures greatly overbalance the pains. Continual nursing & petty details hurt a woman's temper, and though Mary is the most exemplary of women as a Mother, the warmth of passion gets deadened by harrassed nights, pangs of child birth, fag of nursing. It is not so with a man, his passions are always ready, and always furious. . . . The case of a husband is hard but the education of his children & his pursuits should have more of his attention than ever. I have no right absolutely to complain, only I must choose between my dearest Mary's life & my own passions. . . .' But he sums up, 'My happiness, my health, my energy have been doubled since matrimony. . . . Hail Wedded Love! and I trust in God I shall keep my honour &

[1] Diary iii. 355, 25 Apr. 1829.
[2] iii. 547, 31 Aug. 1831.

fidelity.'[1] Mary's illnesses recur (after childbearing ceased) and so do Haydon's prayers for continence and fidelity. In 1842, 'My wedding day! God bless it, & grant my dearest Mary & myself many happy returns of it! I have had the greatest happiness & my dear love much misery, but she has born it like a Heroine, & saved my brain & health.'[2]

The second of two crises which disturbed the marriage was just over, or almost so. The first was Haydon's infatuation for Mrs. Norton—the strangest revelation in the *Diary*. The other, perhaps more serious, was dissension over Haydon's elder stepson, Orlando. The Mrs. Norton affair was previously known only from what Haydon told Miss Barrett in confidence and she confided to Robert (p. 105). It obsessed him from early in 1833 to the end of 1835, and indeed much later, after he had 'escaped'. It is the most remarkable manifestation of his vanity and capacity for self-delusion—or so it would seem. His assertions and reflections are directly at odds with his own record of the stages of the infatuation.

Haydon's Reform Bill portraits, as he often remarked, brought him again into high life. The introduction to Mrs. Norton was from Melbourne. While Brougham was sitting for his portrait his stepdaughter and Mrs. Norton called to see it. The fascination was instant. 'She is like Mary in her bloom, every body else looked ugly by her side—pale, intelligent, & extremely delicate. She looked like a bit of Greek sculpture come to life. . . . It is extraordinary how beauty & genius irritate the species. I am much fatigued.'[3] Ten days later, 'Tomorrow I call upon that marble beauty, with pale passion & deep feeling marked on her brow, Mrs Norton. Her face & dear Mary's would have made Eve jealous indeed.'[4] He calls. Three days later he dines at Storey's Gate and meets Melbourne and Disraeli. Another dinner is described; Haydon makes frequent calls till July, when he went too far, and as he says later, was 'very properly' dismissed. He records his reactions. 'Give me a beautiful woman gifted with Genius! to talk with, to look at, and feel for.' And, 'When I am with her I am confused. When I am absent I do nothing but muse, and think how much more agreeable I might have been.'[5]

Haydon also met Mrs. Norton's beautiful sisters, Mrs. Blackwood (afterwards Lady Dufferin) and Lady Seymour (afterwards

[1] *Diary* iii. 560, 10 Oct. 1831. [2] v. 209, 10 Oct. 1842.
[3] iv. 47, 14 Feb. 1833. [4] iv. 49, 24 Feb.
[5] iv. 107, 112, 2 and 13 July.

Duchess of Somerset). He visits them, they come to his painting room, and he gets Lady Seymour to sit to him. 'Dear Lady Seymour sat . . . she wished to be God-Mother to my dear little *just-born*. This is a great honour. These ladies literally combine the wit of Sheridan with the beauty of Miss Lindley' [*sic*] (their grandparents). 'Three such women as Mary, Lady Seymour, & Mrs Norton would be Paradise.' He longs to possess them all. Frank's comment: 'Thou silly Gentleman!'[1] In August he records: 'I have been thrown back lately by a quarrel with Mrs ——, which, when I feel inspired, I will state in my journal.'[2] In September, 'Mrs N—— is confined of a boy. In spite of myself felt wretchedly anxious. Sublime creature, without wishing to be unfaithful to Mary, I cannot help a passion for her.'[3]

Mary suffers terribly. 'She is uneasy at seeing me musing about Mrs Norton—she knows every thing of my unfortunate infatuation. She relies on my honour, but I confess my folly', Haydon wrote in May.[4] To overcome his passion (he says), which grows by absence, he blackmails Mrs. Norton into sitting for his picture of Cassandra. 'We have made it up again—Huzza! She is a fine Creature. I worried her well & myself more. I told her . . . if she would not sit for Cassandra, my family would be ruined. This is her noble answer [her letter]. I knew that would hit her at last. . . . By seeing her I shall vanquish my intense passion—by absence it only grew worse. . . . I confessed every thing to Mary, but having a Wife saved me—had I been single I should have gone mad.'[5]

'My infatuation about Mrs Norton gives me pain of mind. It is wicked, loving Mary as I do, behaving as she has behaved. But I conceal nothing. . . . "How can I forget you my dearest love? In the first place I believe *her* to be good—and you know *me*—" "I deserve it—because I gave you great pain on account of Sir Willoughby Cotton before marriage." . . . She then sobbed hysterically. We both kissed & loved. . . . At my time of life, to think of my infatuation for dear Mrs Norton—What can I do? She has very properly kept me at a distance for a year, but it is no use, and I am perfectly convinced of her sympathy for me if there be truth in female expression. . . . I very much suspect M—— [Melbourne] insisted on my dismissal, for her dear preference was visible. . . . Dearest Woman—I *do* love thy head [Frank: 'thee' was written

---

[1] *Diary* iv. 105, 109, 28 June, 5 July 1833. [2] iv. 119, 10 Aug. 1833.
[3] iv. 127–8, 3 Sept. 1833. [4] iv. 189, 19 May 1834.
[5] iv. 190, 19 May 1834.

first and 'head' added], beautiful creature, . . . you do love me. I need not Vanity. I have been too much all my life loved. It is a fact that *all* Women have advanced half way—& most, more.'[1] By his own showing Mrs. Norton had not.

Mrs. Norton posed for Cassandra (in a fatiguing position), but very occasionally and did not keep appointments. 'I love her to distraction' (13 June). 'Dearest Mrs Norton did not come' (23 June). In August Mary wrote in a book given her by 'Dear Benjamin . . . to put down my thoughts, as relief to my feelings that can no longer contain themselves. . . . I ask for redress from the Almighty for the deep deep misery I have suffered and suffered without cause.'[2] In September Haydon went to Hampstead for air. 'Dearest Mary came. . . . She said she was perfectly happy, and so was I, and she promised never again to be jealous of Women of Fashion—dearest Mary!—thou hast no *real* occasion!'[3]

In July Haydon had been to two charade parties at Mrs. Leicester Stanhope's. 'Spent a delightful evening . . . charades—written and acted by that extraordinary creature for beauty & Genius, Caroline Norton.' He was entranced;'Had Mary been there it would have been glorious, too'. And on the second occasion 'Mrs Norton did the Lady of Fashion in a style which no actress could accomplish. . . . I was highly delighted . . . to find myself in such high Life again, after such humiliations.'[4]

Taylor says of 1835, 'I find constant mention of dinners and routs and charade parties.' These must be from notes of invitation, not from the *Journals*, where only occasions where Mrs. Norton was met or discussed are recorded. The social side of Haydon's life is rarely mentioned though there are complaints of its distractions. Haydon was seeing a good deal of Lady Blessington, who was not received in society (an exclusion approved by Haydon). By January 1835 he was listening to her malicious gossip about Mrs. Norton, though he knew it was 'spitish', and on an earlier occasion it had displeased him. 'We talked of Caroline. . . . Caroline's Power is dreadful. She nearly destroyed me in struggling to get free. Nothing but such superior beauty as my dear Mary's could have preserved me, because Mary's beauty is embalmed in innocence. . . . But I behaved very thoughtlessly & gave my sweet great unhappiness. We both bless our God I escaped. . . .' Here is the transition from sublime creature to temptress. ' "How

---

[1] *Diary* iv. 191, 25 May.   [2] iv. 219 n.
[3] iv. 223, 15–17 Sept. 1834.   [4] iv. 210, 213–14, 15, 31 July 1834.

cruel—does she not know what I have gone through for you? How cruel!" Then the fervent denunciations of Vengeance burst out, violent hystericks & tenderest & most pouting love' (Frank: 'Yah!'). Haydon goes on, 'I tell her all—& ever will as my only security. It is hardly to be credited the offers I have had from Women of Fashion—but Mary's face awes the dear husseys.'[1] (Frank: 'Pretty well for a man of 49 with some of his front teeth gone, bad breath, a pot belly & bald headed.' At this time Frank was twelve and the description of his father may be from later memories. Frederic's description of Haydon at fifty-two is very different (p. 120).)

In April more scandal from Lady Blessington. 'Good God! If what I heard of Caroline yesterday is true! What an escape! But I cannot doubt it.'[2] He was by no means free. One sitting for Cassandra is recorded in November, seemingly the last: '. . . succeeded in Caroline's head. She sat with the kindness & simplicity, & amiability of a beauty. . . . Dear Mary's head is different, without her depth, but more of the Angel.' A four-line 'Impromptu' follows: 'When Caroline at Hampton Court reposes, / E'en Raphael leaves his glory in the Skies. . . .'[3] Mrs. Norton was living there with her mother. This seems to have been the occasion of which Haydon wrote in 1837, 'The agony she [Mary] suffered the last time I had Caroline alone & was sketching her resolved me at once to cut the infernal connection.'[4] It was not completely cut. On 19 December there was a dinner at the Stanhopes' when 'Caroline sang with great & deep feeling "Would I were with thee" . . . .'. And on the 27th Haydon called on Lady Seymour and Caroline: 'Surrounded by her Children I could not help thinking of the continued calumnies about her. I spent a delightful hour with her & admired her sketches.'[5]

The gutter press had been busy with scandals arising out of the very public quarrels between the Nortons. Then came Norton's suit for divorce by which he hoped to get large damages from Melbourne. Haydon believed the worst. On the eve of the trial he wrote, 'She appears to have been all I have suspected her to be from the 1st moment I saw her, & yet with my eyes open I sank into a species of infatuation. . . she has passed her whole life in trying to disturb the peace of domestic happiness. . . . To *me* &

[1] *Diary* iv. 254–6, 7 Jan. 1835.   [2] iv. 282, 20 Apr. 1824.
[3] iv. 324, 20 Nov. 1835.
[4] iv. 418, 2 July 1837.   [5] iv. 327, 330.

Lord Melbourne & Lord Mulgrave in *public* hardly a word passed; to me especially she *submitted* her opinion & shrunk from collision, sang when I asked her, hung over me while I sketched, but always with distance before others—happy to see me, yet when my name was announced, *to the servants* said to reply "what a *bore*". I came often & too unreservedly, and endangered that character for virtue she was too anxious of keeping.'[1] That Haydon was a tiresome intruder on Mrs. Norton and Melbourne one can believe.

A little before this he had written, 'I pity Lord Melbourne. He has been her complete victim. On me she failed entirely, but it was a singular evidence of character to watch how she varied her plans of attack, always keeping her ultimate object in view. When all failed, she tried to wind herself into the affections of my dear Mary, & when Mary told me she had assured her nothing like a connection could take place from the nature of a *complaint* she was subject to, I really felt as if my hair was creeping over my skin. However, I'll wait before I detail'[2] (he never did). Can Mary have invented this?

Haydon crowned these distorted reflections by a letter to Melbourne: 'I wrote him yesterday & hinted that he ought not to be too sure. I told him a Cousin of mine had dined with the Attorney for Norton . . . [who] told my Cousin there was evidence enough from the Servants to convict him twice over. . . .'[3] With this horrifying and scarcely credible intrusion Haydon's agreeable visits to Melbourne cease.

The trial (22 June) was a triumph for Melbourne. The evidence of dismissed servants (harboured and bribed by Lord Grantley) was easily discredited. No evidence was called for the defence. The jury did not leave the box. Melbourne was cheered in court, Norton was hooted. The trial suggested to Dickens the case of *Bardell* v. *Pickwick*. Haydon noted: 'Caroline was acquitted yesterday—but surely not in the mind of any impartial person. I have read the evidence through & knowing her habits as I do, I could not have sanctioned such a verdict.'[4] How can what seems an aberration, or worse, be explained? One can only guess. That he and she were on different wave-lengths—social and personal—and that Haydon, like many others, misinterpreted Caroline Norton's unconventional ways? Haydon's belief that he was irresistible and his conscious or unconscious resentment at having been resisted?

---

[1] *Diary* iv. 352–3, 20 June 1836.   [2] iv. 347, 14 May 1836.
[3] iv. 353–4, 20 June 1836.   [4] iv. 354, 23 June 1836.

That to cure his infatuation and to console Mary he made himself believe that he had escaped from a temptress?

As with the Infernal Woman of 1812 he could not keep Mrs. Norton out of his *Journal*. 'My dear Love's health after so many children & so much anxiety is in a delicate state. She has never recovered the blow it received by the heartless vice of Caroline. There was something in the heartless attempt of that Devil to seduce me from my love, after what we had both gone through, of a nature so cruel & so fiendish that nothing would or could shew to what a pitch the passions of Women of fashion drive them from their habits of continual unrestraint.'[1]

A week later there is a new twist. 'I neglected dear Mary from pique. She flirted before marriage with Cotton, put me in a rage, and when Caroline made advances I thought it no harm to shew my love I could pique her.'[2] (After twelve years of married life!) Apart from Mary's hysterical self-accusation there is no other mention of Cotton[3] in the *Journals*.

Five years after the trial the Duke of Sutherland sent opera tickets; Mary and her daughter went. 'Who should Mary meet as she walked about in her smart, maternal beauty, but Caroline Norton, hollow cheeked & worn down, in Company with an old Wretch, as a contrast. Ah Caroline! You felt how awful Virtue is! What an extraordinary meeting! Good God! Mary ruined her, & she knows it, & she brought it on herself. Poor Caroline—she is to be pitied. What a fate, a history, & an example!'[4] Whatever Mary may have conveyed to Norton's attorney was no part of the 'evidence'. And she could have had no part in inducing the proceedings: the motives were Norton's hope for damages or to be bought off, the rancour of his family against his wife, the intrigues of some 'low tories'—notably Lord Wynford—for a scandal that would harm Melbourne. And Mrs. Norton was not 'ruined'; she was wronged and unhappy but still a beauty—fifteen years younger than Mary—a London hostess, received at Court, and with a reputation as poetess and novelist. Mary's vengeance seems pure fantasy. But in 1838, in a long denigration, Haydon wrote, 'Caroline came athwart a Woman of Spirit, her superior in perfect beauty, though not her equal in expression, her match in energy

---

[1] *Diary* iv. 417, 25 June 1837.   [2] iv. 418, 2 July.
[3] Sir Willoughby Cotton, 1783–1860, General (Lt.-Col. 1821), C.-in-C. Bombay 1847–50, Governor of Jamaica 1829–34, etc. (*D.N.B.*).
[4] v. 76, 30 July 1841.

& her superior in principle—and she was baffled, defeated & blasted!
—exposed, exposed to the World, driven from fashion, &
deprived of her children & deserted by her husband. . . . If I live
thy story shall be told as well as the strange events that led to
thy exposure!'[1]

But Haydon's final musing on the affair was sober, if hardly
candid. 'Romantic youths with down for indications of beard are
liable to Brain infatuations. As Manhood devellopes, the physical
gives symptoms, and after puberty I think few are the Imaginative
infatuations, though Caroline Norton's head certainly infatuated
my imagination & nothing more, for there was more of the
Painter than the Lover then in me—& even that was sinful, because
it gave my sweet & only Love exquisite torture.'[2]

The pattern of the Infernal Woman of 1812 is strangely repeated. Both are very attractive married women, surrounded by
admirers at their husband's table. Both are 'fiendish', both compared to Messalina; both (Haydon says) use their children to cover
their intrigues. To both Haydon writes letters which he is anxious
to recover. From both he escapes with difficulty. The first was the
model (from memory) for the wicked mother in *Solomon*. And
when Haydon saw Lockhart looking at Wordsworth as the Devil
might look at Adam & Eve, he was seized with an idea: 'Caroline
Norton's Eyes, Lockhart's Melancholy, Byron's Voluptuousness,
Napoleon's mouth, Haydon's forehead, and Hazlitt's brows, will
make a very fine Devil.'[3]

A note of tragedy was added to the Norton episode by the fact
that it coincided with a rapid sequence of deaths and births. Alfred
died in May 1833, and in June Georgiana Caroline Elizabeth Sarah
Seymour was born—the names of Mrs. Norton and her sister must
have pained Mary. In April 1834 Harry, Haydon's favourite child,
died. The baby Georgiana died in June 1835; two months later,
the last child, Newton, was born and lived for nine months.
Added to this, 1834 and 1835 were years of extreme financial
anxiety and distress.

To go to other domestic troubles. These are anxieties about
Frank, and Haydon's uneasy relations with his elder stepson,
Orlando—which caused the second crisis with Mary. There is
relatively little about family matters in the *Journals*, and such

---

[1] *Diary* iv. 516, 31 Aug. 1838.   [2] v. 284, 12 June 1843.
[3] v. 163, 29 May 1842. This is the only mention of Mrs. Norton in Taylor's
version, with C—— N—— and L—— for the names.

entries as there are seem compulsive. In 1818 Haydon had noted, apropos Leigh Hunt's 'perpetual whining' about his wife and children, 'no Nation feels greater disgust at a man's obtruding on the World what regards his domestic concerns only.'[1] (The passions of a man of genius Haydon did consider of public interest.)

Births, deaths, and illnesses are frequent entries, but in general are briefly recorded, though they cause anguish. Haydon was a devoted father. Frederic and Mary gave no trouble, nor did Simon, the younger stepson. It was otherwise with Orlando, whose full name (not in the *Journals*) was Orlando Haydon Bridgman Hyman. When Haydon first saw Mary and her two-year-old child, he was absorbed in *Orlando Furioso*. The Orlando may belong to Bridgman and be a mere coincidence, but how did he get the Haydon? Was he christened after the marriage?

At the time of the marriage—which he may have resented—Orlando was a clever and precocious child of seven. When Haydon was walking in Devonshire with Mary (a visit not otherwise mentioned) 'Orlando turned all of a sudden & crying out, said, "Mamma, I wish you & Mr Haydon would make haste & *not loiter kissing so!*" '[2]

The boys went away to school at eight, after some teaching of classics by Haydon. Dissatisfied with his own education, he was determined to do his best for stepsons and sons alike, but found school fees a burden. In 1840, after listening to accounts by Dr. Lushington of 'vice' at Eton and public schools generally, he comments, 'But still I am for public Schools—and what a race they produce in Statesmen, Generals, Admirals &c. Boys should be brought up with each other. . . . I know I saved my boys by early precaution, & they went to School knowing & despising the horrid vices they were to see—and they were never taken by surprise, nor did they ever give into them, as they have assured me, and therefore though not one in 100 may be the average who become celebrated, I should be disposed to take the chance. Boys should not be kept too innocent or ignorant. I explained the fatal consequences of the school vice—they went dreading it, & as much aware of it, as Men. It was an experiment, & it succeeded.'[3]

Orlando went first to Hayes, then at fourteen to Dr. Valpy's

[1] *Diary* ii. 196, 5 Apr. 1818.
[2] iii. 469, 5 July 1830.
[3] v. 15, 11 Nov. 1840.

school at Reading,[1] where in 1830, aged sixteen, he got a scholarship at Wadham, became a Fellow at twenty-one, and as Fellow remained there till his death in 1878. 'Orlando, for whose schooling I have been imprisoned twice & arrested once, has won a scholarship at Wadham College, Oxford. There is some pleasure in suffering for a boy like this. . . .' 'It is curious, I have pushed him through his education like a Lion, suffering all sorts of insults. I only hope God will enable me to do that for my own dear Children He has enabled me to do for my Children in Law.'[2] This was written in prison. Next October he got £50 from Lord Stafford 'to get my son matriculated'. For this he was to paint a picture. He did so, a *Waiting for the Times*,[3] with which his patron was pleased.

Orlando was often in money difficulties, though he must have become more or less self-supporting. Haydon's complaints are not of his College bills. In June 1831, 'Went to Oxford about my Son, who had suffered great privation, & lived on bread & water for breakfast, when he was not invited out. . . .' He tells the Warden this. 'Hyman will be distinguished, I am convinced.'[4] A year later, when returning from Birmingham, 'called at Oxford & saw Orlando, who looked pale & studious. He was affected at seeing me after 8 months. He looked interesting with his tattered gown & torn cap. He will be eminent.'[5]

Haydon expected a kind of gratitude he did not get. Seven years later, in June 1839: 'This day, after 18 years of devotion to me, during which she has never left her home without her children, & never left them for a single hour . . . my dearest love has with my consent *taken a holiday*. She is gone to Oxford to see her Son & rest from domestic fag. . . . I fear he has a bad heart, though with great talents.'[6] Next March, when Haydon went to Oxford to lecture, and was entertained by several Heads of Houses and Senior Tutors (pp. 220–1), there is no mention of either Wadham or Orlando. In April Haydon's exasperation breaks out, but this time he says, 'he has a good heart & great simplicity, but a very improper person to have the management of Youth'. Hyman, who was in Orders,

---

[1] Dr. Richard Valpy (1754–1836), very successful Master of Reading School, 1781–1830.

[2] *Diary* iii. 469–70, 5 July 1830.

[3] iii. 590, 31 Dec. 1832. The original was for Kearsey. Both are extant, one owned by *The Times*.   [4] iii. 524.

[5] iii. 621, 21 June 1832.   [6] iv. 564–5, 17 June 1839.

had profoundly shocked his stepfather by saying at breakfast after he had dined out, that he had been asked to say grace, but *did not know what to say! He thought this a good joke. . . .*' This story is inset in a lengthy complaint: 'My Step Son Hyman tries my mind very much. He comes up in the Vacation with nothing to do, & passes his time in eating, Idling, lolling, smoking, and disturbing the economy of a family regularity. He is in that detestable state of mind when sophistication takes the place of Roligion & common sense. . . . When I hear a Young Man whose station in life is owing to my keeping him at it, say he smokes a cigar because he does not know what to do!—it is to me such infamous sacrilege.' To this passage there is a sequence of five notes by Frank. 'You never liked him. His cynicism was bitterer than your own. His conversational readiness in sarcasm greater; his knowledge of books infinitely superior. . . . He owed much to you (rather you owed much *for* him) but you expected . . . an amount of gratitude which no human being ever yet paid to any other.' Whatever the truth of these remarks, Frank seems to have misinterpreted his father in the matter of cynicism and sarcasm, which Haydon disliked. Another note: 'The plain English of all this outburst of virtue is that Hyman was better educated than my father, & did not vest all his assertions with that "dropping-down-deadness" of acquiescence which my father exacted from all his children, whether under or over age. Frank Haydon.'[1]

Tension reached a climax in the following October, when a letter dated 1 February 1833 is attached to the *Journal*. Orlando writes that he is in debt, without a farthing, and hopes Haydon will send him £10, though anything would be appreciated. He regrets not having become a clerk. Haydon comments that in 1827 he rejected a clerkship for Orlando, because of his talents, from a rich and powerful merchant, since bankrupt. 'Had I from temporary pressure[2] accepted the Clerkship to help myself, Hyman would have been turned adrift upon the world, & now he is a Fellow of Wadham & stands high as a Tutor! Yet this boy's base ingratitude to me, his subsequent insolence & fiendish behaviour, I record with sorrow.' (Frank's note: 'There are two sides to every quarrell. I hope this bit of ill humour will be passed over by the Editor. F. S. Haydon.') 'Twice was I imprisoned for his schooling, the Second time *ruined*, yet he has been the sole cause of embittering my happiness, and the only cause of any disagreement with my

[1] *Diary* iv. 621–2, 16 Apr. 1840.   [2] Haydon was in prison.

dear Mary, who, though saying the other day when I went where there was danger, "Take care of yourself my love, for if any thing happens, you will leave me at the mercy of such a poor, rhodomontant irresolute creature as Orlando", yet her affections sacrifice me always when he is near her. Now he is on the brink of adultery, & she signed a letter with me of remonstrance, & yet the moment he comes up she undoes all the good done by her signature, & sacrifices as usual my authority—and the result must be separation. . . .' he wrote in October 1840. He added a note— 'I foresee it. London July 3 1841.'[1]

That Haydon could have thought separation from Mary probable is startling. Though, as he says, 'of a sanguine disposition', he was also apt to anticipate the worst. He is as reticent over the relations with Mary in this crisis as he was the reverse over Mrs. Norton. Between the two dates of these forebodings, in February 1841, 'My dearest Mary, who has been so often alluded to in these Journals as the Source of so much happiness, is now broken down in health, and yesterday as I myself washed her pale face & hands, for she would let no one else touch her, as I looked at her beautiful, shrunk face, the tears trickled over my cheeks, and seeing me crying, she wept bitterly herself. After having born up so heroically, followed me to prison, never left me, saved my brain & my health, in poverty, in struggle, with a house full of Babies, nursing by day, watching by night, & harrassed always— now, when my circumstances are better . . . when we pay our way & are in comparative Comfort, down breaks her health, her dear health! But she will weather it, & I support her under it, there is nothing I would not do for her, to make her happy. God bless her & save her and let us descend to the Grave together. Amen.'[2]

She did recover. Next July she was at the Opera 'in her smart maternal beauty'. And the trouble with Orlando subsided. The last trace of it, except for a remark in November, is in a prayer in the following August. 'Awaken my deluded Step Son Hyman from his ingratitude, his sophistries, his idleness, his Scepticism, which must end in vice & ruin.'[3] Haydon may have realized that Hyman was grown up and independent. He was proud of him. In October 1842 he transcribed in his *Journal* a quotation from Plato beginning ' "My constant care is how I may be able to present to my Judge a pure & spotless soul", and ending "Socrates—Georgias"

[1] *Diary* v. 6–7, 1 Oct. 1840.   [2] v. 34–35, 22 Feb. 1841.
[3] v. 76, 1 Aug. 1841.

[*sic*]. Hyman's translation.'[1] He sent a copy to Miss Barrett, and in November she wrote to Miss Mitford, 'Talking of Greek Mr Haydon has sent me lately a translation of the Gorgias of Plato, prepared for the press by his son-in-law. It is an excellent and spirited translation, but I venture to think it inelegant & have said so.'[2]

And on Christmas Day there was a family dinner with Hyman and Frank (both argumentative) and another Cambridge under-graduate, 'and a very pleasant day we had'. This is almost the first record of table talk since the immortal dinner, and the meeting with Shelley, some scraps of conversation at the Nortons excepted ('I could have talked better than any but did not like to intrude'). 'Hyman, who is an able Scholar, seemed disposed to deny the Genius of Milton on account of his eternal display of learning (but the hatred of the Churchman was quite apparent) .... Hyman said his learning was a pimple in a splendid face. I said a splendid face always affected me so I never saw the pimples. .... I have greater pleasure in extracting the beautiful from the Evil than in omitting the beautiful on account of the pimples. You, my dear, see pimples in every thing." This was too true not to touch him, & he became silent. But I am highly pleased to hear a boy I had brought up & taught his Verbs, so able, well read, & give other proofs of first rate scholarship.' 'He ridiculed the Lyrical Ballads, said the Enthusiasm for Wordsworth would pass like that for the Germans, & that he could not read the Excursion.' Haydon successfully challenged his knowledge of Wordsworth's 'finest productions'. 'Hyman is of that peculiar nervous temperament that he is sure to fall on subjects which he knows produce dispute. He did not mean to provoke severity from me. I was pleased with his remarks, but had I not forborn, we should have clashed in a moment.'[3]

This was a pleasant interlude in the hopes, fears, and anguish of the cartoon contest. But another family trouble had become recurrent.

[1] *Diary* v. 214, 1 Oct. 1842.
[2] Betty Miller, *Elizabeth Barrett to Miss Mitford*, p. 143 (18 Nov. 1842).
[3] v. 232–4.

4. FATHER AND SON

What anxieties a Father has!—up to the grave! (8 Nov. 1845)

EXCEPT for the difficulties with Mary over Orlando, relations with Frank were more disturbing. As a young man
Haydon had mused on paternity—on 'the necessary indifference of children' and 'the agony of affection' of their parents.[1]
'My dearest Mary is with child! I always prayed God I might know
the sweet name of parent. . . .'[2] He was deeply moved at Frank's
birth. 'I have never been so affected since the death of my Mother.'[3]
He doted on his first-born and Frank's future became a main
preoccupation. 'God grant me life till dear Frank is a man. He is
getting a sweet boy. . . .'[4] The child had a succession of illnesses.
'I thought I should have gone mad at the prospect of losing
dearest Frank—a fellow string of the same instrument as myself!
Oh Frank, dear little intellectual, keen, poetic soul!'[5] He was five.
Ten months later, 'Dear Frank, who is all eye, ear, & Soul for
every thing above, about, or underneath him, has had an attack
from mere excitement. This has distressed & distracted me.'[6]

'He was [our] first child and I overwhelmed [him] with eager
interest which broke him down', Haydon wrote when Frank first
went to school.[7] School must have been too much for Frank,
though the only indication of this is a *Journal* entry when the boy
was twelve. 'Sunday. Read Prayers & went over all the Greek,
Latin, French & Italian lessons of my dear Boy Frank, as in consequence of my difficulties the Masters had refused to come till I had
paid up my arrears.'[8] Counting his blessings on the last day of
1836: 'My children are improved & good. My Eldest Boy has
undoubted & high Genius, and my Lovely Mary is spared to me
in health & happiness.'[9]

---

[1] *Diary* ii. 188, 8 Feb. 1818. [2] ii. 365, 1 May 1822.
[3] ii. 393, 12 Dec. 1822. [4] iii. 160, 21 Oct. 1826.
[5] iii. 252, 1 Feb. 1828. [6] iii. 327–8, 28 and 29 Dec. 1828.
[7] iii. 518, 22 May 1831.
[8] iv. 284, 10 May 1835. In April 1838 Haydon called on Frank's tutor to
inquire about a quotation from Plato.
[9] iv. 394.

At sixteen Frank made his start in life. In March 1839 Haydon took him to Manchester to be an engineering pupil with his friend Sir William Fairbairn, a brilliant inventor and famous engineer. 'It is a complete sacrifice, though his passion for engineering is invincible. . . . I suffered so much from the opposition of *my* Parents, I resolved he should have none in any pursuit wherein he shewed direct & positive evidence of talent & desire. It is his own choice & God bless him in it. No Boy ever issued from his Father's care with more dependance on his God, more chastened by the degradations of his Parents, more timid from bad health, or more believing Religion. God prosper him. Amen.'[1] Next May, on a lecturing tour, Haydon 'flew off to Manchester, saw Frank, paid off his arrears, dashed off to Warrington, & was home to tea. Good Heavens what superb travelling. . . .'[2] The next we hear of Frank is on the last day of the year, 'Frank is not yet recovered to renew his pursuits'.[3]

By the following May Frank had left Manchester, his health had broken down. 'My dear Frank is a fine Youth of great acquirements [Frank's note, 'Acquirements only of course. No member of the Haydon Family possessed Gee-nious except my father. F.S.H.'] but no energy or self will. He was first to be an Entomologist, then a Parson,—then an Engineer; he went to Fairbairn's & broke down.' Frank adds another note, scarcely consistent with the first: 'He was fond of collecting insects . . . at the mature & profoundly reflective age of 13!—he was as active a sceptic as Hume at 15, & laughed at Religion & its Professors—his father among the rest—he took a fancy to steam engines at 17—& having been coddled & caged all his life, very naturally as soon as he got a little freedom, became slightly fond of amusement & dissipation—& for the same reason, was unable to combine work hard enough for a blacksmith with irregularity of life—& fell into bad health—everything was "au sérieux" and every child's fancy which a sensible father would have left to die a natural death was taken up as a symptom of high genius.' Haydon goes on, 'his brother Hyman, an old Bachelor, good heart, but like snarling indigestion in preference to all things—has persuaded him to come to College after all'. Frank's comment on this involves the whole of his career at Cambridge and after, and must be given later. Haydon then breaks into (unserious) doggerel, a dialogue in which

[1] *Diary* iv. 549, 25 Mar. 1839.   [2] iv. 553, 7 May 1839.
[3] iv. 600.

'Parson Snarle' invites 'Dawdle' to Wadham. Frank capped his father's verses; 'Says Dawdle to Sneer, I very much fear/That I've only the foibles of each—/Like you—freely I think/Like him—freely I drink/But like him I can't pray—like you preach, and added the note 'Specimen of the profound meditation of a great artist & an affectionate father'. Haydon did not drink 'freely' but—Frank writes—'[his] tipple is Port—Which one owes for—in Chancery Lane'.[1]

Frank matriculated at Caius in December 1840, went up in October 1841, and in the following January migrated to Jesus. In February 1841 Haydon writes, 'My dear Frank again started for Life. God bless him—to private Tutor . . . before going to Caius'.[2]

For the next four years two torturing anxieties were added to all the others. Frank's health—mental and physical—and how to pay his College bills. When Orlando went to Oxford, Haydon had said, 'No boy of mine can go to College but such as earn it, as Orlando has done'.[3] Frank went as a pensioner, but he was 'to make his living at College', that is, I suppose, become a Fellow like Orlando. At all events, Cambridge meant the Church. In March 1842, 'I prayed with all my heart & all my Soul for relief. I knew if my debt to the Tutor of Caius was not paid, the mind of my son Frank would be destroyed, from his sensitiveness to honour & right.' Desperate efforts were successful. After attempts to raise money on 'sketches at less than half their value', and on the unpublished engraving of the Duke at Waterloo, of three begging letters, one—to a duke—succeeded.[4]

Next May there was a triumph followed by bitter disappointment. 'My dear boy 1st in Mathematics, 7th in Classics. Dear Frank—this is a fine beginning.' (This was a first-year College examination.) News followed that Frank had been appointed Chapel Clerk and would have a foundation scholarship for 'his considerable mathematical ability'. But almost at once he had a breakdown which caused intense anxiety. He went with Mary to Gravesend to recover—his 'exertions at Cambridge have shaken him'. He grew worse. Haydon 'Found his dear Mother exhausted & ill with watching. Brought Frank home, & left her to recover'. Next day, 'My dear Frank, on whom my hopes were concentered, in all probability seriously affected. We were too proud of him. . . .'[5]

[1] Diary iv. 628–30, 20 May 1840.   [2] v. 33, 10 Feb. 1841.
[3] iii. 524, 18 June 1831.   [4] v. 135, 7 Mar. 1842.
[5] v. 163, 171, 183, 185, 186, 30 May, 20 June, 12 July, 21 and 22 July 1842.

In September frantic efforts to collect money for Frank's bills, including an appeal to the Archbishop (Howley): 'not a rich man I have appealed to has consented to advance 56. 2. 10 to save the 1st prize Man in Mathematics from destruction at Jesus. How little must they value education.'[1] The next news of Frank is in the following April, 'Thank God my dear Boy Frank has passed his little-go, so his second examination is over.'[2] In June came the shattering blow of failure in the cartoon contest: 'It has given a great shock to my family, especially my dear Boy Frank. . . .'[3]

In September 1844 another illness caused extreme anxiety: 'Frank my Son, ill, very anxious . . . he has knocked himself up by hard work.' Next day, 'Exceedingly harrassed about my son.' Frank got better, but Haydon reflects, 'I question if Religion & reason are a match for inherent organization, defect of education, or results caused by transmission of tendency from Father to Son, or the state of the nervous system of the Father & Mother at the instant of Propagation! They ought to be but are they?'[4] This, with other passages, shows that Haydon feared for Frank's sanity as he feared for his own, and thought his instability inherited from himself. The illness coincided with a money crisis. 'The Tutor having resigned at Jesus, requires the balance at 4 days notice of my Son's college acct—£140. 4. 6. The trouble & anxiety are dreadful. Frank is just recovered from a nervous fever, & I dared not tell him—& the misery of having him degraded, if I were not punctual, was agonizing.' Next day, 'Three whole days have I been racing to raise the money to save my dear boy at Cambridge & succeeded—God be thanked! . . . Thus ends the week in which I ought to fall down on my knees & bow my head to the Earth for raising up such Friends to me as Bennoch & Twentyman.'[5]

'O Lord have mercy on me. I am now in anxieties & petty troubles of the most tormenting description', Haydon wrote in December. He had been lecturing hard, pot-boiling hard, had published lectures, but Frank's bills were a crushing burden. 'Racing the Town all day for money to meet Dear Frank's fees, & thank God, got it. Shall be out again tomorrow. . . . He is going

[1] *Diary*, v. 201–2, 13–15 Sept. 1842.
[2] v. 258, 1 Apr. 1845. The Little Go was then taken in the fifth term, the final examination in the tenth.
[3] v. 293, 30 June 1843.
[4] v. 389, 9, 10, 12 Sept. 1844.   [5] v. 390–1, 20, 21 Sept. 1844.

up for examination & his degree—his fees must be paid & his arrears. . . .' Next day, 'Out all day on Frank's business. Duty to a Son is a paramount duty—a moral duty is of more consequence than the exercise of Genius.'[1]

Frank had become Haydon's paramount anxiety. His address to the Almighty on the last day of the year ends, 'Bless my dear Boy Frank through his examination & degree, & bless me with the means to carry him through. Bless my Art, & advance the glory & greatness of England. Amen, end of 1844.'[2] Frank's health was not preserved. Anxiety was again acute in January. 'Eight days I have lost. Frank was taken ill & feared his examination. I rushed down & cheered him up, & brought him through.' Two more January entries: 'Considering the extreme delicacy of Frank's health, the risk he had of giving in, the dreadful condition of my finances after the Cartoon blow, nothing, it is my active belief, but the goodness of God could have brought Father & Son through so completely.' But a few days later (Wednesday), 'Great domestic anxiety. Saw Frank off. Since Tuesday I have had intense suffering. This dear Boy has thus occupied me 14 days precious [sic]—he is very like Cowper, & I fear I occupied him too early for his nervous system.'[3]

There was yet another blow in May: 'Passed the day in excruciating anxiety about my Son Frank, who for neglecting Chapel has been *sent down*—when getting a good Income & 3 pupils —how provoking! I hope he will have sons of his own!'[4] Frank had taken his degree, a pass, as we hear from himself—at that time a mere farce. In August Haydon notes, 'Dear Frank has a prospect of a Curacy.'[5] The next blow was in November: 'my dear son Frank, shrinking from the display of the Pulpit, after 860.10 expense for a College Education, in anguish of mind I wrote Sir Robert— and told my anguish.' 'What anxiety a Father has!—up to the grave!' Peel's answer was swift, the offer of a clerkship in the Record Office, 'as from your description of him, as a young man of retiring and literary habits, he thinks it will suit him'. Haydon was profoundly grateful, 'I have always said of Peel he had a tender heart . . . after all our row about Napoleon & I said bitter things to him.'[6]

---

[1] *Diary* v. 404, 405, 19, 23, 24 Dec. 1844.   [2] v. 408.
[3] v. 411, 413, 419, 14–22 Jan., 23 Jan., 26 and 29 Jan. 1845.
[4] v. 440, 13 May 1845.
[5] v. 467, 3 Aug. 1845.   [6] v. 490–1, 8 Nov. 1845.

The last mention of Frank is on 21 May 1846: 'Uneasy, as I could not give my dear Boy Frank money to go & see his old friends at Cambridge once more.'[1] Except for a reference to 'dearest Mary', on 16 June, this is Haydon's last allusion to his family (apart from his farewell letters).

Frank makes no comment on these entries. His side of the melancholy tale is in a single note to the entry for 20 May 1840, already referred to.

This is not true. Hyman did nothing of the kind. He persuaded me *against* going to College—he too well remembered the degradation which he had suffered from my father's unpunctuality—my father suspected that Hyman had persuaded me to relinquish Manchester for Cambridge or Oxford— . . . the real fact is *my father* persuaded me to go to College. *Hyman* was against it. As soon as I became aware of the frightful expense I voluntarily offered to give it all up for a Government appointment—this was after I had suffered the degradation of seeing a Bill which he gave my Tutor in Northamptonshire dishonoured, while I was living in the good man's house at the expense of himself & his wife—but my father would listen to nothing—he came up to Cambridge, made a vulgar row in my room, shouting & stamping like a costermonger, actually *falsified* the amount of his income for the previous year, making it out to be larger than it was by including in the estimate *borrowed* sums, in order to quiet me when he saw that noise did not influence me except against him—& persuaded me to stay. I had not been at College a year before I had amply compensated him for his anxiety by winning a scholarship, librarianship, clerkship, exhibition & prizes, & gaining a high reputation with the first tutors in Cambridge for original power in mathematics and real promise in classics—the return for all my labour was that my College bills were unpaid, promise after promise to Tutors, Bankers, Solicitors, broken, & my name became disgraced—or worse. I was *pitied* as the son of a man without a particle of honour in his character. My College Tutor had to pay, *out of his own pocket*, (this he did on the promise of my father to pay the bill at a certain time—which was never kept), on leaving the College & squaring accts, with his Successor a large arrear [140. 4. 6] on my 1st year's bills. My father dishonoured the bill wh. he had given the Tu or for the amount, & the letters which he wrote to my father having been long unanswered, he applied to me, with so much gentleness & sympathy for my painful position, that I confess I was fairly disgusted with my father's conduct from first to last. My health failed, & the high expectation which had been formed, & fairly, of my distinction, sank down as my power of application diminished. I took a

[1] *Diary*, v. 545.

common degree to avoid the mortification of seeing my name below
the place which my talents deserved in the Honour Lists, & after all
the struggling, suffering, & pecuniary disgrace of my College Career,
was placed in a Government office by Peel about five years too late to
gain the average advantages of such a position.

He does not say that on 30 June 1846 (eight days after his father's
death) he left the Record Office, without resigning, for a place
under the Customs Board.[1] He left the Customs and on 16 November
ber 1846 was reappointed a Junior Clerk in the Record Office, by
Treasury Letter (as before),[2] showing that though Peel was out
of office there were still sympathizers with Haydon's family in
power.

Among the puzzling aspects of Frank's statement is the fact that
his father seemed the person who could deal with him in one of
his breakdowns—'cheer him up', persuade him to take his degree
and not 'give up'. Another is the large total of Frank's College
expenses (£860. 10s. for—at most—twelve terms, in the last of
which he was getting 'a good income'), at a time when the expenses
of rich and poor undergraduates differed widely. In 1850 the
necessary expenses for an undergraduate were from £50 to £80
a year or rather more. This does not include fees for coaching—
necessary for Honours men because of the inferiority of College
teaching. For those aiming at high mathematical honours this
might amount to a total of £150, for those aiming at lower
honours, £40 to £60. This made the average expenses of an
undergraduate £137 a year,[3] but Frank's were (at least) £215
a year, besides his scholarship, etc. This was paid by the Steward
quarterly according to the number of weeks in residence. Frank
was paid a total of £30. 16s. 10d. for two years ending in December 1844 (after that the Steward's book is missing). As a scholar
his rooms would be rent free and his tuition fees lower. As Chapel
Clerk he might get as little as £2 a year (the eighteenth-century
rate), as an assistant librarian as much as £10 (the rate in 1849).
For the exhibition there is no evidence but Frank's statement.[4]

[1] This was a better-paid post as landing-waiter, given by Peel, A. Hayter,
A Sultry Month (1965), p. 130.

[2] I am much indebted to Mr. E. K. Timings, Principal Assistant Keeper of
the P.R.O., for this information and for other facts about F. S. H.'s career there.

[3] J. P. C. Roach, in *Victoria County History, Cambridge*, iii (1959), 245-7.

[4] I am greatly indebted to Mrs. T. K. Jones, Assistant Archivist, Jesus College,
for details of Frank's College career and about the University routine of the
period.

His standard of living would seem to have been that of a rich young man. His father described him as 'Handsome, intellectual, witty and mathematical'.[1]

Only once does Haydon admit awareness of his son's attitude to himself, when, 'in an agony for want of money', he came home 'wet & exhausted' from a whole day spent in trying to raise it. 'I am almost born down by the difficulties of my situation—the brutality & insults of one of my children, & the fiendish ingratitude of another [Orlando].'[2] Perhaps this reflects the stormy visit to Cambridge, not mentioned in the *Journals*. One has the impression that where Frank was concerned only the tip of the iceberg is visible, in contrast with the lush landscape of the Caroline Norton episode. Four months later, thanking God for the blessings of the week, Haydon ends: 'To find your Sons honouring you, to have educated them thoroughly, though they exhaust your pocket & keep you poor, are also blessings, & these I have.'[3] Well, Frederic honoured him.

Two of Frank's not very numerous notes to his father's *Journals* stand out as brutal and insulting, and except for those saying he remembers incidents of childhood recorded by Haydon all have a note of contempt or dislike. One of Haydon's most flamboyant addresses to God ends: 'and when my grand Soul is sufficiently refined through the furnace of affliction, thou knowest I shall be ready, for I shall then have done that for which thou inspired me! In *thee* I trust, glorying! Amen!' Frank: 'And the result of trusting "*thee*" & "glorying" was despair & suicide. F.S.H.'[4]

A press cutting on General Tom Thumb is attached to the *Journal* for April 1844, saying that a performance of Napoleon musing at St. Helena had 'elicited great mirth'. Haydon notes, 'I do not like this, B.R.H.', with every reason, since this might seem to be, and perhaps was, a parody of the picture which had become a chief source of income. Frank's comment, 'What uneasy vanity',[5] made *after* the tragic coincidence of Tom Thumb and the calamitous last exhibition, has a note of singular heartlessness. 'Uneasy vanity' seems more applicable to Frank's note on Haydon's assessment of his son as 'a youth of great acquirements', not to speak of the reason he gives for not attempting an honours degree.

[1] Quoted, evidently from a letter, in Olney, *Haydon*, p. 236.
[2] *Diary* v. 227, 28 Nov. 1842.   [3] v. 257, 26 Mar. 1843.
[4] iv. 249, 1 Jan. 1835.   [5] v. 355, 9 Apr. 1844.

There was probably less—perhaps much less—family unease than all this might suggest. There was the agreeable Christmas dinner in 1842. In January 1844, 'My boys & I passed a very talented evening.'[1] In August 1845, 'Went with the boys to the Old Ship Tavern, Greenwich, to eat whitebait, and enjoyed myself immensely. . . . It did my Sons good though it was expensive.'[2] And the only mention of a family 'row' does not sound very serious. 'Had a row with my family, who swore Napoleon was not beaten at Waterloo. I told Mary & all they *lied*. All ran out except my daughter, who like a dear sat still and read.'[3] Here is a more normal family scene. 'These little evening Sketches, made in the bosom of my family, with my dearest Mary & daughter & son, are of the greatest use next day.'[4]

We hear very little of the younger Mary except that she was beautiful and good. In a prayer for his family—Mary, Frank, and Frederic—on the last day of 1841, Haydon wrote, 'My dear Daughter Mary I do not mention, but she is so good, diligent, religious, prudent & Discreet, that she is not an anxiety. . . .'[5] D. T. Coulton, a recent friend of Haydon's, wrote a sonnet, 'The Painter's Daughter', 'Addressed to Miss Mary Haydon', which ends, 'Nature . . . / Embodied all his dreams of loveliness / In a sweet girl's angelic form & face; / Faultless in blushing Innocence she stood / Part of his Soul, Mind, Being, heart & blood.' Haydon transcribed it without comment in the entry for his fifty-ninth birthday.[6]

The calamitous state of the family finances is reflected in a letter from Miss Barrett to Miss Mitford in September 1844. 'And do you know of anyone who, having a young child of four to ten years of age, wished [it] to be taught French, English, Italian, and music, by a daily governess? Miss Haydon is anxious to undertake the teaching of such a child—and her father has written to me to do what I can to meet her wishes. I!—what can I do? . . .'[7] Nothing seems to have come of this—it is not mentioned in the *Journal*—but there is a sad little sequel eight years later. Having 'learnt truth and goodness from her many trials', 'Poor Miss Haydon' was a daily governess at eight shillings a week.[8]

[1] *Diary* v. 340, 7 Jan. 1844.   [2] v. 470–1, 18 Aug. 1845.
[3] v. 474, 4 Sept. 1845.   [4] v. 23–89, 7 Jan. 1843.
[5] v. 108.   [6] v. 412, 25 Jan. 1845.
[7] Betty Miller, *Elizabeth Barrett to Miss Mitford* (1954), pp. 221–2.
[8] Ibid.

Frank's last contribution to his family history was a letter to Buxton Forman in 1884 which illustrates his character. Walking with his father on the day before his death, he asked him 'if he had asked his sister for [money]; he said that he had done so & that she had never answered his letter! Thank the—whoever or whatever it is—that manages this muddle of a world, my dear aunt applied to me quite recently for a loan of £200, & I had the supreme felicity of refusing her request. I never "kick up a row" about my own wrongs, or those which I make my own, but always wait for the chance which, sooner or later, gives me my revenge. And I always take it, for having a very retentive memory for what is disagreeable, I don't forgive.'[1]

Tragedy and frustration were Frank's lot. He married two years before he reached the grade of Senior Clerk in 1860. His children came even more quickly and disastrously than Haydon's. His elder daughter, who inherited the *Journals* and died unmarried in 1935, was born in 1859. In less than a year a son was born and died. Just a year afterwards a daughter was born and died, and ten days later his wife died.

The frustrations of Frank's Record Office career are illustrated by a comparison with a near-contemporary, one Alfred Kingston, seven years younger than Frank, who had become a Junior Clerk in 1844 at fifteen. Both reached the grade of Senior Clerk (£250 a year) in 1860, Kingston taking two years longer than Frank. But Kingston became an Assistant Keeper (£520 a year) in 1878, Frank not till 1885, when he was sixty-three.[2] Two years later he shot himself. Yet Frank was a scholar who had edited (officially) two medieval Latin texts.[3]

The evidence of his daughter and his doctor at the inquest shows that, as his father had feared, he died insane. Since Frederic's death (in Bedlam) he had been 'very emotional and violent'. He had had a stroke (7 August 1887); since then he had been under

[1] *Diary* v. 551 n. The aunt, a widow, died in 1884.

[2] Information from Mr. E. K. Timings.

[3] It is remarkable that the work which has earned him an entry in the *Cambridge Bibliography of English Literature* was published in part while he was a Junior Clerk and completed twelve years before he became an Assistant Keeper: *Eulogium Historiarum* [Creation to 1413], ed. F. S. Haydon, 3 vols., Rolls Series 1858–63. He belonged to the London Mathematical Society, the Camden Society, and the Royal Archaeological Institute of Great Britain. *Diary* v. 569; information from Mr. J. H. Hopkins, Librarian of the Society of Antiquaries.

the delusion that he was being followed and would be arrested for a criminal offence and had said, 'When they came for him they should not take him alive'.[1]

To end this family chronicle on a different note. Though Frederic's career was unfortunate his descendants prospered. He married a daughter of Haydon's old friend, Sir Peter Fairbairn of Leeds, brother of Sir William, and also an inventor and manufacturer (of textile machinery) on a large scale. She died four years later, and when Frederic died in 1886 he left a son of seventeen and a daughter of sixteen. The son was educated at Charterhouse and Trinity, Cambridge; he married a Miss Blanche Greville but left no children. The daughter, Lina Frederica Marie Mordwinoff Haydon, married the second of the five sons of the very popular Bishop of Ripon. She lived till 1961, leaving a son, a grandson, and a great-grandson, all Boyd Carpenters.[2] 'In a letter, written with all the spirit of her grandfather, [she] . . . granted her full permission for publication' to Professor Pope.[3]

[1] *The Times*, 1 Nov. 1887.   [2] *Diary* v. 569–70.
[3] i. xiii.

5. FRIENDS AND ENEMIES

I write these faults in a passion (20 Jan. 1817)

THE unexpurgated Haydon is inevitably more uninhibited, more passionate, more vindictive than the Haydon of Taylor's abridgement. He made a feature of 'denunciations'. How far they were seriously intended is a matter of surmise. They give an impression of being—in part at least—a safety-valve, a letting off of steam, or an exercise in invective. But they also correspond to crises in Haydon's life. They are so characteristic that they demand attention. Three targets stand out, Northcote, Fuseli, Seguier.

Northcote has the full treatment. He is always the embodiment of spiteful malice. 'The attempt of this little creature to mortify others is quite amusing, he exists on it'. Haydon calls him 'the withered poison' and attributes his venom to 'the malice of Nature' which had made him dwarfish and shrivelled. 'Manliness, deformity, genius, or stupidity he equally hates, because they are equally *human* characteristics. In addition to this inherent malignant depravity, I was his Townsman. This was unpardonable! I had genius! This was a crime! The instant I entered his room in 1804, my face as if prophetic of my power, attracted the piercing viper glitter of his contracting little eyes. He darted a look into me that pricked my feelings as a needle does the skin, and when he read the letter of introduction from his Brother, his "What, be a come to starve!" proved my anticipation to be conclusive. From that moment to the present hour I have been on his fears, his hopes, his reputation, like a shadow that pursued him! When Solomon sold, he sank into a fever and nearly died. The success of Jerusalem brought on a retention of urine, and when I called he shrunk up like a withered leaf by the side of a burning iron, saying, "what dye call on me fore? . . ." '[1] So Haydon wrote in his first imprisonment, after a visit from Hazlitt, whom he had asked to tell him what Northcote said about him.[2] How differently

[1] *Diary*, ii. 417-18, 25 June 1823.
[2] Cf. Hazlitt, *Conversations of James Northcote Esq. R.A.*, Conversation XII, where H. and N. exchange very disparaging judgements on Haydon, who is 'X'.

he was to describe that first visit in the *Autobiography* (pp. 19–20), where the letter of introduction is from Prince Hoare, not North-cote's brother.

Haydon's rejection by the Academy in 1827 after he had spent much time and tact in propitiatory visits to R.A.s in 1826 ('the most humiliating event in my life') is recorded in his *Journal* as a set piece—a quiz—which is a sort of *Dream of Somniator* (pp. 109–10) in reverse, though equally flattering to himself. The meeting for the election of an Associate is described by 'our Reporter'. The R.A.s give their reasons for excluding Haydon: 'little N——' is the first to speak. 'His dialect was broad Devonshire, his looks keen, malignant & weasel-like, his figure wrisled, shrunk & mean, yet a look of living malice seemed to nourish his exhausted frame. Every thing he said or did or thought was steeped in spite.' '. . . he had the impudence to study the Art on the principles of Michel Angelo & Lionardo da Vinci, and not on the principles of us, the members of this Academy. . . . we all hoped he was at last destroyed! [by the second imprisonment] Well, but he is out again! & has nearly done a Picture which it must be our business to prevent being sold, as we did the Entry into Jerusalem.' With a very great deal more from Northcote, Turner, and others.[1]

In June 1831 Haydon wrote a verse 'Epitaph on Northcote by Anticipation'. 'Here lies of men the most malignant, / . . . a . . . . mass / Of Envy, Malice, spite, & brass', etc. etc. Northcote died shortly afterwards. With minor variations the verses were published under Haydon's name in *The Civil Engineer and Architect's Journal* of September 1844 as 'Epitaph on a deceased Academician'[2] Yet in the *Autobiography*: 'I liked Northcote and used to call frequently, he was very entertaining. . . .'

The treatment of Fuseli is even more remarkable. The delightful account of Haydon's first visit in 1805 is in the *Autobiography* only. The *Journal*, 12 December 1808: '. . . called on Fuzeli, staied three hours, talking of the Art, Italy, Michel Angelo, Homer, Virgil, Horace, enough to make a man mad. When Fuzeli dies, where shall I meet "his like again"? I do not know any body I feel a greater affection or reverence for. From my first entrance into the Academy he noticed me in a particular manner. . . .' Haydon quotes this in the *Autobiography*, but not the note dated 27 November 1815: 'I have since found Fuzeli a Traitor—mean, malicious,

---

[1] *Diary* iii. 232–6, 14 Nov. 1827.
[2] iii. 519–20 and n., 8 June 1831. Northcote died 13 July 1831.

cowardly & debauched.'[1] In January 1814 he had thanked God that he had 'escaped in time, that I had purified my soul from the influence of his dark & dreary fancy'.[2] Next December, 'The Engines in Fuzeli's Mind are Blasphemy, Lechery, and blood. His women are all whores, and men all banditti. . . . Such a monstrous imagination was never propagated on lovely woman. No, Fuzeli was engendered by some hellish monster, on the dead body of a speckled hag. . . .'[3]

All this might suggest that Haydon broke with Fuseli. But John Lane, a fellow student of Haydon, told Farington in 1811 that Fuseli 'had signified to *Haydon* His desire that He (Haydon) should no longer call upon him'. The reason for this was an abusive paragraph in the *Examiner* on a picture of Fuseli's seen only by Haydon and two others, both of whom had denied having written it.[4] The paragraph was probably by Robert Hunt on information from Haydon. There was also the *Examiner*'s advice to Fuseli to study and learn from Haydon (pp. 35-6).

But, in 1825, 'Fuzeli is dead, and in my opinion is an irreparable loss.' A long and balanced appreciation follows—'How many delightful hours have I passed with him in one continual stream of quotation, conception, repartee, & humour.' Taylor quotes and praises, deleting a sentence here and there and a long description of Fuseli's house—'that wizard's tavern'—very different from the one in the *Autobiography*. 'Few knew him better than Haydon, or appreciated him, as it seems to me, more justly or more kindly.' Had he read the early *Journals*? After the funeral, where Haydon wept: 'Farewell! To thy powerful mind I am greatly indebted & feel thy loss.'[5]

In Taylor's version Seguier appears as an old friend, who, as Keeper of the King's Pictures, was helpful over the purchase of the *Mock Election* in 1828 (p. 188). In the full text it is otherwise. Haydon distrusted him, but enjoyed his company, with its humour and mimicry and malicious gossip about the Court and grandees, and there are records of visits to Seguier, with dwindling relish, between 1825 and 1829. Some of these are printed by Taylor, where Seguier is S., but already in 1824 there is an elaborate denunciation of 'Mr ——', 'a secret enemy' who is unmistakable: '. . . risen from the lowest depths of Society, illiterate, . . . a

---

[1] *Diary,* i. 37-38. [2] i. 335. [3] i. 488-9.
[4] *Farington Diary,* ed. Greig, vii. 58-59, 9 Nov. 1811.
[5] iii. 14-19, 16 and 25 Apr. 1825.

Cockney in his dialect & vulgar in his address, influenced by the meanest in revenges, guided by the lowest cunning, sleek & slavish in the presence of a nobility he despises, & humbly acquiescing in the dictation that he ridicules in private for the amusement of his Friends—this poor, miserable, puffed up bit of vanity, is so essential to their wants, their vanities, & their necessities, & no nobleman of my acquaintance ventures to purchase a pot de chambre without desiring Mr ——, with his best compliments, to try it first himself. . . . There is not a man of rank he has not quizzed.'[1]

With the purchase of his picture, after a burst of gratitude, Haydon soon developed doubts, and he came to believe, possibly correctly, that Seguier had tried and failed to dissuade George IV. The story is complicated; it is impossible to disentangle the rights and the wrongs of it. But Haydon was convinced that in 1830 Seguier's trickery had prevented the King from buying *Punch* and thus deprived him of the commissions that would (he believed) have followed. Seguier was a remarkable man and Haydon's assessment, though prejudiced, is interesting. Apropos of one of his petitions for the public employment of artists, he writes, in 1826, 'The apparent Friend & private thwarter, I fear, is Seguier. It is extraordinary the influence, the deadly influence, of this man. He is the torpedo of Modern Art! Where his deadly sneers are put forth there ceases all interest for Modern Genius! I & Wilkie have known him for 22 years. . . . What a character I could draw of him! How I could set the King on his guard! & open the eyes of the Nobility.'[2] In the matter of the *Mock Election* distrust soon overpowered initial gratitude. 'There was when I was at the Palace, in Seguier, an uneasiness lest I should stay. It seemed as if he had been ordered to do what he did, as if it was not his own interference or intention. God knows! We all suspect Seguier. Artists and every body.'[3]

When it came to *Punch* (p. 189) in February 1830, Seguier fails to act on the King's order to see Haydon's pictures (on the private day) 'and if worth seeing *to bring them down*'. 'Is this not shameful & though Seguier pretends to do these things for me, is it not evident he tries to obstruct?'[4] When, at last, the picture went and was refused, he believed that this was due to Seguier. On the King's death, Haydon (in prison) first gave vent to an outburst of

[1] *Diary* ii. 459–60, 1 Feb. 1824.   [2] iii. 93, 29 Apr. 1826.
[3] iii. 272, 26 Apr. 1828.   [4] iii. 427, 22 Feb. 1830.

frenzied rage in prose and verse—'Epitaph of a Malicious Man'—
in which the recurrent word is 'sneer'. 'The King is dead!—and
may the curses of a just God light on you and your posterity. . . .
I was almost the last individual he obliged, and while my heart
was quivering with gratitude who led him to believe I was as base
as yourself & as ungrateful as others? Whose infamous treachery,
whose mean duplicity, whose low intrigue, whose base falshoods
was it that blasted my prospects on the brink of royal favour, &
sent me ruined to a Prison?'

Next day Haydon wrote a long character sketch of Seguier and
his attitude to modern art, with a pencil drawing of 'William
Seguier Esq., the Traitor!' 'The King does nothing without
Mr Seguier's advice. At the B. Gallery he is keeper, hanger, judge,
secretary, & factotum. At the National Gallery he is director &
every private collection is under his controul, his management &
protection.' The only exaggeration in this is the word 'every'.
The *D.N.B.* adds that he arranged the summer exhibitions of the
old masters at the British Institution (or Gallery), and the winter
ones of living artists, and had collected pictures for Peel and
others with great expertise. He and his brother had inherited
and developed a very successful business as picture cleaners, dealers,
and connoisseurs. The firm employed artists who restored the
pictures brought back by Wellington from Spain. Seguier had
started as a painter, doing skilful imitations—not copies—of old
masters. On marrying a rich wife he had turned to connoisseurship.

To return to Haydon. 'Seguier I never liked. There was always
a nasty sarcasm, & tattling scandal, an undervaluing sneer, against
every body, even his most intimate Friends. . . . Yet with all this
there is something in Seguier so apparently sincere, he judges so
soundly, he idles so agreeably, he waits so patiently, and speaks
with apparent candour while he is spinning the web that is to en-
tangle you that one does not & cannot wonder that the nobility or
the Sovereign feel disposed always to unbend with him, for no one
has such exquisite tact of how far to go with familiarity, and how
long to remain in silent respect. . . . He talks of nothing but what
he is wanted to talk about, & his hideous cockneyisms, his barbar-
ous French, & his savage Italian are all overlooked, or rather born
with some satisfaction, because, as I have said, his inferiority is undeniable & irrefutable the moment he opens his mouth. . . . They
are no more offended at Seguier's illiterate dialogue than they
would be in the Stables with their Grooms. . . . They seek him for

what they want, & he can inform them, & here is the whole secret of his influence.' Haydon is clearly thinking of his own very different conversational style. 'Wherever he goes, like the Torpedo, he dulls all desire, all enthusiasm, all elasticity, for Modern Artists of admiration. . . .' A long, intricate, and circumstantial account follows of Seguier's manœuvres over the *Mock Election* and *Punch*. Though this is Haydon's biased version it seems far from unlikely that the *Mock Election* was George IV's choice, and that this being so, Seguier would contrive that the King, then almost on his death-bed, did not buy another Haydon. In other words, he followed his aesthetic judgement without regard to the necessities of the Haydon family. 'One word from him would have made my fortune. He knew my dreadful danger, he knew Mrs Haydon had lost her 1000, he knew I was on the borders of ruin, and instead of holding out his hand & helping an old Friend, who never in all his life said or did one thing to hurt him . . . gave him a secret push that hurled him to the bottom.' 'All my previous suspicions of this Villain are thus realised. Nature has given me an exquisite perception of character, but accompanied with a distrust of my own perceptions that renders my convictions nugatory & of no avail. Sir George & Lady Beaumont told me he it was who obstructed the sale of Jerusalem, that I might depend upon it he was my bitterest enemy. . . .'[1] This truly Haydonian mixture of self-pity, rancour, reason, and unreason was followed by an equally characteristic remark on Seguier's death in 1843. 'One of my earliest Friends, Seguier, is dead. He was an intimate of the Clique . . . They are all gone except Lady Mulgrave [and] myself.'[2] Not that he had forgotten. 'The King was kind to me', he wrote in 1845, '& would have been kinder but for a Villain.'[3]

The most overtly venomous of Haydon's quarrels was with Shee. He was obnoxious as an R.A.—from 1830 P.R.A. ('to think of Shee occupying the throne of Reynolds!')[4] as a fashionable portrait painter and a poor draughtsman, and above all as one of the hanging committee that had displaced *Dentatus*. The quarrel boiled over in Shee's examination by the Ewart Committee in 1836, but this has been obscured by the record of the official minutes and by

[1] *Diary* iii. 450–1, 453–61, 9 and 10 June 1830. George IV died on 26 June and Haydon recorded it (again) on that day.
[2] v. 327, 15 Nov. 1843.
[3] v. 402, 4 Dec. 1844.   [4] iii. 413, 9 Jan. 1830.

the biography of Sir Martin Archer Shee by his son:[1] 'The day', writes Martin Shee, 'was an easy triumph for the P.R.A.; at no point did he address himself to Haydon.'[2] According to Haydon's *Journal* the day (16 July) was a humiliation for Shee—'justice indeed triumphed'—and it is clear that Shee lost his temper and was rebuked. Haydon had noted on the 5th, 'The evidence is not yet printed to send to Shee. As soon as it is he will come. . . . I warned them he is quick & voluble. I have got a set of questions ready for him. Ewart said my evidence was the thing—the very thing. . . .'

The day came. 'I placed myself right opposite to Shee, which seemed to disturb him. . . .' 'He accused the evidence of being personal & partial. . . . Shee shaking his hand at me across the table in the most extraordinary manner, "That's the *respectable* man", alluding of course to my misfortunes.' A proposal by Mr Pusey that the court should be cleared was abandoned on the understanding that no altercation or personalities took place. Of course Haydon's evidence had been 'personal and partial' (p. 214), but what he says of Shee is supported by two letters of H. T. Hope, one of the committee, attached to the *Journal*. The first, expressing disapproval of Shee's personalities, evoked a request by Haydon for a commission. The second (12 August): 'Though I might otherwise hesitate, yet having witnessed some of the bitterness which has been displayed towards you, I accept your offer to paint a picture for me to the value of the enclosed, the subject of which I leave to yourself.' (Haydon decided on a Falstaff, which, if painted, is unrecorded.)

To Haydon the proceedings of the committee were a personal triumph over his enemies as well as a blow to the prestige of the Academy. 'The very men, the very hangers—Shee, Phillips & Howard, who . . . used me so infamously by hanging Dentatus in the dark—by which all my prospects were blasted for ever. . . . Ah, they are deservedly punished.'[3]

But what about the official minutes, which tell a different story? Mr. Bell has shown that the witnesses were given transcripts of

[1] Quentin Bell, 'Haydon versus Shee', *Journal of the Warburg and Courtauld Institutes* xxii (1959), 347–58.

[2] T. S. R. Boase, *Oxford History of English Art*, accepts this. 'It was undoubtedly the P.R.A., Shee, who came well out of the case. He kept his temper. . . .'

[3] For the committee see pp. 212–15, and *Diary* iv. 355–69, 29 and 30 June, 1, 5, 16, 17, 19, 21, and 29 July, 13 Aug. 1836.

their evidence and allowed to edit them. They did this in such a wholesale way, removing much and adding much—in Shee's interest—that the resulting scandal produced a Select Committee on Printed Papers.

The background of this Shee–Haydon clash was an exchange of letters in 1829, provoked by Haydon, venomous on both sides, in which Shee was the more deadly. 'I wrote Mr Shee frankly, asking him if he was or was not on the Committee of 1809 which hung Dentatus', Haydon records. A stinging rebuff followed. Shee begs 'leave to decline all farther communication with you on any subject relating to the Arts or the Royal Academy'. Insults from Haydon—who ends 'God bless you Mr Shee. I heartily wish you long life, better drawing and [a] little more self-command'—provoked a rejoinder on (inter alia) the crawling meanness, [the overtures to R.A.s in 1826] which so happily alternates with insolent presumption in your degraded career . . .'. A torrent of rancorous self-pity and contempt for Shee's work follows in the Journal. 'God forbid I should ever wish you, despicable & impotent wretch as you [are] in your Art, such calamities [as mine], or if ever they overtook you should have the heart to jeer at their agony.'[1] Did he get a certain satisfaction from this opportunity of brooding over his sufferings and the malice of his enemies? He told the Duke of Sussex, when sketching him for the Reform Banquet picture, 'Shee & I had had a tremendous quarrel, and that we belaboured each other, at which he shrugged his shoulders and laughed.'[2]

Taylor's discretion is at its most misleading over the relations between Haydon and Charles Eastlake (by 1853 P.R.A. and Sir Charles), a vital element in the tragedy of the cartoon contest. Favourable comments on Eastlake are printed in full; in neutral ones—if printed—the name is a blank. All criticisms, even the mildest, are cut out. In the abridgement there is no hint of the doubts of Eastlake's loyalty expressed after Haydon's death (p. 277). In the Diary we can now follow the painful sequence from 'my dear Pupil' to 'my bitterest enemy'. This could be regarded as yet another instance of Haydon's way with his friends, and of course there are analogies—Haydon was Haydon. But this was different from the self-destroying rancour over Dentatus and other grievances. There is not the studied invective of his 'denunciations'. Haydon was delighted that Eastlake was to be Secretary

[1] Diary iii. 329–32, 6 Jan. etc. 1829.   [2] iv. 65, 23 Mar. 1833.

of the Fine Arts Commission. After getting from Barry (the architect) 'the extent that could be employed in fresco'; 'My dear old
Pupil Eastlake I went to First. He was much affected at seeing
me.'[1] (Taylor deletes the 'much'.) Then, 'Eastlake called & thought
my Fresco successful'.[2] Some months later, 'Eastlake's kindness
as can be seen is great . . . he freely writes me his continual knowledge about Fresco . . . as I did him in early life about Art. Now
Wilkie is gone, his mind is the only mind I think of.'[3]

But doubts soon creep in. 'I said to Barry yesterday, "Shall I be
employed?" He replied, "Yes." "Is Eastlake my Friend?" "I do
not know why he should not be, but he is a cold man; there is no
knowing what he means." '[4] A week later, after talking over old
times with Eastlake, Haydon reflects that he has not *yet* repaid the
£18 with which he 'assisted me . . . at different times . . . Had I
been just to myself instead of being kind [to] others I need not
have had this sum of him, had I made his Father pay me 200 gs. for
the instruction I gave Charles, this would have been right.'[5] But
suspicions are in abeyance. Eastlake makes a Sunday call, 'kind &
affectionate, & begged me to be *Quiet*'.[6] Two months later, 'Called
on Eastlake, who was in high spirits. The Commission had met,
& they asked who was ready to paint Fresco. He replied I was &
read my Statement. . . . On the whole I am glad to find so timid
a Man so animated. He begged me to keep our *meetings Secret*. If
we Devonshire boys accomplish this great Reform, it will be a
grand point.' Next day, 'O God, spare me 20 years to produce
greater works than since Rubens. I know I shall do it if I live.'[7]

Suspicions reawaken, but are immediately dismissed. 'I fear
Eastlake will deceive me. . . . I hope Eastlake wont prove a
Traitor. He has risen by amiability or hypocrisy. His Family were
marked for hypocrites & sneerers. I trust he is not so—Heaven
only knows.'[8] Eastlake's announcement of the terms of the competition (a press cutting attached to the *Journal*) removed all
Haydon's doubts, and he added a note 'All this suspicion is a restless & eager apprehension as *unjust* as *cruel*.' Here were Haydon's
own principles of art—the figure, anatomy. 'Here is my Pupil,

[1] *Diary,* v. 72, 11 July 1841.
[2] v. 84, 21 Aug. 1841.
[3] v. 104, 10 Dec. 1841.
[4] v. 117, 7 Jan. 1842.
[5] v. 120, 13 Jan. 1842.
[6] v. 125, 23 Jan. 1842.
[7] v. 137–8, 20 and 21 Mar. 1842.
[8] v. 145, 23 Apr. 1842. There is a favourable account of Eastlake's father in
the *Autobiography.*

Eastlake, whom I instructed . . . putting forth a code by my influence & the influence of his own sound understanding which will entirely change the whole system of British Art.'[1]

Misgivings returned because Eastlake never mentioned Haydon in his examination and had not brought Cornelius to see his fresco. 'These may be flying fancies—indigestion or bile—but I feel it. I have lost reliance & think I can perceive a cold, calculating diplomacy which is to baffle me. . . . Eastlake has had now the power to return the obligations of early life, but he has shrunk from it, and at the last interview he said, "*Of course you & I must be secret in our Visits.*" '[2] A few days later, 'Eastlake called & we had a long & interesting conversation on the Style of Art, the proceedings of the Commission, the taste of the Nobility, & prospects of Art. Still, he listens with a sort of impatience, when I just hint at my claim from having fought the battle for so many years, by my sufferings, by my attacks, by my petitions. . . .'[3] At the end of May Haydon sums up, 'The great Cause is advanced. State Support has been decided on. My dear Pupil has been the Manager, following my footsteps with more temper & prudence. There can be no doubt that my perpetual agitation of the principle kept it alive, but these journals bear testimony I have never shrinked, & will, if not burned, bear evidence of my tenacity.'[4]

A series of incidents shook Haydon. Eastlake had promised him an autographed copy of his Report, but did not send it, and when Haydon wrote, answered that he had not enough and that one could be bought. The contents were a greater shock. 'Eastlake, who owes to me the direction of his mind to me [*sic*] . . . who knows that the Committee & the Commission . . . are only carrying into force my plans & my evidence of 1836, never in his whole evidence alluded to me, & now in the Report has kept the same dead silence. Good God, what a heart!' To make things worse it was 'hideously hot', which always affected Haydon, and his want of money was dreadful. 'Thus I raised up this Man in all probability to supercede me, & to take the very prize I have fought for. But in God I trust. . . .'[5] Five days later he asks himself, 'Will God damn a Soul which cannot express its innate virtue, solely owing to a physical deficiency? And will God d——n a Soul which owing to a physical derangement so affects the Soul as to paralize

---

[1] *Diary* v. 146–7, 25 Apr. 1842. [2] v. 149–50, 8 May 1842.
[3] v. 152, 14 May 1842. [4] v. 164, 31 May 1842.
[5] v. 194, 16 Aug. 1842.

its power to controul the brain to impel the brain to destroy itself? Human responsibility in such a System is out of the question, but *yet* I believe Human responsibility, though I cannot see its justice or possibility in the present system.'[1] This was a time of intense anxiety about Frank.

Another cause of dissension. Eastlake had been sponsoring German art and German fresco—anathema to Haydon, who wrote (31 October) accusing him of pro-German tendencies. 'The above letter may separate Eastlake & I but it was necessary. His conduct to me has been base. In fact, you may say he never opens his mouth but to conceal his real intentions. He is a Talleyrand.'[2]

By next March they were on good terms again, though Haydon reflects, 'Ah, Eastlake, neither you or your Masters know what I am enduring, & my dear Mary too, for the sake of Art. God bless me through. Amen.'[3] Then came the day for placing the competing cartoons in Westminster Hall. (Some months earlier Haydon had reflected 'The blessing is—if I were to drop dead, what is done of my Cartoons is enough to assure my dear Country I was up to the Mark.') 'I found Eastlake, my Pupil, walking about. He was most happy to see me.' They talked about old times. 'How interesting that we were both from Devon, both having finished our education at Plympton Grammar School, where Reynolds was educated.'[4] Doubts soon returned. 'My suspicion is that both the Minister & his Commission Secretary are determined if possible to lower my rank in public estimation.' He repeats his grounds for suspecting Eastlake. 'I believe Eastlake to be jealous of my leading the public mind in Art. . . . Amidst such conflictions [Court influence], what chance have I?' 'Taking every thing into consideration, though Eastlake owes the Elements of Art to my unreserved communication . . . he does not like my position in the English mind, the Academy back him in secret, & they will influence Sir Robt, Rogers & Lansdowne to do just as they will. . . .'[5]

The blow fell in a letter from Eastlake dated 27 June to say his 'drawings are not among those that have been rewarded'. From the passage quoted (p. 271) Taylor has deleted 'In such humours Men shoot themselves—but not me'.[6] Haydon reacted with great courage. 'Went & removed my Cartoons. Saw Eastlake, who

[1] *Diary*, v. 195–6, 21 Aug. 1842. [2] v. 216.
[3] v. 253, 10 Mar. 1843. [4] v. 280, 1 June 1843.
[5] v. 286, 288, 290, 17 June 1843. [6] v. 302, 14 Aug. 1843.

certainly was agitated. . . . We shook hands though he has treated me with base ingratitude.'[1]

'. . . passed the day in taking a review of my probable destiny', Haydon recorded in September. 'There can be no doubt at all that by my energy & appeals to the Government and the people, I pushed the one to their enthusiasm, & the other to State patronage —and one would have thought that some thing like a reward would have been bestowed on one who had fought so hard a battle & suffered so much for so noble a cause, but alas, I had been so uncompromising. . . . If not encouraged for Cartoons which had indisputable merit, what chance have I to get any in my future attempt? Eastlake could burke my name in his Reports, when it would have availed, but he was ready enough to announce me as among the unsuccessful Candidates by a Circular . . . alas, it is shocking! . . . . The deep, cautious, diplomatic duplicity with which in every way he is trying to break down my station in the public feeling is a pitiable instance of ingratitude & heartlessness. *We shall see* if God will let such conduct *prosper*. In him I trust, & do not believe I shall be deserted. Amen.' Haydon believed that the decision against him was pre-determined, and states that Eastlake, 'to prevent the possibility of mistake', wrote his name in a little book 'when he put their *sizes* down, saying "It is useless to conceal you" ', although secrecy was 'passed in a law by the Royal Commission, of which our well beloved Charles was Secretary'.[2]

Next April, 'I called on Barry, the most amiable of God's creatures, & had a long & interesting conversation. . . . Barry said "what I admired your Cartoons for was that they were *filled*. I told every body so. However angry you may be with Eastlake, by hints I *know* he thinks you ill-treated." . . . "The fact is", said Barry, "you say what you think so completely, & carry it to such an extent, that they are afraid of you." "Who—the Nobility?"— "Yes"—"But I am not in a responsible position—if I was my policy would be altered." '[3]

Another slight from Eastlake followed in June. Haydon wrote to ask Eastlake why he had not sent him a ticket for an exhibition. The answer was 'he had not enough tickets to satisfy all'. The two letters are pinned 'to the *Journal* with the comment, 'Ah my worthy Secretary, supposing I had neglected thee in Early Life—as you have me in Maturity. What would have become of ye? Through

---

[1] *Diary* v. 307, 4 Sept. 1843. [2] v. 309–11, 15 and 19 Sept. 1843.
[3] v. 357–8, 24 Apr. 1844.

me, when an unknown boy, I got you to the Stafford & Bridg-
water Collections, & Grosvenor & Hope, when admission was a
privilege & honour. It is pitiful to complain of such things, but
shocking to be guilty of them. We shall see how it will all
prosper.'[1]

The 'agonising disappointments' of the cartoon contest were
exacerbated by these encounters with Eastlake. '. . . pained occasionally at the treachery of Eastlake—when I think of my openness
to him, & advancing him as fast as I could.' 'Eastlake's base
hypocrisy haunts me. I felt my heart beating at waking this morning.'[2] But Haydon could be generous. A few days later, inspecting
eight frescoes commissioned by Prince Albert for a pavilion in the
garden of Buckingham Palace, he found 'Eastlake's a fine &
beautiful Fresco—but the rest should be all cut out'.[3]

Two days later, he saw no prospect for himself in the decoration
of Parliament. 'Peel hates me . . . Eastlake hates me because he
owes his principles of Art to my instruction, & knows he never
paid me 1/-, & to the Royal Academy I am a perpetual indigestion
because I first shook their roots in public estimation & left them
like a set of teeth loosened by a blow. . . .'[4] Then he found a letter
from Eastlake of 1824, expressing gratitude for Haydon's early
kindness. 'My early impressions in Art. . . . I owe entirely to you
. . . I look back with pleasure & gratitude to the time when I began
the study of a happy profession under your guidance.' Haydon
annotated it, 'This will do Master Charles', and pathetically
thought he possessed a talisman. 'Found a letter of Eastlake's 1824,
fully acknowledging his obligations to my instructions, saying all
I could wish—Providential.'[5]

There was no open split. 'Xmas day. . . . Eastlake called—a good
sign. Eastlake & David Wilkie never call unless it is a safe thing
so to do.' Five days later, 'Called on Eastlake. God knows what this
sudden graciousness means. My suspicion is he is acting under
orders. . . .'[6] 'Called on Eastlake & found him quite bitten by
aristocratic manners—dipping his head & jerking it back, like a
Royal Person who condescended to recognise your physical
existence!'[7]

With the fateful decision to exhibit his pictures separately—the

---

[1] *Diary*, v. 372–3, 29 June 1844. [2] v. 383, 15 and 16 Aug. 1844.
[3] v. 386, 27 Aug. 1844. [4] v. 387, 29 Aug. 1844.
[5] v. 394, 13 Oct. 1844; 508, 10 Jan. 1845 (copy of letter).
[6] v. 405, 407. [7] v. 412, 25 Jan. 1845.

last chance 'of connecting myself with a great public Commission *by opposition* and interesting the public . . .', he prayed for 'energy & vigour to seize the moment. . . . Thou knowest I educated with fearless indifference to my own interest the bitterest Enemy that has crossed my Path! Shall *he* with thy approbation, blast the talents thou hast blest me with? Shall he revel in the malignant chuckle of having power to baffle energy he dreads & Genius he crouches under? No, no—— if thou hast said, "*Fear not, I will be with thee*", thou never will *permit* such an Incarnate Treachery to flourish & triumph! I wait. In thy justice I trust & never did I *trust* in vain. Amen.'[1]

Despite the persecution mania of this final outburst against his 'bitterest enemy', Haydon's suspicions, however exaggerated, cannot be dismissed as groundless. Eastlake was *persona gratissima* with Prince Albert and determined to remain so. Haydon had offended by his repeated attacks on German art (pp. 276–7; the rebuff over the article on fresco is not mentioned in the *Journal*). Hence, one surmises, Eastlake's anxiety not to appear on friendly terms with Haydon, his requests for secrecy, the slights in not sending the promised autographed Report or the ticket for the exhibition. Trifles, but significant trifles. More important, the real injustice in making no mention of Haydon, either in his evidence or the Reports, though many obscure names were there. The contrast with the Ewart Committee (pp. 212–15) was painful. It may even be that his cartoons *were* prejudged and for the same reason. If so the instrument was Eastlake. It seems unlikely that they were worse than all the twenty-one which got awards. Besides the praise quoted (p. 269), there was Frith, who thought them 'very fine'. Watts, though severely critical of Haydon (pp. 157–8), thought 'that his expression of anatomy and general principles of form. . . . the best by far that can be found in the English school'. Conceivably there may have been something of the jealousy that Haydon came to suspect. His prestige was still considerable. The first volume of his Lectures was published (1844) and favourably reviewed in the *Quarterly*. Of course, as usual, he had precipitated disaster by his repeated and untimely attacks on German art, which Eastlake had praised and practised. A *Journal* entry of 1812 spotlights the nature of the wound: 'Let me for a moment indulge the privilege of Genius and revel with delights in the picture of my own Imagination. Let me conceive the House

[1] *Diary* v. 507-8, 8 Jan. 1846.

of Lords with its spacious & ample sides clothed with illustrious examples of Virtue & Heroism.'[1] This was part of an impassioned plea, eleven pages long, for the state support of High Art, addressed to the readers of his *Journals*.

The anguish of the cartoon contest and its aftermath coincided with the 'excruciating anxieties', emotional and financial, of Frank's Cambridge career.

[1] *Diary* i. 270, 21 Dec. 1812. The opening of Parliament by the Regent (30 Nov. 1812) is described, i. 255-6, but the conception of decorating the House of Lords (p. 52) is in the *Autobiography* only.

6. HAYDON ON HAYDON

Painters & Poets are liable to the erruptions of different feelings (Oct. 1809).

DOES Haydon's darker side, the hypochondria and the fits of despair, editorially muted by Taylor, affect the question of his sanity? He brooded on insanity as he brooded on suicide, expected Leigh Hunt to die insane, feared the same fate for Frank, and thought Frank's instability inherited from himself. Hypochondria, like suicide, he attributed to indigestion. 'What machines we are. Digestion is the great cause of every virtue & every vice . . .',[1] he wrote in June 1845. A few months earlier he had prayed; 'Spare me, O God from a failing brain.'[2] The preservation of his sanity he ascribed to marriage and to his religion, and the direct intervention of the Almighty. But for religion, he told a clergyman, 'I should have gone mad.'[3] And, 'It is wonderful to me I have held out so long to 56. Had I been debauched or drunken I never could, and the Religion of my mind has saved my intellect often.'[4]

Haydon's religion, intertwined with superstition, was a lifeline, a talisman, his prayers an incantation, and a blend of entreaty and confession and self-justification ('Thou knowest . . .') that became a necessity. In the aggregate they fill many many pages. The superstition he admitted: 'Men of Genius are considered superstitious, but the fact is, the fineness of their nerve renders them more alive to the supernatural than ordinary men.'[5] Thus in 1830. Ten years later, 'Danger is the very basis of Superstition. It produces a searching after help, supernaturally, when all human means are no longer supposed to be available.'[6] His frequent resort to the *sortes Biblicae* he did not regard as superstitious. The comforting text always turned up, just as—till the very end—the timely cheque or commission seemed a direct answer to prayer.

His religion was peculiar and highly characteristic. He was a pragmatist, yet had a mystical sense of communion with the Almighty. 'God be praised! If this perpetual belief in the

[1] *Diary* v. 456.
[2] v. 402, 6 Dec. 1844.
[3] iv. 525, 2, 3, 4 Oct. 1838.
[4] v. 152, 9 May 1842.
[5] iii. 429, 12 Mar. 1830.
[6] iv. 619, 6 Apr. 1840.

protection of God be a weakness, it is a weakness that tends to great good.'[1] 'Carry me through the ensuing week, the ensuing month, the ensuing Year!' he prayed in 1845. 'In *thee* I trust with an unfailing splendour of Vision in my brain, as if I saw a light mortals cannot see, & heard a harmony that makes me faint.'[2] His horror of scepticism was not fundamentalist. On the contrary: 'I have known Deists, Atheists, Sceptics, Baptists, Protestants, Unitarians & Catholics, & always found the Catholics ready with damnation & never wrong, but all the rest acknowledging that they could not explain, candidly.'[3]

After much musing on the problem of evil he came to the conclusion that the Almighty was not omnipotent. On his fifty-first birthday, 'I find now my judgment matured—conviction at last arrived at that the Deity cannot eradicate Evil, & that the Mortal can only check or compromise with it. But that is no reason it should not be opposed, or checked, resisted & turned aside, if possible.'[4] In a bitter mood in 1842: 'Evil certainly has more power than good, is a match for virtue, & though it cannot overturn, it seems as if it maliciously *baffled* the Almighty.'[5] What shook his confidence in the justice of God was not his own manifold injuries (as he thought them) but the massacre of 500 men, women, and children in Algeria, which 'really shakes one, as to the moral justice of the Great Creator, to allow so many innocent people to be butchered in so horrid a way. It is a mystery. Prayed to be eased of agonising doubts.[6]

Haydon was saved (till 22 June 1846) by his faith and by his vitality and his natural resilience and buoyancy. His capacity, not only for putting a good front to the world, but for enjoying simple pleasures in the middle of adversity, was remarkable. In July 1845, 'Dined with my dear Friend Peter Fairbairn, & he took me to the play. I had not been so long I laughed & cried like a child.'[7] And, three weeks later, that dinner at Greenwich with his boys—'I enjoyed myself immensely.'

There are wild outbursts of misery that seem less than sane, but, strangely, only in 1824, a year of domestic bliss and relative freedom from money troubles, owing to Kearsey (pp. 173–6) and portraits. One of these Taylor quotes, deleting the more extreme

[1] iii. 181, Jan. 1827.
[2] v. 448, 25 May 1845.
[3] v. 37, 10 Mar. 1841.
[4] iv. 401, 25 Jan. 1837.
[5] v. 119, 10 Jan. 1842.
[6] v. 464, 20 July 1845.
[7] v. 467, 28 July 1845.

passages, and it is quoted here (p. 171). It ends: 'Adieu for ever, unadulterated happiness! purity of thought! ardour of heavenly love! & welcome bloody, bawdy madness! endless, torturing, fierce, ungovernable agony,—welcome!'[1] More wild, more raving, is a long passage some months earlier which is worked up to a climax of surrealist nightmare. It begins: 'Of what use is my Genius—to myself or others? It has brought me to prison—of what use is that fame which a breath may destroy as a breath has created it? . . . My Youth is gone! . . . I am ruined! I wonder my frame has born this so long—the mere agitations of the conceptions one's mind has flushing one's brain with blood, & bathing one's body in perspiration, must wear it, and then in addition the necessities of poverty are dreadfull. If I were alone again I would leave my Country for ever—buried in Italy or Greece, I would pass my days in the lowest avocations, could I get peace! ay, peace!' Finally, imagining himself sinking into 'the sloth & superstition, the dreary praying, the solemn imbecility of a cowled monk!', he would plunge into the wild, vent his rage on trees, stones, birds, and animals, and 'glory with ecstatic rapture to meet a *solitary human being without defence*', whom he would murder in the most savage, ghastly, and gory way. 'Ah, ah, Revenge, Revenge, thou dear, dear, dear passion! . . . Genius! the nectar of a soul parched & dried up by poverty & ruin! Curses, Curses, Curses, endless, withering, Hellish, from that lower Hell where the most Hellish rebels down are deeper thrown—light [? blight], blast, scathe those who could dim a brain so brilliant & a heart so tender to such bitter, bitter, solace. B. R. Haydon.'[2] (Abridgement here mitigates the savagery.) Was this a brainstorm, or fantasy, or a safety-valve? Haydon describes his distress (in 1824) at seeing a rabbit shot.[3]

The summing up of the year on the last day of December is also strange. Taylor prints the optimistic reflections—'My domestic happiness is doubled. . . . My mind calmer, my principles of honour firm, & Religion deeper than ever.' But then comes a wild despairing cry on the human condition which he omits: . . . 'ye came into breath without consciousness and ye go out cursing your fate that ye possess it! Heroes, Poets, Painters, Mathematicians, Fanatics, Priests, or what ye may be! . . . Oh humanity, humanity, can there be a being who can . . . bear to hang over thy filth! who is

---

[1] *Diary* ii. 499, 6 Oct. 1824.   [2] ii. 474–5, 26 Apr. 1824.
[3] iii. 107, 30 June 1826.

alive to lovely thoughts? can bear thy murders, thy malice, thy base desires.' There is much more. The entry ends, 'Pardon me if too Presumptuous, Worldly, & vain. Amen. I leave all to thy mercy. Amen.'[1] The contrast between Haydon in his *Journals* and in contact with the world is pointed by an undated letter of about December 1824, printed by Taylor. 'I must own that the comforts and ease and tranquillity which attend portraits and the misery and insults which have always attended my history-painting, begin to affect me.'[2]

The note of wild despair is never struck again. (It was in 1824 that he told Miss Mitford (p. 7) '. . . die I shall at last from the agonies of racked ambition'.) 'I do not think any man on Earth ever suffered more agony of mind than I have done, & so would the World think if it knew why, and yet I always had an abstracting power, & that saved my mind & made me look down & meditate, as it were, on my own sufferings. They became a matter of curious speculation.'[3] Haydon called himself 'of a sanguine disposition' (*Autobiography*) and 'naturally happy tempered'.[4]

The despair was doubtless caused by the realization—sometimes allusively recorded—that with a family and without his large lofty painting room,[5] his dream of greatness was but a dream. 'What I could produce if seconded by Public encouragement! I dread to dwell on it! It pains me so.' (The occasion was an abortive proposal to paint a Crucifixion for Liverpool Town Hall.)[6] 'I look back on the glories of my past life with desponding enthusiasm. Here I am now in a snug carpeted parlour!—but alas! where is now the magnificent grandeur of my solitary & extended Painting Room! . . . My feelings perhaps are deeper now, perhaps higher, but I look back & ever shall (though then unblessed by Mary's face) with desponding remembrance to days & nights which are passed—*for ever!*' And he breaks into free verse beginning 'Solitude—Farewell!' and ending '. . . Would human / Effort fail if not roused by hoping / To do more than it can do?'[7]

'I am one of those beings born to bring about a great object through the medium of suffering', he wrote in 1829. 'I shall accomplish what I was born for, and die in all probability without

---

[1] *Diary* ii. 502–7. [2] *Autobiography and Memoirs* (1926), i. 358.
[3] iii. 38, 13 Aug. 1825. [4] iii. 117, 10 July 1826.
[5] It still exists, or did recently, called Welbeck Hall, and is used as a chapel by a group of Plymouth Brethren at 1 Rossmore Road. ii 129 n.
[6] iii. 8, 21 Feb. 1825. [7] iii. 94–95, 30 Apr. 1826.

sharing its worldly benefits. I only hope, if I should, my Children will not be forgotten by my Country.'[1] He compares his hypochondria to Johnson's: 'O God, assist me to get rid of this insane condition of mind. I take it, I feel the want of *discipline* in my early life. I was an only son, & ever had my own will, like Byron, & left to my own impulses. This has produced all the good and all the vice of my character.'[2] 'Whenever I have been encouraged I have met it by desperate exertion, but I have been so ill used and so cruelly treated that my feelings are melancholy & exasperated, and I have occasional fits of sluggish disgust. My face, with its energy & colour conceals my feelings. My Mary only knows them.'[3] (Apart from specific grievances, by ill treatment or cruelty Haydon means the absence of commissions for High Art.) He was again upset by reading—passionately—Bourrienne's *Memoirs*, 'the Boswell of Napoleon'. 'Remembering him as I do from 1796, it is peculiarly interesting to me, and I awoke this morning despising myself for my present pursuits [he was painting *Punch*] and agitated by all my former ambitious feelings.'[4]

In 1834, distraught by financial dangers and family troubles, 'I must "who aspire to greatness" shew form of being able "*greatly to suffer*". . . . I fear a curse hangs over me, for leaving my Father to pursue Art—whenever I touch "high Art" it seems in force.'[5] A few days later, after a timely cheque, 'These anxieties are proper corrections! They keep the creature dependant to his Creator. . . . Continued prosperity would make me impudent, voluptuous & ungrateful. I see the value of affliction to a character like mine, if he has a soul to be saved.'[6] And, in the desperate plight of 1836 (from which he was to be extricated by Newton). 'Though more hopeless than ever in situation, I despair less than ever and trust in thee O god, with all my Soul, & know I shall be delivered. Amen.'[7]

All this Taylor omits, as he does expressions of pure pessimism. Even in the early raptures of marriage, after 'indigestion': 'Such is human Nature!—sleeping, rising, eating, drinking, purging, propagating, suffering, dying & rotting!—but there is one little matter in "Life's else bitter cup distilled" that makes us bear the rest.'[8] 'Next to the agony of being born is the horror of belonging to *such a species!*', he writes, on realizing that though he had wept

[1] *Diary* iii. 334, 15 Jan. 1829.   [2] iii. 359, 10 May 1829.
[3] iii. 373, 21 June 1829.   [4] iii. 390–1, 25–27 Aug. 1829.
[5] iv. 221, 30 Aug. 1834.   [6] iv. 221, 30 Aug., 3 Sept. 1834.
[7] v. 373, 27 Aug. 1836.   [8] ii. 377, 19 Aug. 1822.

bitterly at the death of his baby Fanny, he 'did not feel less hungry of my dinner.'[1] In the bitter aftermath of the cartoon contest, after revelling in sea-bathing at Dover, 'swimming always braces me—but then comes this calamity—Life.'[2] Nine days later, 'Rubbed in Uriel, but harrassed so much my brain becomes turgid with apprehension.'[3]

In these days of 'torturing petty anxieties' as well as of anguish —'I feel I have suffered so much my Imagination is diseased about ruin'[4]—optimism has a forced note and is largely omitted by Taylor. 'Weather, indigestion, a glass of wine beyond my three, oversleeping, not working hard—all these causes help to depress the physique & then the mental—yet what a Blessing is life!'[5] A year later, 'Who for fear of Pain would lose their intellectual being? If there be happiness on earth it is mine. To sit, with a Sketch one side, my Literature the other, & a grand work before me —meditating alterations & improvements—"Seeing Him who is invisible" & hearing Immortal Chauntings no Earthly Ear can Catch.'[6]

Haydon prided himself on his courage—his bottom—but not, apart from his tenacity in pursuing high art, on strength of character. 'The same follies, the same weaknesses, the same want of self-command, the same——.'[7] And, 'I am the same Man as ever, 30 years [ago] I had just the same feelings, the same delusions!'[8] One impulse which he knew to be a weakness, and which became an addiction, was the urge to polemics in the press. Tempted by 'a pompous announcement in the Times...' 'After a struggle I conquered my evil Genius.' 'Writing to me is no trouble; it is pouring out my thoughts only, as I would talk, but the consequences are deep. I tell too many truths, make enemies, & lose my time.'[9] After spending a week on 'a memorial for Lord Grey, about the Academy, which has disturbed my thoughts.... Why cannot I, as Buckingham said, consider myself blessed by God with high gifts & be content to exercise them—why cannot I indeed?'[10] 'O God restore my intellect to its sound condition', he prayed, 'its passion for painting, root out this appetite for Controversy & writing, except on subjects of Art, calm & useful, for Jesus Christ's sake,

[1] *Diary*, iii. 582-3, 22 Nov. 1831. [2] v. 373, 6 July 1844.
[3] v. 376, 15 July 1844. [4] v. 310, 16 Sept. 1843.
[5] v. 383, 15 Aug. 1844. [6] v. 465, 22 July, 1845.
[7] iv. 449, 14 Nov. 1837. [8] iv. 493, 16 June 1838.
[9] iii. 395, 10 Sept. 1829.
[10] iv. 23, 15 Dec. 1832. B is James Silk Buckingham.

Amen.'[1] 'Wrote, but neither drew or painted, I regret to say, I ought never to write, because if I say what I know to be truth, I hurt myself, if I do not I hurt my conscience.'[2] 'Many years more of effectual practice I can hardly expect', he reflected in 1844, 'and is it not time to think only of my dear Art, and let her do her duty by the Pencil alone—as well as my family. The fact is, the Cause is so linked up with me, that both Pencil & pen I fear will ever go together.'[3] In 1845 Haydon sketched in his *Journal* a pen and a palette and brush, which he called 'The bane & Antidote', with the comment, 'Unless I am constantly Painting, I give vent with the pen. The moment my mind is not excited by the brush, it turns right round & pours out a torrent of thought for the pen.'[4] How different his life would have been if he had never embarked on his polemical career with those two articles in the *Examiner* in 1812 (p. 45).

Haydon came to deplore his intervention in politics over Reform which he regarded as a public desertion of the Tories in favour of the Whigs. His politics were peculiar and characteristic—a complex of concern for the Art, self-interest, public spirit, Academy-phobia, regard for rank, Radical leanings, John-Bullishness, hero-worship of Wellington, then, admiration (this side idolatry) for 'dear Lord Grey'. In 1827 he had declared himself a Reformer, 'that is, a man whose abstract notions of right & wrong are too intensely strong to yield to the whispers of self-interest! or be blind to the sophistry of Power!'[5] Haydon's zeal for Reform (which makes a first appearance in the *Journals* in December 1819) was based on hatred of the corrupt corporation—embodied of course in the Academy—and therefore of the nomination borough. He told Lord Althorp that the Academicians were 'the Boroughmongers of the Art'.[6] The 'Radical Junior'[7] letters of which he was so proud (p. 211) were anonymous. 'I would wish to keep well with all in hopes of getting some of the Rascals to do something for Art.'[8]

The Reform Banquet picture changed that. Haydon's expectations soared. 'The immortality conferred upon me by Lord Grey in giving me a Picture connected with Reform—the glory of that

[1] *Diary* iv. 578, 26 Aug. 1839.   [2] v. 208, 3 Oct. 1842.
[3] v. 361, 8 May 1844.   [4] v. 440, 13 May 1845.
[5] iii. 231, 6 Nov. 1827.   [6] iv. 16, 25 Nov. 1832.
[7] 'Junior' because of a series of influential letters in *The Times* from December 1830, signed Radical. They had been attributed to Lord Durham, but were by Lt.-Col. Leslie Grove Jones.
[8] iii. 570, 22 Oct. 1831.

night at Guildhall—the return of fortune . . . but I regret to say
the materials I have to work with for Art—King, Nobility &
People—are materials from which little good can be expected.'[1] The
abortive Newhall Hill picture (p. 206) had inspired more spon-
taneous enthusiasm. Here are his conflicting views on the Radicals.
'If we were left to the Radicals, God help Art, science, knowledge
or honour.'[2] Some five years later, 'The Radicals, men of honest,
abstract Virtue, despise worldly ways, & leaving principles to act
for themselves, fall before Men less honest, who know the World
better'.[3] His social attitude had similar conflicts: '*I* should be happy
to *enlighten* the lower classes but not to *dine* with them [he must
have been thinking of Johnson]. . . . This is, I daresay, wrong, but
I cant help it. I prefer Tasso or Virgil, Propinque maribus, champagne, & the order of the Bath. I know it is wrong, & in reality
perhaps I don't, but "*the ribbon paints well*". Times are coming
when it won't be the thing, & I don't see why the Queen [Adelaide]
should have 100,000 a year. There is Poetry in the *People*, but there
is also Poetry in *nobility*, the Elect, the Choice, the Adorned, the
Refined. I can't deride [? decide] & yet I can. The Rights of Thousands, & the privileges of some.—"an ounce of civet".'[4] (One of
Haydon's favourite quotations from *Lear*.)

Haydon can hardly be called a *staunch* Tory. 'If the English
People again submit tó the Tories', he wrote in May 1833, 'may
they be ground to dust & crushed to atoms, may Russians, Prus-
sians & Austrians help to enslave, and may their old enemies the
French come in at the Crisis & complete their destruction . . . [etc.
etc.] these things & worse is my ardent prayer. Amen.'[5] (How
little his verbal explosions could mean. He feared a popular up-
heaval and blamed it on Tory policy after 1815.) With less
extravagance: 'Church & King—means pluralities & the Pension
List', but annotated it four years later, '1838 October. This was
Radical cant. It does not mean that in essence, but it comes often
to that in abuse.'[6] In essence, Haydon was a Church and King man.

Disillusion with the Whigs set in. Talking to his friend,
William Hamilton, 'I said I did not think the Whigs so fit for
business as the Tories, and I found a great deal of Aristocratic feeling among the Whigs. Lord Grey would leave me to go to lunch
& never ask me, though he knew I must be feeling faint. Lord

[1] *Diary*, iv. 27, 31 Dec. 1832. [2] iv. 126, 26 Aug. 1833.
[3] iv. 486, 3 June 1838. [4] iv. 33, 24 Jan. 1833.
[5] iv. 84–85, 20 May 1833. [6] iv. 242, 26 Nov. 1834.

Mulgrave always made me frankly dine, breakfast & lunch with him, and yet Lord Grey knew it was my habit, because when he left town he gave orders for my having a lunch at the time I painted in Downing Street.'[1] 'I never dined but once with a Whig, and yet the Tories, with all their pride, were always having me at their tables, and the only Minister who has invited me to dine during the fever for me is a *Tory* (*Palmerston*)—curious, certainly. Johnson said the first Whig was the Devil. Why? From a love of Liberty—no. From a hatred of controul, & a passion to rule others. This is the secret of Whiggism.'[2]

'Lord John's saying that an open Window was enough air & exercise for a Prisoner has shewed me the real despotism of his nature, & the conduct of the Whigs to me in settling the School of Design that I first proposed, never consulting me, & putting no Artists but Academicians has disgusted me much. It shews they have no real desire to open a new Aera, and that if they could have helped it, they never would have passed the Reform bill.'[3] Two weeks later, 'The Whigs are evidently sinking . . . they will go without regret from any body. This comes from playing *Tories* . . . As to myself, I have been rightly served for belying my real heart & rushing forward to honour them because I believed they passed the Reform bill, when I found on close contact they were as much annoyed at being obliged to do it almost as the Tories themselves.'[4]

'The Unfortunate Banquet! it ruined me, has ruined the Engraver, & thus my enthusiasm for the cause, which they never would have carried except for *the people*, and which they have lamented carrying *ever since, has been my bane!*'[5] By 1838 Haydon was violently anti-Whig, hated the new Poor Law, resented and dreaded their foreign policy. 'I am in a devil of a rage with the Whigs for the want of decision they display in every thing but keeping their places.' This ends a long, extravagant tirade in the vein of the anti-Tory explosion.[6] In 1839, 'I *do certainly* regret the part I took about the Reform Bill'. (This is annotated 'I do not (1841). I would do it again, if the Duke acted so again.') I believe it was more revenge for ill usage & spirit because the Duke said *no Reform* was necessary than genuine Patriotism. *I do not know.* . . . I hate Radicalism & Whiggism. I hate Intermediation, & believe

[1] *Diary* iv. 245, 21 Dec. 1834.   [2] iv. 195–6, 31 May 1834.
[3] iv. 403, 8 Feb. 1837.   [4] iv. 407, 22 Feb. 1837.
[5] iv. 442, 29 Oct. 1837.   [6] iv. 492–3, 16 June 1838.

I shall end my Life a Conservative Reformer. If the Duke comes to sit & gives me a commission, I am done for! At any rate *this* is honest. . . . The real truth, I court all Parties to get one [or] other to do *something* for the Art, but I am more a Duke's man than any other, and under every other pretence *have always been so*, and *that is from my heart!* . . .'[1]

But he thought himself committed to the Party. 'It is impossible for me now after my devotion & enthusiasm for the Whigs, after the absurd Catalogue I wrote about them (pp. 209–10) ever to mingle again in political matters without deserved Ridicule. It is the Duke's fault. . . .'[2]

By 1841 Haydon was veering to the Whigs. 'If there be a dissolution what shall I do? The Whigs have not done *all* I could wish, but they have done a great deal. Will Peel do as much? I fear not. . . . The Whigs granted me a Committee . . . [Ewart's]. They have formed a Central School as I advised in my evidence. They have begun branch Schools, as I recommended. Ought I not to be grateful & pleased?'[3] Peel's ministry is mentioned (1 September) without enthusiasm, and after that politics are submerged by a complex of anxieties—Mary, Orlando, Frank, the cartoons. He remarks in 1842, 'The reign of the Tories has always been a curse to me. I never get employed when they are uppermost.'[4] Not that Haydon lost interest in public events. On the eve of the fatal last exhibition: 'The Victories of the Punjaub are the grandest thing since Waterloo, & by Pupils of that illustrious Man!' He prophesied that 'its entire civilization & final Christianity will be the result.'[5]

Thrice Haydon recorded his political creed. First, a plea for Church and monarchy, '& the Nation will gradually arrive at an Amalgamation of Classes, without blood, violence or folly'.[6] Then, twice, in almost identical terms. 'Of the Two Evils, Monarchy is preferable to Democracy [still a word of ill-repute]. It is an evil that any given number of human beings should be fed & pampered & made believe it is the duty to feed & pamper them, but when property & religion & Liberty are more secure under a Sovereign as an abstract head of the Law than under a plurality of Tyrants as abstract heads of Democracy, Monarchy in the long run will be the selected Government of the Earth.'[7]

[1] iv. 556, 19 May 1839. [2] iv. 557–8, 28 May 1839.
[3] v. 52–53, 24 May 1841. [4] v. 134, 28 Feb. 1842.
[5] v. 528, 3 Apr. 1846. [6] v. 40, 23 Mar. 1841.
[7] v. 277, 28 May 1843. The entry for 16 Sept. 1842 is almost the same.

Though the *Autobiography* shows a vivid memory for details of early life, there are strange lapses in the *Journals*. Haydon says (in 1845) that his name 'had been down 4 times [for the Academy,] 1810 & 1811, 1826, 1827—& never had a single vote'.[1] He told the Ewart Committee that he had been rejected for the Associateship in 1810, 1811, and 1820 (p. 214). The minutes of the R.A. confirm what the reader of the *Autobiography* and the *Journals* suspects, that he applied only in 1810 and 1827.[2] Then, when Mary went to Brighton for her health in March 1846 (p. 281)—'My dearest love who has never left me for 25 years'; he forgot that other momentous first separation, after eighteen years, when Mary went to Oxford to see Orlando.

Haydon was torn by conflicts ('I try to like Portrait, & I try not to like it')[3]—between solitude and family life, between the People and the elect, between life as a calamity and life as a blessing, between a death-wish and desire for long life. Two of Haydon's musings on suicide demand quotation. In 1835 in a verse on 'The Painter's Blessings' addressed to Mary: 'Oh hail my three blessings of Life, / My pencil, my Book, & my Wife, / Never mind the alloy, / While these I enjoy, / I defy both the bullet and knife.' This was the outcome of prolonged musings on mind and body, immortality, Revelation, and suicide induced by reading Brougham's *A Discourse of Natural Theology*. The book 'threw my mind entirely off its balance for painting . . .'.[4] In 1842:

Nothing is so dreadful as the inexorability of Time! The half of the Year was last week. . . . Oh Time, Time—dreadful. If the falls of Niagara were near, I would go over them shouting to put an end to this horror of living *here!* Would it put an end? *Here* it might, but where would you *wake?*

This is sheer '*stomach strain*' from foul air & anxiety.

I am ashamed of myself, but such is life!—and such is a Lord of Creation when his *stomach* is deranged—that's the power after all, the identical thing which can & does baffle the mind—is surely the strongest of the two, and regulates its deductions. I am not well & do not know how it will all end. Let us draw the Curtain— & all to meditation.[5]

---

[1] *Diary* v. 438–9, 11 May 1845.
[2] I am much indebted to Mr. Hans Fletcher for this information.
[3] iii. 355, 2 May 1829.   [4] iv. 321, 3 Nov. 1835.
[5] v. 173, 27 June 1842. Haydon adapts *Henry VI*, Part II, III. iii. 32–33.

A. HAYDON'S PICTURES: CASUALTIES AND RESTORATIONS

THE year 1960—year of the publication of the first two volumes of the *Diary*—is a landmark in the annals of Haydon's pictures. The lost *Judgement of Solomon* reappeared in the saleroom and was recognized. This was announced in *The Times* (21 July) four days after the paper had recorded the rescue and restoration of *Wellington Musing on the Field of Waterloo*.

Solomon, returned to Haydon by the assignees in bankruptcy of the last owner, had been stored in London, Newton paying the rent. At the Haydon sale in 1852 (of which more later) it was bought by a dealer or agent and then acquired by Landseer. In 1853 it was exhibited at the British Institution. Lord Ashburton lent it to the International Exhibition of 1862. At the Ashburton sale at Melchet Court in 1911 it was in the servants' hall, unframed, by an unknown artist and fetched thirty shillings.

Before the reappearance in the sale room (Bonham's, 30 June 1960, catalogued by the auctioneer as Italian School, *c.* 1730) it had undergone a truly remarkable transformation. Folded and crumpled, with flaked and flaking paint, heavily coated with dark-brown varnish and backed by a blue and white basket-weave tablecloth, it had nevertheless been recognized by Mr. Jack Gold, a picture restorer, as Haydon's lost masterpiece. His craftsmen worked on it for over a year. Varnish and tablecloth were removed, it was relined with canvas and repainted. The glazes were gone, but all but two faces were intact. From a dark-brown picture it was revealed as brightly coloured with reds and yellows predominating.

In April 1962 there was an article in the *Burlington* by Mr. Frederick Cummings, 'Poussin, Haydon and the Judgement of Solomon'. He sees the picture as a change in the direction of English art away from Reynolds, Romney, Fuseli, and others. Reproductions show its striking resemblance to Poussin's picture of the same subject (1649), both in the architectural background and the general disposition of the figures. Mr. Cummings also reproduces preliminary sketches by Haydon and the charming oil study of a sleeping boy, the origin of the dead child in the picture, which went to Russia in Haydon's lifetime—he does not say how or why—and is still there, in a museum in Vladivostock.

In the same month *Solomon* was reproduced in *The Times* with an article, 'Haydon's Masterpiece restored'. The anonymous author attributes the general design to Raphael's cartoon of the Blinding of Elymas (which Haydon knew well), with the good mother taken from Titian's *Noli me Tangere* and the executioner from Poussin's picture. Neither critic mentions Haydon's own account: 'There is hardly any thing new. I never literally stole but one figure in my life (Aaron) from Raphael. Yet today I found my Olympias, which I had dashed in, in a heat, exactly a repetition of an Antigone, & the first thing I saw in the Louvre was Poussin's Judgement of Solomon—Solomon nearly in the same position. Yet I solemnly declare I never saw even the print when I conceived my Solomon, which was done one night, before I began to paint at 19, 1805, when I lodged in Carey Street, & was ill in my eyes. I lay back in my chair, and indulged myself by composing my Solomon. I will venture to say no Painter but Wilkie will believe this, though it is as true as that 2 & 2 make 4 so help me God!'[1] Wilkie had discussed the composition with Haydon and they had visited the Louvre together.

Wellington Musing on the Field of Waterloo (pp. 236–42) has the characteristic sub-title *or, A Hero and the Horse, which carried him in his grandest Battle, imagined to be on the Field again, after Twenty Years*. It hangs in St. George's Hall, Liverpool, for which it may have been intended. It was not exactly lost, but suffered a series of humiliations, starting with the inability of the Committee to raise more than 400 guineas when their commission had been for 600. It was in the Liverpool Collegiate Institution before 1907, when it was banished to the corridor of a school in Lodge Lane, exposed to the penknives of schoolboys. It was afterwards rolled and stored in a coach-house, then nailed on the wall and destined for a bonfire. At this point it was rescued by a group of people, including Professor Pope and the Duke of Wellington, who subscribed for its restoration.[2] It was exhibited at the Walker Art Gallery before being removed to St. George's Hall. Haydon would have been proud to know that the head sketched at Walmer for this picture, and an unrecorded copy, are now owned by the

[1] *Diary* iii. 114, 5 July 1826 (printed by Taylor).
[2] *The Times*, 17 July 1960.

Duke of Wellington and by the United Service Club[1] (said to be the Duke's favourite club).

Altogether there were five versions of *Wellington Musing*, the fifth being one of a pair of sketches for window panels at Chatsworth, the companion being Napoleon at St. Helena. They were commissioned for £50 by the Duke of Devonshire to help towards Frank's Cambridge bills, and Haydon was grateful: 'I hope he will be pleased, I have painted them with great gusto.'[2] (They are still at Chatsworth, attached to the shutters of a window.) Shortly before, 'Worked like a Hero, & nearly finished Duke & Horse at the *wholesale* price, 3 Napoleons & a Duke going home in a day or two, 10 gs each.'[3]

Christ's Triumphal Entry into Jerusalem has had its vicissitudes since its departure for America (p. 194), when Haydon wrote, 'I trust in God it will be preserved from fire and ruin.'[4] Cephas Childs, the engraver, and Henry Inman, the portrait painter, bought it from Binns to be the nucleus of the American Gallery of Painting in Philadelphia, to which they lent it. In 1846 there was a bad fire, the picture was cut from the frame and 'dragged out like a wet blanket'. It was later shown in the Franklin Gallery, then acquired by the Roman Catholic Archbishop of Cincinnatti and hung in the cathedral there, and finally reached the St. Mary's Seminary of the West in Norwood, Ohio. In 1941 it was restored by members of the Cincinnatti Art Museum.[5] Recently it has been promoted to a permanent position in the foyer of the new administrative building of the Athenaeum of Ohio, Saint Gregory's Seminary, Cincinnatti.[6]

An important letter by Haydon discovered in the archives of the Pennsylvania Academy of Fine Art[7] corrects erroneous (contemporary) identifications and the 'so-called Key in the Boston Public Library'. It also corrects and adds to the suggested identifications on page 309. Haydon writes, 'I consider the Penitent Girl & Centurion except the head of Lazarus the best things in all my life, the best things I ever did.' 'On the right of Christ is a Mother bringing

---

[1] The original is reproduced in *Iconography of Wellington*, by the 7th Duke of Wellington, 1935, the club portrait in *Country Life*, 3 May 1962.

[2] *Diary* v. 406, 28 Dec. 1844; 409, 2 Jan. 1845.   [3] v. 395, 19 Oct. 1844.

[4] iii. 556, 23 Sept. 1831.   [5] Olney, *Haydon*, pp. 112–13.

[6] Information from the Registrar, the Revd. Donald A. Tenoever, who has kindly sent me a photograph of the picture and the building.

[7] Maria Allentock, *Art Bulletin*, Mar. 1962.

a Penitent—her sister & boy [John Hunt's son] are behind.' 'There is a belief the Penitent Girl from Mrs Haydon. . . . When I had painted . . . [her] I had never seen Mrs Haydon.' Her portrait is 'the middle one of three female heads looking up [where?]; between the stems of the Palm trees is a head bawling loudly into the Ears of another figure who is turning back to catch the sound, the head calling is poor Keats the Poet'.

Wordsworth, Voltaire, and Newton, standing together on the right, are well known and unmistakable. 'Newton & Wordsworth are Believers. Voltaire is a Sneerer. . . . Above St John is a face scrutinizing Christ.—This is Hazlitt & very like. . . . Behind Christ's right shoulder is a part of a bald head & one eye—This is from Sharp the Engraver. . . . The hands of our Saviour are from Wilkie who has very fine hands. . . . The Centurion from my own Servant' [Sammons]. Lazarus 'kneeling & bending to the Earth' my old Corporal of the 2d Life Guards [Webster]. The Samaritan Woman from a female model I used to have, but of course elevated.'

Aristides and *Nero* (see p. ix) are no longer in the Melbourne Aquarium, which was burnt down in the late 1940's. Both belong to Sir Harold Jengoult Smith, but are stored in the Exhibition Building. The *Journals* show that Bennoch (whom Haydon calls Bennock) and Twentyman were indeed 'Haydon's main financial supporters' from 1843 to his death. After Haydon's death Twentyman (who went to Australia in 1846 or 1847) accepted both pictures at Haydon's valuation in part payment of his debt—£840 for *Aristides* (Haydon's top price achieved in the raffle for *Xenophon*), £420 for *Nero*. In the early 1850's he offered them to the National Gallery of Victoria for £250; they were refused. He then built a gallery at his house for Haydon's pictures—there were other smaller ones—open to the public at weekends for a small charge. During the last war *Nero* and *Aristides* were on the landing at the top of the stairs in the Aquarium, which then housed R.A.A.F. trainees. They used the *Aristides* as a target. The picture was not at first restored—a large panel of plywood was nailed across the foreground.[1] That has been removed, and there have been repairs, but the picture is in bad condition.[2]

---

[1] Transcript of a broadcast (n.d., lent to me by the Clarendon Press) by Sir Clive Fitts, who saw the pictures in the Aquarium and, before that, the

[Notes 1 (cont.) and 2 overleaf]

The *Napoleon Musing at St. Helena* commissioned by Peel in 1830 (pp. 192-3) has had a short but remarkable history as—apparently—the only work by Haydon downgraded since 1948. It remained in the Peel family till 1900, when it was bought by Pierpont Morgan, who presented it to the Metropolitan Museum of Art, New York. It was there till 1950, when it was sold by auction for $140 to Mr. Maurice Solow, of Mamaroneck, New York.[1]

Professor Pope lists fifteen paintings not mentioned in the *Journals*. Among these is the portrait of Leigh Hunt (pp. 164-5). Although not by name, it is mentioned: 'April 10 [1815]. I painted a Portrait of a Friend, a long promise! Then did I miserably feel the different sensations after concluding the one to those after a day's work on my Picture. The one was all the timid, mean sensation of a face similist[?]; the other all the swelling bursting glories of realizing a [host] of visions of imaginations. I feel the beauties of individuality as much as any one, the sharpness and softness of flesh, the delicacy of touch, and calm sweetness of breadth & melting racy flush of colour; but if all these tend to elicit a mean character, of what value are they?'[2] I learn from the National Portrait Gallery that the portrait was painted for John Hunt (who had lent Haydon £30) and that 1815 is a probable date. Doubt is removed by Haydon's letter to Leigh Hunt (12 February 1816): 'do not forget that *your* Portrait is the only one I have painted, or probably ever will.'[3]

collection in the Twentyman house, where it remained till the death of Twentyman's grandson. With it was a locked wallet containing the 1853 edition of the *Journals*, with 400 letters from Haydon (mostly to Twentyman, a few to Bennoch) which he was allowed to read.
   [2] Information from Dr. Ursula Hoff, Curator of Prints and Drawings, National Gallery of Australia.

---

[1] *Diary* iii. 525 n.
[2] i. 420.
[3] Quoted by Olney, *Haydon*, p. 89, from a letter in the British Museum.

B. THE SALE: HAYDON AND NEWTON

THE Catalogue of the sale, at Foster's, Pall Mall, 18 March 1852,[1] is a poignant document, both for the derisory prices and for the fact that, with two exceptions,[2] all belonged to Newton, 'my old Friend Billy, the dearest Friend I ever had'.[3] They were pictures he had bought or commissioned, pictures individually pledged to him, or part of the contents of the house at Haydon's death. 'The furniture in my house was 3 times seized by him & released, & I gave him a power to enter again 1836—for the same claims. Great additions have been made since.' (Haydon's will.) The principal items in the Catalogue and the first 37 lots out of 78 were 'Some important Gallery and Cabinet works, Sketches and Sketch books of the late B. R. Haydon'. Sketches ranged from Elgin Marble drawings (some by pupils) to '95 Studies in Physiognomy including heads of Wordsworth the Poet and Sir C. L. Eastlake, P.R.A.' There were also oil sketches and pen-and-ink designs for many of his pictures. These lots went for under £2 except for the Physiognomies—£3. 15s.

The principal items were 'Finished Pictures' arranged in the auctioneer's ascending order of merit or size, the last being *Solomon* at the top price of 57 guineas. The first two were a *Napoleon at St. Helena* (£2. 10s.) and a *Napoleon in Egypt* (£1. 10s.). Then came *Mercury and Argus* (£1). The first mention of Newton in the *Journals*, 21 July 1830, is: 'My worthy Landlord Newton gave me a commission to finish Mercury and Argus for 20 guineas.' It had been begun in 1823 and was exhibited in 1831 at the British Gallery.

The next, *Christ raising the Widow's Son* (£16. 5s. 6d.), together with *Achilles discovered by Telymus*[4] (£5. 10s.), had been a munificent commission from Newton—£420 each—when Haydon was in dire straits in 1835. Haydon prayed for the success of these two

---

[1] Marked Catalogue in the Victoria and Albert Museum, prices and names of owners and purchasers in pen.

[2] Belonging to the late T. H. Illidge (1799–1851), portrait painter. One is the portrait of Haydon (£50), painted in 1838 (*Diary* iv. 531), which he said made him look like 'an old daddy'.

[3] iv. 277, 29 Mar. 1835.

[4] 'by Ulysses' in the checklist; 'Achilles' only in the text.

pictures, to make them 'beneficial to my dear Landlord Newton, for whom . . . they are painted'. And on the last day of 1835, 'I have cause for the deepest gratitude towards my Great Creator for raising up such a Friend as my dear Landlord, who has helped me when the nobility forsook me as usual, and employed me to paint the Widow's Son & Achilles, paying me 5 guineas weekly, to the amount of 100 gs each, and then striking off 400 gs. each from the gross debt.'[1]

Between these two in the list is *Samson breaking his bonds* (£4. 4s.). Newton's 'Sampson' had been *Samson and Dalilah*: 'Settled the subject for Newton, Sampson & Dalilah', in February 1835; it was begun in July 1836 and finished in February 1837. The next picture, *Christ's Agony in the Garden* (pp. 104, 172), has some claim to be Haydon's most unfortunate painting; he thought it his worst. Taylor omitted the wounding incident of a letter from Sir George Philips who 'informs Mr Haydon that he may have his picture of Christ's Agony whenever he may be inclined to send for it, as Sir George has no intention of hanging it up either in his house in town or in the country'. Haydon, after recording a favourable opinion of Sir George and hatred of Lady Philips: 'The Caprice of these people is extraordinary. Here's a man who approves of the subject before I painted it, allows me to finish it, is so pleased he writes a long puff *himself* in the Globe, & now says he will hang it up nowhere. One can only laugh like Andromache' [smiling through her tears: *Iliad*].[2] The price fell from the original 500 guineas to 5 guineas. It was unfortunate for Haydon's post-1926 reputation that Aldous Huxley chose this picture on which to assess Haydon's work and exercise his gift for ridicule.

A *Curtius leaping into the Gulf* (pp. 260, 265–6) at £22. 6s. must have been large. Besides the original (126 × 90 in.), exhibited at the British Gallery and sold, now in the Royal Albert Memorial Exhibition, Plymouth, there were (at least) five others, some small. Haydon writes, 1 December 1844 '. . . painted Napoleons and Curtiuses at so much the dozen'. This one is probably 'My Curtius at the Pantheon on which there is a lien of 80 to my Landlord Newton', and which he valued (in his will) at 200 guineas.

Edward the Black Prince thanking James Lord Audley for his Gallantry at the Battle of Poictiers, for which Newton had struck off £525

---

[1] *Diary* iv. 304, 330, 26 Aug. 1835, 31 Dec. 1835.
[2] iv. 342, 12 Apr. 1836.

of debt in 1842 (pp. 227–8), fetched £26. 5s. From the full text it appears that this was not the picture commissioned by Lord Audley in 1836 and left on Haydon's hands, but another, commissioned in 1840: '3 June. Began the Poictiers for dear old Billy.' It was exhibited at the R.A. in 1842. What happened to the first one does not appear.[1]

Last but one is the large unfinished canvas of *Alfred and the British Jury* which was splashed with Haydon's blood (p. 294). It is moving to find that Newton *bought* this picture (£8. 18s. 6d.). The last, *Solomon*, has already been noted. A clause in Haydon's will clarifies the situation which the many *Journal* entries leave obscure. 'I owe a great sum to my Landlord, William Newton. . . . He holds Pictures, Books & Prints & the Judgment of Solomon, which is the property of the assignees of the late Mr Prideaux, Bankrupt. He took possession of the Picture at the Western Exchange, paid the rent due in my insolvency of 1830. His claim is for warehouse-room, for which he paid. He has been a good landlord to me.'

Doubtless prices would have been higher if advantage had been taken of the wave of sympathy immediately after Haydon's death.[2] The delay of nearly six years must surely be another instance of Newton's 'innate goodness of heart'. A query about the house by which Newton lost so heavily. Haydon signed the lease on 5 January 1824 and moved in at once. The address of this corner house was changed in February 1828 from 58 Connaught Terrace to 4 Burwood Place. Haydon incurred criticism (as he resentfully records) for its size and expense. Seguier asked him if he was going to take a house in St. James's Square. The rent, £120, was high, in view of the fall since then in the value of money. Carlyle paid £35 a year for his house in Chelsea. Haydon moved in just after a distraint for rent (£4. 10s.) from the 'two old reptiles' in the lodgings to which he went after losing the Lisson Grove house on his first imprisonment. (The rent of that house and studio was also £30 a quarter.) How did Haydon manage to obtain such a lease? The answer, presumably, is again Newton's 'innate goodness of heart', but he is not mentioned in the *Journals* till 1830.

[1] In Professor Pope's 'Checklist of Pictures begun by Haydon' both are bought by Newton for £525. This hardly seems possible, even for Newton.

[2] See A. Hayter, *A Sultry Month* (1965), pp. 137–9.

INDEX

REPRINTED LITHOGRAPHICALLY IN GREAT BRITAIN
AT THE UNIVERSITY PRESS, OXFORD
BY VIVIAN RIDLER
PRINTER TO THE UNIVERSITY

PLATES

2. The Assassination of Dentatus, 1808–9. Wood engraving by William Harvey

British Museum

(Basil Gray, *The English Print*, 1937, p. 67)

3. The Assassination of Dentatus, 1808–9

By courtesy of the Marquess of Normanby

4. Study for the head of Solomon
By courtesy of the Trustees of the Tate Gallery

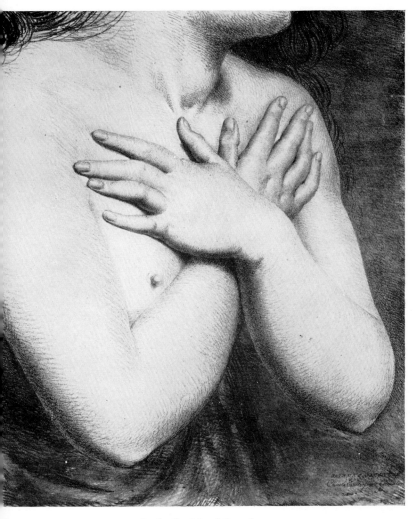

5. Study for Jairus' Daughter
British Museum

6. Christ's Triumphant Entry into Jerusalem, 1814–20

7. The Raising of Lazarus, 1820–23
By courtesy of the Trustees of the Tate Gallery

8. Wordsworth Musing upon Helvellyn, 1842
National Portrait Gallery

9. Leigh Hunt, 1815
National Portrait Gallery

10. Benjamin Robert Haydon, self portrait, n.d.
National Portrait Gallery

11. Punch, or May Day, 1829–30
By courtesy of the Trustees of the Tate Gallery

12. The Mock Election, 1827

13. Robert Hawkes, Mayor of Norwich, 1823
By courtesy of the City of Norwich

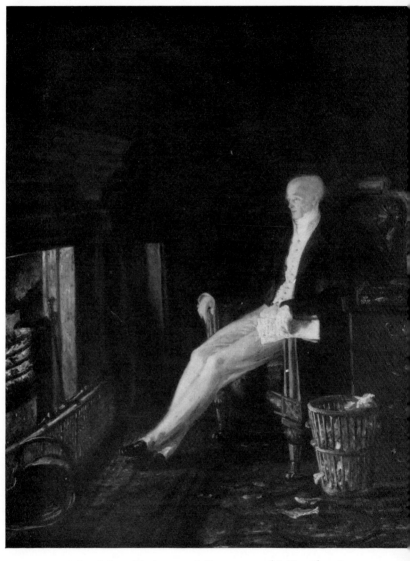

14. Lord Grey Musing, or, A Statesman at his Fireside, 1832–4
By courtesy of the Laing Art Gallery Committee, Newcastle-on-Tyne

15. The Meeting of the Unions on Newhall Hill, Birmingham, 1832

By courtesy of the City of Birmingham

16. The Reform Banquet, 1832-4

17. The Judgement of Solomon, 1812–14

By courtesy of Jack Gold Esq.

(As in others of Haydon's large canvases the reproduction does not do justice to the picture. A negro crouching on the left in deep shadow is invisible.)

18. Curtius leaping into the Gulf, 1836–42
By courtesy of the Royal Albert Memorial Museum, Exeter

19. Wellington musing on the Field of Waterloo, 1838-9
By courtesy of St. George's Hall, Liverpool

20. Benjamin Robert Haydon, 1833, by T. H. Illidge

By courtesy of the Victoria and Albert Museum

From a negative of 1868